Comprehensive COBOL

Andrew S. Philippakis

Leonard J. Kazmier

Arizona State University

 Mitchell **McGRAW-HILL**

New York St. Louis San Francisco Auckland Bogotá Caracas Hamburg
Lisbon London Madrid Mexico Milan Montreal New Delhi Paris
San Juan São Paulo Singapore Sydney Tokyo Toronto Watsonville

Comprehensive COBOL 4th Edition
Vol I: Fundamentals of Cobol Programming
International Edition 1991

Exclusive rights by McGraw-Hill Book Co.–Singapore for
manufacture and export. This book cannot be re-exported
from the country to which it is consigned by McGraw-Hill.

2 3 4 5 6 7 8 9 0 BJE SW 9 8 7 6 5 4 3 2

ISBN 0-07-049828-8

The sponsoring editor was Steve Mitchell.
The production supervisor was Betty Drury.
The production manager was Greg Hubit, Bookworks.
The text and cover designer was Gary Palmatier.
The Compositor use Ideas to Images.

Library of Congress Catalog Card Number 90-83377

When ordering this title use ISBN 0-07-112767-4

Printed in Singapore

Contents

Preface xi

COBOL in the '90s and Beyond 1

PART I — Fundamentals of COBOL Programming 5

Chapter 1 Introduction 7

> Business Data Processing vs. Scientific Computing   8
> Levels of Computer Languages   8
> The Operating System and the Execution of Computer Programs   10
> Characteristics of Good Programs   13
> Steps in a Programming Project   14
> Program Structure Charts   15
> Pseudocode   16
> Debugging and Testing a Program   16
> Overall Structure of COBOL Programs   19
> Data-Names   19
> Sample COBOL Program   21
> > *Summary*   30
> > *Exercises*   31

Chapter 2 Basic Commands 33

> The Sample Report Program   34
> An Outline for Your COBOL Programs   42
> PROCEDURE DIVISION for the Sample Report Program   42
> Input-Output Verbs   46
> The MOVE Instruction   49
> The Arithmetic Verb: ADD   49
> Control Verbs   50
> A Logic Template for Input Processing Loops   53
> The STOP RUN Statement   53
> > *Summary*   55
> > *Exercises*   56

Chapter 3 Data Definition and Editing 63

Introduction 64
Overall Structure of the DATA DIVISION 64
Data-Names and Constants 64
Defining an Elementary Data Field 66
FILLER—A Nonspecific Data-Name 67
Defining Initial Contents with the VALUE Clause 68
Using Level-Numbers to Define Group Structures 69
Record Layout 73
FILE SECTION 76
WORKING-STORAGE SECTION 78
The PICTURE Clause for Data Description 80
The PICTURE Clause for Data Editing 84
The BLANK WHEN ZERO Clause 91
The CURRENCY AND DECIMAL-POINT Clauses 91
Sample DATA DIVISION 93
Summary 96
Exercises 97

Chapter 4 Writing Complete Programs 101

COBOL Language Formats 102
IDENTIFICATION DIVISION 103
ENVIRONMENT DIVISION 105
DATA DIVISION 107
File Input and Output 108
The MOVE Statement 112
The PERFORM Verb 115
Arithmetic Verbs 117
Conditional Statements 120
Sample PROCEDURE DIVISION 121
Summary 125
Exercises 128

Chapter 5 Conditions and Conditional Statements 133

The IF Statement 134
Relation Conditions 136
Condition-Name Conditions 139
The SET Verb for Condition-Names 143
Nested Conditions 145
The END-IF Scope Terminator 149
Compound Conditions 151
Summary 153
Exercises 154

Chapter 6 Structured Programming in COBOL 159

Basic Program Structures 161
Partitioning Program Modules 165
Levels of Abstraction and Structure Charts 166
Alternative Forms of Structure Charts 171
Formatting Rules for Programs 174
Summary 178
Exercises 179

PART II — Additional COBOL Instructions 181

Chapter 7 Additional PROCEDURE DIVISION Statements 183

The Four Arithmetic Verbs   184
The COMPUTE Verb   190
Additional PERFORM Options   193
The GO TO Verb   197
The ACCEPT and DISPLAY Verbs   198
Qualification and the MOVE CORRESPONDING   201
Character Processing Verbs   205
Sample Program   216
Summary   219
Exercises   220

Chapter 8 More About Conditional Statements 227

The IF Statement and Nested Conditions   228
The CONTINUE Statement   232
Class Conditions   233
The Sign Condition   237
Switch-Status Conditions   237
Compound Conditions   238
The EVALUATE Statement   241
The GO TO . . . DEPENDING ON Statement   246
Verb-Related Conditions   250
Sample Program Using COBOL '85   251
Summary   251
Exercises   253

Chapter 9 Control Break Processing for Reports 257

The General Structure of Reports   258
Control Breaks in Report Writing   260
Logic of Report Programs   262
A Simple Report Program   263
A More Advanced Example   270
The WRITE Verb with the LINAGE Clause   281
Summary   283
Exercises   284

Chapter 10 Sequential File Processing 289

File Organization   290
File Storage Devices   291
File Labels   296
COBOL Instructions for Sequential Files   298
The FILE-CONTROL Specification   298
The File Description Entry   302
The OPEN and CLOSE Verbs   304
The READ, WRITE, and REWRITE Verbs   306
Sample Program to Create a Sequential File   308
Sequential File Updating   313
Sample Sequential File Update Program   315
Summary   325
Exercises   325

Chapter 11 Sorting and Merging Sequential Files 329

Introduction 330
The COBOL Sort Feature 331
DATA DIVISION Format Specifications 341
PROCEDURE DIVISION Format Specifications 342
File Merging 345
File Merging in COBOL 349
Summary 351
Exercises 351

Chapter 12 Single-Level Table Handling 355

Introduction 356
Subscripting and the OCCURS Clause 356
Reading Values into a Table 360
Entering Constant Values into a Table 360
The PERFORM Verb and Table Handling 363
Sample Program I—Forecasting 369
Sample Program II—Printer Graphic Output 370
Summary 376
Exercises 376

Chapter 13 An Expanded Example of Sequential File Processing 379

Introduction 380
Overview of the Task 380
The Program to Create the Master File 380
Daily Master Processing 386
Monthly Processing 398
Summary 406
Exercises 406

PART III — Vol II Advanced COBOL Programming 407

Chapter 14 Program Design 409

Cohesion in Programs 410
Types of Cohesion 411
Levels of Cohesion 416
Program Design 417
Top-Down Design 429
Summary 431
Exercises 432

Chapter 15 Program Testing 435

Introduction 436
Top-Down Program Development and Testing 437
Bottom-Up Program Development and Testing 441
Top-Down vs. Bottom-Up Approaches to Testing 442

Testing Procedures   444
Common Errors   447
Converting Unstructured Programs to Structured Form   451
Summary   460
Exercises   461

Chapter **16** **Special Data-Oriented Features** **465**

Multiple Data Records in the FILE SECTION   466
The REDEFINES Clause   468
The RENAMES Clause   469
Reference Modification   471
Data Representation   474
The USAGE Clause   480
The SIGN Clause   484
The SYNCHRONIZED Clause   486
The JUSTIFIED RIGHT Clause   487
Collating Sequences and Alphabets   488
Summary   492
Exercises   493

Chapter **17** **More About Sequential File Processing** **497**

A General Programming Model for Updating Sequential Files   498
Sequential Update Sample Program   503
Processing Variable-Length Records   513
Use of Declaratives for I/O Exception Processing   519
Master File Maintenance   521
Transaction Records and File Maintenance   525
Activity Ratios and File Maintenance   529
Summary   531
Exercises   532

Chapter **18** **Multilevel Table Handling** **537**

Two-Level and Higher-Level Tables   538
Mapping Subscripted References to Storage Locations   542
The PERFORM Verb and Table Handling   545
Sample Program with a Two-Level Table   551
Sample Program with a Three-Level Table   555
Summary   560
Exercises   560

Chapter **19** **Searching and Sorting Tables** **571**

Table Searching   572
Linear Search   572
Binary Search   574
COBOL Language Options in Table Searching   578
Examples of Table Searching   584
Sample Program with Indexing and Searching   589
Internal Sorting   592
Summary   600
Exercises   601

Chapter 20 Indexed Files **613**

Introduction   614
Indexing Methods   615
The Indexed Sequential Access Method (ISAM)   615
The Virtual Storage Access Method (VSAM)   619
An Example of Creating an Indexed File   623
ENVIRONMENT DIVISION Instructions for Indexed Files   626
PROCEDURE DIVISION Instructions for Indexed Files   629
An Example of Processing an Indexed File   637
     Summary   643
     Exercises   643

Chapter 21 Relative File Processing **647**

Relative File Organization   648
The Division Remainder Method   650
Other Key-to-Address Transformation Methods   652
COBOL Statements for Relative Files   654
An Example of Creating a Relative File   659
An Example of Updating a Relative File   664
Using Buckets with Relative Files   672
     Summary   677
     Exercises   678

Chapter 22 Interactive Processing **681**

Introduction   682
ACCEPT and DISPLAY   682
Programming Concepts for Interactive Processing   684
Sample Interactive Program for Standard COBOL   689
Sample Interactive Program for Nonstandard COBOL   698
     Summary   703
     Exercises   704

Chapter 23 Subprograms and Nested Programs **705**

Introduction   706
Calling and Called Programs   707
Subprogram Data Linkage   710
Transfer of Control   716
Sample Program with a Subprogram   720
The Concept of Nested COBOL Programs   724
The COMMON and INITIAL Options   726
EXTERNAL and GLOBAL Items   727
Sample Nested Programs   731
     Summary   735
     Exercises   736

Chapter 24 The Report Writer Feature **741**

Introduction   742
The Report Writer Feature—A Basic Example   742
Report Writer with Control Breaks   752
Report Writer Using Declaratives   760
Language Specifications for the Report Writer   764
     Summary   769
     Exercises   769

Chapter 25 Data Structures **771**

    Introduction   772
    Logical Data Structures   772
    Pointer Structures   778
    Sample COBOL Program   786
    Indexing and File Inversion   793
    Database Management Systems   796
        Summary   798
        Exercises   799

Chapter 26 A Comprehensive File Processing Example **801**

    Overview of the Task   802
    Student Master Update   802
    Registration Processing   817
        Summary   829

Appendix A COBOL Reserved Words **831**

Appendix B Complete COBOL Language Formats **833**

Index **863**

Note: Pages 407–829 are found in
    Vol II: Advanced COBOL Programming

Preface

The title of this book, *Comprehensive COBOL,* accurately indicates its contents. Increasingly, courses in COBOL are taken by students who have a *serious* professional interest in business programming, and for this purpose a casual acquaintance with the language is not sufficient. Students interested in a general introduction to programming typically choose to study a language other than COBOL. On the employer side, the need is for graduates who have had a *rigorous* exposure to COBOL concepts and programming techniques.

In this environment, there is a need for a textbook that can support courses intended for professional preparation. This classroom-tested book is unique in its thorough coverage of *both* the COBOL language features and the underlying information processing concepts and methods.

Although the content of the book is comprehensive, we have made special efforts to assure that it is *user friendly*. Every chapter begins with clearly stated **learning objectives**. Included with every main section of every chapter are **interactive reviews**, so that the student can combine review and self-testing throughout the chapter. The **summary** at the end of each chapter then reviews and reinforces all of the concepts and techniques. There are **extensive end-of-chapter** partial and complete **programming exercises**, with **sample data and tested program solutions available on disk to text adopters.**

The organization of the book reflects a spiral-learning approach. By Chapter 4 the student has covered a complete, though limited, set of COBOL instructions. Thus the student's self-confidence develops through the ability to write complete programs for simplified exercises early in the course. Later chapters impart successively broader views and more detailed methods and concepts. Overall, this book emphasizes long-lasting learning by presenting fundamental concepts first, *followed* by programming details, rather than focusing on programming minutia.

One-Semester Course

The book is structured to that it easily accommodates either a one-semester course or a two-course sequence. The first 13 chapters are intended for the first course and present a complete set of topics, including basic commands, structured programming concepts in COBOL, extensive coverage of conditional statements, control break processing, sequential files, file sorting and merging, and single-level table handling. Chapter 13 consists of an expanded "case" example of sequential file processing and serves as a capstone for the one-semester experience.

Enriched courses for those with previous programming experience can include one or more topics from later chapters, such as additional file processing techniques, multilevel table handling, or program design and testing.

Full Year Course

The second semester in a two-semester course typically would cover Chapters 14 through 26. However, complete coverage of all 13 chapters requires an intensive effort. Typically, some chapters would be omitted or covered lightly, with the selection of such chapters depending on instructor preference. File processing, which is the "heart" of business information systems, has five of the 13 chapters devoted to it, including the comprehensive "case" example that constitutes the last chapter in the book. The example involves multiple files, all three file organization methods, and the application of concepts concerned with a "system" of interrelated programs.

Coverage in the last half of the book extends beyond language features, in that file processing is also studied in terms of *information systems* processing concepts and procedures. Interactive processing and subprograms/nested programs are developed well beyond the level that is common in other COBOL books, while the inclusion of a chapter on data structures provides instructors with the opportunity to lay a foundation for a subsequent database course.

Instructor's Guide

An *Instructor's Guide* is available to adopters of the textbook. It comes with the aforementioned data disk as well as the program solutions on disk. Documentation and overhead transparency master information is contained in the *Instructor's Guide*.

ACKNOWLEDGMENTS

We express appreciation to Marian Lamb for her technical editing assistance with the original manuscript and preparation of the book index. We thank Deepa Luthra for her outstanding programming support during the development of this book. The timely publication of this book would not have been possible without the commitment of Greg Hubit and his staff at Bookworks, the editorial planning of Raleigh Wilson, and the coordinating activities of Denise Nickeson at Mitchell Publishing.

COBOL is an industry language and is not the property of any company or group of companies, or of any organization or group of organizations.

No warranty, expressed or implied, is made by any contributor or by the CODASYL Programming Language Committee as to the accuracy and functioning of the programming system and language. Moreover, no responsibility is assumed by the contributor, or by the committee, in connection therewith.

The authors and copyright holders of the copyrighted material used herein

FLOW-MATIC (trademark of Sperry Rand Corporation), Programming for the UNIVAC® I and II, Data Automation Systems, copyrighted 1958, 1959, by Sperry Rand Corporation; IBM Commercial Translator Form No. F28-8013, copyrighted 1959 by IBM; FACT, DSI 27A5260-2760, copyrighted 1960 by Minneapolis-Honeywell

have specifically authorized the use of this material in whole or in part, in the COBOL specifications. Such authorization extends to the reproduction and use of COBOL specifications in programming manuals or similar publications.

COBOL in the '90s and Beyond

QUESTIONS AND ANSWERS

YOU ARE ABOUT TO MAKE *a large investment of your time and effort by studying COBOL programming.*

The length of this book tells you something obvious: COBOL is a language for the professional programmer. Whether you spend one semester studying about half this book, or you complete the whole book in two semesters, you will undertake a serious learning task.

It is only natural that you should want to know if the study of COBOL represents a good investment. We try to give you a realistic assessment using a question-answer approach.

Question: *Who uses COBOL today?*

Answer: The main users of COBOL are medium and large organizations, to do their "business" processing. Manufacturing, retailing, insurance, banking, government agencies, hospitals, school districts, colleges, and universities are typical extensive COBOL users. In fact, information processing in medium and large organizations throughout the world is based on COBOL, and this has been true for the last two decades.

Question: *What about the use of other languages for information processing?*

Answer: There are many programming languages in use. Many small companies use the RPG languages rather than COBOL. But as small companies grow, they often join the larger ones in also using COBOL. Other languages, such as BASIC and Pascal, are used by both small and large organizations, but usually on a limited basis and for specialized projects. More recently C, and to a lesser extent Ada, are finding increasing use in developing new computer applications.

Information processing is a multilingual environment, to be sure. And the trend of using more than one language in the same organization is well established. A successful computer professional should be familiar with more than one language. Most programmers tend to develop their main competency in one language, but the successful ones can move to another language when the need arises.

Question: *Why do you think that COBOL will continue to be the language of business information processing?*

Answer: It may be useful to consider an analogy. If you visit an old city and look at the way its streets are laid out, it's not practical to contemplate changing the layout of the streets. You may think of changes and improvements in transportation systems, but the basic infrastructure is already there.

Something analogous has happened with COBOL. Organizations have made heavy commitments over the past two decades in developing COBOL-based computer applications. The cumulative total of these developments represents a major asset. To see this point, consider Table 1, which estimates the total dollar investment for different combinations of number of years and number of programmers in an organization. The numbers in the table are based on a reasonable average of $30,000 per person per year, which is low for today's salaries, but high for the long past.

The cumulative investment in COBOL-based programs in organizations is so large, and the applications are so extensive, that COBOL is here to stay for a long time. Any notion of "clearing the decks" and starting over again with some other language is no more practical than thinking of redesigning the street layout for an established city.

Question: *What is happening in terms of improved use of COBOL?*

Answer: The use of COBOL is not static. New things are happening to increase the productivity of COBOL programmers. Companies are acquiring a variety of "productivity tools" to facilitate the design, coding, and revision of COBOL programs. Some of these tools facilitate writing reports (report generators), others make it easier to write interactive programs (screen formatters), to re-use similar code across several programs (libraries), to re-use data definitions (dictionaries), and to correct errors (on-line debuggers). Such productivity tools increase the programmer's output per hour of work, improve the quality of the programs, and enrich the programmer's job.

TABLE 1
Cumulative Investment in Millions of Dollars

TOTAL NUMBER OF YEARS	NUMBER OF PROGRAMMERS EMPLOYED				
	5	10	25	50	100
10	$1.50	$3.00	$7.50	$15.00	$30.00
15	2.25	4.50	11.25	22.50	45.00
20	3.00	6.00	15.00	30.00	60.00

Many of these productivity tools are available on personal computers, as well as large, shared computers (minicomputers and mainframes). Unfortunately, colleges and universities often do not have such productivity tools available for instruction. This is due both to limited budgets and to the objective of teaching fundamental concepts rather than training the student to become a fluent programmer. A recent survey that we conducted revealed that the vast majority of colleges use large computers to teach COBOL, and this limits the availability of many productivity tools that are less expensive when purchased for use with personal computers.

Question: *What else is happening in the use of COBOL today?*

Answer: Many organizations find that program "maintenance" has become an overwhelming activity. Maintaining a program means that it is changed to adapt to the changing needs of the organization. As programs undergo multiple changes over the years, they become complicated and difficult to keep changing. Therefore organizations are gradually redesigning their old systems. One approach to redesigning programs is to take the old programs and convert them to modern forms of program structure. The practice of *reverse engineering* relies on the use of specialized programs that take existing COBOL programs and help convert them to well-structured programs that are less complex and more understandable.

Another development is the use of *Computer Assisted Software Engineering* (CASE). CASE relies on methods and special programs that automate much of the design and coding of COBOL programs. Use of graphics is common in CASE, since visual tools increase the conceptual power of the programmer. CASE tools are in limited use at colleges, partly because they are new, and partly because the hardware and software required to implement CASE are rather expensive.

Question: *What are the prospects for COBOL over the next 10 years?*

Answer: The most likely occurrence during the next ten years is a high level of activity in organizations aimed at modernizing their program libraries and designing new or redesigning existing major application systems. Increasing the use of power tools will be a high priority as organizations try to manage the costs of these major undertakings. More important for the prospective student is the fact that organizations will need well-educated and open-minded professional programmers. From this standpoint, experience is not as much a factor. In fact, many experienced programmers, who grew up thinking in the old ways, have difficulty adapting to the new features of COBOL. Through this course you will be educated in the current version of the language and the modern ways of conceiving and designing high-quality structured programs. In this respect you can expect to have something of a competitive advantage as you graduate and enter the market as a programmer-analyst.

Of course, computing is a dynamic field that has had a continuing stream of changes in conceptual and physical tools. To compete and succeed as a professional programmer, you need to keep learning new methods and adopting new tools. Learning COBOL now will provide you with a solid foundation for business uses of computers. As time goes on, you will need to keep adding to your store of knowledge, including the ability to use other languages that may interface with COBOL.

In summary, over the next ten years we foresee COBOL remaining the main language for business applications of computers in medium and large organizations. However, it will continuously be supplemented by capabilities and tools that will require frequent updating of your knowledge of how to use COBOL in a particular programming environment.

It is impractical to try to predict the more distant future with a high degree of confidence. But if any major changes do occur, it is almost certain that they will develop over long periods of time. There are too many existing programs, and all of these systems have a huge human component. The bottom line is that the time and effort that you spend in learning COBOL programming is an investment that will yield positive long-run returns to you.

I

Fundamentals of COBOL Programming

Introduction

BUSINESS DATA PROCESSING VS. SCIENTIFIC COMPUTING

LEVELS OF COMPUTER LANGUAGES

THE OPERATING SYSTEM AND THE EXECUTION OF COMPUTER PROGRAMS

CHARACTERISTICS OF GOOD PROGRAMS

STEPS IN A PROGRAMMING PROJECT

PROGRAM STRUCTURE CHARTS

PSEUDOCODE

DEBUGGING AND TESTING A PROGRAM

OVERALL STRUCTURE OF COBOL PROGRAMS

DATA-NAMES

SAMPLE COBOL PROGRAM

IN THIS CHAPTER *you will first briefly consider the differences between business data analysis and scientific computing. Then you will study some **general issues** in computer programming. These include levels of computer languages, the operating systems of computers, characteristics of good computer programs, and steps in a programming project.*

*After this general foundation you will be introduced to some **design and testing concepts** for COBOL programs. Included are the use of program structure charts, use of pseudocode, and procedures of debugging and testing a COBOL program.*

*In the last several sections of the chapter you will focus specifically on the COBOL **language.** Included is an introduction to the overall structure of COBOL programs, the use of data-names and constants, and finally, a complete sample COBOL program.*

BUSINESS DATA PROCESSING VS. SCIENTIFIC COMPUTING

Business data processing has distinct characteristics and requirements. Business operations involve such transactions as sales, payments, shipments, and purchases. *Transaction processing* involves the input of data for transactions, and the output of reports that reflect the consequences of the transactions. For example, when a product is sold, input data about the sale transaction are used to change (update) the customer file, the inventory file, and the accounts receivable file. As a result of transaction processing, various output reports also are generated. For example, the daily sales transactions can be reported according to categories of products and according to different retail store locations.

Business data processing reflects the structure and operations of an organization. Since organizations consist of many interrelated parts (departments, divisions, etc.) that have a large variety of operations, it follows that business data processing involves a great variety of input data, many and varied data files (personnel, materials, sales, financial, and so on), and a complex series of programs to process transaction data in order to update the multiple files. Finally, most organizations have a variety of scheduled activities that involve data processing, such as payroll every two weeks, billing of customers every month, and financial reports every quarter. This time-associated processing is another major distinguishing feature of data processing.

By way of contrast, *scientific computing* has quite different characteristics. Scientific computing tends to focus on individual projects rather than interrelated organizational operations. Such projects tend to involve extensive calculations. If they involve a lot of data, such as do geological and space exploration projects, the data tend to be limited in form, consisting mostly of numeric values. Business data tend to be varied in form, consisting of long records containing large numbers of fields of both numeric and character data.

In general, business data processing is different enough from scientific computing that there are distinct computer programming concepts and methods for each type of computing. Reflecting the specialized needs of business data processing, a special computer language, COBOL (COmmon Business Oriented Language), has been developed.

LEVELS OF COMPUTER LANGUAGES

A *computer program* is a set of instructions that directs a computer to perform a series of operations. A *computer language* is a set of characters, words, and rules that can be used to write a computer program.

Every computer model has its own language, which is determined by its hardware structure. Such "native" computer languages are referred to as *machine languages*. These languages are, of course, machine dependent. They appear highly obscure because they consist of strings of numeric codes. Early computer programming was almost exclusively machine-language programming. Although machine language is natural to the hardware of a computer, it is quite unnatural to people. A step in the direction of making computer programming easier was taken with the development of *symbolic languages*. Symbolic languages use codes that are easier to remember, such as ADD, to represent machine instructions. For instance, a machine instruction such as 21300400, meaning to add (indicated by "21") the value stored in location 300 to the value stored in location 400, could be written as ADD AMOUNT1, AMOUNT2.

Such codes as ADD are not directly understood by a computer. They have to be translated into machine-language form. An *assembler* is a machine-language program that translates symbolic-language instructions into machine-language instructions. Symbolic languages are machine dependent in that a set of such codes is applicable only to a particular computer model; therefore the programmer has to be familiar with the particular instruction set of the machine being programmed. This is a serious disadvantage when programming efforts are extensive and hardware is continually changing.

The next stage in the development of programming language was the advent of *higher-level languages* that are procedure oriented rather than machine oriented. Such languages focus on the data processing procedure to be accomplished rather than on the coding requirements of particular machines. Further, higher-level languages are *not* machine dependent; such programs are not restricted to use with particular computer models.

Even though such instructions are not designed to correspond to the way a particular computer model operates, they must, of course, ultimately be executed on some particular machine. Again the process of translation is used to obtain the required machine-language program. A computer program written in a higher-level language is referred to as a *source program*. A *compiler* is a machine-language program that translates (or compiles) the source program into a machine-language program. This machine-language program is referred to as the *object program*. The object program is then input into the machine to perform the required task. Thus a compiler is a program whose function is to convert source programs into object programs. The main difference between a compiler and an assembler is that compilation is a more complex process than assembly. Assembly typically involves a one-for-one translation from a word code to a machine code; compilation involves a many-for-one translation: one higher-level instruction may be the equivalent of several machine-level instructions.

Figure 1-1 illustrates the compilation and execution process. In the first phase the source program and the compiler serve as input. The output includes the object program, which is stored on disk, and a listing of the source program on

FIGURE 1-1
COBOL Program Compilation-Execution Process

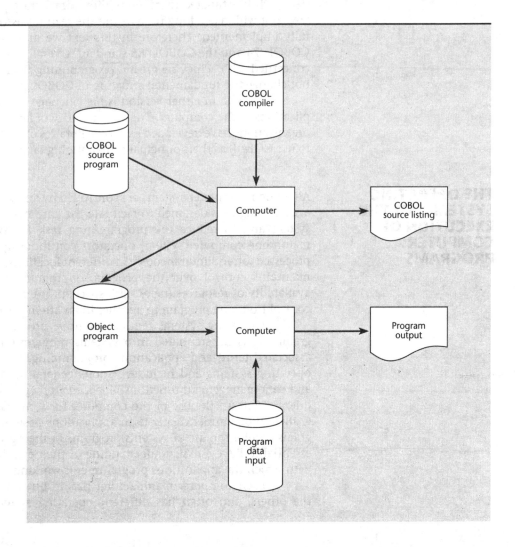

the printer, along with diagnostic error messages, if any. If no serious errors are detected, the object program is entered into the computer. Based on the program instructions, input data are then read and processed, and output data are written onto files or printed reports.

COBOL is a programming language that has been designed expressly for data processing. It is a higher-level language and, as such, is designed to be machine independent.

The idea of developing the language was conceived at a Pentagon meeting in May 1959. At that meeting representatives from the U.S. government, from business users, and from computer manufacturers decided that it was feasible to proceed with the development of a higher-level language that would satisfy the specific needs of administrative data processing, as contrasted to scientific computing. A preliminary version of COBOL appeared in December 1959. This version was followed in 1961 by COBOL '61, which became the cornerstone for the development of later versions of the language. In 1968 a standard version of the language was approved by what now is called the *American National Standards Institute* (ANSI), and revised versions were adopted by ANSI in 1974 and again in 1985. Thus, the three standard versions of the language are COBOL '68, COBOL '74, and COBOL '85. The language is continuously evolving and being enhanced by the addition of new programming capabilities and the deletion of obsolete functions. Proposed changes in the COBOL language are documented annually in the *Journal of Development*. These changes are tentative, however, until ANSI adopts a new standard.

It is estimated there are millions of existing programs written in COBOL '74, so it will take a long time before the features associated with COBOL '85 are fully implemented. Therefore in this text we make a clear distinction between COBOL '74 and the COBOL '85 standard. Overall, the new standard is principally concerned with achieving greater programming flexibility and capability; it does not change the fundamental structure of COBOL programs.

COBOL in either version is *the* language of choice for administrative applications of the computer. The vast majority of large business and governmental organizations have developed extensive libraries of COBOL programs and continue to use COBOL as their principal programming language for data processing.

THE OPERATING SYSTEM AND THE EXECUTION OF COMPUTER PROGRAMS

All modern computer systems are controlled by an *operating system* that consists of a set of programs designed to facilitate the automatic operation of the computer system and to reduce the programming task for system users. In a modern mainframe computer system, operators continuously input the programs to be processed (often simultaneously in different locations), while the operating system maintains control over the program-to-program execution sequence, checks availability of resources (tapes, disk space, printers), and, when needed, transfers control from one program to another in an attempt to maximize throughput.

Operating systems require extensive programming efforts. In fact, programming is differentiated into systems programming (systems software is an associated term) and applications programming. *Systems programming* relates to operating systems and includes various general-purpose machine management and data management functions. *Applications programming,* on the other hand, is oriented toward the use of the computer for some data processing task. Thus a COBOL programmer clearly is an applications programmer. All applications programs require the use of systems programs in their processing, and therefore it is essential to have a basic understanding of the operating system of the computer with which the applications programmer is working.

Each computer manufacturer has an operating system that differs from the others, and often has different operating systems for different computer models. Therefore we cannot explain the specifics of particular operating systems in this text. We will, however, discuss the general concepts that relate COBOL programming to operating systems, and we assume that the reader has access to information about the specific operating system used by his or her computer. Our comments concern large mainframe computers shared by many users. The basic concepts apply to personal computers as well, but many things are simplified for personal computers.

In order for a COBOL program to be run, the programmer needs to communicate certain things to the operating system. Typical areas of information include the following:

- Identify the user as a legitimate user of the machine.

- Indicate the fact that a COBOL program is being used. (In a typical installation, programs are written in several languages and they need to be differentiated.)

- Request compilation of the COBOL source program into object-program form.

- Indicate whether the compilation output (object program) is to be saved on disk, tape, etc.

- Request the use of tapes, disks, printers, and other devices.

- Request execution of the compiled program.

The communication process between the programmer and the operating system is effected by means of system commands known collectively as the *Job Control Language (JCL)*. The JCL, of course, is not standardized. Figure 1-2 portrays a typical COBOL program setup. In the past, the JCL statements were punched onto cards referred to as *program control cards*. Although punched cards as such are

FIGURE 1-2
Typical COBOL Program Setup

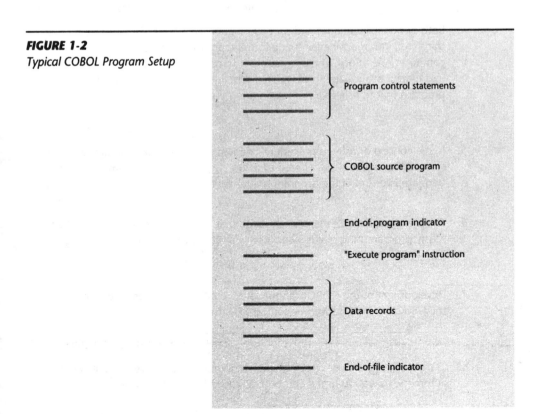

Program control statements

COBOL source program

End-of-program indicator

"Execute program" instruction

Data records

End-of-file indicator

not used anymore, it is still not unusual to refer to "cards" in this context. In general, the first card identifies the user by account number or by name and may set parameters on maximum time, maximum number of pages, and the like. Then there are one or more JCL statements to invoke the compiler and to indicate the disposition of the object program. The source program follows, possibly with an end-of-program indicator. Then there are one or more JCL statements to ready the object program for execution. The "execute" type of instruction often is followed by the data and by an end-of-file indicator.

Overall, then, program control statements serve to transmit certain categories of information to the operating system. On the basis of this information, execution of the program is scheduled and monitored.

R E V I E W . . . .

1. A computer program is essentially a set of instructions that directs the operation of a machine. When the set of instructions is written in a language that consists of a series of numeric codes that can be used with a particular computer model only, the language is referred to as a _____ language.

    machine

2. The next stage in the development of computer languages made possible the use of word codes, such as ADD, in place of numeric codes. As is the case for machine languages, such languages are also machine dependent. Because of the type of code system used, such languages are called _____ languages.

    symbolic

3. The third stage in the development of computer languages was the formulation of higher-level, or procedure-oriented, languages that [are also / are not] machine dependent. An example of such a language is _____ .

    are not; COBOL (or BASIC, FORTRAN, Pascal, etc.)

4. Both symbolic languages and procedure-oriented languages have to be translated into machine-language form before they can be used to direct computer operations. The program that translates a symbolic-language program into machine-language form is called a(n) _____ , whereas the program that translates a procedure-oriented language program is called a(n) _____ .

    assembler; compiler

5. In the context of using a procedure-oriented language, the program written in such a language is often referred to as the _____ program, whereas the translated version of the program is referred to as the _____ program.

    source; object

6. The major procedure-oriented language that has been designed specifically to satisfy programming needs associated with administrative data processing is _____ .

    COBOL

7. Development of the COBOL language is a continuing process. New versions of the language are approved periodically by the _____ .

    American National Standards Institute (ANSI)

8. The set of programs designed by the computer manufacturer to facilitate the automatic operation of the computer is called the _____ .

    operating system

9. The types of computer programs that are concerned with such functions as disk-space allocation and copying data from tape to disk are called _____ programs.

systems

10. The types of computer programs concerned with actual data processing tasks are called _____ programs.

applications

11. A programmer who uses COBOL as the programming language is a(n) [systems / applications] programmer.

applications

12. An applications programmer communicates with the operating system of a computer through the use of a set of commands called the

_____ .

Job Control Language (JCL)

* * * * * * * * * * * * * * * * * * * *

CHARACTERISTICS OF GOOD PROGRAMS

The traditional approach to the programming process was to view a computer program as a personal creation by an individual. The distinguishing characteristic of a good programmer was the ability to write clever programs—"clever" often being synonymous with complex and obscure. The trouble with such programs is that it is difficult for persons other than the author of the program to understand them, and even the author may have difficulty when months or years have passed. Therefore particular emphasis is now given to the principles and concepts by which good programs can be written. The following is a list of several characteristics associated with a good computer program:

1. It is correct.

2. It is understandable.

3. It is easy to change.

4. It has been written efficiently.

5. It executes efficiently.

Of course, the identification of these characteristics does not in itself tell us how to write such programs. However, the following sections of this chapter are directed toward describing some of the concepts and techniques by which these objectives can be achieved.

The first, and usually most important, characteristic of a good program is that it is *correct*. The program should carry out the task for which it was designed and do so without error. To achieve this objective, a complete and clear specification of the purpose and functions of the program must be developed. Thus program "errors" can be due to outright mistakes on the part of a programmer or to a lack of a clear description regarding the processing detail and the required output of the program.

The second characteristic of a good program is that it is *understandable*. Although a computer program is a set of instructions for a computer, it also should be comprehensible to people. A person other than the author should be able to read and understand the purpose and functions of the program. Higher-level programming languages such as COBOL are intended for direct comprehension by people, and are intended for machine use only indirectly, through compilation.

Third, a computer program should be *easy to change*. Changes in products, changes in company procedures, new government regulations, and the like, all lead to the necessity of modifying existing computer programs. As a result most established computer installations devote considerable time and effort to changing, or *maintaining,* existing programs. A good program not only fulfills its original purpose but also is adapted easily in response to changing needs.

The fourth characteristic of a good program is that it has been *written efficiently*. This refers to the amount of time spent in writing the program. Of course, this objective is secondary to the program being correct, understandable, and easy to change. In practice, the easiest way to write a program quickly is to write it partly correct, leave it difficult to understand, or allow its obscurity to make it difficult to change, but none of these ways is cost effective. The main cost of a programming project is the programmer's time. Thus the best programming techniques economize this time while still satisfying the objectives that the program be correct, understandable, and easy to change.

The final characteristic of a good program that we consider is that it *executes efficiently*. The program should be written so that it does not use more computer storage nor more computer processing time than is necessary. This objective also is secondary to the primary objectives that a program be correct, understandable, and easy to change. Furthermore, as hardware costs have decreased relative to programmers' salaries, overall cost considerations often justify reducing the concern about a high level of efficiency in program execution. A programmer should be alert, nevertheless, to the techniques by which efficient program execution can be achieved.

STEPS IN A PROGRAMMING PROJECT

A programmer goes through a number of steps in completing a COBOL program. These steps are summarized in Table 1-1.

We begin the project by first designing the *overall program structure*. This is achieved by preparing a structure chart and associated pseudocode for the programming project, as explained and illustrated in the following two sections of this chapter. Then the actual first draft of the program is written on the *COBOL Coding Form*. This coding form is included as Figure 1-9 with the sample COBOL program in the last section of this chapter. After these first two steps in Table 1-1 are completed, the third step begins a process of review and revision of the program that continues with the rest of the steps in the listing.

All of the steps beginning with the third step are collectively called *program debugging and testing*. We shall return to this topic, and to Table 1-1, after the next two sections on structure charts and pseudocode.

TABLE 1-1

Steps Included in a Programming Project

- Design the overall program structure.
- Write the program on a COBOL coding form.
- Review and correct the handwritten program.
- Key-in the program in machine-readable form.
- Obtain a listing of the program for review.
- Compile the program and review any diagnostic error messages.
- Recompile the program until no error diagnostics are issued.
- Execute the program with some limited test data.
- Review the output for the test data and determine the causes of any erroneous output.

PROGRAM STRUCTURE CHARTS

A *structure chart* is a visual representation of the main functions and subfunctions of a program. Figure 1-3 presents a structure chart for a typical COBOL programming task. The single block at the top of the chart stands for the entire programming task. Having identified the overall task, we then ask, what are the main functions that need to be carried out to do the task? The four functions identified at the second level of the structure chart in Figure 1-3 are *Print report heading, Read customer record, Process customer detail,* and *Print report footing.* The completion of these four functions would constitute the complete program.

Next, we consider each of the main functions individually and determine what subfunctions need to be carried out to complete that function. For instance, we could ask, what activities need to be carried out to accomplish the function *Print report heading*? Because this task is a simple one, we conclude that it is not necessary to break it down into subordinate functions in Figure 1-3. However, when the function *Process customer detail* is considered, four subfunctions are identified. In other words, we conclude that to accomplish the function *Process customer detail,* four specific tasks have to be completed: *Compute net sales, Accumulate totals, Print customer detail data,* and *Read customer record.* Because *Read customer record* is a function that is used in more than one place in the structure chart, the upper-right corner of the block is shaded to indicate such repetition.

The programmer continues the process of considering each function and subfunction in turn to determine if it can be broken down into more specific tasks. For example, for the function *Compute net sales* in Figure 1-3 we would ask, what needs to be done to compute net sales? The answer is that the unit price needs to be determined, and the units sold need to be multiplied by the unit price. We could have chosen to show these two tasks as subordinate functions of *Compute net sales* in Figure 1-3. We chose not to do so because showing the additional detail would not add much to the usefulness of the structure chart. At what level of detail should the analysis of functions be stopped? This judgment is based largely on experience with similar programming projects. As a general rule, the structure chart should have sufficient detail to be a useful guide in developing the program but not so much detail that the blocks in the structure chart are direct alternatives to COBOL program statements.

Structure charts provide a comprehensive overview of the functions to be performed. Notice that no consideration is given to the timing or sequence of

FIGURE 1-3

Structure Chart for a Typical COBOL Programming Task

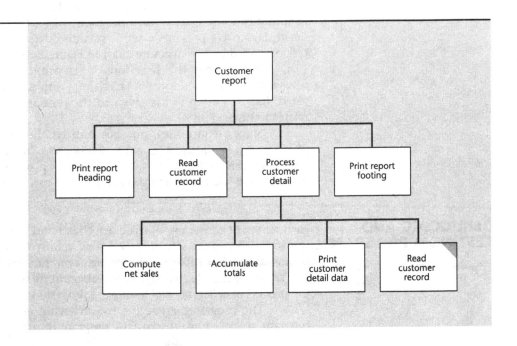

FIGURE 1-4
Pseudocode for the Programming Task Example

CUSTOMER REPORT PROGRAM

PERFORM

    Print the report heading

    Read a record from the customer file

    PERFORM UNTIL the end of customer file

        Determine appropriate price

        Compute net sales

        Accumulate totals

        Print customer detail line

        Read a record from the customer file

    END-PERFORM

    Print the report footing

END-PERFORM

Stop execution of the program

tasks in developing a structure chart. In contrast, such a concern is fundamental in the development of flowcharts, as described in the Sample Program section at the end of this chapter. The matter of the time flow of the specific tasks to be performed is also considered in the use of pseudocode, as described in the following section.

PSEUDOCODE

After development of a structure chart, it may be useful to write the program outline in *pseudocode*. As the name implies, we do *not* write the program code according to the rules of COBOL. Instead we concentrate on the logical flow of the program, using ordinary language to represent the main functions in the program.

Pseudocode is incomplete and limited, but it is very useful because it can communicate the essence of a program without being bogged down in precise detail. Figure 1-4 presents a set of pseudocode statements for the programming task described by the structure chart in Figure 1-3.

Notice that the functions taken from the structure chart are listed *sequentially* in the pseudocode. That is, not only are the functions to be performed listed, but also attention is given to the time flow and the program logic as it relates to time.

Since pseudocode is not standardized, there is not much point in trying to offer exact rules on how to write pseudocode; however, some organizations do have in-house guidelines to follow. A common-sense rule is to write pseudocode in a way that has meaning for its author and can be understood easily by others.

DEBUGGING AND TESTING A PROGRAM

Having described the use of structure charts and pseudocode as aids in designing the overall program structure, we now return to the steps in a programming project as listed in Table 1-1 shown again on the next page. As we indicated when this table was first discussed, the steps beginning with the third step all constitute the process of *debugging and testing* the program initially written.

The programmer begins by reviewing and correcting the handwritten program, followed by entering the program into the computer system by the use

TABLE 1-1 *(Repeated)*
Steps Included in a Programming Project

- Design the overall program structure.
- Write the program on a COBOL coding form.
- Review and correct the handwritten program.
- Key-in the program in machine-readable form.
- Obtain a listing of the program for review.
- Compile the program and review any diagnostic error messages.
- Recompile the program until no error diagnostics are issued.
- Execute the program with some limited test data.
- Review the output for the test data and determine the causes of any erroneous output.

of a terminal, and obtaining a program listing that is again reviewed. Only after such a "double review" should the programmer compile the program. Use of the COBOL compiler results in the source program written in COBOL being translated into the machine-language object program. Given that there are some *diagnostic error messages,* which is typical, the program is recompiled until no error messages are issued.

The absence of diagnostic error messages indicates that the technical requirements of the language have been satisfied. However, the absence of such errors in itself says nothing about whether the data processing objectives of the program have been achieved. Although the test data used for trial execution of the program are described as being "limited" in Table 1-1, they are limited only in the number of data items. The test data should include not only all of the extremes of values for each type of data item, but also combinations of extreme values for different data items. Finally, these extreme values should include "impossible" values, such as an hourly employee having a work week of 140 hours.

If the test run gives erroneous output, the programmer can find the source of the problem by a process called *tracing.* This procedure often is the most difficult part of programming. The programmer "walks through" or "desk checks" the program step by step by applying each program instruction sequentially and checking the results at each step. This includes a listing of program output for every step of processing in the program. If the nature of the output error indicates that the program error probably occurred in a particular routine, we trace and compare program execution in the suspected routine first, rather than starting from the beginning of the program. There may be an early error, however, that does not surface until later in the program. For instance, it may be that a total is incorrect at the end of program execution because we forgot to set an accumulator equal to zero at the beginning of the program.

Experience and insight are very useful in debugging and testing; however, the best way to avoid debugging and testing problems is to be very careful in the initial design and writing of the program. It is a fact that the student who writes a program with little design and review effort is the one who gets involved in seemingly endless attempts to correct a poorly written program. A programmer who spends 10 hours designing, writing, and reviewing a program may spend two hours correcting compiler diagnostics and program testing. On the other hand, a programmer with similar abilities who spends just five hours designing, writing, and reviewing the same program will likely spend 15 hours in debugging the program.

R E V I E W . . . .

1. The most important characteristic of a good computer program is that it is
    _____ .

    correct

2. Probable later reference to the program by individuals other than the original
    programmer dictates that it should be _____ , while
    unavoidable changes in data processing requirements in most organizations
    make it desirable that the program be _____ .

    understandable; easy to change

3. To economize the programmer's time, a program should be _____
    efficiently; to economize the use of computer hardware, the program should
    _____ efficiently.

    written; execute

4. The type of chart used as a programming aid that is a visual representation of the
    main functions and subfunctions of a program is the
    _____ .

    structure chart

5. In a structure chart the entire programming task is represented by the single
    block at the [top / bottom] of the chart.

    top

6. The upper-right corner of a structure-chart block is shaded for functions that are
    _____ in the chart.

    repeated

7. The analysis of functions and associated subfunctions to be carried out in a
    programming project is fundamental to the development of a
    _____ chart.

    structure

8. A program outline written in approximately ordinary language that concentrates
    on the logical flow of the program is described as being outlined in
    _____ .

    pseudocode

9. A program outline using pseudocode generally would be written immediately
    following development of the program _____ chart.

    structure

10. The overall process of checking a program for correctness is called program
    debugging and _____ .

    testing

11. After the keyed-in version of the program is listed and reviewed, the program is
    compiled to obtain a printout of the COBOL source program and a listing of
    diagnostic _____ messages.

    error

12. Corrections and changes to the program are made by reviewing all of the
    diagnostics. When no diagnostic error messages are obtained upon recompiling
    the program, the program is then executed using limited _____ .

    test data

13. When a programmer arranges to list every record or the result of every sequential
    processing step that is associated with an output error, the procedure is called
    program _____ .

    tracing

. . . .

OVERALL STRUCTURE OF COBOL PROGRAMS

Every COBOL program consists of four *divisions* that are included in the following order:

- IDENTIFICATION DIVISION

- ENVIRONMENT DIVISION

- DATA DIVISION

- PROCEDURE DIVISION

The *IDENTIFICATION DIVISION* identifies the COBOL program to the computer by providing a program name.

The *ENVIRONMENT DIVISION* specifies the computer equipment and operating environment that are required to execute the program.

The *DATA DIVISION* includes all of the data format specifications for input, output, and temporary storage. This includes the assignment of data-names and the definition of constants, as will be described in the following sections of this chapter.

The *PROCEDURE DIVISION* is the executable part of the COBOL program. That is, this division contains the specific input, data processing, and output statements that are to be executed to achieve the overall data processing objectives.

The next two sections of this chapter explain the assignment of data-names and the definition of constants in COBOL. Following these explanations the final section of the chapter presents a sample COBOL program that includes, in order, the IDENTIFICATION DIVISION, ENVIRONMENT DIVISION, DATA DIVISION, and PROCEDURE DIVISION. Also included for the program are the program structure chart, pseudocode, COBOL Coding Form, and flowchart.

DATA-NAMES

A *data-name* in COBOL is analogous to a *variable* in algebra. It is a general symbol or name that can have different values. Another way of viewing a data-name is that it is a label for a storage location that may contain various, and different, values at different times. In this sense any computer program consists of a set of instructions to manipulate central storage areas that are referenced by their corresponding data-names. In COBOL, data-names and their formats are specified in the DATA DIVISION.

Data-names are coined at the discretion of the programmer, except that there are certain rules that must be followed:

1. A data-name can be up to 30 characters in length and can include alphabetic characters, numeric characters, and hyphens.

2. At least one character must be alphabetic.

3. The only special symbol permitted is the hyphen. A hyphen must always be *embedded;* that is, it cannot be the first or last character of the data-name.

4. Blanks cannot be included in the data-names.

5. Within the above rules the programmer may use any data-name, with the exception of the approximately 300 COBOL *reserved words* listed in Appendix A. (Manufacturers often add some of their own words to the ANSI list.)

Some examples of legitimate data-names are these:

HOURS	PREMIUM
ENDING-INVENTORY	A527157
SALES-TAX-TOTAL	31576X5

As illustrated above, data-names do not have to be meaningful English words. A programmer can choose to use such data-names as X, Y, Z, X1, X2, and the like. However, even though such data-names are typically shorter than those that are inherently meaningful as names, they increase the likelihood of subsequent confusion. COBOL was designed specifically to allow *self-documentation,* which means that by reading the program one should be able to understand what the program does and what data it uses. The problem with using terse data-names is that their meanings are forgotten by the programmer and are difficult to understand by others even if a list of definitions is supplied.

In addition to data-names, *constants* also are defined in the DATA DIVISION. We defer discussion of the types of constants and their use until Chapter 3, which focuses particularly on writing the DATA DIVISION of a COBOL program.

R E V I E W . . . .

1. Of the four divisions of a COBOL program, the one that identifies the COBOL program to the computer by providing a program name is the _____ DIVISION.

   IDENTIFICATION

2. The division of the COBOL program in which the computer equipment to be used is specified is the _____ DIVISION.

   ENVIRONMENT

3. The division that includes the data format specifications for both input and output is the _____ DIVISION.

   DATA

4. The division of a COBOL program that includes the executable instructions directly concerned with the overall objectives of the program is the _____ division.

   PROCEDURE

5. The order in which the four divisions of a COBOL program appear is _____ , _____ , _____ , and _____ .

   IDENTIFICATION; ENVIRONMENT; DATA; PROCEDURE

6. IN COBOL a label for a field of data that can contain different values at different times is called a(n) _____ .

   data-name

7. A data-name must not be more than _____ (number) characters in length and can include [alphabetic characters only / alphabetic and numeric characters].

   30; alphabetic and numeric characters

8. Every data-name must include at least one [alphabetic / numeric] character, and the only special symbol permitted is the _____ .

   alphabetic; hyphen

9. Place a check mark before each of the following that is a legitimate data-name in COBOL.

   a. _____ INVENTORY

b. _____ END OF YEAR BALANCE

c. _____ 2735B5

d. _____ 27-35B5

e. _____ BALANCE-DUE-

f. _____ 57

g. _____ END-OF-YEAR-BALANCE-DUE-ON-ACCOUNT

h. _____ DATA

i. _____ BALANCE

a. ✔

b. spaces not allowed

c. ✔

d. ✔

e. hyphens must be embedded

f. at least one alphabetic character must be included

g. must be less than 30 characters in length

h. a reserved COBOL word (a bit of a trick question—see Appendix A)

i. ✔

10. Each field of internal storage has a unique data-name, or label, associated with it. Each data-name [must / need not] be unique and [must / need not) imply something about the meaning of the content.

must; need not

. . . .

SAMPLE COBOL PROGRAM

In this section you will study the sample program from a broad point of view only, not in terms of the meaning and function of each of the specific COBOL statements included in the program. In the next chapter, Basic Commands, you will focus on the specific commands included in another sample program.

Program Function

The function of the sample program is simply to read all the student records in a file and to print each name on the printer.

Input

The student file consists of records that have the following format:

- Columns 1-10:   Contains the first name

- Columns 11-25:   Contains the last name

- Columns 26-80:   Contains other data, not used by this program.

The sample input looks like this:

J	O	S	E	P	H					A	N	D	E	R	S	O	N								
R	O	B	E	R	T	A		J	O	B	R	O	W	N											
D	A	N	I	E	L					C	A	S	T	E	L	L	O	R	I						
L	I	N	D	A						C	H	R	I	S	T	I	A	N	S	O	N				
K	A	T	H	E	R	I	N	E		D	R	I	N	K	W	A	T	E	R						

Output

The output will be a printed listing with the following format:

- Columns 1-10:   Will contain blank spaces
- Columns 11-20:   Will contain the first name
- Columns 21-22:   Will contain blank spaces
- Columns 23-37:   Will contain the last name
- Columns 38-132: Will contain blank spaces

Based on the sample input on the preceding page, the corresponding output would differ by the fact that there will be at least two blank spaces between the first and the last name. Short first names, of course, will have more than two blank spaces following since the last names will be vertically aligned.

Structure Chart

Figure 1-5 is a structure chart for the sample program. The MAIN-LOGIC module has two immediate subordinate modules: READ-STUDENT and PRINT-STUDENT. The READ-STUDENT module then also is subordinate to PRINT-STUDENT because after each customer record is printed the next input record needs to be read.

The number at the top-right of each module identifies the paragraph number in the corresponding PROCEDURE DIVISION of the COBOL program. Of course, this number can be known only after the program is written. Thus a structure chart evolves through several stages. Initially, which is the point we are at now, it serves as a graphical tool in designing the main functions of the program and their relationships. After the program is completed and the paragraph numbers are inserted, another reviewer of the program can compare the structure chart with the program code to understand more easily the program and the relationships of the main functions (paragraphs). We will refer back to the structure chart in Figure 1-5 after the COBOL program is presented to you.

FIGURE 1-5

Structure Chart for the Sample Program

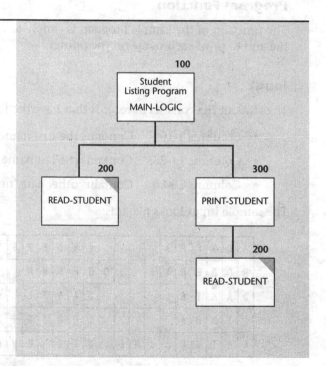

Pseudocode

Figure 1-6 presents pseudocode for the sample program. In part (a) of the figure the pseudocode is written in a general way, while in part (b) the pseudocode is written to correspond rather closely to the COBOL language. As we stated earlier in this chapter, pseudocode is not standardized. Its main function is to help the

FIGURE 1-6

Pseudocode for the Sample Program

Part (a) — Generalized Pseudocode

STUDENT LISTING PROGRAM

PERFORM

    Open the input and output files

    Read student record

    PERFORM UNTIL end of student records

        Clear the output print report record

        Move the name from the input to the output record

        Write the output record on the printer

        Read the next student record

    END-PERFORM

    Close the files

END-PERFORM

Stop program execution

Part (b) — COBOL-Oriented Pseudocode

STUDENT LISTING PROGRAM

100-MAIN-LOGIC.

    Open the input and output files

    PERFORM 200-READ-STUDENT

        to read the first record from the student file

    PERFORM 300-PRINT-STUDENT

        UNTIL the end of the student file

    Close the files

    Stop run

200-READ-STUDENT.

    Read a record from the student file

        and if it is the end of the file, set a flag on

300-PRINT-STUDENT.

    Clear the print report record

    Move the first and last name from the input

        student file record to the report record

    Write the report record (on the printer)

    PERFORM 200-READ-STUDENT

        to read the next record from the student file.

End of Program

programmer develop the program. You can think of part (a) in Figure 1-6 as the first-pass pseudocode; you would develop such a pseudocode when your main focus is on the programming task. Later, as you think about translating the task into COBOL statements, you might develop pseudocode such as in part (b) of Figure 1-6, where we have chosen to use paragraph names that are the same as the function names in the structure chart. Further, we anticipate the syntax required in COBOL programs by assigning unique numbers to the paragraphs. In fact, each of the three numbered paragraph names exactly follows the required COBOL format, including the use of the period at the end of each paragraph name. However, the detail under each paragraph name follows no special format, but does list the subfunctions in logical, sequential order.

The COBOL Program Listing

Figure 1-7 presents the COBOL program to accomplish the desired task. The four divisions that you considered earlier in this chapter are included in the required order: IDENTIFICATION DIVISION, ENVIRONMENT DIVISION, DATA DIVISION, and PROCEDURE DIVISION.

The IDENTIFICATION DIVISION gives the name of the program in the PROGRAM-ID paragraph as being STUDLIST.

The ENVIRONMENT DIVISION identifies the SOURCE-COMPUTER and the OBJECT-COMPUTER in their respective paragraphs. The FILE-CONTROL paragraph is concerned with specific hardware assignments.

FIGURE 1-7
Sample COBOL Program

```
***************************************************************
*   This is a sample program that reads a student file       *
*   and lists its contents (student names) on the printer    *
***************************************************************
*
 IDENTIFICATION DIVISION.
*
 PROGRAM-ID. STUDLIST.
*
*
 ENVIRONMENT DIVISION.
*
 SOURCE-COMPUTER.   ABC-480.
*
 OBJECT-COMPUTER.   ABC-480.
*
 INPUT-OUTPUT SECTION.
*
 FILE-CONTROL.
*
     SELECT STUDENT-FILE  ASSIGN TO   STUDFILE.
     SELECT REPORT-FILE   ASSIGN TO   PRINTER.
*
*
 DATA DIVISION.
*
 FD   STUDENT-FILE
```

FIGURE 1-7
Sample COBOL Program
(continued)

```
                LABEL RECORDS ARE STANDARD.
 *
    01    STUDENT-RECORD.
          05   FIRST-NAME-IN        PIC X(10).
          05   LAST-NAME-IN         PIC X(15).
          05   FILLER              PIC X(55).
 *
    FD   REPORT-FILE
         LABEL RECORDS ARE OMITTED.
 *
    01   REPORT-RECORD.
          05   FILLER              PIC X(10).
          05   FIRST-NAME-OUT      PIC X(10).
          05   FILLER              PIC X(02).
          05   LAST-NAME-OUT       PIC X(15).
          05   FILLER              PIC.X(95).
 *
    WORKING-STORAGE SECTION.
 *
    01   END-OF-FILE              PIC X(03) VALUE 'NO '.
 *
    PROCEDURE DIVISION.
 *
    100-MAIN-LOGIC.
 *
          OPEN INPUT    STUDENT-FILE
          OPEN OUTPUT   REPORT-FILE
 *
          PERFORM 200-READ-STUDENT
 *
          PERFORM 300-PRINT-STUDENT
              UNTIL END-OF-FILE = 'YES'
 *
          CLOSE STUDENT-FILE
          CLOSE REPORT-FILE
 *
          STOP RUN.
 *
    200-READ-STUDENT.
 *
          READ STUDENT-FILE RECORD
             AT END MOVE 'YES' TO END-OF-FILE.
 *
    300-PRINT-STUDENT.
 *
          MOVE SPACES         TO REPORT-RECORD
          MOVE FIRST-NAME-IN TO FIRST-NAME-OUT
          MOVE LAST-NAME-IN  TO LAST-NAME-OUT
 *
          WRITE REPORT-RECORD AFTER ADVANCING 1 LINE
 *
          PERFORM 200-READ-STUDENT.
```

The DATA DIVISION includes the specification of data-names to be used in the PROCEDURE DIVISION, including special FILLER fields that describe fields not referenced by the PROCEDURE DIVISION, but needed for certain data description purposes. An explanation of what the data specifications mean is included with the sample program in the next chapter. For now we continue focusing on an overall, broad understanding of the program. Notice that the DATA DIVISION includes detailed specifications for the input in the STUDENT-RECORD description and detailed specifications for the output in the REPORT-RECORD description.

The PROCEDURE DIVISION includes the statements that are executed to achieve the desired data processing and data output. The 100-MAIN-LOGIC paragraph begins with the required OPEN statement for the INPUT and OUTPUT files. Then the program goes through the sequence of read and print for each record in the input file. The detail associated with the input process, including the necessity to test for the end of the file, is contained in the 200-READ-STUDENT paragraph. Similarly, the detail associated with the output process is contained in the 300-PRINT-STUDENT paragraph. In the 100-MAIN-LOGIC paragraph execution of the first PERFORM statement results in the reading of an input record, and the subsequent execution of the second PERFORM statement results in the printing of an output record. Each execution of the 300-PRINT-STUDENT paragraph includes the next READ operation, because the last statement in that paragraph is PERFORM 200-READ-STUDENT. Notice how this second reference to the 200-READ-STUDENT paragraph corresponds exactly with the relationships shown for the functions in the structure chart in Figure 1-5. Notice also the correspondence between the paragraph numbers in the program and the numbers entered at the top-right of the modules in Figure 1-5.

The sample program in Figure 1-7 complies with the 1974 COBOL standard. Use of the features available in the 1985 standard can result in a PROCEDURE DIVISION that is somewhat different from that in the figure. The PROCEDURE DIVISION for our sample program based on COBOL '85 is presented in Figure 1-8. Using COBOL '85, we could write the entire PROCEDURE DIVISION as one paragraph, and therefore the program in Figure 1-8 does not correspond to the structure chart in Figure 1-5. This need not always be the case; it occurs for this example only because the programming task is such a simple one. In any event a program written using the rules of COBOL '74 can always be compiled by a COBOL '85 compiler. Such a relationship is called *upward compatibility*. Because most existing COBOL programs in organizations have been written using the 1974 version, and given the upward compatibility, it is important that you be familiar with COBOL '74 as well as COBOL '85.

The COBOL Coding Form

The COBOL Coding Form for our sample program is presented in Figure 1-9. Blank copies of this form are included in the back of this book for your use. Historically this form was designed to coincide with the standard 80-column format of the punched card. Of course, nowadays input terminals are used to enter COBOL programs into a computer.

The first six positions of the COBOL Coding Form are reserved for the optional *sequence number*. The programmer may assign a sequence number to each program line so that the lines are numbered in order. A common practice has been to use the first three columns as a page number corresponding to the number of coding form pages used. Then the next three columns can indicate line numbers, such as 010, 020, 030, and so on, leaving gaps in the numbering for possible program changes. Given that this program is quite short, we chose not to assign any sequence numbers in Figure 1-9. In any case the practice of using sequence numbers in a COBOL program is now generally unnecessary. Most programs are

FIGURE 1-8

PROCEDURE DIVISION for the Sample Program Based on the 1985 ANSI COBOL Standard

```
*
PROCEDURE DIVISION.
*
PRINT-STUDENT-REPORT.
*
    OPEN INPUT   STUDENT-FILE
    OPEN OUTPUT  REPORT-FILE
*
    PERFORM UNTIL FILE-END
*
        READ STUDENT-FILE RECORD
*
            AT END SET FILE-END TO TRUE
*
            NOT AT END
*
                MOVE SPACES TO REPORT-RECORD
                MOVE FIRST-NAME-IN TO FIRST-NAME-OUT
                MOVE LAST-NAME-IN  TO LAST-NAME-OUT
*
                WRITE REPORT-RECORD
                    AFTER ADVANCING 1 LINE
*
        END-READ
*
    END-PERFORM
*
    CLOSE STUDENT-FILE
*
    CLOSE REPORT-FILE
*
    STOP RUN.
*
```

now keyed-in using a text editor or word processing program. Such programs allow for insertion and deletion of individual lines and automatically keep track of line numbers.

Column 7 is used to indicate that a line contains a *comment* entry, shown by entering an *asterisk* (*) in that column. Whatever is written on such a line is listed with the source program but is not compiled. Comments can be used to enter explanations about a portion of the program; however, a well-written program should have a limited need for comments. Back in Figure 1-7, the first four lines were comment lines that gave a brief description of the program. Several lines throughout the coding form in Figure 1-9 have an asterisk in column 7, but with nothing else on the line. The effect is that when the program is listed, these lines will be left blank, thereby enhancing the readability of the program listing.

Finally, readability of a program listing can be enhanced by causing a portion of the program to be listed on a *new page* on the printer. This can be accomplished by entering a *slash* (/) in column 7, as illustrated at the top of the second page of Figure 1-9. Incidentally, it is coincidental that the signal for the page break in the program listing happened to be exactly at the top of the second

FIGURE 1-9

COBOL Coding Form for the Sample Program

```
IDENTIFICATION DIVISION.
PROGRAM-ID. STUDLIST.
*
ENVIRONMENT DIVISION.
CONFIGURATION SECTION.
SOURCE-COMPUTER. ABC-480.
OBJECT-COMPUTER. ABC-480.
INPUT-OUTPUT SECTION.
FILE-CONTROL.
    SELECT STUDENT-FILE ASSIGN TO STUDFILE
    SELECT REPORT-FILE  ASSIGN TO PRINTER.
*
DATA DIVISION.
FILE SECTION.
FD  STUDENT-FILE LABEL RECORDS ARE STANDARD.
01  STUDENT-RECORD.
    05 FIRST-NAME-IN    PIC X(10).
    05 LAST-NAME-IN     PIC X(15).
    05 FILLER           PIC X(55).

WORKING-STORAGE SECTION.
01  END-OF-FILE         PIC X(3) VALUE 'NO '.
    88 FILE-END         VALUE 'YES'.
```

```
PROCEDURE DIVISION.
100-MAIN-LOGIC.
    OPEN INPUT    STUDENT-FILE
    OPEN OUTPUT   REPORT-FILE
    PERFORM 200-READ-STUDENT
    PERFORM 300-PRINT-STUDENT
        UNTIL END-OF-FILE = 'YES'
    CLOSE STUDENT-FILE
    CLOSE REPORT-FILE
    STOP RUN.
*
200-READ-STUDENT.
    READ STUDENT-FILE RECORD
        AT END MOVE 'YES' TO END-OF-FILE.
*
300-PRINT-STUDENT.
    MOVE SPACES TO REPORT-RECORD
    MOVE FIRST-NAME-IN TO FIRST-NAME-OUT
    MOVE LAST-NAME-IN TO LAST-NAME-OUT
    WRITE REPORT-RECORD AFTER ADVANCING 1 LINE
    PERFORM 200-READ-STUDENT.
```

page of Figure 1-9. The point at which we would like a page break in the program listing generally is unrelated to where we happen to begin a new page on the COBOL Coding Form.

Program Flowchart

Figure 1-10 presents the flowchart for the sample program. Flowcharts are useful for *understanding* the overall logic and the sequential relationships of functions in

FIGURE 1-10

Flowchart for the Sample Program

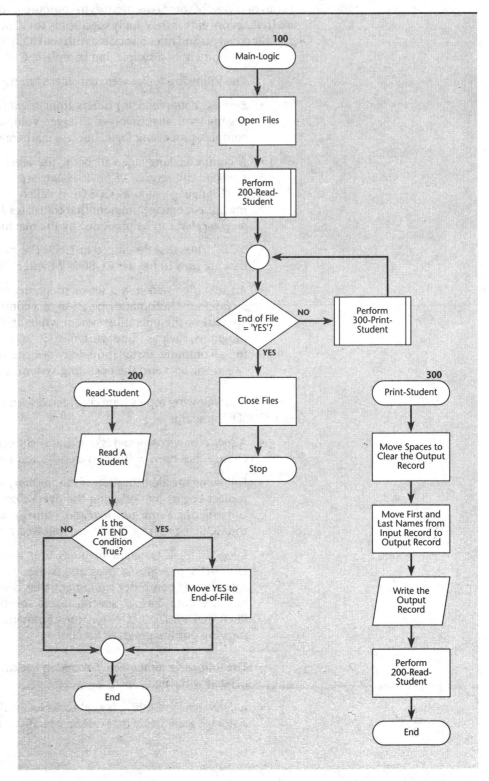

a program, and therefore are important for program documentation. However, flowcharts are not as useful in *designing and writing* a COBOL program as are the combined use of structure charts and pseudocode.

SUMMARY

The contents of this chapter were designed to provide you with a broad but thorough introduction to COBOL programming by focusing on three categories of topics: (1) an overview of some *general issues* in computer programming; (2) program *design and testing* concepts as they apply specifically to COBOL programming; and (3) some specific concepts and rules associated with the COBOL *language,* including the review of the development of a simple, but complete, COBOL program.

The following topics were considered in the category of *general issues:*

- *Business data processing* differs from *scientific computing* in that data processing typically involves a larger volume and variety of data, more complex processing logic, but less mathematical manipulation.

- A computer language can be at the level of being a *machine language, symbolic language,* or *higher-level language.* A program written in a higher-level language such as COBOL is called a *source program.* A *compiler* is a machine-language program that translates a source program into an *object program* that can be processed by the machine.

- COBOL was first developed in 1959. The two standard versions of COBOL that are now in use are COBOL '74 and COBOL '85.

- An *operating system* is a set of programs supplied by a manufacturer to facilitate the automatic operation of a computer system. *Systems programs* are part of the operating system while *applications programs* are end-user programs, such as those written in COBOL. The *Job Control Language* (JCL) for a computer installation provides the means of communication between the user and the operating system.

The following topics were considered with respect to the *design and testing* of a COBOL program:

- A *good computer program* is one that is correct, understandable, and easy to change, has been written efficiently, and executes efficiently.

- Following the identification of the *program function,* a COBOL programming project begins by designing the overall program structure, preferably by constructing a *structure chart* and writing *pseudocode.* Then the first draft of the COBOL program is written, followed by *program debugging and testing.*

- Every COBOL program includes four divisions. The IDENTIFICATION DIVISION provides a program name. The ENVIRONMENT DIVISION specifies the computer equipment that is required. The DATA DIVISION has the data format specifications for both input and output. The PROCEDURE DIVISION has the commands specifically concerned with carrying out the program function.

The following topics were covered in the category of specific concepts and rules associated with the COBOL *language:*

- A *data-name* in COBOL is analogous to a variable in algebra. It is a label for a storage area (field) that can be referenced by the program.

• The last section of the chapter includes a complete COBOL program for reading a set of customer records and printing the name of each customer. Use of a *structure chart* and *pseudocode* are illustrated. Following the program listing, a *COBOL Coding Form* and a *program flowchart* are included.

EXERCISES

1.1 Describe some of the main characteristics of business data processing and contrast those with scientific computing.

1.2 Give examples of some data processing tasks that would be done in one of these types of organizations: a library, a college, a hospital, a retail store, a manufacturing plant. What are some typical files and typical transactions that would take place in the organization of your choice?

1.3 Name and briefly discuss three levels of computer languages.

1.4 Explain these three related concepts: source program, object program, and compiler. Draw a diagram to illustrate how these three entities are related to one another in a typical COBOL program run.

1.5 What does it mean when we say: "COBOL programs should be substantially self-documenting"?

1.6 What is the operating system of a computer? What is the usual name for the type of language that we use to give commands to the operating system?

1.7 Programming is not a single step but is best thought of as a process. Describe the main steps included in the programming process.

1.8 Give the name and the role for each of the divisions that make up a COBOL program.

1.9 Take the sample program in Figure 1-7 and use it as a basis for learning how to compile and execute a COBOL program with your computer.

1.10 Modify the sample program in Figure 1-7 so that the order of the first and the last name is reversed in the output report.

2 Basic Commands

THE SAMPLE REPORT PROGRAM

AN OUTLINE FOR YOUR COBOL
    PROGRAMS

PROCEDURE DIVISION FOR THE
    SAMPLE REPORT PROGRAM

INPUT-OUTPUT VERBS

THE MOVE INSTRUCTION

THE ARITHMETIC VERB: ADD

CONTROL VERBS

A LOGIC TEMPLATE FOR INPUT
    PROCESSING LOOPS

THE STOP RUN STATEMENT

THE MAIN PURPOSE *of this chapter is to provide you with a working knowledge of a basic set of executable commands in COBOL.*

As discussed in Chapter 1, each COBOL program consists of four divisions. The first three— IDENTIFICATION, ENVIRONMENT, and DATA DIVISION—contain specifications about the program rather than executable statements as such. They set the stage for the fourth division, the PROCEDURE DIVISION to contain the commands that will be carried out during program execution.

In this chapter you will focus your attention on the PROCEDURE DIVISION and study a limited number of basic commands: OPEN, READ, WRITE, CLOSE, MOVE, ADD, PERFORM, and STOP RUN. A sample program is first described and then referenced throughout the chapter, so that you can relate the use of these commands to a concrete example.

THE SAMPLE REPORT PROGRAM

Program Function

This is a simple program designed to read records from a customer file and to print a report about those records. The report will consist of a *report heading,* a set of *detail records* corresponding to the records in the customer file, and a *report footing* consisting of a total value. Figure 2-1 is a sample printed report that specifically identifies the three report groups.

Data Definition

There are three main categories of data in any COBOL program: *input data* read from one or more input files, *working storage data* used during program execution, and *output data* written to one or more output files. Although the typical form of output is a printed report, outputting to magnetic disk, to magnetic tape, or to a terminal screen is also common.

For our sample report program, the *input file* is a disk file that contains customer records. Each customer record is described by means of the *record layout chart* in Figure 2-2. Each customer record consists of three fields:

- Columns 1–13:   Customer name
- Columns 14–16: Number of units sold for a particular product
- Columns 17–80: Other data not used by this program

Following is a listing of sample input data:

```
SAMPLE INPUT DATA
ADAMS        100
BROWN        075
GROVER       030
MOORE        025
PETERSON     060
WILLIAMS     010
```

FIGURE 2-1
Desired Output for the Report Program

```
CUSTOMER NAME        UNITS SOLD   } Report Heading

ADAMS                   100       ⎫
BROWN                    75       ⎪
GROVER                   30       ⎬ Customer Detail
MOORE                    25       ⎪
PETERSON                 60       ⎪
WILLIAMS                 10       ⎭

TOTAL                   300       } Report Footing
```

FIGURE 2-2
Record Layout Chart for the Report Program

Field name	Customer name	Units sold	Unused
Field positions	1–13	14–16	17–80

The desired program output is described by means of the *printer spacing chart* shown in Figure 2-3. Blank copies of this chart are included in the back of this book for your use. The printer spacing chart provides an effective means of defining report data. Typically, these charts provide 132 columns because this is the number of print positions on "computer paper" that is 13½ inches wide. As you can see in Figure 2-3, we wish to print the report heading starting with column 11 and extending through column 43. The "H" at the left margin of line 1 on the print chart indicates that the first line of the report is a heading.

Next, the chart shows the layout of the detail (D) lines on line 3, following one blank line below the report heading. Each detail line consists of four *fields*. The first field consists of blank spaces in columns 1–10. The Customer Name is in columns 11–23, followed by a field of 13 blank spaces in columns 24–36, and the numeric field for the Units Sold in columns 37–39. The report detail records repeat for as many lines as there are customers in the input file. Therefore it is not possible to specify the line number for the third type of report group, the report footing. Again referring to Figure 2-3, you can see the spacing designed for the report footing (F), which gives the total units sold to all of the customers listed on the report. There are 10 blank spaces in columns 1–10, the word TOTAL in columns 11–15, 20 blank spaces in columns 16–35, and then the Total Units Sold field in columns 36–39. Note that the Totals field in the report footing consists of four columns instead of the three columns allocated to the Units Sold field in the detail lines. The reason is that a total field is likely to need more positions than the individual values.

The record layout chart for the input data and the printer spacing chart for the output constitute the two main data definitions for this program. There is

FIGURE 2-3
Printer Spacing Chart for the Report Program

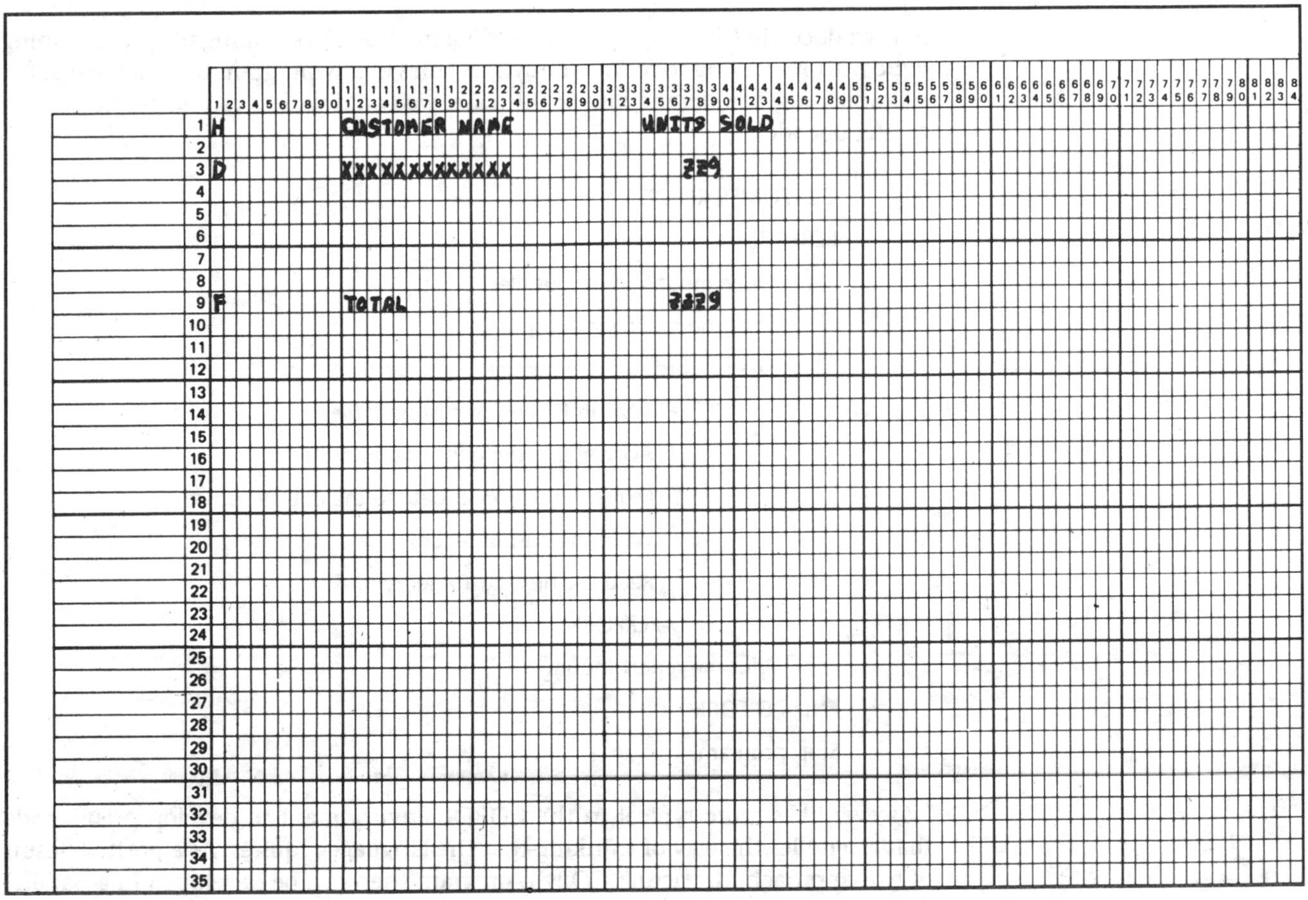

also a need for some other data fields to be used in the program, and these are described in the WORKING-STORAGE of the program. However, we will not discuss them at this point, in order to attend to our main objective, which is to learn some basic PROCEDURE DIVISION commands.

Structure Chart

Figure 2-4 is a structure chart designed for the sample program. It consists of just four modules for the relatively simple program function. The module for the overall programming task, or *root module,* is labeled PROGRAM-SUMMARY. The root module has two immediate subordinates, the READ-CUSTOMER-RECORD and the PROCESS-CUSTOMER-DETAIL modules. Each module has an identification number at its top right for cross-reference with the corresponding paragraph in the COBOL program. As explained with the sample program in Chapter 1, we develop the structure chart *before* writing the COBOL program, and therefore we would not know the paragraph numbers at the time that the structure chart is constructed. However, here we show the structure chart as it would look *after* the program is written. Thus a structure chart initially is used to help us design the program, and then subsequently it can also serve as a reference for a person reading the program. The READ-CUSTOMER-RECORD module is shaded in the upper right corner to mark it as a module that is used in more than one place. In this case it is subordinate to both PROGRAM-SUMMARY and the PROCESS-CUSTOMER-DETAIL modules.

Pseudocode

As introduced in Chapter 1, pseudocode is a method of describing the programming logic without having to follow the syntax rules of any programming language. For a simple program like the one in this case, we could write a rather simple version of pseudocode:

        CUSTOMER REPORT
        PERFORM
                Open input and output files
                Print the report heading
                Read record in customer file
                        PERFORM UNTIL end of customer file
                                Accumulate the units sold into the total
                                Move the customer data to the output record
                                Write the output record
                                Read the next customer record
                        END-PERFORM
                Print the report footing
        END-PERFORM
        Stop program

However, it is more typical in the COBOL environment to develop pseudocode that resembles the way of thinking that the language requires. As a positive result of this approach, the actual COBOL program then can be developed in a parallel

FIGURE 2-4

Structure Chart for the Report Program

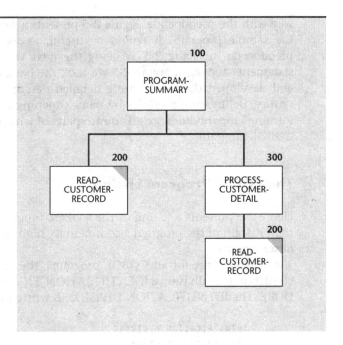

FIGURE 2-5

Pseudocode for the Report Program

Pseudocode for the Customer Report Program

    Written by Chris Anthony

    Date: 06-10-89

100-PROGRAM-SUMMARY

    Open the input and output files

    Print the report heading

    Perform 200-READ-CUSTOMER-RECORD
        to read the first record from the customer file

    Perform 300-PROCESS-CUSTOMER-DETAIL
        until the end of the customer file

    Print the report footing showing the total units sold

    Close the files

    Stop

200-READ-CUSTOMER-RECORD

    Read a record from the customer file
        and if it is the end of the file, set a flag on

300-PROCESS-CUSTOMER-DETAIL

    Accumulate the total units

    Move the customer name and units sold to the output record

    Print the output record

    Perform 200-READ-CUSTOMER-RECORD to read the next record.

END OF PROGRAM

way with the pseudocode. Figure 2-5 presents a set of pseudocode statements for the sample program. It would be useful, as well as typical, to think of the pseudocode in Figure 2-5 as being the next version of the set of pseudocode statements above. In Figure 2-5 we took the basic concepts in the above sample and developed them into more detailed descriptions that parallel the COBOL syntax. Delineating modules by name, opening and closing the files, and "performing" the modules are all counterparts of what eventually will be written as a COBOL program.

The COBOL Program Listing

Figure 2-6 presents a listing of the COBOL program written for the task. On the right margin of the program a commentary highlights the meaning of each group of statements.

As is true for all COBOL programs, the complete program in Figure 2-6 consists of four divisions: IDENTIFICATION, ENVIRONMENT, DATA, and PROCEDURE. The IDENTIFICATION DIVISION is written first:

```
IDENTIFICATION DIVISION.
PROGRAM-ID.  CUSTRPRT.
```

It consists of one paragraph-name, in this case PROGRAM-ID, which then identifies this program by the name CUSTRPRT.

The ENVIRONMENT DIVISION is written next. The basic function of this division is to make reference to the computer system and the file devices required for this program. We defer any study of this division until Chapter 4.

The DATA DIVISION follows. It is used to identify the data-names that will be used in the program. This division consists of a FILE SECTION and a WORKING-STORAGE SECTION.

The last division is the PROCEDURE DIVISION, which constitutes the executable part of the program. In this division the programmer writes the specific data processing instructions to be carried out by the computer.

The purpose of this chapter is to focus on a basic set of PROCEDURE DIVISION commands. However, a few comments are necessary with respect to the DATA DIVISION, because it defines the data-names that are used in the PROCEDURE DIVISION.

Notice the definition of the input file in Figure 2-6:

```
FD  CUSTOMER-FILE
    LABEL RECORDS ARE OMITTED
    RECORD CONTAINS 80 CHARACTERS
    DATA RECORD IS CUSTOMER-RECORD.
01  CUSTOMER-RECORD.
    05 CUSTOMER-NAME      PIC X(13).
    05 CUSTOMER-UNITS     PIC 999.
    05 FILLER             PIC X(64).
```

The input file is called CUSTOMER-FILE, and each record is referenced by the name CUSTOMER-RECORD. Referring to the input record layout chart presented earlier, it is easy to see the correspondence between the record layout chart and the data description in the program. This correspondence is made explicit in Figure 2-7.

Figure 2-8 presents an analysis of one of the data description entries used. The *level-number* indicates whether a field is part of another field. The highest level-number in the hierarchy is 01. Thus 05 CUSTOMER-NAME indicates that the

FIGURE 2-6
Listing of the COBOL Program

```
        IDENTIFICATION DIVISION.                        The beginning of the program and the
        PROGRAM-ID. CUSTRPRT.                           program name.
    *
        ENVIRONMENT DIVISION.
    *
    *
    *
        CONFIGURATION SECTION.                          This section identifies the computer
        SOURCE-COMPUTER. ABC-480.                       system being used.
        OBJECT-COMPUTER. ABC-480.
    *
        INPUT-OUTPUT SECTION.
        FILE-CONTROL.
            SELECT CUSTOMER-FILE  ASSIGN TO CUSTFILE.   Designation of the two files and their
            SELECT REPORT-FILE    ASSIGN TO PRINTER.    hardware assignment.

        DATA DIVISION.
    *
        FILE SECTION.
    *


        FD CUSTOMER-FILE                                Description of the input
            LABEL RECORDS ARE OMITTED                   customer data file.
            RECORD CONTAINS 80 CHARACTERS
            DATA RECORD IS CUSTOMER-RECORD.
        01 CUSTOMER-RECORD.
            05 CUSTOMER-NAME      PIC X(13).
            05 CUSTOMER-UNITS     PIC 999.
            05 FILLER             PIC X(64).
    *
        FD REPORT-FILE                                  Description of the output report file.
            LABEL RECORDS ARE OMITTED
            RECORD CONTAINS 132 CHARACTERS
            DATA RECORD IS REPORT-RECORD.
        01 REPORT-RECORD          PIC X(132).
    *
        WORKING-STORAGE SECTION.
    *
        01 END-OF-FILE            PIC XXX VALUE 'NO'.    A "flag" field used to signal the end of file.
    *
        01 REPORT-HEADING.                              A record containing the report heading.
            05 FILLER             PIC X(10) VALUE SPACES.
            05 REPORT-HEADING-LINE PIC X(31)
            VALUE 'CUSTOMER NAME     UNITS SOLD'.
    *
        01 REPORT-FOOTING.
            05 FILLER             PIC X(10) VALUE SPACES.   A record containing the report footing.
            05 FILLER             PIC X(5)  VALUE 'TOTAL'.
            05 FILLER             PIC X(18) VALUE SPACES.
            05 REPORT-TOTAL-UNITS PIC ZZZ9.
    *
```

FIGURE 2-6
Listing of the COBOL Program (continued)

```
01 REPORT-DETAIL-RECORD.                              A record consisting of the report
   05 FILLER              PIC X(10) VALUE SPACES.     detail data fields.
   05 REPORT-CUST-NAME    PIC X(13).
   05 FILLER              PIC X(10) VALUE SPACES.
   05 REPORT-UNITS        PIC ZZ9.
01 TOTAL-UNITS            PIC 9999 VALUE ZERO.        A units accumulator.
/
PROCEDURE DIVISION.
*
100-PROGRAM-SUMMARY.
*
   OPEN INPUT    CUSTOMER-FILE                        Declare the input/output files and get
        OUTPUT   REPORT-FILE.                         them open.
*
   MOVE REPORT-HEADING TO REPORT-RECORD               Print the report heading on
   WRITE REPORT-RECORD AFTER ADVANCING PAGE.          a new page.
*
   MOVE SPACES TO REPORT-RECORD                       Print a blank line to double space.
   WRITE REPORT-RECORD AFTER ADVANCING 1 LINE
*
   PERFORM 200-READ-CUSTOMER-RECORD.                  Read the (first) customer record.
*
   PERFORM 300-PROCESS-CUSTOMER-DETAIL                Keep processing customers until the
           UNTIL END-OF-FILE = 'YES'.                 end of the file.
*
   MOVE TOTAL-UNITS TO REPORT-TOTAL-UNITS             Print the report footing, double
   MOVE REPORT-FOOTING TO REPORT-RECORD               spacing after the last line.
   WRITE REPORT-RECORD AFTER ADVANCING 2 LINES
*
   CLOSE CUSTOMER-FILE                                Close the files.
         REPORT-FILE.
*
   STOP RUN.                                          Terminate the program.
*
200-READ-CUSTOMER-RECORD.
*
   READ CUSTOMER-FILE RECORD                          Read a record from the customer file. If
        AT END MOVE 'YES' TO END-OF-FILE.             it is the end, set a flag to YES.
*
300-PROCESS-CUSTOMER-DETAIL.
*
   ADD CUSTOMER-UNITS TO TOTAL-UNITS                  Accumulate total units.
*
   MOVE CUSTOMER-NAME TO REPORT-CUST-NAME             Move data from the input record to
   MOVE CUSTOMER-UNITS TO REPORT-UNITS                report detail.
*
   MOVE REPORT-DETAIL-RECORD TO REPORT-RECORD         Print a customer detail line.
   WRITE REPORT-RECORD AFTER ADVANCING 1 LINE.
*
   PERFORM 200-READ-CUSTOMER-RECORD.                  Read (another) customer record.
```

FIGURE 2-7

Relationship of the Defined Data-Names to the Record Layout Chart

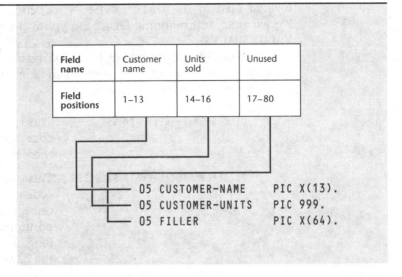

Field name	Customer name	Units sold	Unused
Field positions	1–13	14–16	17–80

```
05  CUSTOMER-NAME    PIC X(13).
05  CUSTOMER-UNITS   PIC 999.
05  FILLER           PIC X(64).
```

FIGURE 2-8

Analysis of One Data Definition Entry

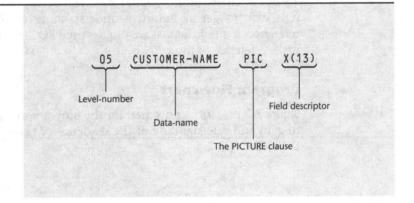

```
05      CUSTOMER-NAME      PIC      X(13)
```
Level-number

Data-name

The PICTURE clause

Field descriptor

name field is under, and part of, the 01 CUSTOMER-RECORD. Similarly, 05 CUSTOMER-UNITS and 05 FILLER are all fields within 01 CUSTOMER-RECORD. Because these three fields all have the same 05 level-number, none of them is part of the other two fields. Chapter 3 will provide you with a more in-depth explanation of the use of level-numbers.

The *data-name* plays the obvious role of naming the field. In Figure 2-8 the data-name is CUSTOMER-NAME. As discussed in Chapter 1, COBOL specifies a number of rules for forming data-names. One data-name used frequently is FILLER, which is a reserved word and is designed to define fields that are not needed to be referenced in the program. In other words, there will never be a statement such as MOVE FILLER in a program. We use FILLER fields in records to define portions of a record that are not of interest in a specific program. We also use FILLER frequently in the WORKING-STORAGE SECTION, to define fields that contain such constant data as headers:

```
05  FILLER   PIC X(5)  VALUE 'TOTAL'
```

In the example the keyword PIC (abbreviation for PICTURE) is used to introduce the field description in terms of a *picture string* that follows. In Figure 2-8 the picture string X(13) specifies that this is an alphanumeric field by using the X code, and that it is 13 bytes long, by the number within the parentheses.

Continuing with the example above, the field of five bytes will contain the characters in quotes. By the way, VALUE, as we will study in Chapter 3, is a *keyword* used in the DATA DIVISION to define the initial contents of fields. For example, in examining Figure 2-6 you will see clauses like VALUE ZERO or VALUE SPACES.

You will study the DATA DIVISION features in greater detail in Chapter 3. For now we can summarize two other main types of PIC clauses, in addition to the PIC X, by the following examples:

`05 CUSTOMER-UNITS PIC 999`	This is a numeric field by use of the 9 code, and it is 3 bytes long because there are 3 9's.
`05 REPORT-TOTAL-UNITS PIC ZZZ9`	This is a numeric edited field. The Z code specifies suppression of leading zeros, if any, in the first three positions. The total field is four bytes long, one byte for each character in the ZZZ9 picture code.

The other data definitions in the DATA DIVISION of the sample program are not discussed at this point. However, because of their self-documenting names it is easy to get an intuitive understanding of their purpose. We will make reference to all of them as we discuss the PROCEDURE DIVISION statements that make reference to these fields.

Program Flowchart

Figure 2-9 presents a flowchart for the program in Figure 2-6. Study this flowchart to gain an understanding of the sequence of tasks included in the PROCEDURE DIVISION.

AN OUTLINE FOR YOUR COBOL PROGRAMS

As a student learning the COBOL language for the first time, you will probably find it convenient to create a program outline similar to the one presented in Figure 2-10. Using a text editor, you can create such an outline and save it as a text file. Then whenever you are about to key-in a new program, copy the outline and add the appropriate instructions. In Figure 2-10 blank spaces indicate the locations of required data, data-names, and so forth in the program. Using a program outline will save you program entry time as well as help to avoid the inadvertent omission of required keywords or sections.

PROCEDURE DIVISION FOR THE SAMPLE REPORT PROGRAM

Reviewing the function for the report program, we begin with a file of customer records, with each record containing a customer name and number of units sold for a particular product. The program is designed to read each record in the file and to produce the report portrayed in Figure 2-1. The complete program in Figure 2-6 is referenced throughout the remainder of this chapter so that you can relate the various types of language statements to a concrete example.

The IDENTIFICATION, ENVIRONMENT, and DATA DIVISION in a COBOL program perform "housekeeping tasks" in that they provide background information so that the program can be executed after compilation. On the other hand, the instructions that directly result in execution of the program are given in the PROCEDURE DIVISION. Most of these executable instructions operate on storage locations, or fields, that have been defined in the DATA DIVISION. The keywords PROCEDURE DIVISION identify the beginning of this division and

FIGURE 2-9

Flowchart for the Report Program

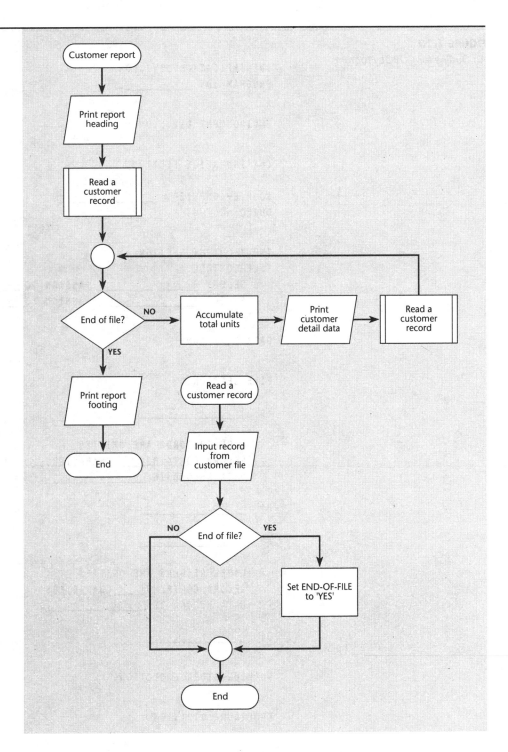

begin at the A margin of the COBOL Coding Form, followed by a period, as illustrated by the following excerpt:

```
SEQUENCE   C  A   B                    COBOL STATEMENT
(PAGE)(SERIAL) O
        0 1    PROCEDURE DIVISION.
        0 2  *
        0 3    100-PROGRAM-SUMMARY.
        0 4  *
        0 5        OPEM INPUT  CUSTOMER-FILE
        0 6             OUTPUT REPORT-FILE
        0 7  *
```

FIGURE 2-10
An Outline for COBOL Programs

```
IDENTIFICATION DIVISION.
PROGRAM-ID. _____.


ENVIRONMENT DIVISION.


CONFIGURATION SECTION.


SOURCE-COMPUTER. _____.
OBJECT-COMPUTER. _____.


INPUT-OUTPUT SECTION.
FILE-CONTROL.
    SELECT _____   ASSIGN TO _____
    SELECT _____   ASSIGN TO _____.


DATA DIVISION.


FILE SECTION.

FD  _____

    LABEL RECORDS ARE OMITTED
    RECORD CONTAINS ___ CHARACTERS
    DATA RECORD IS _____.


01  _____


FD  _____

    LABEL RECORDS ARE OMITTED
    RECORD CONTAINS ___ CHARACTERS
    DATA RECORD IS _____.


01  _____


WORKING-STORAGE SECTION.


PROCEDURE DIVISION.
```

The PROCEDURE DIVISION consists of paragraphs, each paragraph containing at least one sentence. Each paragraph starts with a paragraph-name beginning in column 8 (A margin) of the COBOL Coding Form and ends with a required period. Paragraph-names are coined by the programmer following the rules of data-name formation, with one additional option: paragraph-names may be all numeric. Sentences and statements are written in the B area of the coding form, which includes columns 12–72.

In the sample report program in Figure 2-6 the PROCEDURE DIVISION consists of three paragraphs:

```
PROCEDURE DIVISION.
100-PROGRAM-SUMMARY.
200-READ-CUSTOMER-RECORD.
300-PROCESS-CUSTOMER-DETAIL.
```

These three paragraphs correspond to the three unique modules in the structure chart in Figure 2-4. Except for the first paragraph, 100-PROGRAM-SUMMARY, the order of the other two paragraphs is not important because they are executed by reference with a PERFORM statement. You can see this by reading the contents of the 100-PROGRAM-SUMMARY paragraph in Figure 2-6. Notice that the last statement in that paragraph is a STOP RUN, which terminates the execution of the program. So the program execution flow is to begin with the first statement in the first paragraph, to branch to and return from PERFORMed paragraphs referenced in that first paragraph, and to stop execution when we reach the last statement in the first paragraph, which normally will be a STOP RUN. Now it is obvious why we used 100-PROGRAM-SUMMARY for the name of the first paragraph. Another common name for such a module is 100-MAIN-LOGIC, although the rules of the language allow us to call any paragraph by any name.

The two most commonly used types of PROCEDURE DIVISION statements are imperative and conditional statements. An *imperative statement* consists of a verb that indicates action, plus appropriate operands involved in the action. In this chapter we will concentrate on imperative statements. The following imperative verbs are described in the following sections of this chapter:

- Input-output verbs: OPEN, READ, WRITE, CLOSE
- Data transfer verb: MOVE
- Arithmetic verb: ADD
- Control verbs: PERFORM, STOP RUN

A *conditional statement* allows the program to test for the existence of a condition, and to execute one or more commands selectively depending on the result of the test. Two basic conditional expressions are covered in this chapter: The AT END and the UNTIL conditional clauses. The AT END is used in READ statements, while the UNTIL is used in PERFORM statements.

R E V I E W . . . .

1. Of the four divisions that make up any COBOL program, the one that always is first in the sequence of presentation is the _____ DIVISION.

IDENTIFICATION

2. The next division in the program, which makes reference to the computer hardware that is required, is the _____ DIVISION.

ENVIRONMENT

3. The division of our sample COBOL program that consists of a FILE SECTION and a WORKING-STORAGE SECTION is the _____ DIVISION.

DATA

4. In the DATA DIVISION the hierarchical relationship of a field with other data fields is indicated by the _____-number that is assigned to the field.

level

5. The name of a field is indicated in the DATA DIVISION by the assignment of a _____-name.

data

6. The field description PIC X(13) in the sample program identifies a field as being [numeric / alphanumeric], and ____ (number) bytes long.

alphanumeric; 13

7. The field description PIC 999 in the sample program identifies a field as being _____ , and ____ bytes long.

numeric; 3

8. The field description PIC ZZZ9 in the sample program identifies a field as being numeric and 4 bytes long, and for which up to 3 _____ , if any, will be suppressed in the printed output.

leading zeros

9. The division of a COBOL program that includes the executable statements directly related to the overall program function is the _____ DIVISION.

PROCEDURE

10. Of the two commonly used types of statements in the PROCEDURE DIVISION, the type that includes a verb that indicates action—such as OPEN, MOVE, ADD, or PERFORM—is the _____ statement.

imperative

11. The type of statement in the PROCEDURE DIVISION that includes use of the AT END or the UNTIL clause is a _____ statement.

conditional

·   ·   ·   ·   ·   ·   ·   ·   ·   ·   ·   ·   ·   ·   ·   ·   ·   ·   ·

INPUT-OUTPUT VERBS

In this section we consider four input-output verbs: OPEN, READ, WRITE, and CLOSE.

Before an input or an output file can be used by the program, it must be OPENed. For the report program the following statement can be seen in the first paragraph of the PROCEDURE DIVISION in Figure 2-6:

```
OPEN INPUT    CUSTOMER-FILE
     OUTPUT   REPORT-FILE.
```

The file named CUSTOMER-FILE is opened as input, so that we can READ from it. The file named REPORT-FILE is opened as output; in our example the printer is assigned as the output file, and we will WRITE on it. Thus the OPEN verb declares the input or output function of the file. As in the above, it is common to write each file-name on a *separate* line rather than on the same line, and *not* to repeat the OPEN verb for each file. This practice makes for better readability than is true for the following alternative version of the above commands:

```
OPEN INPUT CUSTOMER-FILE OPEN OUTPUT REPORT-FILE.
```

At this point we should note that the file names appear in two other divisions of the program. In the ENVIRONMENT DIVISION the two files are referenced in the corresponding entries in Figure 2-6:

```
SELECT CUSTOMER-FILE ASSIGN TO  CUSTFILE.
SELECT REPORT-FILE   ASSIGN TO  PRINTER.
```

The statements above designate the hardware assignment for each file. CUSTFILE and PRINTER are assumed to be the names of the two files in the operating system; CUSTOMER-FILE and REPORT-FILE are the chosen file-names within the COBOL program. Then in the DATA DIVISION the FD entries name and describe certain characteristics of each file. For instance, in Figure 2-6 we have the following:

```
FD  REPORT-FILE
    LABEL RECORDS ARE OMITTED
    RECORD CONTAINS 132 CHARACTERS
    DATA RECORD IS REPORT-RECORD.
```

Thus when references to files are made in the PROCEDURE DIVISION, it is understood that the above type of information about the files has already been given in the ENVIRONMENT DIVISION and DATA DIVISION.

The basic format of the READ instruction is

READ file-name RECORD

    AT END imperative-statement.

In Figure 2-6, in the 200-READ-CUSTOMER-RECORD paragraph of the PROCEDURE DIVISION, the input instruction is

```
READ CUSTOMER-FILE RECORD
    AT END MOVE 'YES' TO END-OF-FILE.
```

Each time the command READ CUSTOMER-FILE RECORD is executed, the data contained in the next record of the customer file on disk is copied into central storage in the area referenced by the record-name CUSTOMER-RECORD. For example, whatever data is in columns 1–13 of the disk record is copied into columns 1–13 of CUSTOMER-RECORD (which is designated by the data-name CUSTOMER-NAME).

Each execution of the READ statement causes the previous content of the corresponding record in central storage to be erased. This means that normally one record at a time is processed, and, when a next record is read, there is no longer any use for the content of the preceding record.

As part of the READ instruction, we also need to indicate what the computer should do after all the input records have been read. The AT END clause serves this purpose. When a record is read, it is examined to see if it is an end-of-file record. The specific form of an end-of-file record differs according to the computer used, but in general it contains data codes that designate it as such. Only when such a record is read, is the "imperative-statement" following AT END executed. Thus AT END is a conditional clause: it indicates that the statement following the AT END should be executed if the record just read is an end-of-file record.

In our sample program, the imperative statement following AT END enters a YES in the END-OF-FILE field so that the program will be able to test the content of this "flag" field and determine when all the data have been read. This test is done by the UNTIL clause in the PERFORM verb discussed later.

The output verb WRITE is similar to the input verb READ, except that reference is made to a *record-name* rather than a file-name:

WRITE record-name AFTER ADVANCING integer LINES

or

WRITE record-name AFTER ADVANCING PAGE.

Consider the following excerpt from Figure 2-6:

```
MOVE REPORT-HEADING TO REPORT-RECORD
WRITE REPORT-RECORD AFTER ADVANCING PAGE.
```

The contents of the WORKING-STORAGE field called REPORT-HEADING are MOVEd (copied) to REPORT-RECORD, which is the record of the output file (recall the OPEN . . . OUTPUT REPORT-FILE). The AFTER ADVANCING PAGE clause in the excerpt above specifies that the printer should skip to the start of a new page and then write the data. PAGE is another reserved word in COBOL and signals the start of a page. As also illustrated in Figure 2-6, we can control the number of lines between printed output. To single space, we say WRITE . . . AFTER ADVANCING 1 LINE. To double space we say AFTER ADVANCING 2 LINES, and so on.

As illustrated in Figure 2-6, in COBOL we do not write data directly. First we transfer whatever is to be written to an output file record, and then we issue the command WRITE. The output record is like a gate through which all output passes. For this reason the description of the REPORT-RECORD in the DATA DIVISION of our sample program specifies one long field of 132 bytes:

```
01   REPORT-RECORD   PIC X(132).
```

There is no point in subdividing the above field of 132 bytes into subfields, since a variety of output may be moved to the field. For instance, we will print a report heading, detail lines, and a report footing. Incidentally, as we mentioned earlier, the choice of 132 bytes is in reference to the common width of printers in mainframe computers. If our output device were a video monitor or a typical, 80-column personal computer printer, we would have used another record size, such as PIC X(80).

We conclude this discussion of input-output verbs with the CLOSE verb, which is used after a file is no longer needed and which must be used before the end of the program. At the end of the PROGRAM-SUMMARY paragraph in Figure 2-6, we see

```
CLOSE CUSTOMER-FILE
      REPORT-FILE.
```

The CLOSE verb is particularly meaningful in the context of magnetic tapes and disk files. File-names are written on separate lines simply to enhance readability, and the CLOSE is written only once by style choice. For the second line it would be equally correct to write CLOSE REPORT-FILE.

R E V I E W . . . .

1. Input of data into the central storage of the computer is accomplished by executing a READ statement. Before a READ statement can be executed, a checking procedure must be carried out to determine file availability by executing a(n) _____ statement.

2. As each record of a file is read into storage, the previous content of that storage location, which typically represents data from the preceding record that was read, is automatically [moved / erased].

erased

3. The part of the READ statement that indicates what should be done after all the records of the input file have been read is the _____ clause.

AT END

4. Output of data from a designated output file is accomplished by executing a(n) _____ instruction.

WRITE

5. Just as is true for a READ STATEMENT, before a WRITE statement can be executed, availability of the output file must be ascertained by executing an appropriate _____ statement.

OPEN

6. An option available with the WRITE statement allows control of the vertical spacing in the printed output. The clause used to designate spacing instruction is the AFTER _____ clause.

ADVANCING

7. When a data processing operation is completed, the availability of both the input and output files that have been used should be terminated. This is accomplished by an appropriate _____ instruction.

CLOSE

.   .   .   .

THE MOVE INSTRUCTION

The MOVE verb is used to copy data from a sending field to a receiving field. Despite what the word MOVE implies, data items are not moved but, rather, are simply copied. Thus the instruction MOVE A to B designates that B should contain a copy of the content of A which also retains its content. Examples of the MOVE instruction in Figure 2-6 are

```
MOVE      REPORT-HEADING TO REPORT-RECORD
MOVE      SPACES TO REPORT-RECORD
MOVE      CUSTOMER-NAME TO REPORT-CUST-NAME
```

The sending field should not be longer than the receiving field, for otherwise some data would be truncated. When a sending field such as REPORT-HEADING is moved to a larger receiving field such as REPORT-RECORD, the extra spaces to the right are filled with blanks. When moving numeric data, the programmer must observe many rules. The MOVE operation will be described in further detail in Chapter 4.

THE ARITHMETIC VERB: ADD

In this section we consider the ADD arithmetic verb which is used in the first line of the 300-PROCESS-CUSTOMER-DETAIL paragraph in Figure 2-6:

```
ADD CUSTOMER-UNITS TO TOTAL-UNITS.
```

The instruction says to add the value in CUSTOMER-UNITS to the existing value in TOTAL-UNITS. If the first field had a content of 30 and the second a content of 20, the ADD instruction would change the content of TOTAL-UNITS to 50 and would leave the value in CUSTOMER-UNITS unchanged.

TOTAL-UNITS in the above example serves as an accumulator. We keep adding to it the values of CUSTOMER-UNITS being read from the CUSTOMER-FILE records. It is important to start the accumulator with a zero value; otherwise we would be adding to an already existing value. Therefore the DATA DIVISION specifies

```
01  TOTAL-UNITS    PIC 9999    VALUE ZERO.
```

The VALUE ZERO clause assures us that the accumulator will have a zero initial value. If we forgot to include the VALUE ZERO clause, we would generate improper totals, since the initial content of the field is not likely to be zero.

The ADD verb, as well as other arithmetic verbs, has many variations. You will study these verbs in some detail in Chapters 4 and 7.

R E V I E W . . . .

1. The verb that is used for data transfer is the _____ verb.

    MOVE

2. Execution of a MOVE instruction results in the content of a sending field being [moved / copied] into the receiving field.

    copied

3. The sending field should not be [smaller / larger] than the receiving field.

    larger

4. The verb that is used to achieve the accumulation of values that are stored in two different fields is the _____ verb.

    ADD

5. When the statement ADD DAILY-SALES TO SALES-TOTAL is executed, the record field whose content remains unchanged because of its position in the above statement is _____.

    DAILY-SALES

6. When the statement ADD DAILY-SALES TO SALES-TOTAL is executed, the field whose content is changed, given that the other field had a nonzero value, is _____.

    SALES-TOTAL

7. The clause in the DATA DIVISION record description that is used to ensure that a field used as an accumulator has an initial value of zero is the _____ clause.

    VALUE ZERO

. . . .

CONTROL VERBS

Program instructions in the PROCEDURE DIVISION are executed in the order in which they are written, from top to bottom, except when control verbs interrupt this normal flow. In this section we describe some basic forms of program control by use of the PERFORM and STOP RUN verbs.

The PERFORM verb provides a powerful mechanism for program control. Referring to the 100-PROGRAM-SUMMARY paragraph of the PROCEDURE DIVISION in Figure 2-6, you can observe the following instruction:

```
PERFORM 200-READ-CUSTOMER-RECORD.
```

The 200-READ-CUSTOMER-RECORD is a paragraph-name. The effect of the above instruction is to branch to the specified paragraph, execute all the instructions in the paragraph, and then resume with the statement immediately following the PERFORM.

When the PERFORM 200-READ-CUSTOMER-RECORD is executed, we read the next record in CUSTOMER-FILE. If that record happens to be the end-of-file record, the field named END-OF-FILE would then contain a YES because of the READ statement that has already been executed:

```
READ CUSTOMER-FILE RECORD
    AT END MOVE 'YES' TO END-OF-FILE.
```

Again a PERFORM statement says "go execute the named paragraph and come back." In the 100-PROGRAM-SUMMARY paragraph in Figure 2-6 we have two PERFORM statements in succession:

```
PERFORM 200-READ-CUSTOMER-RECORD.
PERFORM 300-PROCESS-CUSTOMER-DETAIL
    UNTIL END-OF-FILE = 'YES'.
```

The second PERFORM statement has a different format from that of the first one, as will be explained below. But apart from that consideration, when the program comes to the second PERFORM, a record has already been read from the CUSTOMER-FILE and the AT END test in the READ statement has been executed.

The PERFORM verb also can be used to execute an *iterative procedure*, or *loop*, as in the second PERFORM statement discussed above:

```
PERFORM 300-PROCESS-CUSTOMER-DETAIL
    UNTIL END-OF-FILE = 'YES'.
```

Recall that the END-OF-FILE contains YES only when the end-of-file record has been read in the CUSTOMER-FILE. The above PERFORM operates as follows: the conditional expression END-OF-FILE = 'YES' is tested; if it is true, the program leaves the associated PERFORM statement and continues execution with the next statement, which starts with MOVE TOTAL-UNITS. If the condition is not true, then 300-PROCESS-CUSTOMER-DETAIL is executed again. The entire process is repeated until the condition is true. At this point, it would be a good idea for you to turn to the flowchart in Figure 2-9 to get a visual view of the interrelationships in the program logic.

It is important to recognize that the specialized conditional UNTIL . . . is executed first, and if END-OF-FILE is YES, then the associated PERFORM 300-PROCESS-CUSTOMER-DETAIL is *not* executed. To understand fully the control structure in the sample program, notice that the last statement in the 300-PROCESS-CUSTOMER-DETAIL paragraph in Figure 2-6 is PERFORM 200-READ-CUSTOMER-RECORD. Thus every time we repeat execution of the PERFORM . . . UNTIL, a new record is read and checked for the end-of-file condition. Furthermore, before the PERFORM . . . UNTIL is executed for the very first time, a record has already been read due to the first PERFORM statement in the 100-PROGRAM-SUMMARY paragraph.

Figure 2-11 portrays the control structure of the PERFORM . . . UNTIL in flowchart form. As an additional aid in understanding the control structure involved, we consider a few special cases in the following paragraphs.

Suppose that the customer file contains only two customer records. How many times would the 200-READ-CUSTOMER-RECORD paragraph be executed? The answer is three times. The first time is caused by the first PERFORM in the 100-

FIGURE 2-11

*Flowchart Showing the Effect of
Executing the Conditional UNTIL*

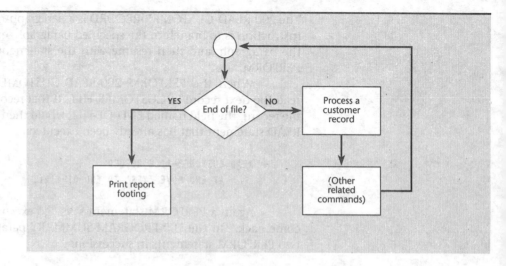

FIGURE 2-12

*Sequence of Program Execution
Steps Involving PERFORM
Statements*

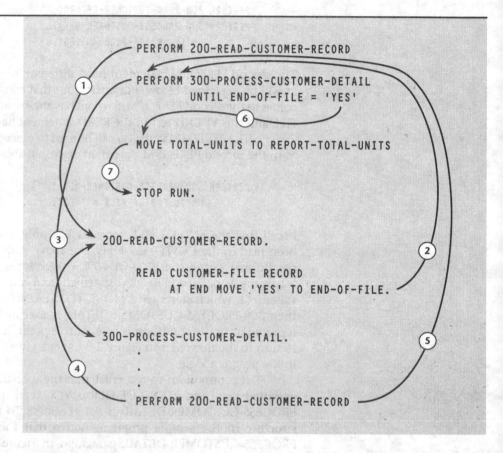

PROGRAM-SUMMARY. The second and third times are caused by the PERFORM in the 300-PROCESS-CUSTOMER-DETAIL paragraph. Of course, the third record would not be a customer record; it would be an end-of-file record that would cause YES to be moved to END-OF-FILE, which in turn would cause the PERFORM . . . UNTIL not to execute 300-PROCESS-CUSTOMER-DETAIL, and would lead to printing of the report footing and the termination of the program via execution of the STOP RUN command.

The flowchart in Figure 2-9 and the examples above may not make it obvious how program control returns to the PERFORM . . . UNTIL statement after each customer record has been read. To illustrate how this occurs, Figure 2-12 portrays the sequence of program execution for the usual data situation in which there is at least one customer record. Study Figure 2-12 as you read the following paragraph.

As a result of executing the PERFORM 200-READ-CUSTOMER-RECORD statement in the 100-PROGRAM-SUMMARY paragraph, the 200-READ-CUSTOMER-RECORD paragraph is executed. The first record is a customer record. As is always the case, program execution now returns to the statement following the PERFORM that was just executed. The next statement is the PERFORM . . . UNTIL. Because the record that was read was *not* the end-of-file record, the 300-PROCESS-CUS-TOMER-DETAIL paragraph is now executed, culminating with the last statement in that paragraph, which is PERFORM 200-READ-CUSTOMER-RECORD. Execution of this statement results in program control returning to the 200-READ-CUSTOMER-RECORD paragraph. If the record that is read is a customer record, the record is then simply available for processing. If the record is the end-of-file record, YES is moved to END-OF-FILE. After executing the 200-READ-CUSTOMER-RECORD command, program execution then would continue with the statement following the PERFORM statement in the 300-PROCESS-CUSTOMER-DETAIL paragraph. But there is no statement following that embedded PERFORM statement, because it is the last statement in that paragraph. Therefore, control returns to the PERFORM . . . UNTIL statement after every record is read.

A LOGIC TEMPLATE FOR INPUT PROCESSING LOOPS

Most COBOL programs are input-driven and involve the following general structure:

> We read a record from an input file, process that record, and then we continue so reading and processing until we reach the end of the input file. At that point, we either terminate the program or we do other tasks, such as print summary totals.

Because this structure is so common, we suggest that you take the time to learn how to code this general logic in a "standard" way so that you don't have to stop and "re-invent the wheel" every time that you wish to do such data processing. Figures 2-13 and 2-14 present two recommended standard templates for handling the logic of iteration for input from a file. Figure 2-13 presents the template based on the 1974 ANSI COBOL standard and follows the procedure used in the sample program. Figure 2-14 presents the template based on the 1985 standard.

The main difference between COBOL '74 and COBOL '85 is that in the 1985 version we have available a number of new features, such as the in-line PERFORM and the NOT AT END clause in the READ statement. The details of these features will be discussed in Chapter 4. For now we will stay with a rough, but simple explanation of some of the COBOL '85 features. The in-line PERFORM does not make reference to another paragraph; instead, it means to say, "perform what follows." Thus in the template in Figure 2-14 you can observe that what follows the in-line PERFORM . . . UNTIL is a READ statement that specifies what to do for both the AT END and the NOT AT END cases. Finally, the END-READ and END-PERFORM are "scope terminators" that define the end of the effect of the corresponding statement. We are proceeding on the assumption that these are intuitive enough features that make sense for now, and we will return to them in Chapter 4.

THE STOP RUN STATEMENT

The STOP RUN statement is the control statement that terminates program execution. When this statement is encountered, program execution terminates immediately. Therefore you should take care to include this command only at the appropriate point or points in terms of the logic of the program.

FIGURE 2-13

*A Logic Template for Handling
Input-Driven Iteration Using
COBOL '74*

Set up a Read-Input-File paragraph that reads the input file and, if it is the end of the file, it sets a flag to a value such as "yes".

Set up a Process-Record paragraph that does the necessary processing.

The last statement in this paragraph performs the Read-Input-File paragraph.

PERFORM the Read-Input-File paragraph
to read the first record from the file.

PERFORM the Process-Record paragraph
UNTIL the end-of-file condition is true.

Example:

OPEN the input and output files.

PERFORM 200-READ-CUSTOMER-RECORD.

PERFORM 300-PROCESS-CUSTOMER-DETAIL

UNTIL END-OF-FILE = 'YES'.

Other instructions, such as processing summary totals, etc.

CLOSE the files.

STOP RUN.

200-READ-CUSTOMER-RECORD.

READ CUSTOMER-FILE RECORD

AT END MOVE 'YES' TO END-OF-FILE.

300-PROCESS-CUSTOMER-DETAIL.

instructions to process the record

PERFORM 200-READ-CUSTOMER-RECORD

R E V I E W . . . .

1. The COBOL verbs that interrupt the normal sequential execution of program statements are called _____ verbs.

control

2. The control verb that makes it possible to branch to a specified paragraph, execute it, and then return to the statement immediately following the statement containing the control verb is the _____ verb.

PERFORM

3. The control verb that is used to terminate program execution is the _____ verb.

STOP RUN

4. The STOP RUN statement [is / need not be] the last statement in a program.

need not be

FIGURE 2-14

A Logic Template for Handling Input-Driven Iteration Using COBOL '85

```
PERFORM UNTIL end-of-file-condition is true

    READ a record from the input file

        AT END SET end-of-file-condition TO TRUE

        NOT AT END

            Process the input record, either by writing the instructions
            right here, or by writing a PERFORM that references a paragraph
            that does the processing

    END-READ

END-PERFORM


Example:

OPEN input and output files

PERFORM UNTIL END-OF-INPUT

    READ CUSTOMER-FILE RECORD

        AT END SET END-OF-INPUT TO TRUE

        NOT AT END

            PERFORM

                instructions to process the record

            END—PERFORM

    END-READ

END-PERFORM

CLOSE the files

STOP RUN.
```

SUMMARY

The overall purpose of this chapter was to introduce you to a basic set of PROCEDURE DIVISION commands. A sample program was referenced throughout the chapter as a concrete example.

The *program function* was to read records from a customer file and to print a report that includes a *report heading*, a set of *detail records*, and a *report footing*. A *printer spacing chart* was used to plan program output. A *structure chart* was prepared, *pseudocode* was written, and a *flowchart* was developed in the process of program design, culminating in a listing of the COBOL program.

As a necessary prerequisite for discussion of the PROCEDURE DIVISION commands, the way that data specifications are written in the DATA DIVISION was briefly described. The elements of such a specification include the *level-number, data-name, PICTURE (PIC) clause,* and the *field descriptor* (such as 999) associated with the PICTURE clause.

After reviewing the overall logic of the sequence of paragraphs in the sample PROCEDURE DIVISION, two types of PROCEDURE DIVISION statements were identified: imperative statements and conditional statements. This chapter focused particularly on imperative statements.

An *imperative statement* consists of a verb that indicates action, plus the appropriate operands involved in the action. The imperative verbs whose uses were described in this chapter are

- Input-output verbs: OPEN, READ, WRITE, CLOSE
- Data transfer verb: MOVE
- Arithmetic verb: ADD
- Control verbs: PERFORM, STOP RUN

A *conditional statement* allows the program to test for the existence of a condition, and to execute one or more commands selectively depending on the result of the test. Two conditional expressions were described in this chapter: the AT END and the UNTIL. The AT END is used in READ statements, while the UNTIL is used in PERFORM statements, and such uses are included in the sample program.

EXERCISES

2.1   Write COBOL statements for the following tasks.

(a) Set the value of a data-name A equal to 150.

(b) Set the value of ACCUMULATOR equal to zero.

(c) Add the value of BONUS to PAY.

2.2   Write COBOL statements to exchange the contents of two fields, A and B. (You may assume any additional data-names that you need.)

2.3   A program contains the statement

```
PERFORM REPORT-PRINTING
        UNTIL END-OF-DATA = 'YES'.
```

Explain how END-OF-DATA is defined in the program, and illustrate how it is used as a control mechanism. Assume that END-OF-DATA refers to an input file called CUSTOMER-FILE.

2.4   The following program segment contains a logical error. Find and correct the error.

```
PROCEDURE DIVISION.
FIRST-PARAGRAPH.
    READ PRODUCT-FILE RECORD
        AT END MOVE 'YES' TO END-OF-FILE.
```

2.5   Write a statement to make an output file called TRANSACTIONS-FILE available for subsequent use.

2.6   Assume that we have the following program excerpt.

```
PROGRAM-SUMMARY.
    ... (other statements of no interest here)
    PERFORM PROCESS-INPUT
        UNTIL END-OF-FILE = 'YES'
```

```
READ-INPUT.
      _____
      _____

PROCESS-INPUT.
      . . . (other statements of no interest here)
      PERFORM READ-INPUT.  (last statement in paragraph)
```

Write statements to determine if an input file called PAYABLES has been read-in completely and, if it has, to terminate the program. Assume that PAYABLES and RECEIVABLES are the input and output files that had been used in the program. Fill in the blank spaces indicated in the program segment.

2.7 Write statements to print two records from a file whose record is called MONTHLY-REPORT, leaving two blank lines between the records. The first record will print the contents of HEADER-1 and the second will print the contents of HEADER-2.

2.8 Consider the following main-logic paragraph of a program.

```
MAIN-LOGIC.
      . . . (other statements of no interest here)
      PERFORM PROCESSING
            UNTIL END-OF-FILE = 'YES'
      _____
      _____

STOP RUN.
```

After the PERFORM PROCESSING instruction, write statements to print the (last) record of a file called FINAL-REPORT. The record-name of FINAL-REPORT is called MONTHLY-REPORT. The record written will be double-spaced from the previous record written and it will contain the data in a field called MONTHLY-SUMMARY.

2.9 Using the PERFORM verb, write PROCEDURE DIVISION instructions to read 10 records from a file called SALES-FILE. Each record contains a field called AMOUNT-SOLD. We want to accumulate the sum of the AMOUNT-SOLD values in a field called TOTAL-AMOUNT. The DATA DIVISION has been written so that TOTAL-AMOUNT has an initial value of zero.

(*Hint:* Set up a field and call it RECORD-COUNTER, to count the records read-in and to test for the value of the counter in the PERFORM . . . UNTIL statement, to determine termination.)

Assume that after the 10 records have been read-in, the program continues with other statements that are not of interest to us.

```
PROCEDURE DIVISION.
PROGRAM-SUMMARY.
      OPEN. . . (etc., not of interest here)
      PERFORM READ-SALES-FILE   (initial read)
      _____
      PERFORM ACCUMULATE-SALES
            UNTIL _____
      (etc., not of interest to us here)
READ-SALES-FILE.
      _____
      _____
```

```
ACCUMULATE-SALES.
    _____
    _____
```

2.10 We have a file on disk that contains employee records. Each record in the input file contains the following fields:

Employee Name in columns   1–15

Hours Worked in columns   16–17

Unused by this program: 18–80

The Employee Name field will not be used directly by the program, so it could be designated as a FILLER field. Nevertheless, we describe the content of this field anyway, to make the exercise more meaningful.

We want to write a program that will read each record in the file, count the number of employee records in the file, and accumulafe the total hours worked by all employees. The output of the program consists of one line that gives these totals. The following input and output samples illustrate these points.

SAMPLE INPUT

```
ANDERSON, P.   40
BROWN, S.      32
GARCIA, M .    40
LORENZO, K.    40
NICHOLSON, J. 36
PHILLIPS, P.   44
REEBOCK, A.    40
```

SAMPLE OUTPUT

```
EMPLOYEE WORK SUMMARY
NUMBER OF EMPLOYEES =  7     TOTAL HOURS =  272
```

Your assignment is to write the required program by completing the missing parts of the program below. After completing the program, compile and execute it on your computer, using the sample input above.

```
IDENTIFICATION DIVISION.
PROGRAM-ID.  EMPLRPRT.
*
ENVIRONMENT DIVISION.
*
CONFIGURATION SECTION.
SOURCE-COMPUTER. ABC-480.
OBJECT-COMPUTER. ABC-480.
*
INPUT-OUTPUT SECTION.
FILE-CONTROL.
    SELECT EMPLOYEE-FILE ASSIGN TO _____.
    SELECT REPORT-FILE   ASSIGN TO _____.
*
DATA DIVISION.
*
FILE SECTION.
*
```

```
FD  EMPLOYEE-FILE
    LABEL RECORDS ARE STANDARD
    RECORD CONTAINS 80 CHARACTERS
    DATA RECORD IS EMPLOYEE-RECORD.
*
01  EMPLOYEE-RECORD.
    05 EMPLOYEE-NAME          PIC X(15).
    05 EMPLOYEE-HOURS-WORKED  PIC 99.
    05 FILLER                 PIC X(63).
*
FD  REPORT-FILE
    LABEL RECORDS ARE OMITTED
    RECORD CONTAINS 132 CHARACTERS
    DATA RECORD IS PRINT-LINE.
*
01  PRINT-LINE               PIC X(132).
*
*
WORKING-STORAGE SECTION.
*
01  END-OF-FILE-TEST         PIC XXX VALUE 'NO'.
*
01  EMPLOYEE-COUNTER         PIC 999 VALUE ZERO.
*
01  TOTAL-HOURS-WORKED       PIC 9999 VALUE ZERO.
*
01  REPORT-HEADING.
    05 FILLER                PIC X(12) VALUE SPACES.
    05 FILLER                PIC X(21) VALUE
        'EMPLOYEE WORK SUMMARY'.
*
01  REPORT-TOTALS.
    05 FILLER                PIC X(5) VALUE SPACES.
    05 FILLER                PIC X(22)
        VALUE 'NUMBER OF EMPLOYEES = '.
    05 REPORT-EMPL-COUNTER   PIC ZZ9.
    05 FILLER                PIC X(5) VALUE SPACES.
    05 FILLER                PIC X(14)
        VALUE 'TOTAL HOURS = '.
    05 REPORT-TOTAL-HOURS    PIC ZZZ9.

PROCEDURE DIVISION.
*
100-PROGRAM-SUMMARY.
*
    OPEN INPUT  _____
         OUTPUT _____
*
    _____
    _____
    _____
    _____
    PERFORM 200-_____
    PERFORM 300-_____
            UNTIL END-OF-FILE = 'YES'
```

Write instructions
to print the report
heading on top of
page and print a
blank line after-
wards. (*Hint:* See
Figure 2-6.)

```
            MOVE EMPLOYEE-COUNTER TO REPORT-EMPL-COUNTER
            MOVE _____
            WRITE _____
                    AFTER ADVANCING PAGE
     *
            CLOSE _____
     *
            STOP RUN.
     *
     *
        200-_____.
            READ EMPLOYEE-FILE RECORD
                AT END _____.
     *
     *
        300-_____.
     *
     *
            ADD 1 TO _____
     *
            ADD  EMPLOYEE-HOURS-WORKED TO_____
     *
     *
            PERFORM _____.
     *
```

2.11 Key-in and run the sample program given in Figure 2-6. Use as input the sample data given below. Even though this exercise will not involve programming effort on your part, it will provide you with the opportunity to familiarize yourself with the ENVIRONMENT DIVISION entries pertinent to your computer, and the program-submission procedures of your installation.

SAMPLE INPUT DATA

```
ADAMS        100
BROWN        075
GROVER       030
MOORE        025
PETERSON     060
WILLIAMS     010
```

2.12 Write a COBOL program that will take a set of input records and list these records double-spaced on the printer. Each source record read in should be moved to the output file and be written in the exact form that was input, double-spacing between records.

Following are parts of the program for the first three divisions. Refer to the "standard" outline for COBOL programs that we showed in Figure 2-10.

```
        FD  SOURCE-FILE   LABEL RECORDS ARE OMITTED
                          RECORD CONTAINS 80 CHARACTERS
                          DATA RECORD IS SOURCE-REC.
        01  SOURCE-REC    PIC X(80).
        *
        FD  OUTPUT-FILE   LABEL RECORDS ARE OMITTED
                          RECORD CONTAINS 132 CHARACTERS
```

```
                                              DATA RECORD IS OUTPUT-REC.
                                01  OUTPUT-REC    PIC X(132).
                                *
                                WORKING-STORAGE SECTION.
                                01  END-OF-FILE   PIC X(3) VALUE 'NO '.
```

2.13   Figure 2-15 provides the first three divisions of a COBOL program. You are
asked to write the PROCEDURE DIVISION for this program and then
compile and execute the entire program.

The function of this program is to read source records containing the
three data fields, NAME-IN, STREET-IN, and CITY-IN, as you can see in the

FIGURE 2-15

*Partial Program Listing for
Exercise 2.13*

```
IDENTIFICATION DIVISION.
PROGRAM-ID.  LABELS.
*

ENVIRONMENT DIVISION.
*

CONFIGURATION SECTION.
SOURCE-COMPUTER. ABC-480.
OBJECT-COMPUTER. ABC-480.
*

INPUT-OUTPUT SECTION.
FILE-CONTROL.
    SELECT ADDRESS-FILE ASSIGN TO INFILE.
    SELECT PRINT-FILE   ASSIGN TO PRINTER.
*

DATA DIVISION.
*

FILE SECTION.
*

FD  ADDRESS-FILE
    LABEL RECORDS ARE OMITTED
    DATA RECORD IS ADDRESS-RECORD.
*

01  ADDRESS-RECORD.
    02 NAME                      PIC X(25).
    02 STREET                    PIC X(25).
    02 CITY                      PIC X(30).
*

FD  PRINT-FILE
    LABEL RECORDS ARE OMITTED
    DATA RECORD IS PRINT-RECORD.
*

01  PRINT-RECORD.
    02 FILLER                    PIC X(2).
    02 PRINT-LINE                PIC X(30).
    02 FILLER                    PIC X(100).
*

WORKING-STORAGE SECTION.
*

01  END-OF-DATA-INDICATOR        PIC XXX VALUE 'NO '.
```

DATA DIVISION under the FD for ADDRESS-FILE. These three fields are located, respectively, in columns 1–25, 26–50, and 51–80 in the source records. The program should print each of these three fields on a separate line, double-spacing between address records.

Output from two sample records would appear as follows:

```
ALLEN M. JOHNSON
1532 E. WASHINGTON ST.
CHICAGO, ILLINOIS 60186

PATRICIA K. WALTON
2252 PALM BOULEVARD
MIAMI, FLORIDA 33322
```

The program can be used with adhesive labels so that a mailing could be made to a group of individuals whose names and addresses are available in ADDRESS-FILE. The input file, called ADDRESS-FILE, has been ASSIGNed to a device assumed to be called INFILE. Obviously this part of the program may have to be changed to adapt it to your own computer. Similarly, the output file, PRINT-FILE, has been ASSIGNed to a device, PRINTER, which may also need revision. A field in WORKING-STORAGE is called END-OF-DATA-INDICATOR and is initialized to a value of 'NO'. It is assumed that in your PROCEDURE DIVISION you will write

```
READ ADDRESS-FILE RECORD
    AT END MOVE 'YES' TO END-OF-DATA-INDICATOR
```

and you will PERFORM the repeated function of the program UNTIL END-OF-DATA-INDICATOR = 'YES'.

3 Data Definition and Editing

INTRODUCTION

OVERALL STRUCTURE OF THE DATA DIVISION

DATA-NAMES AND CONSTANTS

DEFINING AN ELEMENTARY DATA FIELD

FILLER—A NONSPECIFIC DATA-NAME

DEFINING INITIAL CONTENTS WITH THE VALUE CLAUSE

USING LEVEL-NUMBERS TO DEFINE GROUP STRUCTURES

RECORD LAYOUT

FILE SECTION

WORKING-STORAGE SECTION

THE PICTURE CLAUSE FOR DATA DESCRIPTION

THE PICTURE CLAUSE FOR DATA EDITING

THE BLANK WHEN ZERO CLAUSE

THE CURRENCY AND DECIMAL-POINT CLAUSES

SAMPLE DATA DIVISION

IN THIS CHAPTER *you will develop an understanding of the purpose, structure, and coding details for writing the DATA DIVISION of a COBOL program.*

Specifically, you will learn (1) how to define elementary and group data fields; (2) how to define initial contents in data fields, including the definition of constants; (3) how to use the features in the FILE and WORKING-STORAGE sections; and (4) how to use the PICTURE clause to define and edit data fields.

With respect to PICTURE description, the material in this chapter is more extensive than what you can reasonably apply at this point in your studies. Therefore you should plan to make continued reference to this chapter as you study examples of, or write, PICTURE descriptions in later chapters.

INTRODUCTION

As you learned in the previous chapters, the DATA DIVISION is that part of the COBOL program in which data fields are defined. The executable programming instructions in the PROCEDURE DIVISION make reference to these data fields, as in, for examples, MOVE A TO B and ADD 1 TO TOTAL. In addition to defining the data fields, the DATA DIVISION is also the place in which we specify desired editing. Editing is used to improve the readability of output on a printed report or video monitor by eliminating leading zeros, entering dollar signs, inserting commas in long numbers, and the like.

OVERALL STRUCTURE OF THE DATA DIVISION

The DATA DIVISION commonly includes two sections: the FILE SECTION and the WORKING-STORAGE SECTION. Figure 3-1 outlines the overall structure of the DATA DIVISION. The FILE SECTION is used to define each file used by the program, as will be explained in some detail later in this chapter. The WORKING-STORAGE SECTION is used to define fields that are used in the course of program execution but are not directly related to input or output files. Examples of WORKING-STORAGE fields are report headings, totals accumulators, and "flag" fields used for testing whether or not certain conditions exist.

Although the FILE SECTION and WORKING-STORAGE SECTION commonly are the only sections included in the DATA DIVISION, there may in fact be as many as three more sections: the REPORT SECTION, LINKAGE SECTION, and COMMUNICATION SECTION. However, these latter three sections are rather specialized. The REPORT SECTION and LINKAGE SECTION will be covered in later chapters. The COMMUNICATION SECTION is so specialized and so rarely used that we consider it to be outside the scope of this book.

DATA-NAMES AND CONSTANTS

As introduced in Chapter 1, a data-name in COBOL is analogous to a variable in algebra. It is a general symbol or name that can have different values. The specific rules that must be followed in choosing data-names were presented in Chapter 1, in the section on data-names.

FIGURE 3-1

Outline of a Typical DATA DIVISION

```
DATA DIVISION.

FILE SECTION.

FD   file-name
     other clauses describing the file

01   record-name
     other clauses describing fields
     within the record

FD   file-name... (as many FDs as there are files)

WORKING-STORAGE SECTION.

77   elementary field description

     (as many 77-type descriptions as needed)

01   field description(s)
     with possible subordinate field descriptions

     (as many 01 descriptions as needed)
```

In addition to data-names, COBOL makes use of constants that also need to be defined in the DATA DIVISION. Up to now we have side-stepped this discussion in favor of describing data-names and covering a basic set of PROCEDURE DIVISION commands.

There are three distinct types of constants in COBOL: numeric literals, figurative constants, and nonnumeric literals.

As an example of a *numeric literal,* suppose that the sales tax rate in a particular state is 0.06 of sales. Within the COBOL program we need a way to multiply the amount of sales by 0.06. One way of accomplishing this without using a numeric literal is to define a storage field, assign to it a data-name, such as TAX-RATE, and input the value 0.06 into the field. Conceptually, the internal storage location has the following structure:

TAX–RATE			Data-name
0	0	6	Content

The decimal point is not shown above, but is understood to be located in the appropriate position. With this approach the reference to TAX-RATE will make available the 0.06 value stored in this field. Another approach that is available in COBOL, however, is simply to write the numeric literal 0.06 in the PROCEDURE DIVISION of the program itself and use this value directly. Conceptually, the internal storage location has the following structure in this case:

0	0	6	Data-name
0	0	6	Content

Numeric literals without a decimal point are understood to be integers (whole numbers). If a decimal point is used, it must not be the last character. Thus, 35. is not correct, whereas 35.0 is acceptable. The reason for this rule is that in COBOL programming, the period is always used to signal the end of a sentence, just as in English. Therefore it would be ambiguous as to whether a point following a number is a decimal point or a period.

The second type of constant used in COBOL is the *figurative constant.* The most common figurative constants are ZERO, ZEROS, ZEROES, SPACE, and SPACES, although a few others are available. These refer to zeros or blanks, respectively. Their general use can be illustrated by the following brief examples. Suppose we want to set the data-name AMOUNT equal to zero. We can write MOVE ZERO TO AMOUNT to accomplish this objective. Similarly, if we wish to ensure that blanks are contained in the field called TITLE, we can write MOVE SPACES TO TITLE.

The third type of constant is the *nonnumeric literal.* As contrasted to numeric literals and figurative constants, the nonnumeric literal is any alphanumeric value enclosed in quotation marks. For example, suppose we want to print the title INCOME STATEMENT as the heading of a report. The words INCOME and STATEMENT are not intended to refer to data-names; rather, we simply want these exact words printed. This can be done by enclosing them in quotation marks and making reference to 'INCOME STATEMENT' in the COBOL command. Incidentally, the COBOL language specifications allow use of the single or double quotation marks for nonnumeric literals. Thus for the example above we could have "INCOME STATEMENT". However, some compilers accept only the single quotes or only the double quotes for nonnumeric literals. Therefore you should check as to what your compiler allows.

As an example of how a nonnumeric literal might be used in a decision context, suppose we want to know if a customer's last name is BROWN. We could write the following:

```
IF LAST-NAME EQUAL 'BROWN' (etc.)
```

Unlike a data-name, a nonnumeric literal can include blanks. The nonnumeric literal also can be composed entirely of numeric characters. This may seem like a contradiction, but it is not. The term "nonnumeric" refers to how the characters are handled within the computer, and not to their form as letters or numbers. For a nonnumeric literal, *the numbers are handled as being symbols, as are alphabetic letters, and not as being quantities or values.*

DEFINING AN ELEMENTARY DATA FIELD

The most basic data definition is that of describing an elementary data field. "Elementary" here means a single field that, unlike "group" fields, is not subdivided into subfields. An example is a field designed to store the last name of a customer:

```
05    LAST-NAME   PIC X(15).
```

The definition consists of three parts:

1. The level-number, in this case 05, which is used to describe the relationship of this field to other fields, as will be explained below.

2. The data-name, in this case, LAST-NAME, which can be used to reference the field. For example, MOVE SPACES TO LAST-NAME. Several specific rules for forming data-names were presented in Chapter 1.

3. The PIC (abbreviation of PICTURE) clause, which is used to define the size and the data type of the field. In the above example PIC X(15) defines a field of 15 alphanumeric positions (X indicates the alphanumeric type of field).

The three parts of the definition above enable us to define individual data fields at the elementary level. To do so, we need to know how to assign level-numbers, how to create data-names, and how to define PICTURE clauses. You will study these topics in subsequent sections of this chapter. First, however, let us consider two other topics for elementary fields: the use of the FILLER generic data-name and how to put initial contents into data fields.

R E V I E W . . . .

1. Of the four divisions of a COBOL program, the one concerned with the identification and description of storage fields is the _____ DIVISION.

DATA

2. The two sections commonly included in the DATA DIVISION are the
_____ and the_____.

FILE SECTION; WORKING-STORAGE SECTION

3. IN COBOL a label for a field of data that can contain different values at different times is called a(n) _____ .

data-name

4. Three classes of constants were described. They are the

_____ , _____ , and

_____ .

numeric literal; figurative constant; nonnumeric literal

5. In the following listing, place an NL before those expressions that can serve as numeric literals in a COBOL program, an FC for figurative constants, and a NON-L for nonnumeric literals; leave a blank for expressions not exemplifying any of the classes of constants.

a. _____ 'DEPRECIATION SCHEDULE' g. _____ 25.32

b. _____ '12%' h. _____ SPACES

c. _____ 237 i. _____ 100.0

d. _____ INTEREST-DUE j. _____ "SPACE"

e. _____ 125. k. _____ '325'

f. _____ ZEROS

a. NON-L g. NL

b. NON-L h. FC

c. NL i. NL

d. no quotation marks j. NON-L

e. cannot end with a decimal point k. NON-L

f. FC

. . . .

FILLER — A NONSPECIFIC DATA-NAME

The use of data-names is an essential part of programming. There are many instances, however, when we need to define a data field in the DATA DIVISION that will not be referenced in the PROCEDURE DIVISION. In such instances we use the name FILLER, which is a reserved COBOL word.

A common use of FILLER is in describing report-record formats. For example, suppose we want to define a record that will be printed at the end of a report to show certain totals. We desire the following format:

- Columns 1-5   filled with blanks
- Columns 6-10   to contain the word TOTAL
- Columns 11-20   filled with blanks
- Columns 21-24   to contain the total sales in units
- Columns 25-32   filled with blanks
- Columns 33-40   to contain the total sales in dollars

We could write the following record description:

```
01  REPORT-FOOTING.
    02  FILLER            PIC   X(05)     VALUE  SPACES.
    02  FILLER            PIC   X(05)     VALUE  'TOTAL'.
    02  FILLER            PIC   X(10)     VALUE  SPACES.
    02  REPORT-TOT-UNITS  PIC   ZZZ9.
    02  FILLER            PIC   X(08)     VALUE  SPACES.
    02  REPORT-TOT-SALES  PIC   ZZZZ9.99.
```

Although parts of the preceding description will not be fully clear at this point, note the four FILLER fields. Through use of the VALUE clause, three of these FILLER fields contain blank spaces, but one contains the nonnumeric literal TOTAL. This is a good place to emphasize that the use of FILLER does *not* imply anything about the contents of that field; specifically, it does not mean a field containing blanks, as the word "FILLER" might imply.

The choice of FILLER in the above example is not necessary, of course. We could have used data-names of our choice instead of FILLER in each case. It is just simpler not to assign unique data names for fields that will not be referenced in the program.

In the 1985 standard the recognition that there are fields in a program that will not be referenced explicitly has led to the option of omitting entirely the generic data-name FILLER. Thus we can specify "nameless" fields, as follows:

```
01  REPORT-FOOTING.
    02                     PIC  X(05)    VALUE  SPACES.
    02                     PIC  X(05)    VALUE  'TOTAL'.
    02                     PIC  X(14)    VALUE  SPACES.
    02  REPORT-TOT-UNITS   PIC  ZZZ9.
    02                     PIC  X(08)    VALUE  SPACES.
    02  REPORT-TOT-SALES   PIC  ZZZZ9.99.
```

For the above entries that contain no data-names, the record description is treated exactly as if FILLER had been specified.

DEFINING INITIAL CONTENTS WITH THE VALUE CLAUSE

The example included in our discussion of FILLER fields in the preceding section illustrates that we often need to define the contents of fields *before* program execution begins. In addition to defining storage fields with respect to their size and type by using the PICTURE clause, it is often desirable to assign initial values to WORKING-STORAGE fields. Such a value may remain unchanged throughout the program, as in the case of a tax rate, or it may change in the course of program execution, as in the case of a totals accumulator. Such initial values must not be assigned to FILE SECTION items, since such fields receive their data either from an external file via a READ instruction, or from some other storage location as the result of program execution.

An initial value can be assigned by the use of the VALUE clause. The VALUE clause is usually written after the PIC definition of an elementary data field, as in this example:

```
05  TOTAL-UNITS   PIC 999   VALUE ZERO.
05  REPORT-TOTALS PIC X(21) VALUE 'TOTAL SALES FOR MONTH'.
```

Actually, the order of the PIC and VALUE clauses is interchangeable; either one can precede the other.

The assigned value can be one of these three choices:

ASSIGNMENT TYPE	EXAMPLE
A numeric literal	VALUE 125
A figurative constant	VALUE SPACES
A nonnumeric literal	VALUE 'CUSTOMER NAME'

A very common use of the VALUE clause is the definition of report formats, as the example in the preceding section illustrated. Data stored on disk or tape are written so as to save space by omitting the kind of spacing that we like to see when we read a report on paper or on a video monitor. It is very common for the WORKING-STORAGE SECTION of a COBOL program to contain a large number of report-related definitions with suitable VALUE clauses to define the contents of report headings, spacing between columns of data, and so on. Rather than elaborate on the VALUE clause at this point, we will let its use become evident as we progress through the chapter and use the clause in conjunction with PICTURE descriptions.

Use of VALUE in the DATA DIVISION is not the only way of defining the initial contents of data fields. It is also possible to achieve the same result by writing instructions in the PROCEDURE DIVISION to enter appropriate contents into a field. For example, instead of writing

```
05  TOTAL-UNITS  PIC 999  VALUE ZERO
```

we could write

```
MOVE ZERO TO TOTAL-UNITS
```

early in the PROCEDURE DIVISION, before the TOTAL-UNITS field is referenced by another instruction. While this is possible, the preferred way is to define initial contents with the VALUE clause in the DATA DIVISION. It is a safer practice to adopt.

R E V I E W . . . .

1. The data-name often used in the DATA DIVISION to define a field that is not referenced in the PROCEDURE DIVISION is the reserved COBOL word
   _____ .

   FILLER

2. If a field has been named FILLER, this indicates that the field [is / is not necessarily] filled with blanks.

   is not necessarily

3. As an example of being filled with something other than blanks, a FILLER field could contain a _____ .

   nonnumeric literal

4. Initial values can be assigned to WORKING-STORAGE fields by use of the _____ clause.

   VALUE

5. The VALUE clause [always precedes / always follows / can either precede or follow] the PICTURE clause in a WORKING-STORAGE entry.

   can either precede or follow

. . . .

USING LEVEL-NUMBERS TO DEFINE GROUP STRUCTURES

Data used in business applications of the computer come in a variety of forms and structure. Such data are commonly organized in the form of records. A record typically consists of several fields, sometimes hundreds of fields. For example, the record of a college student will involve fields such as name, campus street address, city and state, zip-code, telephone number, home address, parents' or guardians' name and address, high school(s) attended, test scores, other colleges attended, courses taken, grades and credits earned, and grade-point average. It is easy to see how such a record may consist of a very large number of fields and possibly be a few thousand bytes in length. In such an environment it is very important to be able to define data in a variety of ways and to be able to structure data fields into logical groups. The PICTURE clauses enable us to define the variety of data types, but it is through *level-numbers* that we define the group structures comprising a record.

Let us begin with a common example. We have records that consist of names. In the course of program execution we may need to refer to individual parts of the name record, such as the last name, first name, and middle initial. Alternately, we may need to refer to the entire name as a unit. We can define the record as follows:

```
01  NAME-RECORD.
    05  LAST-NAME        PIC X(15).
    05  FIRST-NAME       PIC X(15).
    05  MIDDLE-INITIAL   PIC X(01).
```

The 01 level-number must be used to define a *record*. It is the highest level-number, and it is used to define a group of fields as a record. The data-name associated with the 01 level-number refers to the collection of all the fields having higher level-numbers until another 01 record is defined (or a new SECTION or DIVISION begins). Level-numbers are allowed in the range 01-49. A level number other than 01 indicates that the field to which it is attached is a subordinate field. In the example above, we chose 05 as the level-number of all three subordinate fields. The choice of 05 is arbitrary. We could have used any number between 02 and 49 inclusive. Many programmers tend to use level numbers that are multiples of 5, but this is not a required practice.

The three fields LAST-NAME, FIRST-NAME, and MIDDLE-INITIAL, are all *elementary* fields, because none of them has any subordinate field. Further, because they all have the same level-number, none of the fields in this group is subordinate to any other field in the group. On the other hand, consider the following example:

```
01  NAME-RECORD.
    03  LAST-NAME           PIC X(15).
    03  NAME-INITIALS.
        05  FIRST-INITIAL   PIC X(01).
        05  MIDDLE-INITIAL  PIC X(01).
```

In this case we have chosen to define a record that is subdivided into the elementary field LAST-NAME, and the group field NAME-INITIALS. A *group field* is defined by the fact that it is followed by two or more fields with a higher level-number, in this case, 05. The main purpose of defining a group field is so that we can reference the whole group by one name. In this example we could write the following type of statements:

```
MOVE NAME-INITIALS TO INITIALS-FIELD
```
or
```
MOVE FIRST-INITIAL TO FIRST-INITIAL-OUT
MOVE MIDDLE-INITIAL TO MIDDLE-INITIAL-OUT.
```

The first MOVE transfers the contents of two fields together as a group, while each of the other two MOVE instructions transfers each field individually. Also by the same reasoning, MOVE NAME-RECORD would transfer the contents of all the subordinate fields of this group field. The subordinate fields in this case are the LAST-NAME elementary field and the MIDDLE-INITIALS group field, for a total of 17 bytes. The length of the NAME-RECORD group can be calculated by adding up the length of all the elementary fields in the group. The length is defined in the PIC descriptions, which in this case are 15 bytes for LAST-NAME and one byte each for the initials fields.

It should be noted that group fields do not have PIC clauses attached to them. PIC descriptions are included only for elementary fields. The group field then is the sum of its parts.

Another important point is that a group field is always treated as an *alphanumeric field,* even if its subordinate elementary fields are defined to be numeric ones, as in the following:

```
05  WEEKLY-SALES.
    10  GROSS-SALES   PIC 999.
    10  NET-SALES     PIC 999.
```

The PIC 999 field descriptions above indicate numeric data. However, writing MOVE WEEKLY-SALES... would transfer both sales quantities as a string of data. Also, writing ADD 1 TO WEEKLY-SALES would be an incorrect instruction (and the compiler would so diagnose the instruction and disallow it). This is consistent with common sense and numeric accuracy. If GROSS-SALES contained 125 and NET-SALES contained 100, the combined field 125100 does not mean a quantity, but rather, consists of two three-digit numbers strung together.

Use of level-numbers to define data records and their appropriate subdivisions is further explained by using the following example. Figure 3-2 represents a 67-byte record designed to contain customer addresses. A glance at the figure shows that there are many fields, they vary in size, and they are organized into groups. For instance, NAME is a data-name that consists of the combination of the two subordinate fields called FIRST-NAME and LAST-NAME. COBOL derives a great deal of its suitability for business applications from the fact that it allows the programmer to construct such hierarchies of data structures.

As we have already discussed, a useful distinction is made between elementary and group items in COBOL. An elementary item has no subordinate parts. With reference to Figure 3-2, FIRST-NAME and ZONE are the first and last of the eight elementary items, from left to right. The data-name NAME, on the other hand, is an example of a group item. A group item can consist of one or more other group items, rather than any elementary items, as is the case with CUSTOMER-ADDRESS in the illustration.

Reference to Figure 3-2 makes the concept of group item rather obvious, but in a programming language we cannot construct figures, and so we need a

FIGURE 3-2
Conceptual Structure of Information in Internal Storage

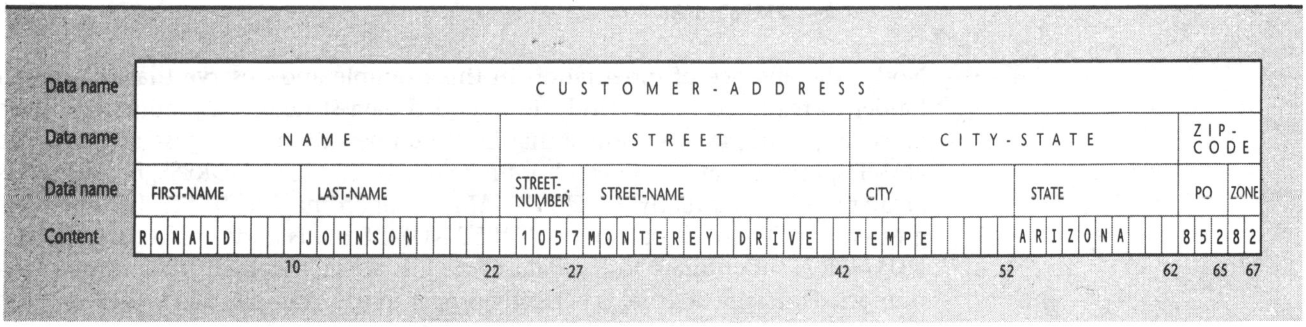

Data name	CUSTOMER-ADDRESS								
Data name	NAME		STREET			CITY-STATE			ZIP-CODE
Data name	FIRST-NAME	LAST-NAME	STREET-NUMBER	STREET-NAME		CITY	STATE	PO	ZONE
Content	R O N A L D	J O H N S O N	1 0 5 7	M O N T E R E Y	D R I V E	T E M P E	A R I Z O N A	8 5 2	8 2

10   22   27   42   52   62   65   67

means of communicating the same information in symbolic form. COBOL provides such a symbolic form by means of level-numbers. Here is an example of how level numbers can represent the same hierarchical (grouping) structure as in Figure 3-2:

```
01  CUSTOMER-ADDRESS
    02  NAME
        03  FIRST-NAME
        03  LAST-NAME
    02  STREET
        03  STREET-NUMBER
        03  STREET-NAME
    02  CITY-STATE
        03  CITY
        03  STATE
    02  ZIP-CODE
        03  PO
        03  ZONE
```

The first level number, 01, is associated with CUSTOMER-ADDRESS. A 01 level number indicates the highest level in a data hierarchy. Reference to the data-name at the 01 level is a reference to the *entire data set,* or *record.* There is only one data-name at the 01 level for each record, as it is the all-inclusive data-name. All data-names that follow this one and are part of this record have level numbers that are higher than 01, and are in the allowable range 02-49.

The 02 NAME introduces NAME as a data-name subordinate to the 01 level. Reading from top to bottom corresponds to left to right in Figure 3-2. We observe a total of four data-names at the 02 level: NAME, STREET, CITY-STATE, and ZIP-CODE. Since they are all at the same level, 02, none of them is subordinate to the others in the group (but each is subordinate to the 01 level).

As in Figure 3-2, we are interested in specifying that NAME is a group item and that it consists of two other data-names, FIRST-NAME and LAST-NAME. This relationship is expressed by assigning the 02 level-number to NAME and the 03 level-number to FIRST-NAME and LAST-NAME. Notice that, as we read from top to bottom, STREET is not confused as being subordinate to NAME because both are assigned to the 02 level.

In terms of format or style, the indentations are preferred but not required. In addition, level numbers need not increase by consecutive values. The following example illustrates these two points:

```
01  CUSTOMER-ADDRESS
03  NAME
05  FIRST-NAME
03  STREET
04  STREET-NUMBER
04  STREET-NAME
```

Notice the absence of indentation in this example and observe that it is much harder to read and understand the intended data structure, as compared to the preceding example. Also notice that level numbers do not increase by 1. The 03 NAME specifies that NAME is subordinate to CUSTOMER-ADDRESS, because 03 is greater than 01. Similarly, 05 FIRST-NAME is subordinate to NAME, because 05 is greater than 03. In the case of 04 STREET-NUMBER, it is understood that STREET-NUMBER is subordinate to the data-name just above it, which has a lower level-number. Thus, the 04 level is perfectly proper in the example, and it preserves the intended grouping of Figure 3-2. Also notice that once NAME is assigned to the 03 level, STREET must also be assigned to the same level, since NAME and STREET have the same immediate superior, CUSTOMER-ADDRESS.

As illustrated in the above examples, level-numbers combine with data-names to represent the desired organization of data. Many times, however, there is no need to describe data in detail. For instance, suppose that we wish to write a program for which the input is the customer file containing the data described in Figure 3-2 and the output is an analysis of the ZIP code information. For such an analysis we are not concerned with the first 62 bytes of data in each record, and therefore we may choose to describe the data record as follows:

```
01  CUSTOMER-ADDRESS.
      02 FILLER          PIC  X(62).
      02 ZIP-CODE.
          03 PO          PIC  999.
          03 ZONE        PIC   99.
```

As explained earlier in this chapter, the reserved word FILLER is a generic data-name. It is not unique and therefore cannot be used in the PROCEDURE DIVISION. In the above example its main purpose is to allow us to specify (although indirectly) that ZIP-CODE begins with byte 63 in CUSTOMER-ADDRESS.

RECORD LAYOUT

As much as COBOL allows great flexibility and ease in describing the organization of data, planning the record layout is a time-consuming and detail-oriented task. When designing a new program or referring to an existing program, it is convenient to use certain graphic representation tools, such as record layout charts and printer spacing charts, to simplify the process.

A *record layout chart* is intended to help specify and visualize the organization of data within a record. The illustration in Figure 3-2 is certainly capable of serving as a record layout chart, but it is too elaborate for such use and too time consuming to prepare. Instead, we prefer a simpler chart, such as the two samples illustrated in Figure 3-3. Figure 3-3(a) is a table-like chart that is rather easy to scan

FIGURE 3-3
Sample Record Layout Representations

COLUMNS	CONTENT	DATA-NAME
1–15	Employee's name	NAME-IN
16	Sex code	SEX-CODE
17–23	Salary	SALARY-IN
24–80	Unused	FILLER

(a)

	EMPL-RECORD			
Data name	NAME-IN	SEX-CODE	SALARY-IN	FILLER
Columns	1 – 15	16	17–23	24 – 80

(b)

and understand. Figure 3-3(b) is a more visually oriented chart that corresponds to the left-right concept of data representation. These are simply illustrations. Many organizations use special forms for record layouts. The main point of this brief discussion is that the supporting documentation for a program should include easy-to-read record layout charts to help convey the organization of data used in the program. Record layout charts are particularly useful for the type of individual records encountered in using disk and tape files. For report files, however, the focus is on the visualization and description of an entire report rather than single records. Since reports are most often printed, we refer to such charts as *printer spacing charts,* as introduced at the beginning of Chapter 2. Actually, their use is equally valid for planning the display of data on a video monitor.

Figure 3-4 presents a *printer spacing chart* for a simple salary report. The underlying programming task involves reading records from an employee file, as described in Figure 3-3, and producing the report form specified in Figure 3-5. The

FIGURE 3-4

Printer Spacing Chart Illustration

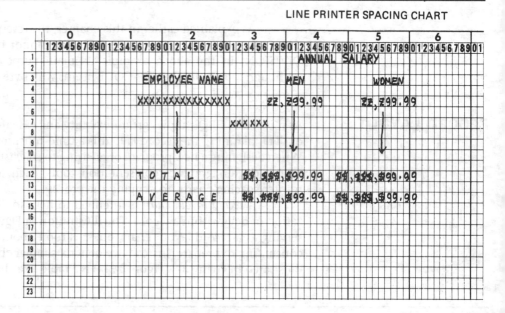

FIGURE 3-5

Sample Salary Report

```
                                  ANNUAL SALARY

          EMPLOYEE NAME        MEN           WOMEN

          JONES, A.         28,200.00
          ANDERSON, P.      22,000.00
          ROBERTS, M.                      25,000.00
          PROUST, K. ******
          NICHOLSON, J.     29,600.00
          PHILLIPS, P.                     28,500.00
          WORK, A.                         30,000.00

          T O T A L        $79,800.00     $83,500.00

          A V E R A G E    $26,600.00     $27,833.33
```

line with asterisks in Figure 3-5 was chosen to represent cases in which there was an error. Employee Proust in Figure 3-5 could not be classified as either male or female because there was an error in the data.

A printer spacing chart such as the one in Figure 3-4 allows a visual summary of a report, and can be used as a valuable aid in writing the corresponding DATA DIVISION specifications. To help you appreciate the value of a printer spacing chart, we ask two questions:

- How many record formats are required in the DATA DIVISION for this report output?

- How many blank columns will separate the last digit of men's salary from the first digit of women's salary in each report detail line?

In answering the first question, one can observe that five different records are portrayed in Figure 3-4: lines 1, 3 , and 5, and the total and average report lines in the report footing. Finally, in response to the second question, one can observe that there are six blank columns separating the two fields in the printer spacing chart, and therefore an appropriate entry in the DATA DIVISION would be

```
...FILLER PIC X(6) VALUE SPACES.
```

As stated in Chapter 2, blank copies of printer spacing charts are included in the back of this book for your use.

R   E   V   I   E   W .   .   .   .

1. In COBOL programming, a data-name that has no subordinate items is called a(n) _____ item, while one that does have subordinate items is called a(n) _____ item.

    elementary; group

2   For a given data set, the all-inclusive data-name generally is defined at the _____ level-number.

    01

3. All fields in the record that are directly subordinate to the overall record commonly are assigned the level number _____ (number).

    02 or higher

4. A data item that is directly subordinate to one at the 02 level [must / need not] be assigned to the 03 level.

    need not

5. The chart that is used to specify and visualize the organization of data in a record is called a _____ chart.

    record layout

6. The chart that is used to portray the layout of a report, whether printed or to be presented on a video monitor, is the _____ chart.

    printer spacing

7. The record layout chart and printer spacing chart are particularly useful with respect to writing specifications in the _____ DIVISION of a COBOL program.

    DATA

FILE SECTION

The function of the FILE SECTION is to describe each file used in the program by specifying four things:

1. The name of the file
2. The name assigned to the record in the file
3. The hierarchical structure of the data fields in the record
4. The field size and type of data in each storage field of the record

The general format presented thus far in the illustrations in preceding chapters is as follows:

```
FD  file-name
    LABEL RECORDS ARE OMITTED
    RECORD CONTAINS integer CHARACTERS
    DATA RECORD IS record-name.
01  record-name.
```

The FD is a COBOL reserved word and designates that this is a file description. There is an FD entry for each file involved in a program, and it includes a complete description of the named record. The description begins with the record name, which is always at the 01 level, and includes the data specifications for the data fields in the record. For instance:

```
DATA DIVISION.
*
FILE SECTION.
*
FD CUSTOMER-FILE
   LABEL RECORDS ARE STANDARD
   RECORD CONTAINS 80 CHARACTERS
   DATA RECORD IS CUSTOMER-RECORD.
*
01  CUSTOMER-RECORD.
    02  CUSTOMER-NAME       PIC X(13).
    02  CUSTOMER-UNITS      PIC 999.
    02  FILLER              PIC X(64).
```

The LABEL clause will be discussed in Chapter 10, "Sequential File Processing." Until then we simply use the LABEL clause to indicate either STANDARD or OMITTED. The RECORD CONTAINS clause is used for documentation. The size of the record is specified indirectly by the sum of the individual PICTURE descriptions, which should correspond to the number of characters identified in the RECORD CONTAINS clause. For the above example the sum of the individual PIC descriptions is 13 + 3 + 64 = 80, which corresponds to the RECORD CONTAINS 80 CHARACTERS. Then the DATA RECORD IS specifies the name of the record, which is described beginning with the 01 level-number.

In COBOL '85, the LABEL, RECORD and DATA clauses in the FD entry are all optional. Therefore we could have written this:

```
FD CUSTOMER-FILE.
01 CUSTOMER-RECORD.
   02 . . . (etc.)
```

Some reasons for making those clauses optional are as follows: The LABEL aspect of a file generally is dependent on the operating system rather than on

FIGURE 3-6

Relationship of File-Names and Data-Names to Hardware Storage

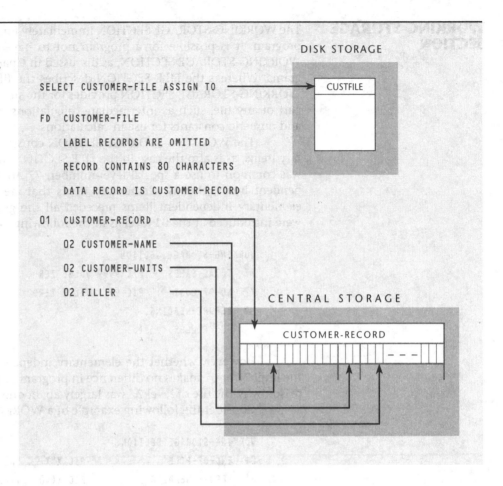

COBOL specifications, even in the 1974 version of the language. The RECORD CONTAINS has always been optional, and the DATA RECORD is redundant, since the subsequent 01 entry always specifies the record-name in any event.

Figure 3-6 should help explain some fundamental concepts about files, records, and fields in a COBOL program. Within the program we use a file-name such as CUSTOMER-FILE. However, that file-name may be designated by other means in terms of the operating system of the computer. In the example the customer file is a disk file and is called CUSTFILE, as illustrated in Figure 3-6.

The 01 record entry describes the central storage area referenced by the record-name CUSTOMER-RECORD. Similarly, the fields CUSTOMER-NAME, CUSTOMER-UNITS, and FILLER also refer to central storage locations, as illustrated in Figure 3-6.

Assuming CUSTOMER-FILE to be an input file, we can give an instruction to copy a data record from the disk into central storage by use of the READ verb. After a READ operation we can then give instructions to operate on the data in central storage by instructions such as ADD CUSTOMER-UNITS TO . . .

CUSTOMER-NAME and CUSTOMER-UNITS are data-names referencing fields in the record. As illustrated in Figure 3-6, CUSTOMER-NAME refers to the first 13 bytes of the CUSTOMER-REC, while CUSTOMER-UNITS refers to the next 3 bytes. The size and type of each field would be specified by the PIC clause. The third field in CUSTOMER-RECORD is named FILLER.

Storage fields associated with the file records receive data from, or are used to send data to, external input-output devices, such as disks, tapes, printers, and video terminals. In addition to such storage fields, there also is a need for storage of header data and the like. The WORKING-STORAGE SECTION is used to define such fields.

WORKING-STORAGE SECTION

The WORKING-STORAGE SECTION immediately follows the FILE SECTION in the program. It is possible for a program not to have either a FILE SECTION or a WORKING-STORAGE SECTION, as discussed in Chapter 23 in the case of subprograms. Whereas the FILE SECTION describes the files used in the program, the WORKING-STORAGE SECTION provides for the storage of data items that are not part of any file, such as intermediate calculations, report headings for printing, and numeric constants for use in calculations.

The WORKING-STORAGE SECTION consists of group items and elementary items, as is also the case in the FILE SECTION. In older versions of COBOL it was common to use a special level-number, 77, to describe all elementary independent items; that is, elementary items that are not part of a group. These elementary independent items preceded all the group (or record) items which were introduced at the 01 level as in the following example:

```
WORKING-STORAGE SECTION.
77  TOTAL-SALES    PIC 9999 VALUE ZERO.
77  NO-OF-CUST     PIC 99   VALUE ZERO.
01  REPORT-HEADING.
    02  FILLER... etc.
```

However, whether the elementary independent items are designated by the level 77 or 01 makes no difference in program processing, and this is the main reason why the use of level 77 was largely abandoned in the late 1970s.

Consider the following example of a WORKING-STORAGE SECTION:

```
WORKING-STORAGE SECTION.
01  END-OF-FILE           PIC XXX    VALUE  'NO '.
01  REPORT-HEADING        PIC X(40)  VALUE
    'CUSTOMER NAME  UNITS SOLD     NET SALES'.
01  REPORT-FOOTING.
    02  FILLER            PIC X(5)   VALUE 'TOTAL'.
    02  FILLER            PIC X(14)  VALUE SPACES.
    02  REPORT-TOTAL-UNITS PIC ZZZ9.
    02  FILLER            PIC X(9)   VALUE SPACES.
    02  REPORT-TOTAL-SALES PIC ZZZZ9.99.
```

Each 01 entry defines a record in central storage. The first entry defines a field called END-OF-FILE that is 3 bytes long (PIC XXX) and is initialized to the value "NO". As we discussed earlier, the VALUE clause is used to define the contents of a record/field at the start of the program execution. Thus the 40-byte REPORT-HEADING is initialized with the desired report heading. Note that the 40-byte literal does not fit on the same line as the data-name and the PIC description, so we switched to the next line to write the literal for the VALUE clause. A nonnumeric literal can be as long as 120 bytes in the 1974 standard (160 in the 1985 version).

If we have a long literal that does not fit on one line, there is a special way to split it across two lines: column 7 of the COBOL Coding Form can be used to signal continuation of an entry to the following line. Recall that in Chapter 1 we first introduced use of this column to signal a comment entry by an asterisk (∗) and to signal that printer output of the source program listing should begin on a new page by a slash (/). When the literal is too long for one line, a *hyphen* (–) is entered in column 7 of the next line, and the entry is continued starting with column 12

FIGURE 3-7

Example of Continuing a Literal on the Next Line of the COBOL Coding Form

SEQUENCE		CONT.	A	B	COBOL STATEMENT
(PAGE)	(SERIAL)				

```
01
02          02  REPORT-HEADING   PIC  X(31)   VALUE  'INFORMATION SYSTEMS COR
03       -            'PORATION'.
04
05
06
```

or to the right of column 12. When a nonnumeric literal is being continued, not only do we enter a hyphen in column 7, but we also start the continued line with a quotation mark in column 12 or to the right of it and conclude with a quotation mark. Figure 3-7 includes an example of continuation for a literal that is split between two lines. Notice the hyphen in column 7 and the opening and closing quotation marks on the second line.

Continuing with the example of a WORKING-STORAGE SECTION above, the first two FILLER fields in the REPORT-FOOTING record specify the characters TOTAL followed by 14 blanks. We used two FILLER fields for convenience, because 14 blanks in a literal are difficult to count visually and may lead to errors. Still, it would have been just as correct to write

```
01  REPORT-FOOTING.
    02  FILLER   PIC X(19) VALUE 'TOTAL
    02  REPORT-TOTAL-UNITS . . .
```

In the above program segment the nonnumeric literal value of FILLER contains 14 blanks to the right of TOTAL and inside the quotation marks.

There is little to say about the organization of the WORKING-STORAGE SECTION except that it is a recommended practice to group related items together under a common group to enhance reader awareness of their relationships. For example, consider the following DATA DIVISION entries:

```
01  SALARY-TOTALS.
    02  MEN-TOTAL-SALARY     PIC 9(7)V99 VALUE ZERO.
    02  WOMEN-TOTAL-SALARY   PIC 9(7)V99 VALUE ZERO.
```

Assuming that we never make use of the data-name SALARY-TOTALS in the program, the 01 group item in this program segment is used only for readability. An alternative to this structure would be to write the two elementary independent items as follows:

```
01  MEN-TOTAL-SALARY    PIC 9(7)V99 VALUE ZERO.
01  WOMEN-TOTAL-SALARY  PIC 9(7)V99 VALUE ZERO.
```

In this alternative program segment, the similarity in the data-names and their physical consecutive order implies a relationship between them, but the association is much clearer when a group data-name is used to indicate the relationship between the two data items.

R E V I E W . . . .

1. The section of the DATA DIVISION concerned with describing each file used in the program is the _____ SECTION.

FILE

2. In the FILE SECTION we designate that an entry is a file description by beginning the entry with the COBOL reserved word _____ .

FD

3. After the name of the file is given, the next item of information given in the FD entry is the name of the _____ included in the file.

record

4. The section of the DATA DIVISION that provides for the storage of such data items as intermediate calculations and report headings is the _____ SECTION.

WORKING-STORAGE

5. In lieu of the older practice of using the special level-number 77 for elementary independent data items in WORKING-STORAGE, current practice favors use of the level number _____ for such items.

01

6. When two or more elementary items are logically related, rather than place them in the program as elementary independent items, documentation is improved by _____

lacing them under a common group (etc.)

7. An initial content can be established in a WORKING-STORAGE field by use of the _____ clause.

VALUE

8. The VALUE clause can be used in the WORKING-STORAGE SECTION to establish field values that are [numeric only / numeric or nonnumeric].

numeric or nonnumeric (for example, a nonnumeric literal such as 'ANNUAL SALARY' can be assigned)

. . . .

THE PICTURE CLAUSE FOR DATA DESCRIPTION

The general form of the PICTURE clause was introduced in Chapter 2, in the example of a complete program. The purpose of this DATA DIVISION feature is to describe the data included in the data items. We use the word PICTURE, or its abbreviated form PIC, and the optional word IS, followed by a string of characters that describe the data. In the following subsections we consider in turn each of the PICTURE characters that can be used to describe data fields that are defined in the DATA DIVISION.

The X PICTURE Character

The X PICTURE character denotes that data contained in that field are treated as alphanumeric. NAME X(20), for example, signifies a field of 20 alphanumeric positions, which can include alphabetic characters, numeric characters, and special symbols. In the following examples a "b" represents a blank space in the storage location. Notice that when the characters do not fill an X field completely, they are left-justified, with blanks filling the remaining positions on the right.

DESCRIPTION	EXAMPLE	REPRESENTED IN STORAGE AS
02 PART-NAME PICTURE XXXXX	DIODE	DIODE
02 PART-NAME PICTURE X(5)	TUBE	TUBEb
02 NAME PICTURE X(20)	JOHN F. ANDREWS	JOHNbF.bANDREWSbbbbb
02 MESSAGE-CODE PICTURE X(8)	AB13C,$M	AB13C,$M

The A PICTURE Character

The A PICTURE character is similar to the X character, except that it indicates that only alphabetic characters and blanks are intended to be contained in a field. Excluded therefore are numeric characters and special symbols. Since the first two statements in the preceding examples concerned storage locations containing only alphabetic information, the A PICTURE character could have been used instead of the X, as indicated in the following table:

DESCRIPTION	EXAMPLE	REPRESENTED IN STORAGE AS
02 PART-NAME PICTURE AAAAA	DIODE	DIODE
02 PART-NAME PICTURE A(5)	TUBE	TUBEb

The reader is cautioned against using the A character in what seems a natural use: a field containing people's names. Names such as O'Neal do not consist of alphabetic characters alone. The X character is better suited for use in such fields. In fact, use of the A PICTURE is rare, because use of the X field is satisfactory for all cases of nonnumeric data fields.

The 9 PICTURE Character

The numeric 9 indicates that a storage position should contain only any of the numeric digits from 0 to 9. In this context a blank is not considered equivalent to the numeric 0 and thus is not a numeric character. The field size of the item is indicated by the number of successively written 9s in the PICTURE clause; thus PICTURE IS 999 means a field of three numeric positions. An alternative is to write a 9 followed by parentheses enclosing the number of positions in the field. For example, the statement 03 AMT PICTURE IS 9(5) indicates that AMT is a five-position numeric field. Some examples of using the 9 PICTURE character are as follows:

DESCRIPTION	NUMERIC VALUE	REPRESENTED IN STORAGE AS
02 SCHOOL-ENROLLMENT PICTURE IS 9(6)	12,327	012327
02 STOCK-ON-HAND PICTURE 9999	8,956	8956
04 POPULATION-OF-CITY PICTURE 9(10)	1,563,813	0001563813
03 UNION-MEMBERSHIP PICTURE IS 9999	285	0285

Again note that a numeric field can contain only the digits 0-9. Blanks are not numeric characters. When entering data, you should be careful to zero-fill a field with leading zeros; otherwise you may be in for some surprising results. Thus in a field of five positions the numeric value 532 should be entered as follows:

0	0	5	3	2

The V PICTURE Character

The V character indicates the position of an assumed decimal point. "Assumed" means that the decimal point is not written as part of the field and therefore is not included as part of the field size. Instead, the information about decimal point location is stored elsewhere (as part of the instructionns that do arithmetic computations), so that any arithmetic computations can be done correctly. For example, if two items are multiplied and each is assumed to have two positions to the right of the decimal, the product will be understood to have four positions to the right of the decimal point.

If the V character is omitted, it is understood that the decimal point is at the extreme right of the numeric field. It is not necessary, therefore, to place a V as the last character in a PICTURE clause. Of course, no more than one V is permitted in a field. Refer to the following table and note that, if we printed HOURS-WORKED without any editing, the value represented in storage, 385, would be printed without a decimal. The V character establishes the position of the decimal for purposes of arithmetic manipulation but does not make the decimal point as such available for printout. Some examples of using the V character are given in this table. The *caret* (∧) indicates the position of the assumed decimal point.

DESCRIPTION	NUMERIC VALUE	REPRESENTED IN STORAGE AS
03HOURS-WORKED PICTURE 99V9	38.5	38∧5
03NET-PAY PICTURE 9(4)V99	452.39	452∧39
02TON-CAPACITY PICTURE 999	550	550∧
02BALANCE PICTURE IS 99999V99	23561.00	23561∧00

The P PICTURE Character

The P PICTURE character is used in conjunction with the V character to indicate the position of a decimal point in cases in which the decimal point is not within the number. This character is used, for example, when it is understood that a value held in storage represents thousands of units and we wish to indicate the decimal position for this value. The following examples indicate the use of this character. As before, the caret indicates the position of an assumed decimal point.

DESCRIPTION	NUMERIC VALUE	ARITHMETIC EQUIVALENT
02 AMOUNT PICTURE IS 99PPPV	12	12000∧
02 AMOUNT PICTURE VP(3)9(4)	1023	∧0001023

The P character is not used very much in administrative applications. It is suited best to scientific computational needs, which are likely to be better satisfied by the use of languages other than COBOL.

The S PICTURE Character

The S character is used to designate a numeric field that is signed; that is, one that can be negative in value. In COBOL all fields are considered positive unless the S has been used. For instance, for a field containing the checking account balance of a bank customer, when the account is overdrawn, the only way the balance will become negative is to designate the balance field as a signed one by use of the S character. Otherwise, if the dollar balance in the field is 23.50 and a check is written for 50.00, the balance will become 26.50!

Only one S character may be used in a field, and it must be the leftmost character. The S is not counted in the size of the field; therefore S99 is a field of two positions. In the following examples the negative sign (−) in machine representation is shown as a "⁻" above the rightmost digit in order to preserve the concept that it does not take up an extra position.

DESCRIPTION	NUMERIC VALUE	REPRESENTED IN STORAGE AS
02 BALANCE PICTURE S9999V99	−1251.16	1251ₐ1$\bar{6}$
02 BALANCE PICTURE S9(4)V99	− 0.10	0000ₐ1$\bar{0}$
02 BALANCE PICTURE 9(4)V99	− 325.18	0325ₐ1$\bar{8}$

The reason for not needing an extra position is related to how numeric values and their signs are represented by specific bit combinations in internal storage. For example, a value of negative 32 might be written as 3K, the K representing the bit combination of the digit 2 and the negative sign. Further, the specific representation would depend on the system in use (as will be further discussed in Chapter 16, "Special Data-Oriented Division Features"). If this seems a bit alarming, keep in mind that in business data processing, input data are almost never negative. Instead, we define categories of positive data that may then be treated as negative in the program logic. Consider this example: A customer returns an item and receives a refund. One could think of this as a negative sale represented by a negative number. But that is not the way it is done. Instead, a "sales" record would have a field that identifies the type of sale, as perhaps purchase or return, by means of a code. When the record is processed, we would specify something like this:

If it is a purchase

add the amount to the customer's balance

else

if it is a return

subtract the amount from the customer's balance.

As the above example illustrates, negative values are not used directly in input files. When we want to show negative values in reports, we use the special editing PICTURE character "-" as explained in the next section of this chapter, on the use of the PICTURE clause for data editing.

R E V I E W . . . .

1. We have discussed thus far six PICTURE characters that can be used in a PICTURE clause to describe the contents of a field. These are the X, A, 9, V, P, and S PICTURE characters. The character used to indicate that a field can contain either alphabetic, numeric, or special symbols is the _____ character, whereas the character that indicates alphabetic content only is the _____ character.

X; A

2. The character that indicates numeric content only is the _____ character. If the stored values can be negative as well as positive, the PICTURE clause should include the _____ character as the leftmost character.

9; S

3. The character used to indicate the position of an assumed decimal point is the _____ character. This character is used only with PICTURE clauses that also contain the _____ PICTURE character.

V; 9

4. When we wish to identify the correct decimal position for a field whose numeric value is understood to be in thousands of units, we use the _____ PICTURE character.

P

5. When a value does not fill a numeric 9 field completely, the value is justified to the [right / left], and the extra positions are filled with [blanks / zeros].

right; zeros

6. When an item does not fill an A field or an X field completely, the item is justified to the [right / left], and the extra positions are filled with [blanks / zeros].

left; blanks

THE PICTURE CLAUSE FOR DATA EDITING

As contrasted to the field definition characters we have described so far, the PICTURE characters that follow are editing symbols. The editing function involves a change in the form of data. For example, we may suppress leading zeros, we may use commas to make long numeric values more legible, we may insert a dollar sign in front of a value, and so forth. *The purpose of editing is to make data more suitable for human reading.* Thus, in its most common use, editing is associated with printing data on the printer. A great many of the applications of COBOL involve the production of reports that are to be read by people, and data editing greatly enhances the visibility of data in such reports.

The $ PICTURE Insertion Character

By use of the $ PICTURE character, the dollar sign is written in the position in which it is to appear in the output. Because the $ sign is counted in the size of the field, the field should be assigned at least one more position than the maximum number of significant digits expected. The $ sign also may be *floated,* by which we mean that it will not necessarily be entered in the leftmost position of a field but, rather, will be entered to the left of the first significant digit in the field and be preceded by blanks. For example, if we have the statement 02 AMT PICTURE $$$99V99, when a data value is to be entered in AMT, a test is performed. The leftmost digit is examined first. If it is zero, the next digit is examined. If this next digit is not zero, then the dollar sign is inserted directly to the left of that digit. For the PICTURE clause above, the $ sign can appear in any one of the first three positions, according to the value stored in the field. The following examples further illustrate the use of the $ PICTURE insertion character. The last example shows that, when the $ sign appears in all positions and the value is zero, the effect is to blank the field.

DESCRIPTION			NUMERIC VALUE	REPRESENTED IN STORAGE AS
02	AMT PICTURE	$999V99	125.13	$125ᴧ13
02	AMT PICTURE	$9(5)V99	100.0	$00100ᴧ00
02	AMT PICTURE	$$99V99	12.49	b$12ᴧ49
02	AMT PICTURE	$$$9V99	150.10	$150ᴧ10
02	AMT PICTURE	$$$$V99	0.15	bbb$ᴧ15
02	AMT PICTURE	$$$$V$$	0.0	bbbbᴧbb

For the example just given let us consider what the result in storage would be if the value to be written in AMT were 0.05. In this case the presence of the V would stop the dollar sign float, and the value would be represented in storage as bbb$ᴧ05. If the decimal point did not terminate the float, the result in storage would be bbbbbᴧ$5, which is clearly not the desired representation. Therefore the presence of the decimal point stops the float except when the entire field is zero. Further examples involving use of the $ PICTURE character are included in the discussion immediately following. Actually, we would not use a $ and a V in the same field, since the V does not result in a visible decimal point. The above examples make more sense if we use the decimal point editing character, discussed next.

The Decimal and the Comma PICTURE Insertion Characters

Each of these insertion characters is used to indicate the position of the indicated character in the storage location. Because the . (decimal) PICTURE character indicates the position of the decimal point and serves to align the actual decimal values in the field, only one such character may appear in a field. Further, a field cannot contain both a V and a . PICTURE character. On the other hand, a field may include more than one , (comma) PICTURE character if the size of the field warrants it.

The following examples illustrate the use of the . and the , PICTURE insertion characters in conjunction with the $ insertion characters. Notice some of these points. The $ float stops when either the first nonzero digit or the . or V is encountered. The only exception is when the $ is written in all positions and the value is zero, in which case the entire field (including any . and ,) is blanked. If a comma happens to precede the first nonzero item, the comma is replaced by the dollar sign, which is the format generally desired for purposes of output.

DESCRIPTION			NUMERIC VALUE	REPRESENTED IN STORAGE AS
02	AMT PICTURE	$9,999.99	2,350.22	$2,350.22
02	AMT PICTURE	$9,999.99	150.31	$0,150.31
02	AMT PICTURE	$$999.99	150.31	b$150.31
02	AMT PICTURE	$$,$$$.99	25.40	bbb$25.40
02	AMT PICTURE	$$,$$$.999	0.019	bbbbb$.019
02	AMT PICTURE	$$,$$$.$$$	0.009	bbbbb$.009
02	AMT PICTURE	$$,$$$.$$$	0.0	bbbbbbbbb
02	AMT PICTURE	$$,$$9.999	2,210.2	$2,210.200
02	AMT PICTURE	$$,999.9	2,210.2	$2,210.2
02	AMT PICTURE	$$,999.9	2,210.256	$2,210.2
02	AMT PICTURE	$9,999.9999	23	$0,023.0000
02	AMT PICTURE	$$,$$$.$$9	0.002	bbbbb$.002

The Z PICTURE Character

The Z PICTURE character is used to replace leading zeros by blanks and thus performs a function identical to that of the floating $ character, except for insertion of the $ itself. As for the floating $, zero suppression terminates when the first nonzero digit or the . character is encountered, whichever occurs first. As with the $ PICTURE character, the only exception occurs when Zs have been designated for all positions in a field and the value to be inserted in that field is zero, in which case the entire field is blanked. The following examples illustrate the use of the Z PICTURE character:

DESCRIPTION		NUMERIC VALUE	REPRESENTED IN STORAGE AS
02 AMT PICTURE	Z99	25	b25
02 AMT PICTURE	ZZZ.99	25	b25.00
02 AMT PICTURE	ZZZ.99	0.10	bbb.10
02 AMT PICTURE	ZZZ.ZZZ	0.052	bbb.052
02 AMT PICTURE	ZZZ.ZZZ	0.0	bbbbbbb
02 AMT PICTURE	$ZZZ.9	13.2	$b13.2
02 AMT PICTURE	$ZZZZ.Z	13.2	$bb13.2
02 AMT PICTURE	$Z,ZZZ,ZZZ.ZZ	156,320.18	$bb156,320.18
02 AMT PICTURE	$Z,ZZZ,ZZZ.ZZ	3,156,320.18	$3,156,320.18
02 AMT PICTURE	$$,$$Z.ZZZ	0.001	bbbb$b.001

The + and – PICTURE Insertion Characters

Each of these editing characters can be inserted into the leftmost or rightmost position in a PICTURE. When the + character is used, positive values receive a + sign and negative values receive a – sign. On the other hand, when the – PICTURE character is used, positive values are represented in storage without a sign, while negative values receive a – sign. In either case a negative sign associated with a value always is represented in storage.

The – PICTURE insertion character differs from the S character in that the use of the S character identifies a field as a signed one for computational purposes, but the sign does not occupy a position as such. An edited field that contains such editing characters as the negative sign (as well as $, ., etc.) is *not* a numeric field and cannot be used in computations. Thus the compiler will issue a diagnostic error if we try to ADD 1 TO A, and the PIC string for A contains editing characters. Use of the – PICTURE character leads to a field in which the sign occupies a character position.

The + character and the – character also can be floated; in this respect they are similar to the $ PICTURE character. However, the +, –, and $ are mutually exclusive as floating characters. If we want to have both $ float and + or – sign representation, we write the + or – to the right of the field, as illustrated in the last two of the following examples:

DESCRIPTION		NUMERIC VALUE	REPRESENTED IN STORAGE AS
02 BALANCE PICTURE	+ 999.9	35.2	+035.2
02 BALANCE PICTURE	999.9 +	35.2	035.2+
02 BALANCE PICTURE	999.9 +	– 35.2	035.2–
02 BALANCE PICTURE	+ + 9.9	– 001.3	b–1.3
02 BALANCE PICTURE	+ + + 9.99	.05	bb+0.05
02 BALANCE PICTURE	+ + + 9.99	– .05	bb–0.05

DESCRIPTION			NUMERIC VALUE	REPRESENTED IN STORAGE AS
02	BALANCE PICTURE	+ + + +.+ +	.01	bbb+.01
02	BALANCE PICTURE	– – – –.– –	0.0	bbbbbbb
02	BALANCE PICTURE	– 99.99	– 10.25	b–10.25
02	BALANCE PICTURE	– 999.99	100.25	b100.25
02	BALANCE PICTURE	999.99–	– 10.2	010.2–
02	BALANCE PICTURE	$$$$.99–	20.35	b$20.35b
02	BALANCE PICTURE	$$$$.99+	20.35	b$20.35+

R E V I E W . . . .

1. Several $ signs included in a PICTURE clause signify that [several dollar signs should appear in the output / the output should contain the dollar sign in one of several possible positions].

    the output should contain the dollar sign in one of several possible positions

2. Both the V PICTURE character and the . PICTURE character indicate _____ positions.

    decimal point

3. The difference in the use of the V and the . PICTURE characters is that the V signifies an _____ decimal point, whereas the . signifies an _____ decimal point.

    assumed; actual

4. Arithmetic computations can be performed with fields whose decimal point designation is [V only / "." only / V or "."].

    V only

5. In general, the $ float stops when the first nonzero digit is encountered or when the _____ PICTURE character is encountered. The only exception occurs when the value in the field is zero and the $ is written in all positions, in which case the field is filled with _____ .

    V or . (decimal); blanks

6. The PICTURE insertion character that is similar to the . PICTURE character but can appear more than once in a field is the _____ PICTURE character.

    , (comma)

7. The character in a PICTURE clause which is used to replace with blanks the leading zeros in a value is the _____ PICTURE character.

    Z

8. Representation of the algebraic sign of a numeric value is accomplished by the use of the _____ or _____ PICTURE character.

    +; –

9. If the – PICTURE insertion character is used, a value held in storage will have associated with it either a – sign or [+ / no] sign. If the + PICTURE character is used, a value held in storage will have associated with it either a + sign or [– / no] sign.

    no; –

10. Fields that contain editing characters, such as $, +, or –, [can / cannot] be used in computations.

    cannot

The DB and CR PICTURE Characters

In accounting applications there is often need to identify values that represent debits or credits. The COBOL language facilitates such differentiation by means of the DB (debit) and CR (credit) editing characters. As indicated in the following examples, the DB or CR symbol is written only to the right of a field in the PICTURE clause, and in both cases it is represented in storage for the purpose of subsequent output only when the value is negative.

DESCRIPTION	NUMERIC VALUE	REPRESENTED IN STORAGE AS
02 RECEIPT PICTURE $999.99DB	135.26	$135.26bb
02 RECEIPT PICTURE $999.99DB	–135.26	$135.26DB
02 RECEIPT PICTURE $,$$9.99CR	–10.50	bb$10.50CR

Notice that the edited field does not provide for negative values as such. A value such as –10.50 would have been stored previously in a signed numeric field and then sent to the edited field. For example, if the original field is described by 03 PAY PICTURE S9(4)V99, then executing the instruction MOVE PAY TO RECEIPT will generate the stored content represented on the last line of the preceding table.

The following table summarizes the effects of the storage location associated with the use of the +, –, CR, and DB PICTURE editing symbols. Note that for positive values the + is included in the edited field only when the + PICTURE character appears in the PICTURE clause. Note also that for negative values the – sign is included in the edited field if either the + or – PICTURE character has been used, and that the CR or DB appears only if the numeric value is negative.

PICTURE CHARACTER USED	STORAGE REPRESENTATION WHEN VALUE IS POSITIVE	STORAGE REPRESENTATION WHEN VALUE IS NEGATIVE
+	+	–
–	Blank	–
DB	Blank	DB
CR	Blank	CR

The B PICTURE Character

This is an insertion editing character resulting in blanks being entered in the designated positions. For example, suppose the first two characters in the storage location NAME always represent the initials of a person's first name and middle name, as follows: RBSMITH. If we wish to print the name with spaces included between the two initials and between the initials and the last name, we can set up the editing field 02 EDNAME PICTURE ABABA(1O). If we then execute the instruction MOVE NAME TO EDNAME and subsequently print the contents of EDNAME, the output will be R B SMITH.

The 0 (Zero) PICTURE Character

The zero insertion character causes zeros to be inserted in the positions in which it appears. For example, we can use this option if the value represented in the storage is understood to be in thousands and we want to edit it to show the full value. Thus if we had 1365 as the value of AMT and we set up EDSUM PICTURE 9(4)000, we could execute MOVE AMT TO EDSUM, giving the following result in EDSUM: 1365000.

The * PICTURE Character

The * character is referred to as a check-protect character and normally is used to protect dollar amounts written on checks or other negotiable documents. As indicated by the following examples, it works very much like the floating $ or the Z PICTURE character. In this case, however, instead of the $ sign being floated or positions being filled with blanks, the * character is entered in each zero-suppressed position as designated in the PICTURE clause.

DESCRIPTION	NUMERIC VALUE	REPRESENTED IN STORAGE AS
02 CHECK-VALUE PICTURE $*** .99	256.18	$256.18
02 CHECK-VALUE PICTURE $*** .99	10.13	$*10.13
02 CHECK-VALUE PICTURE $*** .99	0.15	$***.15

The / (Stroke) PICTURE Character

Each / (stroke) in the PICTURE character string represents a character position into which the stroke character will be inserted. For example, suppose we have

```
02 NUMERIC-DATE      PIC 9(6) VALUE 040792.
02 EDITED-DATE       PIC 99/99/99.
```

The instruction MOVE NUMERIC-DATE TO EDITED-DATE will cause EDITED-DATE to contain 04/07/92.

R E V I E W . . . .

1. The editing characters that can be used in a PICTURE clause to identify debits and credits, respectively, are the _____ and the _____ characters.

   DB; CR

2. In order for a DB or CR to be included in an editing field, the value entered in that field must be [positive / negative / positive for DB but negative for CR].

   negative

3. The insertion editing character that results in blanks being entered in the designated positions is the _____ PICTURE character, whereas the insertion editing character that results in zeros being entered in designated positions is the _____ PICTURE character.

   B; 0

4. The insertion editing character that is referred to as the check-protect character is the _____ PICTURE character.

   *

5. Use of the / (stroke) insertion character results in the stroke character being inserted in designated character positions [only when those positions are blank / to achieve visual separation of values].

   to achieve visual separation of values

TABLE 3-1

Types of Characters Available for Use in Picture Clauses

TYPE OF CHARACTER	SYMBOL	USE
Field definition characters	9	Numeric field
	A	Alphabetic field
	X	Alphanumeric field
Numeric field special character	V	Assumed decimal point
	P	Decimal scaling
	S	Operational (arithmetic) sign included
Editing characters	$	Dollar sign
	Z	Zero suppression
	*	Check protection
	.	Decimal point
	,	Comma
	+	Plus sign
	–	Minus sign
	DB	Debit
	CR	Credit
	B	Blank insertion
	0	Zero insertion
	/	Stroke insertion

Summary of PICTURE Clause Options

Table 3-1 lists all the PICTURE characters. As indicated, the characters that identify the type of content in a storage field are the 9, A, and X characters. Special-purpose characters associated with numeric fields only are the V, P, and S characters. All the other characters listed in Table 3-1 are used for editing purposes.

Instead of listing the characters that can be used in PICTURE clauses, another way of summarizing the material presented in this section is to consider the categories of data that can be contained in a storage location and the PICTURE characters that can be used with each category. Accordingly, Table 3-2 identifies five categories of data: numeric, alphabetic, alphanumeric, numeric edited, and alphanumeric edited. Notice that the PICTURE clause for alphanumeric items cannot contain all 9s or all A's; all 9s would be indicative of a numeric field, and all A's would indicate an alphabetic field. Note also that numeric edited items can include appropriate combinations of all 12 editing characters included in Table 3-1. On the other hand, alphanumeric edited items can include the B and 0 (zero insertion) and / (stroke) editing characters only.

R E V I E W . . . .

1. Three of the PICTURE characters discussed are used for the purpose of defining the type of content in a storage field, namely, the _____, _____, and _____ characters. On the other hand, the three special characters used

TABLE 3-2
The Five Catagories of Data

Numeric items	The PICTURE may contain suitable combinations of the following characters: 9 V P and S.
Alphabetic items	The PICTURE clause contains only the A character.
Alphanumeric items	The PICTURE clause consists of A 9 and X characters. It cannot contain all A or all 9 characters, but it may contain a mixture of A and 9 characters.
Numeric edited items	The PICTURE clause can contain suitable combinations of the following characters: B P V Z O 9 , . + – CR DB $ and /.
Alphanumeric edited items	The PICTURE clause can contain combinations of the following characters: Z X 9 B O and /.

in conjunction with computational numeric fields are the _____ , _____ , and _____ PICTURE characters. (Refer to Table 3-1 if you wish.)

9, A, X; V, P, S

2. The only editing PICTURE character used in conjunction with an alphabetic field is the _____ character, whereas the three editing characters that can be used in conjunction with an alphanumeric field are the _____ , _____ , and _____ PICTURE characters.

B; B, 0, /

. . . .

THE BLANK WHEN ZERO CLAUSE

Use of this clause achieves the same result as Z PICTURE, but it is more general. Consider the statement 02 AMOUNT PIC ZZ9.99 BLANK WHEN ZERO. If AMOUNT contains a zero value, the field will be blanked (six blanks); otherwise the PICTURE string will provide the editing.

THE CURRENCY AND DECIMAL-POINT CLAUSES

These two clauses actually refer to the ENVIRONMENT DIVISION. However, they are directly applicable to the subject of this chapter because they define aspects of the operating environment that have a direct impact on DATA DIVISION features associated with PICTURE strings for editing.

COBOL includes provisions for international usage with respect to monetary currencies and numeric values. Changing the dollar sign and using a comma in lieu of a decimal point can be accommodated by the use of two special clauses, as explained below.

By use of the following format specification in the SPECIAL-NAMES paragraph of the CONFIGURATION SECTION of the ENVIRONMENT DIVISION, one can thereafter use a sign other than $ in PICTURE clauses that are included in the program.

CURRENCY SIGN IS literal

For example, suppose that 'F' is the appropriate currency sign. We could write:

```
ENVIRONMENT DIVISION.
CONFIGURATION SECTION.
SOURCE-COMPUTER. . . .
OBJECT-COMPUTER. . . .
SPECIAL-NAMES.
    CURRENCY SIGN IS 'F'.
```

Then in PICTURE clauses we would use 'F' in place of $ as in the following two contrasting but equivalent examples:

```
02  AMOUNT  PIC FF,FFF,FFF.99.

02  AMOUNT  PIC $$,$$$,$$$.99.
```

The currency sign cannot be chosen from the following:

1. The digits 0 through 9

2. The alphabetic characters consisting of the uppercase letters A, B, C, D, P, R, S, V, X, Z; the lowercase letters a through z; or the space

3. The special characters ∗ + − , . : ( ) " = /

In many countries outside of the United States the functions of the decimal point and comma are reversed. Thus the values 1,35 and 2.534,99 would be equivalent to the U.S. 1.35 and 2,534.99, respectively. The format of the clause in the SPECIAL-NAMES paragraph to accommodate the difference in these conventions is

DECIMAL-POINT IS COMMA

Once this clause has been used, the function of the comma and period are interchanged in the character string of the PICTURE clause and in numeric literals. Suppose we use the following specification in the ENVIRONMENT DIVISION:

```
SPECIAL-NAMES.
    CURRENCY SIGN IS 'F'
    DECIMAL-POINT IS COMMA.
```

Given the above specification, the following PICTURE definition is valid in the DATA DIVISION:

```
02 AMOUNT-1 PIC FF.FFF.FF9,99.
```

The floating currency sign in the PICTURE definition above is the character 'F' and the roles of the decimal point and comma have been reversed. Thus in the statement MOVE 1000,56 TO AMOUNT, the value is one thousand units and fifty-six hundredths of the F-currency units.

Keep in mind that given the CURRENCY and DECIMAL-POINT specifications above, a PICTURE definition cannot include the floating $ sign nor the "usual" use of the comma and decimal point in a PICTURE definition.

R E V I E W . . . .

1. Changing the dollar sign to a symbol associated with another currency can be achieved by use of the _____ clause.

CURRENCY

2. The clause that makes it possible to interchange the meaning and function of the comma and decimal-point symbols in PICTURE strings is the _____ clause.

DECIMAL-POINT

3. The specification of the CURRENCY and DECIMAL-POINT clauses is written in the _____ paragraph of the _____ SECTION of the ENVIRONMENT DIVISION.

SPECIAL-NAMES; CONFIGURATION

. . . .

SAMPLE DATA DIVISION

We conclude our discussion with a sample DATA DIVISION that includes many of the features described in this chapter. The sample is based on a salary-report programming task. The task consists of reading records in an employee file and producing a report such as that previously illustrated in Figure 3-5. The input record layout chart was presented in Figure 3-3, while the printer spacing chart was presented in Figure 3-4. Finally, Figure 3-8 presents the DATA DIVISION written for the programming task. The PROCEDURE DIVISION for the task is presented and discussed at the end of the following chapter.

FIGURE 3-8
DATA DIVISION for the Salary Report Program

```
      DATA DIVISION.
     *
      FILE SECTION.
     *
      FD   EMPLOYEE-FILE
           LABEL RECORDS ARE OMITTED
           RECORD CONTAINS 80 CHARACTERS
           DATA RECORD IS EMPLOYEE-RECORD.
      01   EMPLOYEE-RECORD.
           02 EMPLOYEE-NAME           PIC X(15).
           02 EMPLOYEE-SEX-CODE       PIC 9.
              88 MALE                 VALUE 1.
              88 FEMALE               VALUE 2.
              88 ERROR-SEX-CODE       VALUE ZERO 3 THRU 9.
           02 EMPLOYEE-SALARY         PIC 9(5)V99.
           02 FILLER                  PIC X(57).
     *
      FD   REPORT-FILE
           LABEL RECORDS ARE OMITTED
           RECORD CONTAINS 132 CHARACTERS
           DATA RECORD IS PRINT-LINE.
      01   PRINT-LINE                 PIC X(132).
     *
      WORKING-STORAGE SECTION.
     *
```

FIGURE 3-8

DATA DIVISION for the Salary Report Program (continued)

```
01  END-OF-FILE-TEST              PIC XXX VALUE 'NO'.
    88  END-OF-EMPLOYEE-FILE      VALUE 'YES'.
*
01  EMPLOYEE-COUNTERS.
    02  NO-OF-MEN                 PIC 99 VALUE ZERO.
    02  NO-OF-WOMEN               PIC 99 VALUE ZERO.
*
01  SALARY-TOTALS.
    02  MEN-TOTAL-SALARY          PIC 9(7)V99 VALUE ZERO.
    02  WOMEN-TOTAL-SALARY        PIC 9(7)V99 VALUE ZERO.
*
01  REPORT-HEADINGS.
    02  HEADING-L.
        03  FILLER               PIC X(36) VALUE SPACES.
        03  FILLER               PIC X(13) VALUE
                'ANNUAL SALARY'.
*
    02  HEADING-2.
        03  FILLER               PIC X(16) VALUE SPACES.
        03  FILLER               PIC X(13) VALUE
                'EMPLOYEE NAME'.
        03  FILLER               PIC X(10) VALUE SPACES.
        03  FILLER               PIC X(3) VALUE 'MEN'.
        03  FILLER               PIC X(13) VALUE SPACES.
        03  FILLER               PIC X(5) VALUE 'WOMEN'.
*
01  REPORT-DETAIL-LINE.
    02  FILLER                   PIC X(15) VALUE SPACES.
    02  REPORT-EMPL-NAME         PIC X(15).
    02  REPORT-ERROR-CODE        PIC X(6) VALUE SPACES.
    02  REPORT-MEN-SALARY        PIC ZZ,Z99.99
                                     BLANK WHEN ZERO.
    02  FILLER                   PIC X(8) VALUE SPACES.
    02  REPORT-WOMEN-SALARY      PIC ZZ,Z99.99
                                     BLANK WHEN ZERO.
*
01  REPORT-TOTALS-LINE.
    02  FILLER                   PIC X(15) VALUE SPACES.
    02  FILLER                   PIC X(9) VALUE 'T O T A L'.
    02  FILLER                   PIC X(8) VALUE SPACES.
    02  REPORT-TOT-MEN-SALARY    PIC $$,$$$,$99.99.
    02  FILLER                   PIC X(4) VALUE SPACES.
    02  REPORT-TOT-WOMEN-SALARY  PIC $$,$$$,$99.99.
*
01  REPORT-AVERAGES-LINE.
    02  FILLER                   PIC X(15) VALUE SPACES.
    02  FILLER                   PIC X(13) VALUE
                'A V E R A G E'.
    02  FILLER                   PIC X(4) VALUE SPACES.
    02  REPORT-AVG-MEN-SALARY    PIC $$,$$$,$99.99.
    02  FILLER                   PIC X(4) VALUE SPACES.
    02  REPORT-AVG-WOMEN-SALARY  PIC $$,$$$,$99.99.
```

The only DATA DIVISION feature in Figure 3-8 that has not been previously discussed is the special level number, 88, which is used to define the condition of a field having a specified value. For example, in the figure we have

```
02 EMPLOYEE-SEX-CODE        PIC 9.
   88 MALE                  VALUE 1.
```

MALE is a *condition-name* that defines a condition that corresponds to the value of "1." Henceforth in the program IF MALE can be used in lieu of IF EMPLOYEE-SEX-CODE = "1." The subject of condition-names is covered more fully in Chapter 5.

For convenience we selectively outline the DATA DIVISION in Figure 3-9, discussing some of the highlights.

FIGURE 3-9

Explanation of Selected DATA DIVISION Entries in Figure 3-8

FD EMPLOYEE-FILE	The input file-name.
01 EMPLOYEE-RECORD.	The name of the input file record.

02 EMPLOYEE-SEX-CODE
    88 MALE
    88 FEMALE
	In the data field identifying the sex category of the employee. Notice use of the 88 level-numbers to specify the condition-names MALE and FEMALE.

88 ERROR-SEX-CODE	Another condition-name, which identifies the condition of EMPLOYEE-SEX-CODE having any of the values of zero or 3 through 9.
01 END-OF-FILE TEST. 88 END-OF-EMPLOYEE-FILE	A data-name used for purposes of testing whether the end-of-file record has been read. Again, a condition-name is used for convenience in testing whether or not the end-of-file condition is true.

01 EMPLOYEE-COUNTERS.
    02 NO-OF-MEN
    02 NO-OF-WOMEN
	The EMPLOYEE-COUNTERS group item is used for documentation purposes. There will be no reference to EMPLOYEE-COUNTERS as such in the PROCEDURE DIVISION. The references will be to either NO-OF-MEN or NO-OF-WOMEN, as appropriate in each case. These counter fields were created in recognition of the need to report the average salary, the computation of which requires a count of the number of men and women, respectively.

01 SALARY-TOTALS.
    02 MEN-TOTAL-SALARY
    02 WOMEN-TOTAL-SALARY
	These data-names were defined in recognition of the fact that the required report presents the total salary for each of the two categories of employees.

01 REPORT-HEADINGS.
    02 HEADING-L
        .
        .
        .
    02 HEADING-2
	The report heading consists of two title lines. For better documentation we coined a group item REPORT-HEADINGS to refer to both of them, and then delineated each heading under HEADING-1 and HEADING-2. Blank lines between these headings can be specified by PROCEDURE DIVISION instructions (. . . ADVANCING . . . LINES), so we do not bother to specify blank line headings in the DATA DIVISION.

01 REPORT-DETAIL-LINE.	This item represents the format for producing each of the detail lines in the report.
02 REPORT-ERROR-CODE	This field is normally blank. However, as illustrated in the sample report in Figure 3-5, we want to print six asterisks in any field for which the employee is not classified as being either male or female. *(continued on next page)*

FIGURE 3-9

Explanation of Selected DATA DIVISION Entries in Figure 3-8 (continued)

02 REPORT-MEN-SALARY	Notice the PIC clause illustrating the use of zero suppression, comma and decimal point insertion, and use of BLANK WHEN ZERO. The thinking is that if an employee record is for a woman, then we want spaces to be in the REPORT-MEN-SALARY, and vice versa for men. Therefore we plan to move zeros to the field, which then are converted to spaces by the BLANK WHEN ZERO clause. (MOVE SPACES TO REPORT-MEN-SALARY would be improper because COBOL does not allow moving inconsistent categories of data. In this example the alphanumeric data, SPACES, cannot be moved to the numeric edited field, REPORT-MEN-SALARY.)

01   REPORT-TOTALS-LINE.
      .
      .
      .
	These are specifications for the last two lines in the report, which constitute the footing, and include the total and average salary for each category.

01   REPORT-AVERAGES-LINE.
      .
      .
      .
	Notice the use of floating dollar signs and the larger field size. Since this is a sum, it should be larger than the field from which we add the data being accumulated. The BLANK WHEN ZERO clause (or the equivalent of $$,$$$,$$$.$$) is not used because we wish to print the zero rather than have a space if the total is in fact zero dollars.

02 REPORT-AVG-MEN-SALARY	

SUMMARY

The purpose of this chapter was to present and explain quite a few of the coding details for writing the DATA DIVISION of a COBOL program. The two sections commonly included in a DATA DIVISION are the FILE SECTION and the WORKING-STORAGE SECTION.

Data fields are defined in both the FILE SECTION and the WORKING-STORAGE SECTION. Therefore the first several sections of this chapter were concerned with defining data fields. In these sections you learned how elementary data fields are defined, the use of FILLER as a nonspecific data-name, the use of the VALUE clause to define initial contents, the use of level-numbers to define group structures, and methodology associated with record layout.

Particular attention was given to *constants* as contrasted to data-names. COBOL has three types of *constants*. A *numeric literal* is a stored numeric value that is analogous to a constant in algebra. A *figurative constant* includes such verbalized constants as ZEROS and BLANKS; these are often used to "fill" a field, such as filling a data field to serve as an accumulator with zeros before it is used. A *nonnumeric literal* is enclosed in quotation marks and typically is used for such functions as a printed heading in a report.

The function of the FILE SECTION is to describe each file used in the program. Each FD entry is followed by a file-name. Then the name assigned to the record in the file is given. The hierarchical structure of the data fields included in the records is defined by use of level-numbers, with the whole record being at the 01 level.

The WORKING-STORAGE SECTION provides descriptions of data items that are not part of any file, such as intermediate calculation values and report headings. Special attention was given to the use of the VALUE clause in defining the initial contents of WORKING-STORAGE fields.

PICTURE clauses are used in both the FILE SECTION and the WORKING-STORAGE SECTION to describe the type of content in elementary data fields. We considered separately the use of PICTURE clauses for data description as contrasted to data editing. These parts of the chapter are quite detailed and include the types of definitions that you will continue to reference in later chapters.

The chapter concluded with a sample DATA DIVISION that illustrates many of the features presented in this chapter.

EXERCISES

3.1 Consider the following record description outline:

```
01  A
       03  B-0
              05  B-1
              05  B-2
       03  C-0
              05  C-1
                     07  C-1-1
                     07  C-1-2
              05  C-2
```

Answer the following questions with respect to the above:

a. How many group fields are described? List them.

b. Which field descriptions should have a PIC clause?

c. Which data-names should be followed by a period?

d. If every elementary field has a PIC of X(5), how long is the entire record in terms of bytes?

3.2 A data field contains social security identification numbers (SSN) and has been defined as follows:

```
01  SOC-SEC-NO-IN  PIC 9(9).
```

We want to MOVE the contents of that field into an edited field that would contain hyphens before the fourth and the sixth digits in SOC-SEC-NO-IN. For example, if the SSN is 233154389, we want to have it available in the form 233-15-4389. Write the data definition for that edited field, name it SOC-SEC-NO-OUT, and explain how you would use the MOVE instruction to accomplish the task.

3.3 Indicate the size of each of the following fields in terms of the number of bytes:

PICTURE	SIZE
99V99	_____
9(3).9	_____
S999V9	_____
ZZ,ZZZ	_____
+(3).99	_____
$***,**9.99	_____
VPP99	_____
ZZZ000	_____

3.4 Complete the DATA DIVISION description for the following WORKING-STORAGE record so that it corresponds to the record layout that follows. Use your own choice of data-names.

```
01  TOTALS-LINE.
    02 _____  PIC _____  VALUE _____
    02 _____  PIC _____  VALUE _____
    02 _____  PIC _____  VALUE _____
    02 _____  PIC _____
    02 _____  PIC _____  VALUE _____
    02 _____  PIC _____
```

1–16	17–25	26–35	36–45	46–50	51–60
Blank	TOTAL	Blank	Men's total salary, showing decimal point and 2 decimal places	Blank	Women's total salary, showing decimal point and 2 decimal places

3.5 Referring to the following schematic representation, write a DATA DIVISION record description using the information:

DEPT	2 letters
NAME	15 characters
RATE	4 digits, 2 decimal places, used for arithmetic
SKILL	1 letter
REGULAR	7 digits, 2 decimal places, used for arithmetic
OVERTIME	6 digits, 2 decimal places, used for arithmetic
SS-TAX	5 digits, 2 decimal places, used for arithmetic

PAY-RECORD					
EMPLOYEE		RATE	SKILL	YEAR-TO-DATE	
DEPT	NAME			GROSS	SS-TAX
				REGULAR / OVERTIME	

3.6 Write DATA DIVISION entries for the WORKING-STORAGE record named SALES-DATA whose description is given in the following table. Data are moved from the items whose PICTURE description is shown.

SOURCE ITEM PICTURE	RECEIVING ITEM-NAME	PRINT POSITIONS	EDITING REQUIRED
99999	SALE-NUMBER	1-5	Suppress all leading zeros.
		6-7	Blank
(X)25	NAME	8-32	None
		33–34	Blank

SOURCE ITEM PICTURE	RECEIVING ITEM-NAME	PRINT POSITIONS	EDITING REQUIRED
S9999V99	DOLLARS	35 – ?	Insert comma, decimal point. Dollar sign immediately to the left of leftmost nonzero digit. Show negative sign if negative.
		2 positions	Blank
S9(3)V9(4)	PROFIT		Show decimal point. Suppress leading zeros. Show negative sign to left of leftmost nonzero digit.

3.7 Following the format below are DATA DIVISION entries for fields that contain the data to be printed as the CHECK-REGISTER record. The output resulting from printing of the CHECK-REGISTER record should have approximately the following format (header titles are shown for clarity only):

VENDOR NAME	VENDOR NUMBER	CHECK NUMBER	DATE	DEBIT	DISCOUNT	CASH
ACME CORP.	1234	12345	01/03/86	$1,030.57	$20.13	$1,010.44

```
01  CHECK-NUMBER    PICTURE 9(5).
01  DEBIT           PICTURE 9(6)V99.
01  DISCOUNT        PICTURE 9(4)V99.
01 CASH             PICTURE 9(6)V99.
01  VENDOR-DATA.
    02  V-NAME      PICTURE X(15).
    02  V-NUMBER    PICTURE X(4).
01  DATE.
    02  MONTH       PICTURE 99.
    02  DAY         PICTURE 99.
    02  YEAR        PICTURE 99.
```

Write DATA DIVISION entries to form the CHECK-REGISTER record so that the output is printed approximately in the desired format. Make sure that the date is in the form MM/DD/YY. Use a printer spacing chart from the supply at the end of the text to assist your output report effort.

3.8 It is required that two lines having the following general format be printed:

```
SUMMARY STATISTICS
AVERAGE BAL.$XXX,XXX.XX  MAX$XXX,XXX.XX  MIN$XXX,XXX.XX
```

Assume the following DATA DIVISION entries:

```
FD  PRINT-FILE LABEL RECORDS OMITTED DATA RECORD IS
        PRINT-LINE.
01  PRINT-LINE   PICTURE X(132).
WORKING-STORAGE SECTION.
01  MAX-BAL      PICTURE 9(6)V99.
01  MIN-BAL      PICTURE 9(6)V99.
01  AVER-BAL     PICTURE 9(6)V99.
```

Write WORKING-STORAGE SECTION entries to set up the required fields to print these two lines.

3.9 Suppose that it has become necessary to change an existing COBOL program. The original version of the relevant DATA DIVISION entries is as follows:

```
02  FIELD-A
    03  FIELD-B
    03  FIELD-C
    03  FIELD-D
02  FIELD-E
```

In the revised version it is required that the fields be restructured so that (a) reference can be made to all the fields as one unit; (b) reference can be made to fields B and C as a unit; and (c) reference can be made to fields D and E as a unit. Show how this can be done.

3.10 Assume that in all cases the following two instructions apply:

```
MOVE A TO B
MOVE B TO C
```

Field C has been defined as follows:

```
01  C  PIC X(11).
```

Show the resulting contents of C in each of the cases included in the following table, assuming that each cell stands for one character position.

CONTENT OF A	PICTURE OF B	RESULTING CONTENT IN C										
10.125	999V99											
10000.00	Z,ZZZ.ZZ											
900.15	$$,$$Z.99											
0.08	$$,$ZZ.ZZ											
50.50	$***.99DB											
−25.25	+,+++.99											
25.25	$$$$.99−											
WELCOME	XXXBXXX											

4 Writing Complete Programs

COBOL LANGUAGE FORMATS

IDENTIFICATION DIVISION

ENVIRONMENT DIVISION

DATA DIVISION

FILE INPUT AND OUTPUT

THE MOVE STATEMENT

THE PERFORM VERB

ARITHMETIC VERBS

CONDITIONAL STATEMENTS

SAMPLE PROCEDURE DIVISION

THE MAIN OBJECTIVE *of this chapter is to develop your knowledge of COBOL to the point that you will be able to write complete programs.*

You will begin by first considering the coding conventions by which COBOL programming options are presented, and then you will review the features of the IDENTIFICATION DIVISION, ENVIRONMENT DIVISION, and DATA DIVISION. Recall that the DATA DIVISION was covered in some detail in the preceding chapter. Your study in this chapter will focus on the PROCEDURE DIVISION, and you will learn how to use a complete set of PROCEDURE DIVISION statements.

The chapter concludes with coverage of the PROCEDURE DIVISION for the employee salary-report programming task for which the DATA DIVISION was written in the preceding chapter.

COBOL LANGUAGE FORMATS

Before turning our attention to PROCEDURE DIVISION statements, we need to describe the method by which programming options are presented in this book. COBOL is characterized by great flexibility in the form of options available to the programmer. To communicate these options, we use a *metalanguage*, a language about a language. The form of presentation used here is not unique to this book but generally is followed in all books concerned with COBOL program statements. The method is used to describe how each type of statement should be structured, and to identify the options available to the programmer for each type of statement. In other words, the style of presentation is necessary because we wish to talk about types of statements in general, rather than about specific and particular program instructions. For this purpose, then, the following set of conventions is followed:

1. Words presented entirely in uppercase letters are always COBOL reserved words.

2. Uppercase words that are underlined are words that are required in the type of program statement being described. Uppercase words that are not underlined are optional and are used only to improve the readability of the program.

3. Lowercase words are used to indicate the points at which data-names or constants are to be supplied by the programmer. In addition to the words "data-name" and "literal," the term "identifier" is used to indicate a data-name, but it has a slightly broader meaning. It refers to either of the following cases: data-names that are unique in themselves, or data-names that are not unique in themselves but are made unique through qualification. Qualification is discussed in Chapter 16. For now, you may safely assume the words "data-name" and "identifier" to be equivalent. Other lowercase words used to indicate items to be inserted by the programmer are

file-name	condition
record-name	statement
integer	any imperative statement
formula	any sentence

4. Items enclosed in braces { } indicate that one of the enclosed items must be used.

5. Items enclosed in brackets [ ] indicate that the items are optional, and one of them may be used at the option of the programmer.

6. An ellipsis (. . .) indicates that further information may be included in the program instruction, usually in the form of repeating the immediately preceding element any desired number of times.

As an example of the use of these conventions, consider the ADD statement. With the COBOL language format a basic form of ADD is

$$\underline{ADD} \begin{Bmatrix} \text{identifier -1} \\ \text{literal -1} \end{Bmatrix} \begin{bmatrix} \text{, identifier -2} \\ \text{, literal -2} \end{bmatrix} \dots \underline{TO} \text{ identifier-m}$$

If we apply the rules just presented, the word ADD is a reserved COBOL word because it is in uppercase, and it is required because it is underscored. The word TO is governed by the same rules. The braces following ADD indicate that one of the two alternatives enclosed must be used. Thus the required word ADD must be followed by either an identifier or a literal. Incidentally, it also is understood that, for this specific instruction, the identifier must be an elementary numeric (nonedited) field and the literal must be a numeric literal. The square brackets indicate that identifier-2 and literal-2 are both optional. In other words, the identifier or literal that immediately follows ADD may or may not be followed by a second identifier or literal. The commas also are optional; they may be included to improve readability, or they may be omitted. The ellipsis indicates that the preceding element (in square brackets) may be repeated as many times as desired. Finally, the identifier-m indicates that an identifier must follow the word TO. Note that it is not enclosed in braces because it is the only option; braces are used when we may choose among alternatives. Utilizing this general format, we see that the following examples are legitimate ADD statements:

```
ADD AMOUNT TO TOTAL
ADD 100 TO TOTAL
ADD REGULAR OVERTIME TO GROSS
ADD 10 BONUS 100.25 TO GROSS
```

R E V I E W . . . .

1. In presenting COBOL statement instructions, words that are entirely in uppercase letters designate _____ words.

    COBOL reserved

2. When a reserved COBOL word is underlined in the format presentation, this indicates that the word [may / must] be used as part of a program instruction.

    must

3. Items to be inserted in the program instruction, such as data-names, identifiers, constants, and expressions, are indicated by [lowercase / uppercase] words.

    lowercase

4. When two or more items are enclosed within brackets [ ], this indicates that one of them [may / must] be included in the program instruction. When two or more items are enclosed within braces { } this indicates that one of them [may / must] be included.

    may; must

5. To indicate that further information, such as additional data-names, can be included in an instruction, a(n) _____ is used.

    ellipsis (. . .)

. . . .

IDENTIFICATION DIVISION

The function of the IDENTIFICATION DIVISION is to supply information about the program to others who may read or use the program. On the COBOL Coding Form we start in column 8 with the words IDENTIFICATION DIVISION. The first and only required paragraph is the PROGRAM-ID, which is followed by the program-name chosen by the programmer. For example, we may have

```
IDENTIFICATION DIVISION.
PROGRAM-ID. CUSTRPRT.
```

In this case the word CUSTRPRT is the name the programmer has chosen to identify the program. This name must start with an alphabetic character and may consist of up to 30 alphabetic or numeric characters unless the specific compiler limits the number to fewer characters. The two lines shown in the example are sufficient content for the IDENTIFICATION DIVISION. All other paragraphs are optional but, if they are used, they must be written in the order shown. The following example includes optional paragraphs. The underlined words are COBOL reserved words, which are required; the other words are a matter of the programmer's choice.

<u>IDENTIFICATION DIVISION.</u>

<u>PROGRAM-ID.</u> SALARY.

<u>AUTHOR.</u> LEE WALTERS.

<u>INSTALLATION.</u> XYZ CORPORATION.

<u>DATE-WRITTEN.</u> JANUARY 14, 1990.

<u>DATE-COMPILED.</u>

<u>SECURITY.</u>   THIS PROGRAM RESTRICTED TO ALL
            PERSONNEL EXCEPT THOSE AUTHORIZED
            BY THE OFFICE OF THE CONTROLLER.

All paragraph-names start in column 8 and, as stated earlier, all paragraphs are optional with the exception of PROGRAM-ID. The compiler does not process what follows the COBOL words but only prints that content. Thus after DATE-WRITTEN we could have written DURING THE SPRING OF 1990. The compiler derives no more meaning from JANUARY or from SPRING than from a nonsense word; therefore the programmer should be concerned simply with choosing verbal descriptions that will be meaningful to the potential readers of the program.

Note that the DATE-COMPILED paragraph is left blank. The compiler will insert the actual date, and the source listing will include that date.

An entry in the IDENTIFICATION DIVISION may extend to more than one line, as illustrated in the case of the SECURITY paragraph. In such a case the lines subsequent to the first line must all start in column 12 or to the right of column 12. The PROGRAM-ID paragraph, however, is restricted to one word, which must not exceed 30 characters in length. (Some exceptions to these rules are discussed in Chapter 23, in connection with subprograms.)

R E V I E W . . . .

1. The order in which the four divisions of a COBOL program appear is:
    _____ , _____ , _____ , and
    _____ .

                                    IDENTIFICATION; ENVIRONMENT; DATA; PROCEDURE

2. Other than the division name itself, the only paragraph required in the IDENTIFICATION DIVISION is the one named _____ .

                                                                          PROGRAM-ID

3. Although other entries in the IDENTIFICATION DIVISION may extend to more than one line, the PROGRAM-ID paragraph is restricted to one word which must not exceed _____ (number) characters in length.

                                                                                  30

4. Overall, the purpose of the IDENTIFICATION DIVISION of a COBOL program is to _____ .

                                              describe the program to potential users (etc.)

. . . .

ENVIRONMENT DIVISION

This division is designed to describe the computer system "environment" in which the program is compiled and executed. With a few important exceptions, this division provides documentation type of information. In the 1985 standard this is an optional division. Still, for the vast majority of programs, and in both the '74 and the '85 versions, there are parts of the ENVIRONMENT DIVISION that define very necessary and important information. This importance will become much more evident in the chapters that deal with file processing (chapters 10, 20, and 21).

The following illustration of an ENVIRONMENT DIVISION is a typical one. Again, as for the IDENTIFICATION DIVISION, the underlined words are COBOL reserved words.

```
ENVIRONMENT DIVISION.

CONFIGURATION SECTION.

SOURCE-COMPUTER.  ABC-480.
OBJECT-COMPUTER.  ABC-480.

INPUT-OUTPUT SECTION.

FILE-CONTROL.

    SELECT CUSTOMER-FILE    ASSIGN TO CUSTFILE.

    SELECT REPORT-FILE      ASSIGN TO PRINTER.
```

There are two sections included in the ENVIRONMENT DIVISION in this example: the CONFIGURATION SECTION and the INPUT-OUTPUT SECTION. The SOURCE-COMPUTER and OBJECT-COMPUTER paragraphs serve documentation purposes. They are intended to provide information about the computer system used for compilation (SOURCE-COMPUTER) and the system used for execution (OBJECT-COMPUTER). The name ABC-480 is fictitious in the example and would be replaced by a manufacturer's name and model number, such as IBM-3081, OR DEC-VAX-8650.

This example has one paragraph in the INPUT-OUTPUT SECTION, the FILE-CONTROL paragraph. The SELECT statement identifies the name of a file, in this case CUSTOMER-FILE. This file-name is the programmer's choice and is formed in compliance with COBOL name formation rules (although some compilers place further restrictions, such as that the first 12 characters must be unique). The ASSIGN statement declares that this file will be associated with the file identification that follows, in this case CUSTFILE. Similarly, REPORT-FILE identifies another file-name, and the hardware device with which this file will be associated is PRINTER (thus this file will include the output information). Device names are neither COBOL words nor programmer supplied; they are *implementor-names,* which means they are specific to the compiler and operating system used. Sometimes the implementor-names can be rather cryptic, as in

```
SELECT CUSTOMER-FILE ASSIGN TO SYS005-UR-2540R-S.
```

We illustrate the common practice in IBM mainframe environments because they are so widely used for business applications in the large corporations that often hire the students who have learned COBOL in college. Figure 4-1 presents an outline of a complete JOB Control Language (JCL) stream for an IBM mainframe system. Included in the figure is an illustration of how file-names in the COBOL program are associated with the operating system file-names. In Figure 4-1 the names in the ASSIGN TO clauses are highlighted, as are the corresponding "DD-names" in the JCL (Job Control Language) stream.

FIGURE 4-1

*Sample JCL Stream for an IBM
Mainframe Computer*

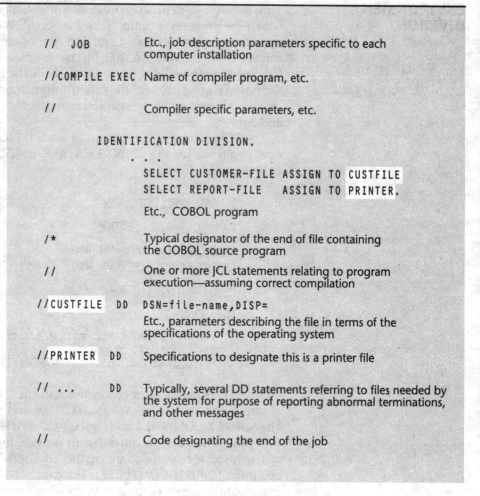

`// JOB`	Etc., job description parameters specific to each computer installation
`//COMPILE EXEC`	Name of compiler program, etc.
`//`	Compiler specific parameters, etc.
`IDENTIFICATION DIVISION.`	
`. . .`	
`SELECT CUSTOMER-FILE ASSIGN TO CUSTFILE` `SELECT REPORT-FILE   ASSIGN TO PRINTER.`	
	Etc., COBOL program
`/*`	Typical designator of the end of file containing the COBOL source program
`//`	One or more JCL statements relating to program execution—assuming correct compilation
`//CUSTFILE DD`	`DSN=file-name,DISP=` Etc., parameters describing the file in terms of the specifications of the operating system
`//PRINTER DD`	Specifications to designate this is a printer file
`// ... DD`	Typically, several DD statements referring to files needed by the system for purpose of reporting abnormal terminations, and other messages
`//`	Code designating the end of the job

Each computer system has its own way of designating computer files. Therefore in this book such entries usually are presented in a general conceptual form rather than in a computer-specific form.

R E V I E W . . . .

1. Of the four divisions of a COBOL program, the one written with an orientation to a particular computer system and its equipment is the _____ DIVISION.

ENVIRONMENT

2. The ENVIRONMENT DIVISION is optional in the [1974 / 1985] standard version of COBOL.

1985

3. Two sections of the ENVIRONMENT DIVISION are the CONFIGURATION SECTION and the INPUT-OUTPUT SECTION. Of these, the one that serves to identify the equipment to be used and is the only section specifically required is the _____ SECTION.

CONFIGURATION

4. The section of the ENVIRONMENT DIVISION concerned with the assignment of specified files to particular devices is the _____ SECTION.

INPUT-OUTPUT

5. The division of a COBOL program that supplies general information about the program is the _____ DIVISION; the division that specifies the equipment to be used is the _____ DIVISION.

IDENTIFICATION; ENVIRONMENT

. . . .

DATA DIVISION

The DATA DIVISION was the main subject of Chapter 3. As a brief review, it serves to define file and working-storage fields and their names. Commonly, it consists of two sections: the FILE SECTION and the WORKING-STORAGE SECTION.

An example FILE SECTION is

```
FILE SECTION.
FD  CUSTOMER-FILE
    LABEL RECORDS ARE STANDARD
    RECORD CONTAINS 80 CHARACTERS
    DATA RECORD IS CUSTOMER-RECORD.
01  CUSTOMER-RECORD.
    05  CUSTOMER-NAME  PIC X(13).
    05  CUSTOMER-UNITS PIC 999.
    05  FILLER         PIC X(64).
```

The FD designation is needed at the beginning of each file description. It is always followed by a file-name—in the case above, by CUSTOMER-FILE.

The clause LABEL RECORDS ARE STANDARD or LABEL RECORDS ARE OMITTED will be discussed in Chapter 10, on sequential file processing. For now we will use it in either the STANDARD or OMITTED versions and will understand that it states whether the file has standard or omitted identifying labels.

The optional statement RECORD CONTAINS . . . CHARACTERS is used to declare the size of the record. In the CUSTOMER-FILE each record is 80 characters in length, and we refer to such a record by means of the name CUSTOMER-RECORD, which is designated in the clause DATA RECORD IS CUSTOMER-RECORD.

Following the FD entry we see the record description. The 01 level-number introduces the record-name CUSTOMER-RECORD, referring to the entire record. Then there are three entries, each starting with the appropriate level-number.

Assuming CUSTOMER-FILE to be an input file, we can give an instruction to copy a data record from the disk into central storage (by use of the READ verb). Subsequent to a READ operation we can then give instructions to operate on the data in central storage—for example, by instructions such as ADD CUSTOMER-UNITS TO . . .

CUSTOMER-NAME and CUSTOMER-UNITS are data-names referencing fields in the record. CUSTOMER-NAME refers to the first 13 bytes of CUSTOMER-RECORD while CUSTOMER-UNITS refers to the next 3 bytes. The third field in CUSTOMER-RECORD is named FILLER.

Storage fields associated with the file records receive data from, or are used to send data to, external input-output devices, such as disks, tapes, printers, and video terminals. In addition to such storage fields, there also is a need for storage of header data, intermediate arithmetic results, and the like. The WORKING-STORAGE SECTION is used to define such fields, as discussed in Chapter 3.

R E V I E W . . . .

1. Of the four divisions of a COBOL program, the one concerned with the identification and description of storage fields is the _____ division.

DATA

2. In the FILE SECTION of the DATA DIVISION, we designate that an entry is a file description by beginning the entry with the COBOL reserved word _____ .

FD

3. After the name of the file, the next item of information given in the FD entry is the name of the _____ contained in the file.

record

4. The level-number assigned to the whole record is always _____ (number).

01

5. All fields in the record that are directly subordinate to the overall record commonly are assigned the level-number _____ (number).

02 or higher

. . . .

FILE INPUT AND OUTPUT

The general functions performed by an input statement and an output statement are, respectively, to transfer data from an external storage medium to central storage, and to transfer data from central storage to an external storage medium. The file storage medium involved in each case is specified in the ENVIRONMENT DIVISION by the corresponding SELECT file-name and ASSIGN TO . . . statements.

The OPEN and CLOSE Verbs

Before a file can be used, we must OPEN that file and designate whether it is an input file or an output file. The format is

```
      ⎧[INPUT file-name-1    [file-name-2 . . . ]]⎫
OPEN ⎨                                          ⎬
      ⎩[OUTPUT file-name-3   [file-name-4 . . . ]]⎭
```

The full meaning and purpose of the OPEN verb is explained in Chapter 10; for now, we simply will say that it must be used prior to writing into or reading from a file.

We can use an OPEN statement for each file, or we can use one OPEN statement for several files as a group:

```
OPEN INPUT  EMPL-FILE
OPEN OUTPUT REPORT-FILE

OPEN INPUT  FILE-A
            FILE-B
     OUTPUT FILE-C
            FILE-D
            FILE-E.
```

The practice of writing only one file-name per line simply enhances documentation. We could also have written all file-names on one line.

Before a program terminates execution with a STOP RUN statement, we must use a CLOSE statement for each file that was opened. The meaning and purpose of this statement will be explained further in Chapter 10.

The following is the format for the CLOSE verb; just as for the OPEN verb, we can use one CLOSE statement for each file or we can reference several files from one CLOSE.

CLOSE file-name-1   [file-name-2] . . .

The READ Verb

One format of the READ verb is

READ file-name RECORD [INTO identifier]

[AT END imperative-statement]

Each execution of the READ transfers the data contained in the subsequent physical record of the file to the internal record described in the 01 entry that follows the FD specification. In effect, the READ is a "copy" command; it copies data from file storage to central storage.

The INTO option is a short form for moving the data from the file-record field to another field so that the data can be copied without a separate MOVE statement. Here are examples of two equivalent versions:

```
READ INPUT-FILE RECORD INTO OUTPUT-RECORD
    AT END MOVE 'YES' TO END-OF-FILE.
IF  END-OF-FILE = 'NO'
    WRITE OUTPUT-RECORD . . .
```

The INTO OUTPUT-RECORD function could be replaced by the equivalent use of MOVE:

```
READ INPUT-FILE RECORD
    AT END MOVE 'YES' TO END-OF-FILE.
IF  END-OF-FILE = 'NO'
    MOVE INPUT-RECORD TO OUTPUT-RECORD
    WRITE OUTPUT-RECORD . . .
```

Thus the INTO OUTPUT-RECORD is simply a "shorthand" substitute for MOVE INPUT-RECORD TO OUTPUT-RECORD. The AT END is indicated as being optional; however, until we discuss alternatives in Chapter 10, we will treat it as being required. Each computer system has one or more special characters for indicating the end of the file. When a record that contains such a character is read, the AT END condition is true and the imperative-statement is executed.

In the 1985 standard the format has been expanded as follows:

READ file-name RECORD [INTO identifier]

[AT END imperative-statement-1]

[NOT AT END imperative-statement-2]

[END READ]

As indicated above, in COBOL '85 the NOT AT END and the END-READ enhancements provide for an IF . . . ELSE . . . type of program structure, as

FIGURE 4-2
Examples of READ Statements

COBOL '74	COBOL '85
| ```
MOVE 'NO' TO END-OF-FILE
READ EMPLOYEE-FILE RECORD
    AT END MOVE 'YES' TO END-OF-FILE.
IF END-OF-FILE = 'YES'
    PERFORM PRINT-SUMMARY
ELSE
    PERFORM PRINT-DETAIL.
PERFORM XYZ.
``` | ```
READ EMPLOYEE-FILE RECORD
    AT END
        PERFORM PRINT-SUMMARY
    NOT AT END
        PERFORM PRINT-DETAIL
END-READ
PERFORM XYZ.
``` |

illustrated in the two contrasting examples in Figure 4-2. In this figure notice that there is no need to use a field such as END-OF-FILE in the revised version since the AT END and NOT AT END allow for the dual alternatives to be expressed in the one READ statement.

The END-READ marks the termination of the READ statement. It could be omitted in the revised language provided that a period is placed after PERFORM PRINT-DETAIL. Such a period terminates the AT END conditional, and there is no ambiguity that PERFORM XYZ is to be executed regardless of whether AT END is true or false.

The WRITE Verb

The WRITE statement, as used with the printer, has the following format:

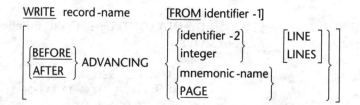

The FROM option is the counterpart of the INTO option for the READ verb. For example, we could write

```
MOVE HEADER TO OUTPUT-RECORD
WRITE OUTPUT-RECORD . . .
```

or we could use the FROM:

```
WRITE OUTPUT-RECORD FROM HEADER . . .
```

The ADVANCING clause is used only with files assigned to a printer, and it is used to control the vertical spacing on the printer. We can write WRITE . . . AFTER ADVANCING 2 LINES to achieve double spacing, for instance. We also can have variable spacing, as the sample in the following paragraph illustrates.

Suppose that a sales invoice form has space for 10 items on each invoice, and we always wish to print the total billing on the last line of the invoice. We can use a storage field (NO-OF-ITEMS) as a counter to keep track of the number of items on each invoice. If an invoice contains four items, the value stored in NO-OF-ITEMS will be 4; if an invoice contains six items, the value will be 6, and so on.

To print the total billing on the last line of the invoice, the number of lines to be skipped (let's call it LINE-COUNT) will always be 10 spaces minus NO-OF-ITEMS. For this example we are assuming that there will never be more than 10 items; therefore the following statements provide the basis for skipping the appropriate number of lines:

```
SUBTRACT NO-OF-ITEMS FROM 10 GIVING LINE-COUNT
WRITE REP-LINE AFTER ADVANCING LINE-COUNT LINES.
```

Use of the AFTER ADVANCING in the above example indicates the "skipping" of as many printer lines as the value of LINE-COUNT.

When a mnemonic-name is used, (see the presence of "mnemonic-name" in the general format for the WRITE verb, at the beginning of this subsection), it is specified in a special paragraph, the SPECIAL-NAMES paragraph of the ENVIRONMENT DIVISION. Such mnemonic-names are specified differently for each operating system. As an example, consider a system where C12 is defined to mean channel 12 on the printer carriage control tape, where channel 12 defines the bottom of a printer page. We could have the following:

```
ENVIRONMENT DIVISION.
    CONFIGURATION SECTION.
    SOURCE-COMPUTER.
    OBJECT-COMPUTER.
    SPECIAL-NAMES.
        C12 IS BOTTOM-OF-PAGE.
INPUT-OUTPUT SECTION.
(etc.)
```

In the PROCEDURE DIVISION the statement

```
WRITE PRINT-RECORD AFTER ADVANCING BOTTOM-OF-PAGE
```

is understood to mean to skip to the bottom of the page. The SPECIAL-NAMES paragraph in the CONFIGURATION SECTION is used to designate such special names as printer spacing codes and "alphabet" designations, as will be discussed in Chapter 16.

R E V I E W . . . .

1. Prior to inputting data from a file, a(n) _____ statement must be executed.

   OPEN INPUT

2. Prior to writing data onto a file, a(n) _____ statement must be executed.

   OPEN OUTPUT

3. Before a program terminates execution with STOP RUN, a _____ statement must be executed for every file that was opened.

   CLOSE

4. Data are entered into central storage by use of the _____ verb.

   READ

5. The option that results in the same data being available in two different places after a READ statement has been executed (often in one input record and one output record) is the _____ option.

INTO

6. Similar to the AT END option available with the READ statement, COBOL '85 also makes available the _____ option.

NOT AT END

7. The verb that is used to output data from central storage onto an external file is the _____ verb.

WRITE

8. In conjunction with a WRITE statement, data are moved from an identifier to the output record being written by use of the _____ option.

FROM

9. Variable vertical spacing of output on the printer can be accomplished by using the _____ clause in conjunction with a WRITE statement.

ADVANCING

• •

THE MOVE STATEMENT

The word "MOVE" in COBOL is, in fact, a misnomer because the function performed is duplicating, not moving. When we write MOVE A to B, the contents of A are duplicated in B, with the contents of A remaining unchanged.

The format for the MOVE instruction is

$$\text{MOVE} \begin{Bmatrix} \text{identifier -1} \\ \text{literal -1} \end{Bmatrix} \underline{\text{TO}} \text{ identifier-2 [, identifier-3] . . .}$$

In any use of the MOVE instruction caution should be exercised so that the receiving field is not smaller than the sending field. If the receiving field is too small, truncation will result in the loss of part of the value or information being transferred. The rules for moving data are many and relate to the form of data moved. One important point to remember is the following: numeric data are aligned according to the decimal point. If the receiving field is larger than the sending, the extra positions are filled with zeros. If the receiving field is smaller, then truncation takes place as needed, to the right, left, or both right and left of the decimal point. In the following illustrations the caret (∧) implies a decimal point:

SENDING FIELD	RESULT IN RECEIVING FIELD
0 1 3 5 2	0 0 1 3 5 2 0
2 5 2 3 5	2 5 2 3 5
2 5 2 3 5	5 2 3 5
2 5 2 3 5	5 2 3

A second important point is that alphabetic or alphanumeric data are left-justified in the receiving field (unless the programmer uses the JUSTIFIED RIGHT clause described in Chapter 16). If the receiving field is larger than the sending field, the additional positions are filled with blanks. If the receiving field is smaller, then truncation takes place from the right. The following examples illustrate some typical cases:

SENDING FIELD   RECEIVING FIELD

| B | O | N | A | N | Z | A | | B | O | N | A | N | Z | A | | |

| B | O | N | A | N | Z | A | | B | O | N | A | N | Z | A |

| B | O | N | A | N | Z | A | | B | O | N | A | N |

Table 4-1 indicates the types of data transfer that are and are not permitted in COBOL. You may want to review Table 3-2 in the preceding chapter, which defines the various categories of data to which reference is made in Table 4-1. Most compilers incorporate the rules presented in this table, so the programmer will be warned of illegal MOVE statements. Still, it is not difficult to internalize most of these rules.

Refer to the last line of Table 4-1. In the 1985 standard it is permissible to move a numeric edited field to a numeric unedited field. This new option allows for *de-editing* of data, something not permitted in the 1974 version. As examples, consider these statements:

```
02  COMP-AMOUNT          PIC 9(5)V99.
02  EDIT-AMOUNT          PIC $$,$$9.99.
    .
    .
    .
MOVE 1234.56 TO EDIT-AMOUNT
MOVE EDIT-AMOUNT TO COMP-AMOUNT.
```

When these statements have been executed, EDIT-AMOUNT would contain $1,234.56 while COMP-AMOUNT would correctly contain 01234$_\wedge$56. The last

TABLE 4-1

Legal and Illegal MOVE Commands

CATEGORY OF SENDING DATA; DATA ITEM	CATEGORY OF RECEIVING DATA ITEM		
	ALPHABETIC	ALPHANUMERIC; ALPHANUMERIC EDITED	NUMERIC INTEGER; NUMERIC NONINTEGER; NUMERIC EDITED
Alphabetic	Yes	Yes	No
Alphanumeric	Yes	Yes	No
Alphanumeric edited	Yes	Yes	No
Numeric integer	No	Yes	Yes
Numeric noninteger	No	No	Yes
Numeric edited	No	Yes	No (Yes in revised language)

statement, MOVE EDIT-AMOUNT to COMP-AMOUNT, strips the data of such editing characters as the dollar sign, the comma, and the decimal point, and moves the numeric data to the numeric unedited field. Such a move is not valid in the 1974 version of COBOL.

It is often assumed that the DATA DIVISION description of a field as being numeric somehow guards against the moving of nonnumeric data into that field. We present the following example to dispel such a notion:

```
01  SAMPLE-FIELD.
    02  A   PIC XX.
    02  B   PIC 99V99.
    .
    .
    .
    MOVE 'ROBERT' TO SAMPLE-FIELD.
```

After the MOVE is executed, B contains the letters "BERT"! How can that be? It is very simple. SAMPLE-FIELD is a group-item that is six bytes long; two of these constitute A and four make up B. Therefore when we move 'ROBERT' into SAMPLE-FIELD, the last four bytes of the field contain the last four characters in the literal.

The above example constitutes a valid action in COBOL and shows the flexibility that the language provides. On the other hand, it would not be correct to do arithmetic involving the B field after the above MOVE. For example,

```
MOVE 'ROBERT' TO SAMPLE-FIELD
ADD 1 TO B
```

would be an incorrect program as far as logic is concerned. However, from the standpoint of COBOL the ADD is a valid statement, because it is phrased independently of the content of B. Fortunately, many compilers add program code to check whether a numeric field does indeed contain numeric data before doing arithmetic with that field. You may wish to test the above illustration on the available compiler to see what happens.

To guard against such possible errors, COBOL provides for class condition tests, discussed in Chapter 8. The following illustrates such a class condition test:

```
IF  B  IS  NUMERIC
    ADD 1 TO B
ELSE
    PERFORM ERROR-ROUTINE.
```

R E V I E W . . . .

1. When data are transferred by use of the MOVE instruction, one might say more correctly that the data have been _____ rather than moved.

   duplicated

2. When numeric data are moved from a sending field to a receiving field, alignment takes place with respect to the _____ .

   decimal point

3. When nonnumeric data are moved from a sending field to a receiving field, alignment takes place at the [left / right] margin.

   left

4. Movement of numeric data into a numeric edited field is valid [in both COBOL '74 and '85 / only in COBOL '85].

in both COBOL '74 and '85

5. De-editing involves movement of numeric edited data into a numeric field and is valid [in both COBOL '74 and '85 / only in COBOL '85].

only in COBOL '85

6. Nonnumeric data can be moved inadvertently into a numeric field when the field is part of a _____-item that is alphanumeric, for example.

group

· · · · · · · · · · · · · · · · · · · ·

THE PERFORM VERB

The PERFORM verb is generally used to specify the sequence of execution of a modular program, represented by paragraphs or sections, or to specify the repeated execution of such modules to achieve program looping. We already have seen the use of the PERFORM verb in the program examples in the preceding chapters. In this section we review and expand our description of the uses of this verb by presenting basic formats associated with the PERFORM verb. This is a highly flexible verb, and additional formats for its use will be presented in later chapters.

The simplest format of the PERFORM is

PERFORM procedure-name

The procedure-name referenced in this format is either a paragraph-name or a section-name (sections are discussed in Chapter 11). Simply stated, the PERFORM directs program execution to the named procedure, at which point the procedure is executed and program execution returns to the next statement following the PERFORM. In this respect it follows that the named procedure must allow the program to return; that is, the procedure must not contain a GO TO (see Chapter 7) or a STOP RUN statement. However, the paragraph that is performed may itself contain another PERFORM instruction.

The PERFORM . . . UNTIL

Another format of PERFORM is shown here:

COBOL '74	COBOL '85
PERFORM procedure-name	PERFORM procedure-name
UNTIL condition	$\left[\text{WITH} \ \underline{\text{TEST}} \ \begin{Bmatrix} \underline{\text{BEFORE}} \\ \text{AFTER} \end{Bmatrix} \underline{\text{UNTIL}} \ \text{condition} \right]$
	[END-PERFORM]

The simplest form of the 1985 version omits the WITH TEST clause and the END-PERFORM terminator, and thereby is the same as the 1974 version. An example is

```
PERFORM PROCESS-DETAIL
     UNTIL END-OF-FILE = 'YES'.
```

In this program segment the UNTIL condition is tested before the procedure is executed. The END-OF-FILE first is tested for 'YES'. If END-OF-FILE is equal

FIGURE 4-3

PERFORM . . . UNTIL with Use of TEST Option

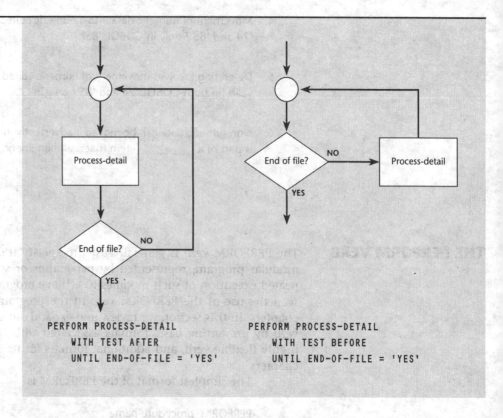

```
PERFORM PROCESS-DETAIL          PERFORM PROCESS-DETAIL
  WITH TEST AFTER                 WITH TEST BEFORE
  UNTIL END-OF-FILE = 'YES'       UNTIL END-OF-FILE = 'YES'
```

to YES, the program continues with the next statement. If it is not equal to YES, then PROCESS-DETAIL is executed, and the process is repeated until END-OF-FILE = 'YES'.

COBOL '85 allows for greater control over the repeated execution of a procedure. If we want to do a procedure and then determine if it should be done again, we use the WITH TEST AFTER option. If we want to determine if a procedure should be done beforehand, then we can either use the TEST BEFORE option or leave the TEST option out altogether. Figure 4-3 presents a flowchart and an example of each of the two TEST options in the PERFORM . . . UNTIL statement.

The In-Line PERFORM in COBOL '85

In the 1985 standard it is also possible to use an *in-line* PERFORM, which does not make reference to a procedure-name. As an example, consider the case in accounting in which we need to form the "sum of the digits" for depreciating an asset over N years, where N has an integer value. We need to form the sum of $1 + 2 + 3 + \ldots + (N - 1) + N$. Thus if N is 5, we have $1 + 2 + 3 + 4 + 5$. Here is a routine for doing this task:

```
MOVE ZERO TO SUM-OF-DIGITS
MOVE 1 TO YEAR-COUNTER
PERFORM UNTIL YEAR-COUNTER > N
    ADD YEAR-COUNTER TO SUM-OF-DIGITS
    ADD 1 TO YEAR-COUNTER
END-PERFORM.
```

Notice the absence of a procedure-name between the words PERFORM and UNTIL. This signifies that the command(s) to be performed follows the basic PERFORM UNTIL statement and is marked by the END-PERFORM terminator.

Thus the two ADD statements constitute the procedure to be executed in the example above. This format of the PERFORM allows for an immediately following "nameless" procedure, in essence. Contrast the above example with the following equivalent one:

```
MOVE ZERO TO SUM-OF-DIGITS
MOVE 1 TO YEAR-COUNTER
PERFORM FORM-SUM UNTIL YEAR-COUNTER > N
        .
        .
        .

FORM-SUM.
  ADD YEAR-COUNTER TO SUM-OF-DIGITS
  ADD 1 TO YEAR-COUNTER.
```

We can see that the in-line PERFORM is more convenient when, as in this example, the procedure is so simple that it does not warrant setting up a separate paragraph.

R E V I E W . . . .

1. The COBOL verb used to execute a paragraph and return to the instruction immediately following that command is the _____ verb.

   PERFORM

2. The format of the PERFORM statement that permits conditional execution of the procedure-name depending on the result of a test is the PERFORM . . . _____ .

   UNTIL

3. In COBOL '74 when the PERFORM . . . UNTIL format is used, the condition is tested [before / after / either before or after] the object of PERFORM is executed.

   before

4. In COBOL '85 when the PERFORM . . . UNTIL format is used, the condition is tested [before / after / either before or after] the object of PERFORM is executed.

   either before or after

5. The version of the PERFORM command that does not make reference to a procedure-name, but rather has the commands to be executed immediately follow the PERFORM UNTIL conditional statement, is the _____ PERFORM.

   in-line

. . . .

ARITHMETIC VERBS

COBOL has five arithmetic verbs: ADD, SUBTRACT, MULTIPLY, DIVIDE, and COMPUTE. The first four verbs are used to execute the arithmetic operations corresponding to their respective names. COMPUTE is a general-purpose verb and can be used in lieu of any of the other four, as well as to write more complex operations that combine several arithmetic steps. A rich variety of statement formats will be studied in detail in Chapter 7, "Additional PROCEDURE DIVISION Statements." In this section we present an overview of arithmetic statements and limit our scope to the very basic options.

We begin with the ADD verb and show three formats:

1.   <u>ADD</u> literal <u>TO</u> identifier
2 .   <u>ADD</u> identifier <u>TO</u> identifier
3 .   <u>ADD</u> two or more literals or identifiers <u>GIVING</u> identifier

The following examples illustrate each of the three formats:

1.   `ADD 123 TO TOTAL`
2.   `ADD STATE-TAX TO TOTAL-TAX`
3a. `ADD 123 AMOUNT GIVING TOTAL`
3b. `ADD STATE-TAX FED-TAX GIVING TOTAL-TAX`
3c. `ADD 0.05 RATE-1 RATE-2 GIVING RATE`

The result of the additions must always be an identifier. Thus in the first example it would be wrong to attempt to write ADD TOTAL TO 123. The identifier following the TO is incremented. If TOTAL contained a value of 100 before the first ADD, then as a result of the ADD, TOTAL would contain 223.

The GIVING option differs from the TO option because the identifier following the GIVING is not incremented. Instead, its former content is replaced by the result of the addition. Considering example 3a above, if TOTAL contained the value 1000 before the ADD and AMOUNT contained 456, TOTAL will contain 579 after the addition. That is, TOTAL would contain 579 after the addition regardless of what it contained before. Thus the GIVING implies a *replace* operation. In essence, it says, "do the addition and then store the result in the identifier that follows the GIVING."

Having discussed the ADD verb in some detail, we now present simplified formats for the other three verbs by means of examples. Detailed coverage of arithmetic verbs will be found in Chapter 7.

Figure 4-4 presents a number of examples. In each example it should be obvious that the generalized format involves arithmetic literals or identifiers in all cases except where the result field is involved. The result must be an identifier, not a numeric literal. For instance, in the case of the SUBTRACT consider these two examples:

```
SUBTRACT TAX 100 FROM GROSS-PAY
SUBTRACT TAX 100 FROM 1000 GIVING NET-PAY
```

In the first case GROSS-PAY is reduced by the sum of TAX and 100, so the item following FROM must be an identifier. In the second case, because of the presence of GIVING, it is permissible to write FROM 1000 because it is NET-PAY that receives the result. As in the case of the GIVING in the ADD statement, the value of the identifier following the GIVING is replaced, not just "changed."

Referring now to Figure 4-4, note that we have labeled a number of columns with simplified data-names, their respective PICTURE definition, and their initial contents. Thus it is possible to follow the change in the contents of the data fields involved in the illustrated arithmetic statements in detail.

The negative sign is shown as a horizontal bar above the last digit in each signed negative field. For example, the initial value of W is negative 10. Also, the assumed decimal point (V PIC character), is shown as a caret (∧) in each case.

Note a few special cases:

• Example 5 illustrates that a negative result is stored as an absolute value (without sign) if the numeric field does not include the S PICTURE character.

FIGURE 4-4

Examples of the Use of Arithmetic Verbs

		W	X	Y	Z
	PICTURE:	S999V99	999V99	999V99	999
	INITIAL VALUE:	010͜0̄0̄	090͜00	030͜00	040
1. ADD X TO Y				120͜00	
2. ADD X Y TO Z					160
3. ADD 5 Y GIVING W		035͜00			
4. SUBTRACT Y FROM X			060͜00		
5. SUBTRACT X FROM Y				060͜00	
6. SUBTRACT X Y FROM W		130͜0̄0̄			
7. SUBTRACT W FROM X GIVING Y				100͜00	
8. MOVE 10 TO X			010͜00		
MULTIPLY X BY Y				300͜00	
9. MULTIPLY X BY Y				700͜00	
10. DIVIDE Y INTO X			003͜00		
11. DIVIDE X INTO Y				000͜33	
12. DIVIDE Z INTO 100 GIVING Y				002͜50	
13. DIVIDE 12.2 INTO Y GIVING Z					002

- Example 6 illustrates the application of the rule of arithmetic that subtracting from a negative value is equivalent to adding the number to be subtracted to that negative value.

- Example 9 illustrates that truncation will occur if the number is larger than the defined field.

R E V I E W . . . .

1. Complete the following table by entering the numeric result of each arithmetic operation:

		W	X	Y	Z
	PICTURE:	99V9	99	99V9	S999V9
	INITIAL VALUE:	15͜0	10	12͜8	100͜0
1. ADD W, Y TO X					
2. ADD W, Y GIVING X					
3. SUBTRACT W FROM Y					
4. SUBTRACT W FROM Y GIVING Z					
5. MULTIPLY W BY Y					
6. MULTIPLY X BY Y GIVING Z					
7. DIVIDE X INTO Y					
8. DIVIDE X INTO Y GIVING Z					

1. X = 37   5. Y = 92ₐ0
2. X = 27   6. Z = 128ₐ0
3. Y = 02ₐ2   7. Y = 1ₐ2
4. Z = 002ₐ2̄   8. Z = 1ₐ28

. . . .

CONDITIONAL STATEMENTS

Conditional statements allow the program to test for a condition and to execute one or more commands selectively, depending on the result. Chapter 5 is dedicated to this subject. Therefore here we provide only a brief introduction to conditional statements.

In the following program segment we determine the appropriate price as follows:

```
IF CUSTOMER-UNITS > 20
    MOVE DISCOUNT-PRICE TO PRICE
ELSE
    MOVE FULL-PRICE TO PRICE.
```

The conditional statement begins with the IF followed by a *conditional expression*. In the example above, the conditional expression is CUSTOMER-UNITS > 20. A conditional expression is either true or false. If it is true, the command that follows the IF statement is executed (MOVE DISCOUNT-PRICE TO PRICE); if it is false, the command that follows the ELSE is executed (MOVE FULL-PRICE TO PRICE).

Although the conditional IF statement often includes the ELSE option, it is not necessary to include the option in the command. In the absence of the ELSE option, when the condition tested by the IF statement is true, the command that follows the IF is executed. When it is false, that command is not executed and program execution continues with the next sentence in the program. For example:

```
MOVE FULL-PRICE TO PRICE.
IF  CUSTOMER-UNITS > 20
    MOVE DISCOUNT-PRICE TO PRICE.
MULTIPLY CUSTOMER-UNITS BY PRICE . . .
```

We conclude this introductory presentation by considering the AT END conditional statement, as in

```
READ CUSTOMER-FILE RECORD
    AT END MOVE 'YES' TO END-OF-FILE.
```

The AT END is a specialized conditional expression that really means "IF END" and refers to the condition of reading the end-of-file record. The specialized AT END conditional statement is used only with the READ verb and specifies what is to be done when our end-of-file type of record is read. In the sample program we MOVE 'YES' TO END-OF-FILE. Just as in any other conditional statement, the period is important, although in this particular example it happens that the AT END statement is also the last statement in the paragraph.

R E V I E W . . . .

1. Whereas the AT END clause is an example of a specialized conditional expression, more general conditional expressions make use of the _____ verb.

2. If the condition specified in the IF clause is met, then program execution continues with [the statement that directly follows the IF / the next sentence / the next paragraph].

> the statement that directly follows the IF

3. If the condition specified in the IF clause is not met, then program execution continues with [the statement that directly follows the IF / the next sentence / the next paragraph].

> the next sentence

4. The option used in conjunction with the IF clause that makes it possible to execute one of two alternative statements is the _____ option.

> ELSE

. . . .

SAMPLE PROCEDURE DIVISION

The sample program task involves reading records from an employee file and producing a report such as the one illustrated in Figure 4-5. This is the same report for which the DATA DIVISION was prepared in the preceding chapter, and presented in Figure 3-8. Each record in the employee file contains the individual's name (columns 1–15), a code classifying the person as a man or woman (column 16), and the annual salary (columns 17–23), as previously presented in the record layout in Figure 3-3. Should there be an error and a record does not include a valid sex code, then asterisks are printed in the report to highlight the error. The occurrence of such an error is illustrated in Figure 4-5 for the case of the employee named PROUST, K., where a group of asterisks appears in the report line.

A structure chart for the program is presented in Figure 4-6, and a more detailed view of the program logic is presented in the pseudocode in Figure 4-7. As usual, the structure chart portrays the overall processing logic for the programming task, whereas the pseudocode goes into detailed program-oriented descriptions and anticipates the eventual program structure.

The PROCEDURE DIVISION is listed in Figure 4-8. Reviewing the sample output in Figure 4-5, we notice that there is need for a report heading at the beginning of the task, and a report footing, showing the total and average values,

---

FIGURE 4-5
Sample Salary Report

	ANNUAL SALARY	
EMPLOYEE NAME	MEN	WOMEN
JONES, A.	28,200.00	
ANDERSON, P.	22,000.00	
ROBERTS, M.		25,000.00
PROUST, K.	******	
NICHOLSON, J.	29,600.00	
PHILLIPS, P.		28,500.00
WORK, A.		30,000.00
TOTAL	$79,800.00	$83,500.00
AVERAGE	$26,600.00	$27,833.33

FIGURE 4-6

Structure Chart for the Sample Program

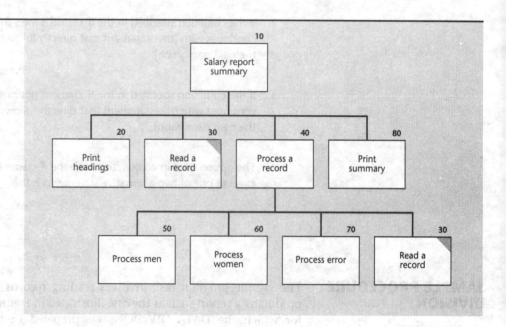

at the end of the task. Corresponding to these two needs, we see the two paragraphs, 20-PRINT-REPORT-HEADINGS and 80-PRINT-REPORT-FOOTINGS. Between these two paragraphs the program logic involves reading employee records, identifying them as pertaining to one of three categories, and processing each category in a separate paragraph. Specifically, employee records are identified as referring to a record whose EMPLOYEE-SEX-CODE meets the MALE, FEMALE, and ERROR-SEX-CODE conditions defined by the respective 88-level condition names. (You may want to refer to Figure 3-9 for a brief explanation of 88-level condition-names in the DATA DIVISION.) Each category is processed in a separate paragraph: 50-PROCESS-MEN, 60-PROCESS-FEMALE, and 70-PROCESS-ERROR-CODE. The content of each of these three paragraphs is simple enough that we could have incorporated their statements into the 40-PROCESS-EMPLOYEE-RECORD paragraph, as in this example:

```
40-PROCESS-EMPLOYEE-RECORD.
    IF  MALE
        MOVE EMPLOYEE-SALARY TO REPORT-MEN-SALARY
        MOVE ZERO TO REPORT-WOMEN-SALARY
        ADD 1 TO NO-OF-MEN
        ADD EMPLOYEE-SALARY TO MEN-TOTAL-SALARY.
    IF  FEMALE...
        etc.
```

However, each employee category represents a distinct logical function in the program and therefore it is a good idea to separate such functions into distinct modules (paragraphs). By this approach it is much easier to change the program if different processing logic is needed for different employee categories in the future. Such a provision is associated with good program design and structure, and will be discussed in Chapters 6 and 14.

The program illustrates use of one more figurative constant, ALL. In 70-PROCESS-ERROR-CODE notice the statement MOVE ALL '*' TO REPORT-ERROR-CODE. The ALL figurative constant signifies that the receiving field should be filled with the nonnumeric literal '*'. This is a convenient way of specifying the move of as many repetitions of the literal as the size of the receiving field in the MOVE statement will allow. Recall that a statement such as MOVE SPACES TO A is

FIGURE 4-7

Pseudocode for the Salary Report Program

PROGRAM-SUMMARY

    Open Files

    Perform Print-Headings

    Perform Read-Record

    Perform Process-Record until no more records

    Perform Print Summary

    Close Files

    Stop

PRINT-HEADINGS

    Write two lines on top of new page and double space after the second line

READ-RECORD

    Read a Record

    If it is the end of the file set an indicator on

PROCESS-RECORD

    If the record represents a man

        Perform Process-Man

    If the record represents a woman

        Perform Process-Woman

    If the record represents neither man nor woman

        Perform Process-Error

    Print a report line

    Perform Read-Record

PROCESS-MAN

    Add 1 to number of men

    Add the salary to the total salary for men

    Move the salary data to the men's column

PROCESS-WOMAN

    Add 1 to number of women

    Add the salary to the total salary for women

    Move the salary data to the women's column

PROCESS-ERROR

    Move asterisks to the salary fields

PRINT-SUMMARY

    Print the accumulated total salaries

    Compute the averages (e.g., divide number of men into total salary of men)

    Print the averages

FIGURE 4-8

PROCEDURE DIVISION for the
Salary Report Program

```
PROCEDURE DIVISION.
*
10-PROGRAM-SUMMARY.
     OPEN INPUT   EMPLOYEE-FILE
          OUTPUT  REPORT-FILE
*
     PERFORM 20-PRINT-REPORT-HEADINGS
*
     PERFORM 30-READ-EMPLOYEE-RECORD
*
     PERFORM 40-PROCESS-EMPLOYEE-RECORD
                UNTIL END-OF-EMPLOYEE-FILE
*
     PERFORM 80-PRINT-REPORT-FOOTINGS
*
     CLOSE EMPLOYEE-FILE
           REPORT-FILE
*
     STOP RUN.
*
20-PRINT-REPORT-HEADINGS.
     WRITE PRINT-LINE FROM HEADING-1
            AFTER ADVANCING PAGE
     WRITE PRINT-LINE FROM HEADING-2
            AFTER ADVANCING 2 LINES
     MOVE SPACES TO PRINT-LINE
     WRITE PRINT-LINE AFTER ADVANCING 2 LINES.
*
30-READ-EMPLOYEE-RECORD.
     READ EMPLOYEE-FILE RECORD
          AT END MOVE 'YES' TO END-OF-FILE-TEST.
*
40-PROCESS-EMPLOYEE-RECORD.
     IF MALE   PERFORM 50-PROCESS-MEN.
*
     IF FEMALE PERFORM 60-PROCESS-FEMALE.
*
     IF ERROR-SEX-CODE PERFORM 70-PROCESS-ERROR-CODE.
*
     MOVE EMPLOYEE-NAME TO REPORT-EMPL-NAME
     WRITE PRINT-LINE FROM REPORT-DETAIL-LINE
            AFTER ADVANCING 1 LINE
*
     MOVE SPACES TO REPORT-DETAIL-LINE
*
     PERFORM 30-READ-EMPLOYEE-RECORD.
*
50-PROCESS-MEN.
     MOVE EMPLOYEE-SALARY TO REPORT-MEN-SALARY
     MOVE ZERO TO REPORT-WOMEN-SALARY
*
```

FIGURE 4-8
PROCEDURE DIVISION for the
Salary Report Program (continued)

```
           ADD 1 TO NO-OF-MEN
           ADD EMPLOYEE-SALARY TO MEN-TOTAL-SALARY.
      .*
       60-PROCESS-FEMALE.
           MOVE EMPLOYEE-SALARY TO REPORT-WOMEN-SALARY
           MOVE ZERO TO REPORT-MEN-SALARY
       *
           ADD 1 TO NO-OF-WOMEN
           ADD EMPLOYEE-SALARY TO WOMEN-TOTAL-SALARY.
       *
       70-PROCESS-ERROR-CODE.
           MOVE ALL '*' TO REPORT-ERROR-CODE.
       *
       80-PRINT-REPORT-FOOTINGS.
           MOVE MEN-TOTAL-SALARY TO REPORT-TOT-MEN-SALARY
           MOVE WOMEN-TOTAL-SALARY TO REPORT-TOT-WOMEN-SALARY

           WRITE PRINT-LINE FROM REPORT-TOTALS-LINE
               AFTER ADVANCING 3 LINES
         *
           DIVIDE NO-OF-MEN INTO MEN-TOTAL-SALARY
               GIVING REPORT-AVG-MEN-SALARY
           DIVIDE NO-OF-WOMEN INTO WOMEN-TOTAL-SALARY
               GIVING REPORT-AVG-WOMEN-SALARY
         *
           WRITE PRINT-LINE FROM REPORT-AVERAGES-LINE
               AFTER ADVANCING 2 LINES.
```

a specialized version of this case, and is equivalent to saying MOVE ALL ' ' TO A, where there is a blank space between the quotes. Thus the ALL can do with any literal what we can do with other figurative constants (such as ZERO and SPACE).

We complete our description of the sample program by presenting a detailed flowchart in Figure 4-9. Normally, a structure chart and a pseudocode are sufficient tools for developing the program. In this case we also show a flowchart as a more detailed aid for the beginning COBOL programmer. Learning to read flowcharts is a useful skill because detailed flowcharts were a strong tradition in the past, and many "old" programs are documented by accompanying flowcharts rather than by structure charts or pseudocode.

SUMMARY

In this chapter we first presented and discussed the set of conventions by which COBOL programming options are presented. This involved such matters as the use of uppercase words, lowercase words, underlining, braces, brackets, and the ellipsis. We then reviewed the functions of the IDENTIFICATION DIVISION, ENVIRONMENT DIVISION, and DATA DIVISION in a COBOL program.

The function of the IDENTIFICATION DIVISION is to supply information about the program. The first and only required paragraph is the PROGRAM-ID, which includes the program-name.

FIGURE 4-9

Complete Flowchart for the Salary Report Program (The numbers in the upper right-hand corner of
some entries serve as cross-references between modules and their respective blocks.)

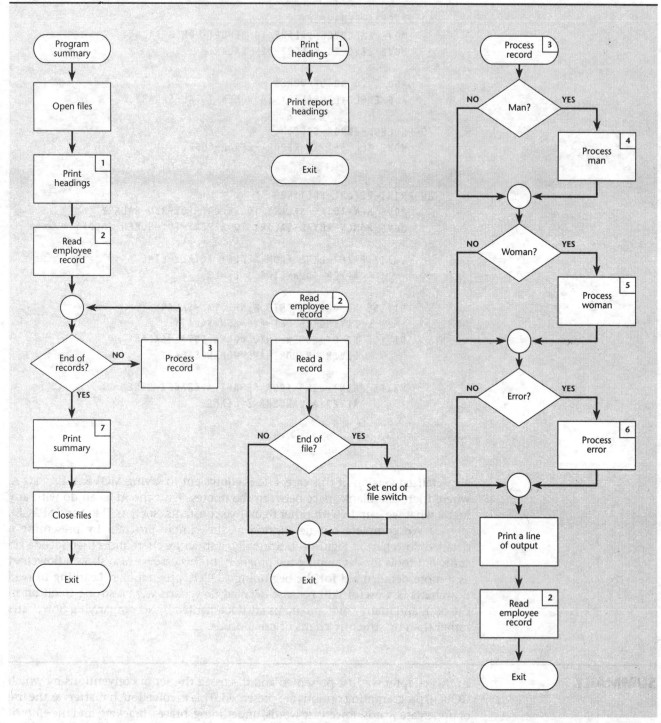

(continued on next page)

The function of the ENVIRONMENT DIVISION is to describe the computer
system on which the program has been compiled and executed. Although this
division is optional in COBOL '85, the information that is supplied is very
important and necessary for most programs. Two sections were included in the

FIGURE 4-9

Complete Flowchart for the Salary
Report Program (continued)

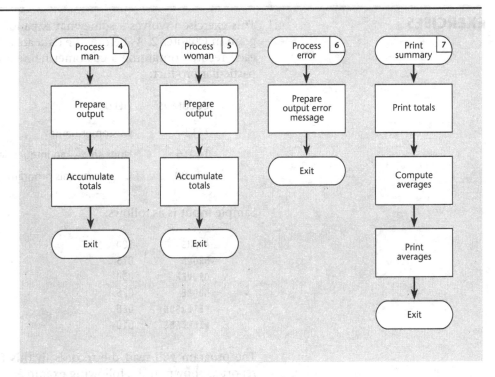

brief chapter example of an ENVIRONMENT DIVISION: the CONFIGURATION
SECTION and the INPUT-OUTPUT SECTION. The CONFIGURATION SECTION
contains the SOURCE-COMPUTER and OBJECT-COMPUTER paragraphs. The
INPUT-OUTPUT SECTION includes the FILE-CONTROL paragraph.

The DATA DIVISION was covered in some detail in the preceding chapter,
in addition to being reviewed in this chapter. It serves to define files and their
records, and working-storage fields. The FD designation is required at the beginning of each file description. Each file description then includes the name of the
file and the name of the record in the file. The level-number assigned to each
record as a whole is 01, with other numbers then assigned to the fields in the
record according to the data structure.

Following the reviews of the first three divisions of any COBOL program,
the chapter focused on the study of the PROCEDURE DIVISION, and specifically,
on the use of various verbs. In the category of file input and output, we studied the
OPEN and CLOSE verbs, the READ verb, and the WRITE verb. Uses of the MOVE
statement were then described, followed by study of the PERFORM and the
associated PERFORM . . . UNTIL option.

The use of arithmetic verbs in COBOL then was described briefly. Examples of using the ADD, SUBTRACT, MULTIPLY, and DIVIDE verbs in arithmetic
operations were studied.

Next, we included a section on the use of conditional statements in the
PROCEDURE DIVISION. The key verb is the IF, followed by a conditional expression. The ELSE option is often included, but it is not required. In the absence of
the ELSE option, if the conditional expression is false, then program execution
continues with the next sentence in the program. The next chapter is devoted to
further study of conditions and conditional statements.

The final section of this chapter presented and discussed the PROCEDURE
DIVISION for the employee salary-report programming task for which the DATA
DIVISION was written in the preceding chapter. Taken together, we have a
complete programming example for the task.

EXERCISES

4.1 This exercise involves a somewhat expanded version of the sample program in Chapter 2. As before, the data are a file of customer records, with each record containing a customer name and number of units sold of a particular product:

COLUMNS	FIELD
1–13	Customer name
14–16	Units sold—an integer field
17–80	Unused by this program

Sample input is as follows:

```
ADAMS         100
BROWN         075
GROVER        030
MOORE         025
PETERSON      060
WILLIAMS      010
```

The program will read the records in this file and produce as output a report as shown in the following example:

```
CUSTOMER NAME     UNITS SOLD     NET SALES

ADAMS                100          950.00
BROWN                 75          712.50
GROVER                30          285.00
MOORE                 25          237.50
PETERSON              60          570.00
WILLIAMS              10          100.00

TOTAL                300         2855.00
```

The NET SALES column in the output results from the following computational basis: If the number of units sold is 20 or fewer, the unit price is $10.00. If the number of units sold is greater than 20, the unit price is discounted to $9.50. The net sales value then is computed by multiplying the number of units sold by the appropriate unit price.

a. Construct a structure chart for the programming task.

b. Write pseudocode.

c. Write, compile, and execute a complete program.

4.2 A file contains data on the number of vehicles passing a certain point on the highway. Each record contains a whole number in columns 1–4 that corresponds to one day's traffic. We are interested in reading the data file and producing a report such as that shown below. For each week we list the daily data and a statistical summary for the week. The last week of data may be a partial week—that is, fewer than seven days. The output format is illustrated by the following, with the report for each week being printed on a new page:

```
               DAILY TRAFFIC REPORT
                  WEEK 03
                  2,345
                  1,000
                    500
                  2,000
                  1,400
                  1,331
                    809
               MINIMUM =   500  MAXIMUM = 2,345 WEEKLY TOTAL =  9,385
```

Note that the program should be able to compute the minimum and maximum value for each week.

4.3   Write a COBOL program to read a file of records containing data about accounts-receivable and to print a summary of the overdue and forthcoming receivables. An extended description follows, including variable names and a partial DATA DIVISION.

The input consists of a set of records having the following content:

COLUMNS	COBOL NAME
1–6	ACCOUNT-NO
7–8	FILLER (blank)
9–11	DAY-DUE
12–13	YEAR-DUE
14–21	AMOUNT-DUE
22–80	FILLER

The records are sorted in ascending sequence on ACCOUNT-NO, and there should be only one record per account. The program checks for correct sequencing. Records out of sequence are to be printed as shown on the sample output below. Note that the data on such records are excluded from the total.

DATA DIVISION entries are provided below, except that you are asked to write WORKING-STORAGE entries to provide the header with the words STATUS, NUMBER OF ACCOUNTS, and DOLLAR VALUE, as shown in the sample output at the end of the description of this assignment.

```
               DATA DIVISION.
               FILE SECTION.
               FD  REC-FILE LABEL RECORDS OMITTED
                          DATA RECORD RECEIV-RECORD.
               01  RECEIV-RECORD.
                   02   ACCOUNT-NO         PIC X(6).
                   02   FILLER             PIC XX.
                   02   DAY-DUE            PIC 999.
                   02   YEAR-DUE           PIC 99.
                   02   AMOUNT-DUE         PIC 9(6)V99.
                   02   FILLER             PIC X(59).
               FD  REPORT-FILE LABEL RECORD OMITTED
                          DATA RECORD REPORT-RECORD.
               01  REPORT-RECORD            PIC X(132).
```

```
        WORKING-STORAGE SECTION.
        01  END-OF-DATA-FLAG              PIC X VALUE 'NO'.
            88  END-OF-DATA                     VALUE 'YES'.
        01  TODAYS-DATE.
            02  THIS-YEAR                  PIC 99.
            02  TODAY                      PIC 999.
    *
        01  PREVIOUS-ACCT-NO              PIC X(6).
        01  NO-OVERDUE                    PIC 9(4).
        01  TOTAL-OVERDUE                 PIC 9(7)V99.
        01  NO-RECEIVABLE                 PIC 9(4).
        01  TOTAL-RECEIVABLE              PIC 9(7)V99.
        01  ERROR-MESSAGE.
            02  FILLER                     PIC X(23)
                VALUE 'ACCOUNT OUT OF SEQUENCE'.
            02  FILLER                     PIC X(3) VALUE SPACES.
            02  ERROR-NUMBER               PIC X(6).
        01  REPORT-LINE.
            02  STATUS-TYPE                PIC X(13).
            02  FILLER                     PIC X(10) VALUE SPACES.
            02  HOW-MANY                   PIC Z(3)99.
            02  FILLER                     PIC X(15) VALUE SPACES.
            02  DOLLAR-VALUE               PIC $$$,$$$,$$9.99.
```

The day on which the account is due is expressed as a 3-digit number (Julian calendar). Thus January 10 is 010 and February 28 is 059.

Use the ACCEPT verb (to be discussed in Chapter 7) to access today's date by writing the following at the beginning of the PROCEDURE DIVISION:

```
ACCEPT TODAYS-DATE FROM DAY
```

The statement above will fill the field TODAYS-DATE with the last two digits of the year in THIS-YEAR and the 3-digit day value in TODAY. Notice that in the WORKING-STORAGE SECTION we have defined the following fields:

```
01  TODAYS-DATE.
    02  THIS-YEAR    PIC 99.
    02  TODAY        PIC 999.
```

Thus if you ran your program on February 18, 1992, as a result of the above ACCEPT statement, THIS-YEAR would contain 92, and TODAY would contain 049.

A few other data-names merit explanation:

PREVIOUS-ACCT-NO stores the previously read account number so that each record can be compared with the preceding one to see that the records are in ascending sequence. Initially, PREVIOUS-ACCT-NO is set equal to zero. NO-OVERDUE stores the number of overdue accounts, TOTAL-OVERDUE stores the total dollar value of overdue accounts, NO-RECEIVABLE stores the number of accounts that are not overdue, and TOTAL-RECEIVABLE stores the total value of accounts that are not overdue.

SAMPLE INPUT FOR DAY 101 OF 1991

```
012345  0909200010000
023467  1509100020020
001234  1409100030030
123456  1309200040040
```

SAMPLE OUTPUT

```
ACCOUNT OUT OF SEQUENCE 001234

STATUS      NUMBER OF ACCOUNTS    DOLLAR VALUE
OVERDUE           02                 $300.20
RECEIVABLE        01                 $400.40
TOTALS            03                 $700.60
```

5 Conditions and Conditional Statements

THE IF STATEMENT

RELATION CONDITIONS

CONDITION-NAME CONDITIONS

THE SET VERB FOR CONDITION-NAMES

NESTED CONDITIONS

THE END-IF SCOPE TERMINATOR

COMPOUND CONDITIONS

COMPUTER PROCESSORS *derive their logic capability from their ability to test for the truth or falsity of conditions. You can appreciate the fundamental nature of this ability by considering what computer programs would be like without conditional logic. It would be impossible to write most computer programs without the use of conditional instructions.*

The COBOL language recognizes the importance of this need and provides a rich set of conditions and conditional statements.

In general, a **condition** *is an expression that is either true or false in a particular circumstance; that is, the condition either holds or it does not hold. You have already studied some conditional statements in preceding chapters.*

In this chapter you will expand your knowledge of conditions and conditional statements. You will begin with a study of the general rules associated with use of the IF statement. Then you will study four specific types of conditional statements that involve use of the IF: (1) relation conditions; (2) condition-name conditions; (3) nested conditions; and (4) compound conditions.

THE IF STATEMENT

In general, the IF statement is used by the programmer to arrange for the conditional execution of one or more statements. A test is made to determine whether or not a condition is true. Depending on the result of that test, one or more statements may or may not be executed. The IF statement is very common, and it is used in a variety of program statements. In this section we will discuss simple IF statements, while in subsequent sections we discuss more complex IF statements. Still, use of even the simple IF comes in a variety of forms.

SIMPLE IF STATEMENT

IF condition-is-true

    executable statement(s).

An example of a simple IF statement is

```
IF  EXAM-SCORE = 100
    ADD 1 TO PERFECT-SCORES.
ADD EXAM-SCORE TO EXAM-SCORE-TOTAL
```

In the above the condition-is-true test is EXAM-SCORE = 100. This is one of several types of conditions that can be tested with the IF and will be discussed later in this chapter. Specifically, it is a relational condition. Execution of the statement ADD 1 TO PERFECT-SCORES, is conditional on the condition being true, as indicated in the following flowchart:

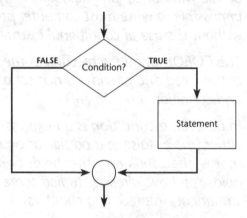

If the condition is not true (false), then the ADD 1 ... statement is not executed; it is bypassed. *The period at the end of the ADD 1 ... statement is significant.* It terminates the scope of the IF statement. Thus, because the statement ADD EXAM-SCORE ... follows the period, it is outside the scope of the IF and it will be executed unconditionally (regardless of what happened within the IF). To see the significance of the period at the end of the IF statement, consider the following example.

```
IF  HOURS-WORKED  >  40
    SUBTRACT 40 FROM HOURS-WORKED GIVING OVER-HOURS
    ADD OVER-HOURS TO TOTAL-OVER-HOURS
    PERFORM COMPUTE-OVERTIME-PAY.
PERFORM COMPUTE-PAY
```

This example illustrates that the scope of a simple IF statement may encompass several statements. Thus, if the condition HOURS-WORKED > 40 is true, three statements will be executed: SUBTRACT ..., ADD ..., and PERFORM. The period at the end of COMPUTE-OVERTIME-PAY terminates the scope of the IF statement, and as a result PERFORM COMPUTE-PAY is executed unconditionally.

A slightly more advanced version of the IF allows us to write *IF-ELSE* types of statements:

SIMPLE IF ... ELSE STATEMENT

IF condition-is-true

       executable statement(s)

ELSE

       executable statement(s).

An IF statement may be written to specify that if a condition is true, one or more statements should be executed, but if it is false, then one or more *other* statements should be executed.

The following flowchart portrays the execution of an IF ... ELSE statement:

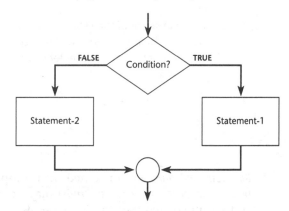

If the condition being tested is true, then we execute one set of statements; if the condition is false, we execute another set of statements. Consider the following example:

```
IF  EXAM-SCORE  =  100
    ADD 1 TO PERFECT-SCORES
ELSE
    ADD 1 TO NORMAL-SCORES.
ADD EXAM-SCORE TO EXAM-SCORE-TOTAL
```

In this example we will ADD 1 either to PERFECT-SCORES or NORMAL-SCORES. Again, the period is significant in defining the *scope* (termination) of the IF statement. Thus, the last statement, ADD EXAM-SCORE ..., will be executed regardless of the truth or falsity of the condition because it is written after the period. A common programming error is to omit the period that terminates the IF statement. In the above example omitting the period would cause the last statement to be executed only when the condition was false!

There can be one or more statements executed in either or both of the "legs" of the IF ... ELSE statement, as in this example:

```
IF  HOURS-WORKED  >  40
    SUBTRACT 40 FROM HOURS-WORKED GIVING OVER-HOURS
    ADD OVER-HOURS TO TOTAL-OVER-HOURS
    PERFORM COMPUTE-OVERTIME-PAY.
ELSE
    PERFORM COMPUTE-REGULAR-PAY.
```

The condition being tested in an IF statement may be of a variety of types. In the following section we discuss one of the most common forms, relation conditions.

R E V I E W . . . .

1. When the condition specified in the IF clause is met, then program execution continues with [the statement that directly follows the IF / the next sentence / the next paragraph].

                                                              the statement that directly follows the IF

2. The option used in conjunction with an IF clause that makes it possible to execute one of two alternative statements without having to use two separate IF conditionals is the _____ option.

                                                                                        ELSE

3. In the absence of the ELSE option, when the condition specified in the IF clause is not met, then program execution continues with [the statement that directly follows the IF / the next sentence / the next paragraph].

                                                                           the next sentence

. . . .

RELATION CONDITIONS

Relation conditions are concerned with comparisons between two items. The items being compared (the *comparands*) may be one of three things: identifier, literal, and arithmetic expression. The type of comparison is indicated by the *relational operator*, which may be in the form of words or symbols. The general format for forming relational conditions is

$$
\text{IF}
\begin{Bmatrix}
\text{identifier -1} \\
\text{literal -1} \\
\text{arithmetic -expression -1}
\end{Bmatrix}
\begin{Bmatrix}
\text{IS [\underline{NOT}] \underline{LESS} THAN} \\
\text{IS [\underline{NOT}] <} \\
\text{IS [\underline{NOT}] \underline{EQUAL} TO} \\
\text{IS [\underline{NOT}] =} \\
\text{IS [\underline{NOT}] \underline{GREATER} THAN} \\
\text{IS [\underline{NOT}] >} \\
\text{IS \underline{GREATER} THAN \underline{OR EQUAL} TO} \\
\text{IS > =} \\
\text{IS \underline{LESS} THAN \underline{OR EQUAL} TO} \\
\text{IS < =}
\end{Bmatrix}
\begin{Bmatrix}
\text{identifier -2} \\
\text{literal -2} \\
\text{arithmetic -expression -2}
\end{Bmatrix}
$$

The last four operators above (greater than or equal, and less than or equal) were added in the 1985 standard, so they cannot be used with earlier compilers.

Studying the format, we see that we can compare one identifier to another, and one arithmetic expression to another. Comparing one literal to another does not make sense since we would already know the "answer." Thus, writing IF 22 > 25, or IF 'MARY' = 'ANN' violates common sense and the rules of the language. The following examples illustrate use of the above general format:

```
IF AMOUNT IS LESS THAN 100
IF AMOUNT < 100
```

```
IF BALANCE IS NOT EQUAL TO CREDIT-LIMIT
IF BALANCE IS NOT = CREDIT-LIMIT
IF HOURS - 40 > ZERO
IF QUANTITY GREATER OR EQUAL MAX-SIZE
IF QUANTITY > = MAX-SIZE
```

As these examples illustrate, one can use either the symbolic (<, =, >) or the verbal (LESS, EQUAL, GREATER) operators; they are equivalent forms, and it is a matter of personal preference as to which is used.

The fifth example above illustrates use of an arithmetic expression (HOURS-40). Rules for forming and evaluating such arithmetic expressions will be discussed in Chapter 7, in connection with the COMPUTE arithmetic verb.

The meaning of relational tests involving numeric values is obvious. If RATE-1 and RATE-2 are numeric fields, the conditional statement IF RATE-1 > RATE-2 PERFORM PAR-A leads to PAR-A whenever the numeric (algebraic) value of RATE-1 is greater than the numeric value of RATE-2, regardless of the field size. In nonnumeric comparisons, however, certain things are not so obvious. A comparison involving two alphabetic items proceeds from left to right in pairs of characters until the first unequal pair occurs. Thus, in comparing

| T | H | O | R | P |

to

| T | H | A | L | E | S |

the first pair of characters to be compared involves two T characters, the second pair involves two H's, but then the first field is determined to be greater than the second when the O-A pair is compared. The size of the fields in this case is irrelevant. But suppose we are comparing the following two fields:

| S | A | N | D | E | R | S |

| S | A | N | D | E | R | S | O | N |

In this case the first field is considered to be smaller in value. The shorter field is treated as if it had enough trailing blanks to make it equal in size to the longer field. Then, when a blank is compared to the letter "O" in the eighth field position, the first field is determined to be smaller in value.

As a third case of alphabetic comparison, consider this:

| S | M | I | T | H |

| S | M | I | T | H | | |

These two items are considered equal, even though their field size is unequal. In this case the first field is treated as if it had enough trailing blanks to be equal in size to the second field.

Now consider the following two alphanumeric fields:

| X | A | - | 1 | 2 | 3 |

| X | . | B | - | 3 |

In this case determining the "larger" of the two fields is not as obvious. Still, these are characters and can be compared in pairs as before. For this purpose, we rely on the *collating sequence* of a computer system. The collating sequence is simply a defined sequence that states the relative "size" of each possible character in a computer's storage. For example, in the widely used IBM large mainframe computers, the EBCDIC collating sequence for some selected characters is as indicated by the following ascending order of listing:

blank
. (period or decimal point)
(
+ (plus sign)
)
– (hyphen or minus)
/ (stroke)
, (comma)
' (single quote)
" (double quote)
letters A–Z
numbers 0–9

Thus, when comparing 3-A/ and Z/9K, the 3-A/ is the greater. In any collating sequence there is a smallest and a largest character. COBOL recognizes that constant fact about collating sequences and provides two special figurative constants as a means of referencing them:

LOW-VALUE

LOW-VALUES

HIGH-VALUE

HIGH-VALUES

In the above the singular and the plural versions have identical meanings. Thus, LOW-VALUE and LOW-VALUES reference the smallest character. Consider an example:

```
02  PREVIOUS-ACCOUNT-NO  PIC  X(5).
        .
        .
        .
    MOVE LOW-VALUES TO PREVIOUS-ACCOUNT-NO.
```

The MOVE statement will fill PREVIOUS-ACCOUNT-NO with as many LOW-VALUE characters as the field size (5, due to the PIC string). It should be noted that LOW-VALUE does not refer to the blank space. Typically, the smallest character is some other character formed by a particular configuration of binary bits, as will be explained in Chapter 16. In fact, in the ASCII collating sequence, the blank space is the 32nd character; there are 31 others that are "smaller" in value than the blank space.

The HIGH-VALUE figurative constant defines the other end of the collating sequence. For example, if we write

```
    MOVE HIGH-VALUES TO PREVIOUS-ACCOUNT-NO
```

then any comparison such as

```
    IF CURRENT-ACCOUNT-NO < PREVIOUS-ACCOUNT-NO
```

will be true, unless CURRENT-ACCOUNT-NO also contains the HIGH-VALUE character.

There are several collating sequences in use, and one should be aware of the possible differences in program results arising from differences in collating sequences. The standard one is the American Standard Code for Information Interchange (ASCII). The subject of collating sequences and character representation is treated in some detail in Chapter 16.

R E V I E W . . . .

1. Relation conditions are concerned with comparisons between two items. The words or symbols that serve to indicate the type of comparison to be made are called relational _____ .

                                                                                      operators

2. As indicated above, relational operators can be in the form of either words or symbols. In the following spaces, enter the symbols that are equivalent to the listed relational operators:

    _____ LESS THAN
    _____ EQUAL TO
    _____ GREATER THAN
    _____ LESS THAN OR EQUAL TO
    _____ GREATER THAN OR EQUAL TO

                                                                   <   =   >   <=   >=

3. Of the following three relation conditions, the one that is invalid as a COBOL expression is the one identified by the letter [a / b / c].

    a. IF GROSS-PAY IS GREATER THAN 99 . . .

    b. IF 100 < ORDER-AMT . . .

    c. IF 500 > 400 . . .

                                                                                      c

4. An ordering that defines the relative rank of all the valid characters in a computer system is referred to as the _____ for the system.

                                                                           collating sequence

5. The smallest-valued character in the collating sequence is referenced by the reserved COBOL word LOW-VALUE or LOW-VALUES, which is a figurative constant. Similarly, the largest-valued character is referenced by the figurative constant _____ or _____ .

                                                                   HIGH-VALUE; HIGH-VALUES

. . . .

CONDITION-NAME CONDITIONS

As discussed in Chapter 1, figurative constants such as ZERO and SPACE are words that signify constant values. For example, the figurative constants ZERO and SPACES mean values of zero and blanks, respectively. In effect, the use of *condition-names* enables the programmer to define additional specialized figurative constants to be used in condition tests in the COBOL program. We begin by considering an example:

```
01  END-OF-FILE-FLAG  PIC  XXX.
    88  END-OF-FILE    VALUE 'YES'.
```

In this case END-OF-FILE is a condition-name. It signifies the condition of END-OF-FILE-FLAG containing the value 'YES'. The condition is true if that field contains YES; it is false otherwise. The statement IF END-OF-FILE is equivalent to the statement IF END-OF-FILE-FLAG = 'YES'. We define a condition-name representing a specified value in a data field and then we can test if the condition is true. That is, we test as to whether the data field associated with the condition-name contains the value defined by the condition-name.

The use of the condition-name option always is indicated by the special level 88 entry, whose format is

$$88 \text{ data -name } \begin{Bmatrix} \underline{\text{VALUE}} \text{ IS} \\ \underline{\text{VALUES}} \text{ ARE} \end{Bmatrix} \text{ literal -1 } [\underline{\text{THRU}} \text{ literal -2}]$$

$$[\text{literal -3 } [\underline{\text{THRU}} \text{ literal -4}]] \ldots$$

For example, we can define condition-names for testing whether an employee is male or female based on data in a record:

```
02  EMPLOYEE-SEX-CODE    PIC  X.
    88  MALE             VALUE 'M'.
    88  FEMALE           VALUE 'F'.
```

Based on this data definition, we could write

```
IF  MALE
    PERFORM  PROCESS-MALE-STATISTICS
ELSE
    PERFORM PROCESS-FEMALE-STATISTICS.
```

The above is equivalent to the following, alternate code:

```
IF  EMPLOYEE-SEX-CODE  =  'M'
    PERFORM  PROCESS-MALE-STATISTICS
ELSE
    PERFORM  PROCESS-FEMALE-STATISTICS.
```

Use of condition-names makes the program more self-documenting. It is much easier to understand the meaning of a condition-name such as "MALE" than a code such as "M". The following example provides a more extended illustration of the documentation feature as well as the general use of condition-names.

Suppose that the personnel record used in a company contains the number of years of education, among other things. The information is contained in a field called EDUCATION and is so coded that the number indicates the last school grade completed. Thus a code number less than 12 indicates that the person did not complete high school, 12 indicates a high school graduate, 13-15 indicate some college education, 16 indicates a college graduate, and a number greater than 16 indicates some graduate or postgraduate work. If we wish to process for educational level using these categories, we could write such PROCEDURE DIVISION statements as

```
IF EDUCATION IS LESS THAN 12 . . .
```

or

```
IF EDUCATION IS EQUAL TO 12 . . . etc.
```

However, an alternative is to define condition-names in the DATA DIVISION that will then stand for the indicated values. Thus we can write

```
01  PERSONNEL-DATA.
    02  ID-NUMBER . . .
    02  NAME . . .
    02  ADDRESS . . .
    02  EDUCATION PICTURE IS 99.
        88  LESS-THAN-H-S-GRAD   VALUES ARE 0 THRU 11.
        88  H-S-GRAD             VALUE IS 12.
        88  SOME-COLLEGE         VALUES ARE 13 THRU 15.
        88  COLLEGE-GRAD         VALUE IS 16.
        88  POST-GRAD            VALUES ARE 17 THRU 20.
        88  ERROR-CODE           VALUES ARE 21 THRU 99.
```

Note the use of the THRU option. It allows us to define a condition-name for a range of values. Thus SOME-COLLEGE is true if EDUCATION contains either 13 or 14 or 15. Thus one advantage of using condition-names is that they allow the programmer to write complex tests in simple form in the PROCEDURE DIVISION.

The use of condition-names improves the readability of a computer program and also makes it easier to change programs. Statements such as IF EDUCATION < 12 and IF SEX-CODE = 'M' require that we remember the arbitrary meaning of the symbolic codes. Their equivalent condition-names, however, are self-documenting when reference is made to LESS-THAN-H-S-GRAD or MALE. In terms of program changes, suppose that we decide to change a code from 1 to 2. In the absence of having used a condition-name, we would have to search the entire PROCEDURE DIVISION to make sure that every instance of the use of this code is changed. If, however, a condition-name has been used, all we have to do is to change the definition of the condition-name from VALUE IS 1 to VALUE IS 2 in the DATA DIVISION.

Next, we discuss another important factor in using condition-names that has to do with the choice of the PIC definition. Let us consider an example:

```
02  EMPLOYEE-CODE       PIC  9.
    88  MALE            VALUE  1.
    88  FEMALE          VALUE  2.
    88  ERROR-SEX-CODE  VALUES ARE ZERO, 3 THRU 9.
```

This example illustrates a potential programming error. One would reason that since EMPLOYEE-CODE is a one-digit numeric field and since MALE and FEMALE account for the 1 and 2 values, ERROR-SEX-CODE correctly covers all other possibilities. However, this is not necessarily true. The PIC 9 specification does not mean that the field must contain numeric data. As we explained in Chapter 4 in conjunction with discussion of the MOVE statement, a PIC 9 field may contain nonnumeric data. So let us write a broader condition-name that covers all possibilities of an error code. Here is a rewritten specification:

```
02  EMPLOYEE-CODE       PIC  X.
    88  MALE            VALUE '1'.
    88  FEMALE          VALUE '2'.
    88  ERROR-SEX-CODE  VALUES ARE LOW-VALUES THRU ZERO,
                               '3' THRU HIGH-VALUES.
```

In the above program segment we allow for the possibility that EMPLOYEE-CODE is not a numeric field in the quantitative sense. The code values are simply characters that identify each employee; they are not measures of quantity. Thus a code of 2 is not a larger value than a code of 1; they are simply different values. Recognizing the nominal nature of the code, it makes more sense to use PIC X rather than PIC 9, and then the 88-level condition-name can be used to capture all error cases. Specifically, we used the LOW-VALUES figurative constant, which refers to the smallest character in the collating sequence, and the HIGH-VALUES, which refers to the highest value. This approach would "sense" any incorrect value in the field. For a review on the LOW-VALUES and HIGH-VALUES figurative constants refer to the preceding section of this chapter, on relation conditions.

As a last point related to the example above, we should notice the use of nonnumeric literals such as '1', '2', and '3'. For example, the MALE condition-name refers to EMPLOYEE-CODE having the character 1 as its content. The PIC X specification defines the field as alphanumeric and we should stay consistent with that definition when using literals. It would not be correct to define VALUE 1 (without quotes) in conjunction with the PIC X specification.

Despite the preceding discussion, it is common practice to use numeric definitions for fields containing such codes as EMPLOYEE-CODE in the above example. The reason that this practice works is that it is typical to test data for correctness when the data are added to a file. For example, we could assume that a "class" test has been performed (as will be discussed in Chapter 8) such as IF EMPLOYEE-CODE IS NOT NUMERIC.... Such class tests can ascertain that the data are indeed numeric, and therefore condition-names that apply to the range 0–9 are a valid programming practice.

R E V I E W . . . .

1. An entry in which a condition-name is defined is always assigned the level-number _____ (number).

                                                                                        88

2. Suppose that for the data-name MARITAL-STATUS the possible values are 1 = married, 2 = divorced, 3 = widowed, 4 = single, and all other values are errors. Assuming numeric data, write suitable 88-level entries to define condition-names for

   a. condition of being or having been married

   b. condition of being single

   c. condition of error code.

   ```
   03  MARITAL-STATUS PICTURE 9.
       88 _____ .
       88 _____ .
       88 _____ .
   ```

                                    a. IS-OR-WAS-MARRIED VALUES ARE 1 THRU 3.
                                                     b. SINGLE VALUE IS 4.
                                    c. ERROR-CODE VALUES ARE ZERO 5 THRU 9.

3. Given that a numeric code is used to identify categories rather than quantities in condition-name descriptions, then the preferred PICTURE for such a one-digit code is [PIC 9 / PIC X].

                                                                                    PIC X

4. When PIC X specification is used for a data item used for condition-names, then a condition represented by the numeric code 3 correctly has the defined value [VALUE 3 / VALUE '3'].

                                                                                VALUE '3'

5. Suppose that for a PIC X field, a value other than 1, 2, or 3 is invalid. Complete the following statement to write a condition-name that defines the condition of invalid.

```
88  INVALID-DATA VALUES ARE _____

                           _____ .
```

LOW-VALUE THRU ZERO
4 THRU HIGH-VALUE

. . . .

THE SET VERB FOR CONDITION-NAMES

COBOL '85 provides for a convenient way to move data into fields for which condition-names have been defined. The 88-level condition-name feature of COBOL is very meaningful for conducting tests as to whether a condition is true. But in COBOL '74 there is something lacking with respect to moving values that correspond to defined condition-names. Consider this example:

```
01  TOTAL-CREDIT-HOURS   PIC 999.
01  STUDENT-CLASS-CODE    PIC X.
    88  FRESHMAN          VALUE  '1'
    88  SOPHOMORE         VALUE  '2'.
    .
    .
    .
    IF  TOTAL-CREDIT-HOURS < 33
        MOVE '1' TO STUDENT-CLASS-CODE
    ELSE
        MOVE '2' TO STUDENT-CLASS-CODE.
```

In the above IF example a statement like MOVE '1' TO STUDENT-CLASS-CODE does not take advantage of the 88 FRESHMAN condition-name specification. But consider the following program revision that uses the specialized SET verb:

```
    IF  TOTAL-CREDITS < 33
        SET FRESHMAN TO TRUE
```

The SET verb above has been used to take advantage of the convenient condition-names provided by the 88-level items.

The general format of the SET verb for this purpose is given below. Other uses of the SET verb are presented in Chapter 19, on table-searching features.

SET {condition-name-1} . . . TO TRUE

In this format the SET verb specifies that the value defined in the condition-name VALUE clause is to be moved to the field associated with the condition-name definition. If a range of values is specified, then the first value is moved, as in the following example.

```
01  STUDENT-CLASS-CODE   PIC X.
    88  UNDERGRADUATE     VALUES ARE '1' '2' '3' '4'.
    88  GRADUATE          VALUES ARE '5' THRU '8'.
```

Use of SET UNDERGRADUATE TO TRUE then is equivalent to saying MOVE '1' TO STUDENT-CLASS-CODE. As the example above illustrates, a range can be specified in detail, as in the first case, or by use of the THRU, as in the second case.

If multiple condition-names are specified in the same SET statement, the effect is the same as using multiple SET statements. This is illustrated in the following example.

```
01   CREDIT-RATING        PIC XX.
     88 DOUBLE-A          VALUE 'AA'.
     88 GOOD              VALUES ARE 'A' THRU 'BB'.
01   ACCOUNT-CLASS        PIC X.
     88 INSTITUTIONAL      VALUE 'I'.
     88 PERSONAL          VALUE 'P'.
         .
         .
         .
     SET DOUBLE-A PERSONAL TO TRUE.
```

The above SET statement is equivalent to

```
     SET DOUBLE-A TO TRUE
     SET PERSONAL TO TRUE.
```
or
```
     SET DOUBLE-A
         PERSONAL TO TRUE.
```

The last two versions are preferred because they make it clear that two condition-names are set to true.

Of course, in either form it would not be logical to use two condition-names from the same field, such as

```
     SET DOUBLE-A TO TRUE
     SET GOOD     TO TRUE.
```

The 88 condition-names included in a given field are mutually exclusive categories, and only one of them can apply. The corresponding data-name cannot contain more than one value at any one time!

R E V I E W . . . .

1. The verb that can be used to move values that correspond to defined condition-names by reference to the condition-name itself is the _____ verb.

                                                                                    SET

2. The SET verb is available in [COBOL '74 AND '85 / COBOL '85 only].

                                                                          COBOL '85 only

3. Given that the DATA DIVISION specification is 88 MALE VALUE '1', then the SET verb statement for an individual that is a male is: SET MALE TO _____ .

                                                                                    TRUE

. . . .

NESTED CONDITIONS

Before discussing nested conditions, let us consider the general format for the IF statement.

$$\underline{IF} \text{ condition THEN} \left\{ \begin{array}{l} \text{statement -1} \\ \underline{\text{NEXT SENTENCE}} \end{array} \right\} \left\{ \begin{array}{l} \underline{\text{ELSE}} \{\text{statement -2}\} \dots [\underline{\text{END-IF}}] \\ \underline{\text{ELSE NEXT SENTENCE}} \\ \underline{\text{END-IF}} \end{array} \right\}$$

The possible unique structures are many, and, since the IF statement is so very common and so very useful an instruction, we will do well to spend some time studying it. Here are some of the forms we can have:

IF condition statement-1.

IF condition statement-1 ELSE NEXT SENTENCE.

IF condition statement-1 ELSE statement-2.

IF condition NEXT SENTENCE ELSE statement-2.

The first case shows that we can omit the ELSE portion as, for example, IF TAX < 5000 MOVE ZERO TO DEDUCTIONS. The statement that follows will be the NEXT SENTENCE, and so it would be redundant to write ELSE NEXT SENTENCE, although it would not be wrong.

As a further review of the IF statements, study the following example.

```
IF  AMOUNT IS GREATER THAN CREDIT LIMIT
    WRITE PRINT-LINE FROM CREDIT-OVERDRAW
ELSE
    MOVE AMOUNT TO BILLING-FIELD
    WRITE PRINT-LINE FROM BILL-AREA.
ADD AMOUNT TO TOTAL-VALUE.
```

The flowchart for this program segment appears in Figure 5-1. The program statements that correspond to the flowchart descriptions are as follows:

FLOWCHART DESCRIPTION	CORRESPONDING PROGRAM STATEMENT
Condition	IF AMOUNT IS GREATER THAN CREDIT-LIMIT
Statement-1	WRITE PRINT LINE FROM CREDIT-OVERDRAW
Statement-2	MOVE AMOUNT TO BILLING-FIELD WRITE PRINT-LINE FROM BILL-AREA
Next sentence	ADD AMOUNT TO TOTAL-VALUE

Notice that statement-1 and statement-2 need not be single statements. Statement-2 illustrates the case in which two statements are included.

The NEXT SENTENCE option is one way of expressing the null leg of a condition, as in this example:

```
IF  DEBITS = CREDITS
    NEXT SENTENCE
ELSE
    PERFORM OUT-OF-BALANCE.
```

FIGURE 5-1

*Flowchart for the Example of a
Conditional Statement*

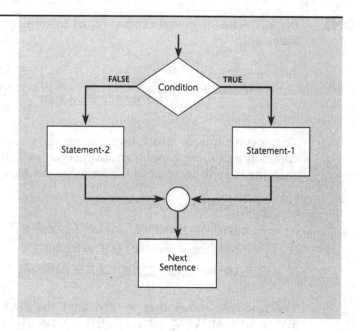

The NEXT SENTENCE in the preceding code provides a clear way of expressing the fact that no action is taken if the condition is true. Contrast the example just given to the equivalent:

```
IF  DEBITS NOT = CREDITS
    PERFORM OUT-OF-BALANCE.
```

The first version is preferred for its clarity.

In the general format for the IF statement, statement-1 and statement-2 are not restricted to being imperative statements; rather, they themselves may be conditional expressions, giving rise to nested IF statements. A relatively simple example of a nested IF statement, or a *nested conditional,* is the following:

```
IF  AMOUNT  <  100
    IF  AMOUNT  >  50
        MOVE 0.3 TO RATE
    ELSE
        MOVE 0.4 TO RATE
ELSE
    MOVE 0.2 TO RATE.
```

This COBOL statement corresponds to the following rule:

AMOUNT	RATE
Less than or equal to 50	0.4
Greater than 50 but less than 100	0.3
Equal to or greater than 100	0.2

A flowchart corresponding to this example is shown in Figure 5-2.

You will find it useful in interpreting nested conditionals to look for the first ELSE; it always pertains to the immediately preceding IF. The second ELSE pertains to the IF just preceding the inner IF, and so on. Schematically, the relationships can be portrayed as follows:

```
IF . . . IF . . . IF . . . ELSE . . . ELSE . . . ELSE . . .
```

FIGURE 5-2

Nested Conditional Structure to Determine Rate

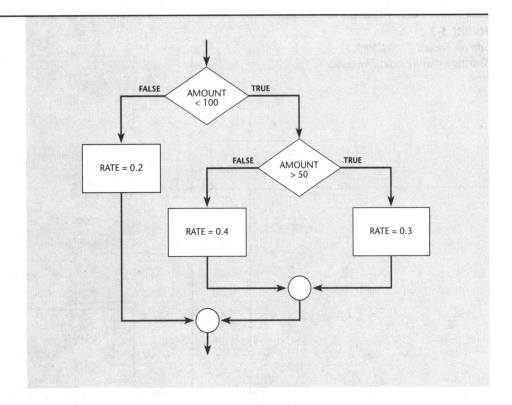

Nested conditions can be very useful in writing program statements, but they also can be misused. This is done by nesting conditions so deeply that program logic is difficult to follow. Because nested conditions are important, we present an additional example.

Consider a code that can have legitimate values in the range 1–5. Figure 5-3 depicts a nested conditional structure that tests for the value of the code and executes a suitable procedure (the strange spelling of KODE is because the more natural CODE is a reserved COBOL word). The corresponding nested IF could be written as

```
IF KODE = 1
   PERFORM ADDITION
ELSE
   IF KODE = 2
      PERFORM DELETION
   ELSE
      IF KODE = 3
         PERFORM CHANGE-ADDRESS
      ELSE
         IF KODE = 4
            PERFORM CHANGE-NAME
         ELSE
            IF KODE = 5
               PERFORM CHANGE-CREDIT
            ELSE
               PERFORM ERROR-CODE.
PERFORM NEXT-P.
```

We have nested to five levels, which tests the limits of our ability to understand the program logic inherent in the nesting. In general, many programming managers

FIGURE 5-3
*Sample Nested Conditional
Structure that Includes Five Levels*

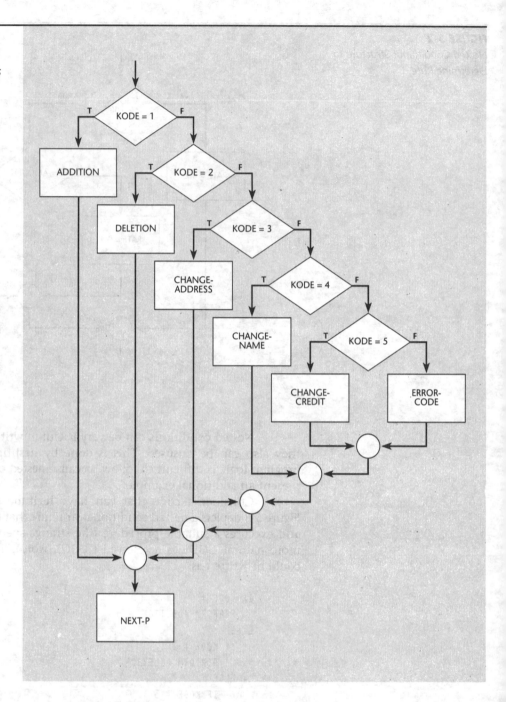

advise against nesting more than three levels. In this particular example the structure is rather easy, however, because of the null alternatives involved. In this sense we can say that, even though we have nested to five levels, it is a "clean" program structure.

The above example represents a "case structure," a subject that will be discussed in the following chapter, on structured programming. One way of implementing the case structure is by means of nested IF statements as in this illustration. Other ways of implementing the case structure will be discussed in Chapter 8 in connection with the GO TO ... DEPENDING ON and EVALUATE statements.

THE END-IF SCOPE TERMINATOR

Nested structures are sometimes a bit awkward to code in the 1974 version of COBOL. Consider the flowchart in Figure 5-4(a). When the GOOD-RISK condition is true, we want to PERFORM GROSS and PERFORM NET regardless of the value of QUANT. Figure 5-4(b) presents the programming statements based on the 1974 standard. The statements PERFORM GROSS and PERFORM NET are written twice to achieve the desired logic. In contrast, Figure 5-4(c) presents the program statements that include use of the END-IF scope terminator. This terminator marks the end of the preceding IF statement, and therefore the PERFORM GROSS and PERFORM NET are executed conditionally on GOOD-RISK being true and unconditionally on the value of QUANT. A second END-IF is used just before the PERFORM INVOICE statement in Figure 5-4(c). A period would play the same role as the second END-IF because a period would also terminate the scope of the main IF GOOD-RISK statement.

While the END-IF plays a useful role, you should not conclude that the 1974 standard is always deficient in ease and clarity of program structure. To make that point, suppose that instead of just the two PERFORM GROSS and PERFORM NET statements we had, say, 20 statements. Duplicating all such statements as was done in Figure 5-4(b) is unappealing, but the following program segment illustrates an improved way of achieving the desired result:

```
IF GOOD-RISK
    IF QUANT > 1000
        MOVE HIGH-RATE TO DISCOUNT
        PERFORM COMPUTATIONS
    ELSE
        MOVE LOW-RATE TO DISCOUNT
        PERFORM COMPUTATIONS
ELSE
    PERFORM BAD-RISK.
PERFORM INVOICE.
COMPUTATIONS.
    PERFORM GROSS
    PERFORM NET.
```

In the above segment we created a new paragraph, COMPUTATIONS, which contains all of the statements whose execution is conditional on GOOD-RISK and unconditional on QUANT. Thus the duplicated code consists of only one statement, PERFORM COMPUTATIONS.

R E V I E W . . . .

1. For the following program instructions, identify the program statement that corresponds to each IF statement element. Refer to the general format for the IF statement if you wish.

```
IF  QUANTITY < 100
    NEXT SENTENCE
ELSE
    MULTIPLY DISCOUNT BY PRICE.
MULTIPLY PRICE BY QUANTITY GIVING NET.
```

FIGURE 5-4

Illustration of Nested IF Without and With END-IF

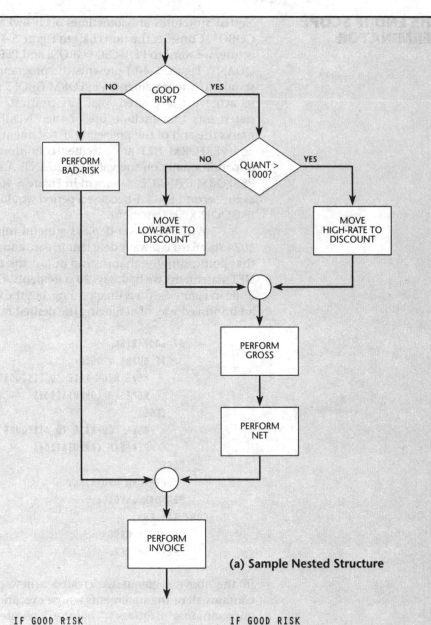

(a) Sample Nested Structure

```
IF GOOD RISK                          IF GOOD RISK
    IF QUANT > 1000                       IF QUANT > 1000
        MOVE HIGH-RATE TO DISCOUNT            MOVE HIGH-RATE TO DISCOUNT
        PERFORM GROSS                     ELSE
        PERFORM NET                           MOVE LOW-RATE TO DISCOUNT
    ELSE                                  END-IF
        MOVE LOW-RATE TO DISCOUNT         PERFORM GROSS
        PERFORM GROSS                     PERFORM NET
        PERFORM NET                   ELSE
ELSE                                      PERFORM BAD-RISK
    PERFORM BAD-RISK.                 END-IF
PERFORM INVOICE.                      PERFORM INVOICE.
```

(b) Without Use of END-IF   **(c) With Use of END-IF**

IF STATEMENT ELEMENT	CORRESPONDING PROGRAM STATEMENT
a. Condition	_____
b. Statement-1	_____
c. Statement-2	_____
d. Next sentence	_____

a. QUANTITY < 100

b. Not used as such (NEXT SENTENCE was used instead)

c. MULTIPLY DISCOUNT BY PRICE

d. MULTIPLY PRICE BY QUANTITY GIVING NET

2. Construct a flowchart corresponding to this program segment:

```
IF  QUANTITY < 100
    NEXT SENTENCE
ELSE
    MULTIPLY DISCOUNT BY PRICE.
MULTIPLY PRICE BY QUANTITY GIVING NET.
```

3. Using the following COBOL statement, complete the table below.

```
IF  GRSPAY < 1000.00
    IF  GRSPAY > 500.00
        MOVE 0.05 TO RETRMNT-DEDUC
    ELSE
        MOVE 0.03 TO RETRMNT-DEDUC
ELSE
    MOVE 0.07 TO RETRMNT-DEDUC.
```

AMOUNT OF GROSS PAY	RETIREMENT DEDUCTION RATE
Equal to or greater than 1,000	_____
Greater than 500 but less than 1,000	_____
Less than or equal to 500	_____

0.07; 0.05; 0.03

. . . .

COMPOUND CONDITIONS

It is possible to combine the simple (individual) conditionals we have described into *compound conditionals* by the use of the logical operators OR, AND, and NOT. OR means *either or both,* and AND means *both.* Consider the following statement:

```
IF  BALANCE < ZERO AND DAYS-OVERDUE > 10
    PERFORM PAR-A.
```

The instruction indicates that the program should execute PAR-A when both the balance is negative and the number of overdue days exceeds 10.

On the other hand, consider the following statement:

```
IF  INPUT-DATA IS NONNUMERIC OR NAME-IS-MISSING
    MOVE 'CANT PROCESS, INCORRECT DATA' TO ERR-MESSAGE.
```

The program will move the indicated message to ERR-MESSAGE if either the condition-name NONNUMERIC condition is true or the condition-name condition defined as NAME-IS-MISSING is true.

There is a rather complex set of rules associated with the writing and evaluation of compound conditionals. In this chapter we shall limit our attention to the use of parentheses to clarify the meaning, whereas in Chapter 8 we shall expand on the subject. For example, we can write

```
IF  (AGE IS GREATER THAN 28) OR ((EXPERIENCE = 4)
    AND (EDUCATION IS GREATER THAN HS)) . . .
```

This condition holds either if age is greater than 28 or if both experience = 4 and education is greater than high school.

As another example, consider the following:

```
IF  ((CUST-CODE = 2) OR (CUST-CODE = 5)) AND (BALANCE = 0)
    PERFORM DISCOUNT-COMP
ELSE
    PERFORM FULL-PRICE-COMP.
```

In this example the first condition is true if BALANCE is equal to zero and CUST-CODE is either equal to 2 or equal to 5.

Using nested IF statements, we might write

```
IF  CUST-CODE = 2
    IF  BALANCE = 0
        PERFORM DISCOUNT-COMP
    END-IF
ELSE
    IF  CUST-CODE = 5
        IF  BALANCE = 0
            PERFORM DISCOUNT-COMP
        END-IF
    ELSE
        PERFORM FULL-PRICE-COMP.
```

Looking at the nested IF above, we see clearly that by the use of compound conditionals we can write conditional tests that otherwise would require very long expressions consisting of several nested IF statements.

R E V I E W . . . .

1. In contrast to the use of simple conditionals, a combination of tests can be included in one statement by the use of _____ conditionals.

                                                          compound

2. The use of a compound conditional requires the use of one of the logical operators: _____ , _____ , or _____ .

OR; NOT; AND

3. When the logical operator OR is used in a compound conditional test, the presence of [either / both / either or both] of the conditional states constitutes a true condition.

either or both

4. When the logical operator AND is used in a compound conditional test, the presence of [either / both / either or both] of the conditional states constitutes a true condition.

both

. . . .

SUMMARY

We began this chapter with a discussion of the general rules associated with the use of the IF statement, and then we covered four specific types of conditional statements: (1) relation conditions; (2) condition-name conditions; (3) nested conditions; and (4) compound conditions.

When the condition specified in the IF statement is met, program execution continues with the statement or statements that directly follow that statement. Otherwise, program execution continues with the next sentence. The ELSE option makes it possible to execute one of two alternative statements (or sets of statements) through the use of one IF before continuing to the next sentence.

Relation conditions are always concerned with comparisons. The words or symbols that indicate the type of comparison to be made are called *relational operators*. We can compare one identifier to another identifier, one arithmetic expression to another arithmetic expression, literals to identifiers or expressions, and identifiers to expressions. For nonnumeric comparisons, it is necessary to know the *collating sequence* of the computer system. The EBDIC collating sequence is used by many IBM mainframe computers, while ASCII is the standard collating sequence.

The use of *condition-names* enables the programmer to define specialized figurative constants for use in condition tests. Instead of testing for a particular value for a data field, one can test for a condition-name instead, such as, IF MALE. Such use of condition-names enhances the readability of programs. The SET verb, available in COBOL '85, can be used to move values that correspond to defined condition-names.

A *nested conditional statement* involves the use of a sequence of IF clauses followed by a sequence of ELSE clauses. The first ELSE pertains to the immediately preceding IF; the second ELSE pertains to the IF just preceding the inner IF; and so on. In using nested designs, care must be taken to ensure that program logic is easy to follow. Use of the END-IF scope terminator available in COBOL '85 can help keep program logic clear.

Compound conditions are formed by joining several simple conditional statements into one statement by use of the logical operators OR, AND, and NOT. Such conditionals make it possible to write conditional tests that otherwise would require very long expressions consisting of several nested IF statements.

EXERCISES

5.1   Write PROCEDURE DIVISION statements to implement the logic included in the following flowchart.

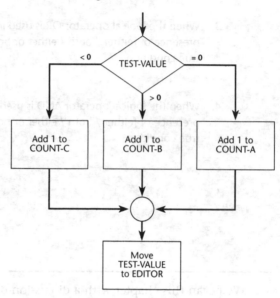

5.2   Using the 88-level-number indicator in the DATA DIVISION and suitable condition-name clauses, the following obvious identifiers have been defined:

MALE	WIDOWED-M
FEMALE	SINGLE-F
SINGLE-M	MARRIED-F
MARRIED-M	DIVORCED-F
DIVORCED-M	WIDOWED-F

Assume we want to tabulate the number of individuals falling into the last eight classes, as, for example, the number of single males (SINGLE-M). We thus want to test the field containing the identifying code and ADD 1 TO the corresponding counter. Assume the following fields are to be used as counters: SM, MM, DM, WM, SF, MF, DF, WF (where SM stands for single males, etc.).

a.   Draw a flowchart corresponding to your program logic.

b.   Write one nested conditional expression to accomplish the required testing and tabulating.

5.3   Consider the following DATA DIVISION entries relating to a personnel record:

```
02  EDUCATION              PIC 99.
    88  H-S GRAD                    VALUE 12.
    88  COLLEGE-GRAD                VALUE 16.
    88  MASTERS-GRAD                VALUE 17.
    88  DOCTORATE-GRAD              VALUE 20.
02  YEARS-OF-EXPERIENCE    PIC 99.
```

```
02  SEX-CODE              PIC 9.
    88  MALE                  VALUE 1.
    88  FEMALE                VALUE 2.
02  GEOGRAPHIC-PREFERENCE PIC 9.
    88  EAST                  VALUE 1.
    88  MIDWEST               VALUE 2.
    88  WEST                  VALUE 3.
    88  SOUTH                 VALUE 4.
    88  WILLING-TO-TRAVEL     VALUE 5.
```

Suppose that we want to find individuals who fulfill one of these three sets of requirements:

a.　Five years of experience, male, high school graduate, willing to travel

b.　Male, one year of experience, master's degree, preferring the West or South

c.　Three years of experience, female, doctorate, preferring the East

Write one compound conditional sentence by which we can check whether a record in question fulfills the first, second, or third of these requirements. If one of these sets of requirements is met, we PERFORM PAR-A. If no set of requirements is met, we execute PAR-B.

5.4　Consider the following table of conditions:

QUANTITY	PRICE	RATING	DISCOUNT
>100	>10	<2	0.05
−100	>10	≥2	0.10
−100	≤10	<2	0.15
>100	≤10	≥2	0.20
≤100	$\begin{cases} < \\ =10 \\ > \end{cases}$	$\begin{cases} < \\ = 2 \\ > \end{cases}$	0.25

a.　Write instructions using nested IF to MOVE to DISCOUNT the value shown depending on the conditions. Do not use END-IF.

b.　Use the END-IF scope terminator to do the task.

c.　Draw a flowchart corresponding to the specifications in the above table.

5.5　Draw a flowchart representing the following nested conditional statements. C1, C2, ... stand for condition names.

```
IF  C1 AND (C2 OR C3)
    PERFORM F1
    PERFORM F2
ELSE
    IF  C2 OR (C6 AND C7)
        PERFORM F3
    ELSE NEXT SENTENCE.
```

5.6 Write a program corresponding to the flowchart in Figure 5-5. Assume that the input file is defined as follows:

```
FD  EMPLOYEE-FILE  LABEL RECORDS STANDARD
                   DATA RECORD EMPL-REC.
01  EMPL-REC.
    02  FILLER           PIC X(5)
    02  HOURLY-OR-SAL    PIC X.
        88  HOURLY            VALUE '1'.
        88  SALARIED          VALUE '2'.
    02  UNION-CODE       PIC X.
        88  UNION             VALUE '1'.
        88  NONUNION          VALUE '2'.
    02  SEX-CODE         PIC X.
        88  MALE              VALUE '1'.
        88  FEMALE            VALUE '2'.
    02  FILLER           PIC X(72).
```

The following sample input and output data serve the purpose of describing the required logic. In summary, we want to count the number of employees who belong to the labor union and to show separately the number of men from the number of women union members.

SAMPLE INPUT

```
111
121
222
211
122
111
121
212
111
112
112
```

SAMPLE OUTPUT

```
UNION MEMBERSHIP

MEN      3

WOMEN    2

TOTAL    5
```

FIGURE 5-5
Flowchart for Exercise 5.6

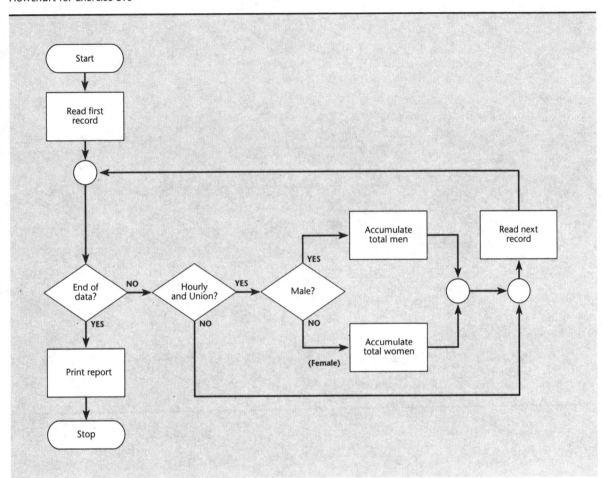

6

Structured Programming in COBOL

BASIC PROGRAM STRUCTURES

PARTITIONING PROGRAM MODULES

LEVELS OF ABSTRACTION AND
    STRUCTURE CHARTS

ALTERNATIVE FORMS OF STRUCTURE
    CHARTS

FORMATTING RULES FOR PROGRAMS

IN EARLY PROGRAMMING *practice, most programs were characterized by "spaghetti bowl logic." This involved the repeated transfer of program execution and control from one part of the program to another, particularly by the use of GO TO types of statements. Programmers had no clear concepts or guidelines on which to rely for writing good programs in a systematic way. Programs differed in their structure depending on the intuition and experience level of individual programmers. By the mid-1970s concepts and methods were developed that could be used to write good programs that have common structural elements.* **Structured programming** *is the label that was given to this development.*

Programs developed under the structured programming approach are less error-prone and can be understood and modified more easily than programs not so developed.

In this chapter you will study the key concepts and techniques associated with structured programming in COBOL. You will begin by considering the several basic types of program structures that you can use. You will then study the application of partitioning to good program design and the use of structure charts in establishing good modular design. You will conclude this chapter by studying a set of rules for formatting COBOL programs.

FIGURE 6-1
Standard Program Structures

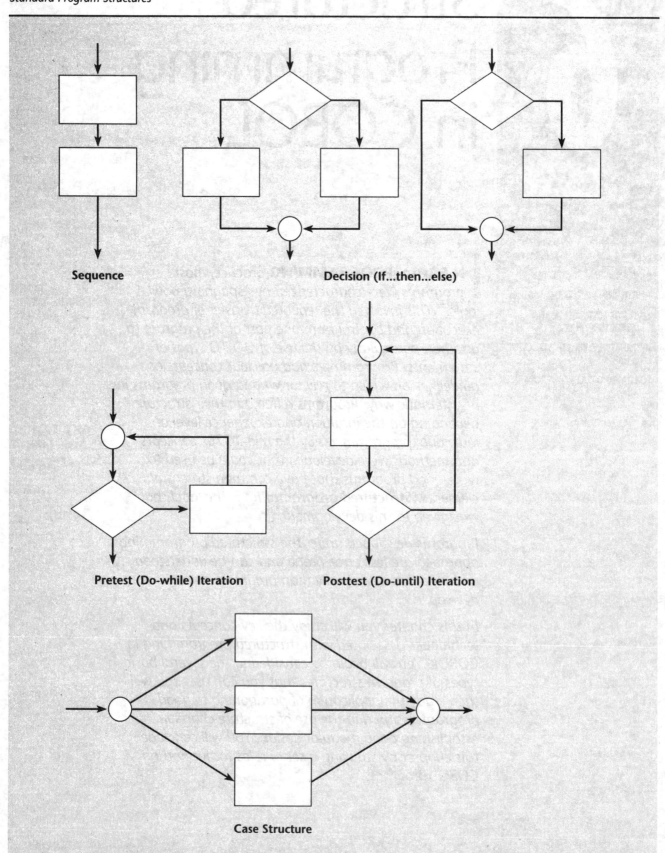

Sequence

Decision (If...then...else)

Pretest (Do-while) Iteration

Posttest (Do-until) Iteration

Case Structure

BASIC PROGRAM STRUCTURES

Briefly stated, structured programming is based on the use of the five standard structures presented in Figure 6-1: Sequence, Decision, Pretest Iteration, Posttest Iteration, and the Case Structure. For a program to be considered structured, one should be able to portray the program by the use of any combination of these five standard structures, and only these structures.

COBOL now provides for convenient implementation of all five basic program structures. In some cases COBOL '74 is incapable of straightforward implementation of all of these structures, but COBOL '85 has removed such deficiencies. A series of examples are presented in this section to demonstrate how COBOL language statements can be used to implement each of the basic structures.

Sequence Structure

Figure 6-2 presents the implementation of the *sequence structure* in COBOL. This is the most basic form of structure, and simply represents the *successive* execution of statements or modules in a program. As exemplified by the set of statements for the second module in that figure, a conditional statement that is properly marked by an END-IF scope terminator in COBOL '85 may be viewed as one step (block) in the sequence. In fact, as we shall see in a later section in this chapter, on levels of abstraction, program can be portrayed as a sequence structure. This is so because all the forms in Figure 6-1 are characterized by one entry and one exit, and can therefore be viewed, in the abstract, as being blocks in a sequence.

The Decision Structure

The implementation of the *decision structure* (also called the *selection* or *if-then-else* structure) is illustrated in Figure 6-3.

There are two forms of the decision structure. The first form is used when we have an IF ... ELSE case. One or more actions are taken given that the condition is true, and another action is taken given that the condition is false.

In the second form one of the "legs" is null, and no action is taken in that case. Either the "true" or the "false" case may be null. An IF without the ELSE, and

FIGURE 6-2
COBOL Implementation of
Sequence Structure

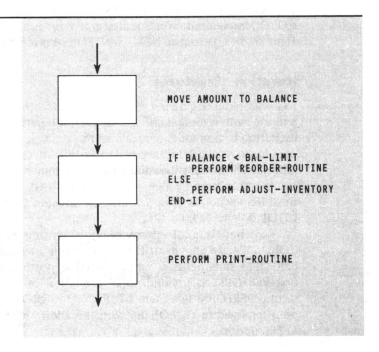

```
MOVE AMOUNT TO BALANCE




IF BALANCE < BAL-LIMIT
        PERFORM REORDER-ROUTINE
ELSE
        PERFORM ADJUST-INVENTORY
END-IF



PERFORM PRINT-ROUTINE
```

FIGURE 6-3
COBOL Implementation of
Decision Structure

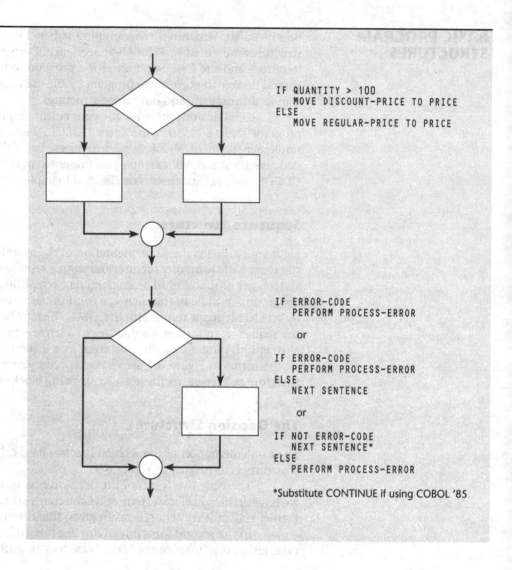

```
IF QUANTITY > 100
    MOVE DISCOUNT-PRICE TO PRICE
ELSE
    MOVE REGULAR-PRICE TO PRICE
```

```
IF ERROR-CODE
    PERFORM PROCESS-ERROR
```

or

```
IF ERROR-CODE
    PERFORM PROCESS-ERROR
ELSE
    NEXT SENTENCE
```

or

```
IF NOT ERROR-CODE
    NEXT SENTENCE*
ELSE
    PERFORM PROCESS-ERROR
```

*Substitute CONTINUE if using COBOL '85

terminating with a period or END-IF, is one way of writing the corresponding COBOL implementation. An alternate way, as shown in the last two examples of Figure 6-3, is use of the NEXT SENTENCE option to indicate the null leg.

Iteration Structures

As presented in Figure 6-4, there are two *iteration structures:* the *pretest* (or *do-while*) and the *posttest* (or *do-until*). In the pretest iteration, a test is performed before any execution of a module, whereas in the posttest iteration, the module is executed once, and then may be executed more times according to the result of the test that follows. The pretest iteration can be implemented with a PERFORM . . . UNTIL command in both COBOL '74 and COBOL '85. The WITH TEST AFTER clause in the 1985 version is optional, and its omission implies exactly what PERFORM ... UNTIL does in COBOL '74.

There is no direct way of implementing the posttest iteration structure in COBOL '74. As shown in the last example in Figure 6-4, we need to write two PERFORM statements to implement the posttest iteration in COBOL '74. The first PERFORM is unconditional execution of the target procedure, while the second PERFORM is a pretest PERFORM ... UNTIL. However, this deficiency has been removed in COBOL '85 with the addition of the PERFORM ... WITH TEST AFTER option.

FIGURE 6-4

COBOL Implementation of
Iteration Structures

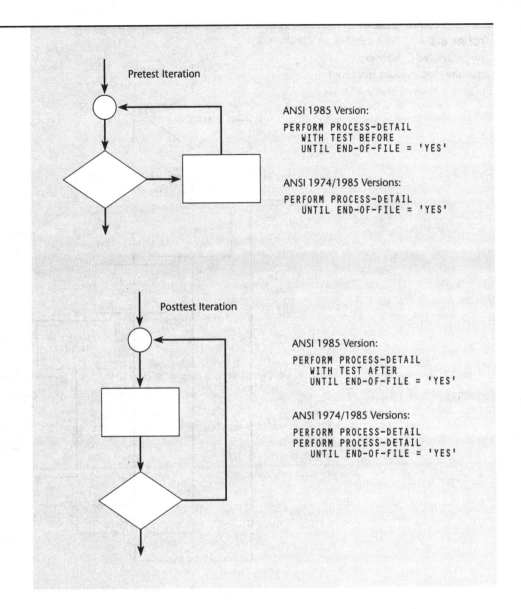

The Case Structure

The *case structure* is useful when we need to select one from among several alternatives. Rather than having one true-false type of condition, we have a number of possibilities, one of which is true, as for example the processing of one of many possible types of transactions in a file update program. Figure 6-5 illustrates case implementation using nested IF statements. Such an approach can be used with both COBOL '74 and COBOL '85.

However, the case structure can be implemented in other ways, as well. A better approach is to use the EVALUATE verb, which will be discussed in Chapter 8. Another possibility is use of the specialized verb GO TO ... DEPENDING ON, also described in Chapter 8. In general, the nested IF illustrated in Figure 6-5 is a good approach when the number of alternatives is relatively small. When the number of alternatives is large, the EVALUATE statement is preferred because it avoids the use of a deeply nested IF structure. The implementation using GO TO ... DEPENDING ON, is suitable only if we have a numeric code that assumes consecutive numeric values ranging as 1, 2, ... , *n*. For instance, if the numeric code represents the last school grade completed from the first grade through the fourth

FIGURE 6-5

Sample Nested Conditional
Structure that Includes Five Levels

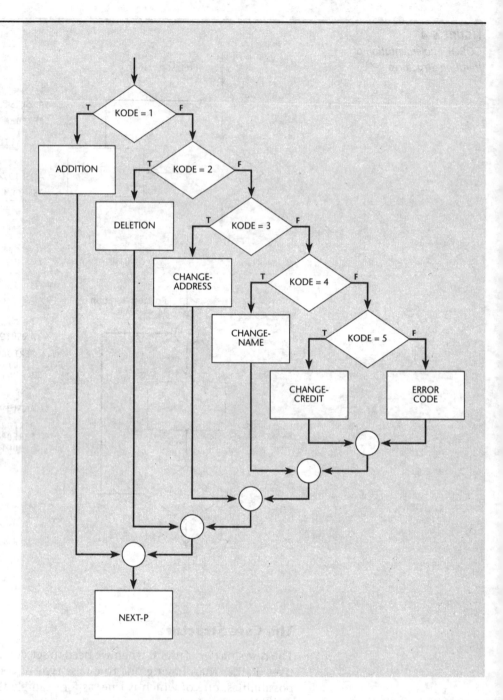

year of college, and we process each of the 16 possibilities separately, then GO TO ... DEPENDING ON implementation would be convenient as well as compatible with both COBOL '74 and COBOL '85.

R E V I E W . . . .

1. Structured programming is based on the use of [any one / any combination] of the standard structures presented in Figure 6-1.

any combination

2. The program structure that simply indicates that processing is to continue with the next statement or module is the _____ structure.

   sequence

3. The type of structure that involves a selection of one of two alternative actions, or of one action versus no action, is the _____ structure.

   decision (or selection, or if-then-else)

4. The two forms of program structure that represent a repeating process, or program loop, are the _____ structures.

   iteration

5. The form of the iteration structure in which a test is done before the execution of a program module is the _____ iteration.

   pretest (or do while)

6. The form of the iteration structure in which the program module is executed once, and then may be executed more times according to the result of a test, is the _____ iteration.

   posttest (or do until)

7. The type of program structure in which selection of program modules is made from more than two alternatives is the _____ structure.

   case

8. When the number of alternative modules is small, the preferred COBOL code to implement the case structure is to use [GO TO ... DEPENDING / nested IF] statements.

   nested IF

· ·

PARTITIONING PROGRAM MODULES

A fundamental concept of program design is that of *partitioning*, which refers to the process of subdividing a large programming task into smaller parts or functions.

The use of partitioning is common in many fields. One form of partitioning in organizations is based on the division of labor, or functional specialization. For example, an automobile manufacturing plant includes departmental units that may be further subdivided according to specific functions. A Painting Department, for instance, could include such separate functions as cleaning, spraying, baking, inspecting, and the like. Similarly, an Information Systems Department could include such separate functions as programming, systems analysis, data entry, and input-output control. In general, we find it not only beneficial, but also necessary, to partition large and complex tasks into smaller and more specialized tasks.

A computer programming task generally is complex enough to make partitioning desirable. In the context of computer programming, a widely used term associated with partitioning is *modularity*. A *program module* is a well-defined program segment. Modular programming has been recognized as a desirable practice for many years. In practice, all programs include some degree of modularity by necessity; no programmer can write a monolithic program that is not partitioned into some kinds of parts, or modules. Thus, it is not just the presence of modularity that is important. Rather, we need to develop an understanding of how to design programs whose modules are so constructed as to lead to good programs.

To be useful, a module should not only be a program segment, but also a *well-defined* program segment. More specifically, a module should be a *named* program segment that carries out a *specific program function*. In the context of COBOL programming, a module eventually is represented in one of four forms in the program:

1. As a single paragraph

2. As a series of two or more consecutive paragraphs that are the object of a PERFORM PAR-A THRU PAR-Z, where PAR-A and PAR-Z stand for the first and last paragraphs in a series (as will be discussed in the next chapter)

3. As a single SECTION (as will be discussed in Chapter 11)

4. As a subprogram (as will be discussed in Chapter 23)

R E V I E W . . . .

1. The process of subdividing a large programming task into smaller, more specific tasks is called _____ .

                                                                              partitioning

2. In terms of its general application, partitioning is a [long-standing / recently developed] concept.

                                                                              long-standing

3. "A named program segment that carries out a specific program function" is a definition of a program _____ .

                                                                              module

4. Program modularity can be described as being effective when it leads to the development of _____ programs.

                                                                              good

. . . .

LEVELS OF ABSTRACTION AND STRUCTURE CHARTS

As we stated in the preceding section, a good program should be partitioned into modules that perform a specific function. For purposes of designing a good program, a module can be viewed as a *black box*. A black box is a means of representing a program task, or procedure, in an abstract way. When we concentrate on the *what* rather than the *how* aspect of a task, we thereby introduce the idea of abstraction, which is concerned with a summary representation, free of detail.

An important consideration in program design is the partitioning of a whole task into smaller, interrelated modules. To achieve effective partitioning of a task, we must be able to look at the parts in abstract form rather than in detail. If a program consists of one hundred modules and each module averages 10 lines of code, it is impossible to comprehend the whole program at once. This is where the black box concept comes in handy. We describe each module as a black box, thus abstracting from its detail. So, for the above example, we would need to consider the one hundred modules rather than the 1,000 lines of code as such. While this is an improvement, we would still find it hard to comprehend the 100 modules viewed all at one time.

The way we manage the large number of modules in program design is to organize them in a systematic fashion. Just as a large college is organized into departments, fields of specialization, and individual faculty, so we organize program modules into a hierarchical structure. *Structure charts* are the best way of depicting

FIGURE 6-6
Rectangular and Angular Structure Charts

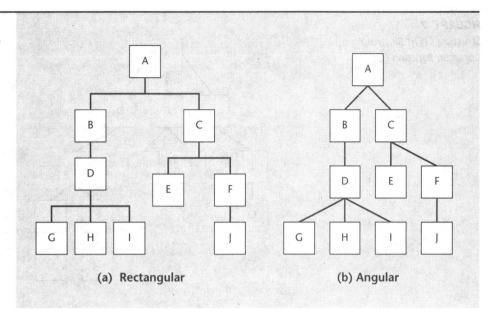

(a) Rectangular   (b) Angular

the hierarchical structure of programs. Figure 6-6 presents two sample hierarchical structure charts, one showing rectangular connecting lines, the second one showing angular connections. The type of connecting lines that are used is simply a matter of preference and has nothing to do with the meaning of a structure chart.

The critical characteristics of a hierarchical structure are

1. There is only one top module (the *root* module), and it represents the entire program. This module is superior to all other modules.

2. Any given module may have subordinate modules. These are shown below their immediate superior and are connected with lines to show this superior-subordinate relationship. In Figure 6-6, for example, D is a module that is subordinate to B and superior to modules G, H, and I.

3. Any given module, except the top one, should have one, and only one, superior in the structure chart. Yet there are situations in which the same module may need to be subordinate to more than one superior. In such cases we draw the subordinate module as if it were a unique subordinate to each respective superior in the structure chart, but we shade the upper-right corner to indicate the fact that it is a duplicate representation. Module Q is such a module in Figure 6-7. Notice that we have included the Q block four times in the structure chart, rather than the alternative of presenting it once and showing four connecting lines leading to the module. By this method of duplicate representation, the requirement that a module should have only one superior shown in the structure chart is satisfied.

In all cases a superior module is superior by the fact that it issues a PERFORM to execute the given subordinate. So in operational terms, a module A is superior to another module B when A contains a "PERFORM B" statement. The PERFORM itself is a means of using abstract references. When a PERFORM is written, it specifies a black box approach; it says what to do, without including the specific procedure of how to do the task. Therefore a structure chart is an abstract representation of a program because it represents a summary of the functions performed by the program.

FIGURE 6-7

Structure Chart Illustrating a Common Function (Q)

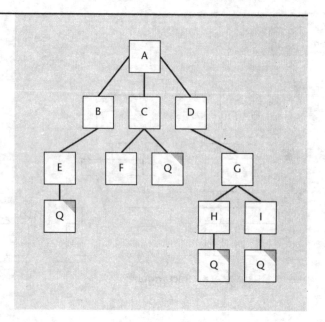

Furthermore, a given module is a summary representation of all of its subordinates. Module C in Figure 6-7 is superior to F and Q, which means it contains "PERFORM F" and "PERFORM Q" statements in it. So when execution of C has been completed, F and Q have also been executed. Similarly, when module A in Figure 6-7 has been executed, the entire program has been executed. Thus a given module provides a high-level, or abstract, representation of its subordinates.

The use of *abstraction* and the *omission of detail* is our best weapon against overwhelming complexity. A structure chart representing a program of 100 modules need not be overwhelming. The hierarchical structure allows us to focus on parts of the total without losing sight of the whole. When we view one module to find out "how it fits in the whole picture," we simply look up to its superior and, if need be, to the superior of its superior, and so on.

In addition to describing the hierarchical relationships, a structure chart can also be enhanced to include

- *Loops* (repetitive execution of subordinate modules)
- *Decision points* (conditional execution of subordinate modules)
- *Data* (input to and output from modules)

Figure 6-8 is a structure chart that includes these additional features. Module A passes X as input data to module B, which returns output data Y to module A. Then modules C and D are executed repetitively, as indicated by the curved arrows below B; the inner loop involves module C while the outer loop involves both C and D. Finally, module F executes modules G and H conditionally, as indicated by the diamond symbol at F.

It may be useful at this point to contrast a structure chart with a *flowchart*. A structure chart is based on hierarchical program structure, whereas a flowchart is based on sequential procedure. To design a good program, first a good structure chart should be developed. After the structure chart has been completed, a flowchart may then be developed as an additional aid for coding the program logic into program procedures; however, a *pseudocode* version of the program is a preferred approach.

We conclude this section with a brief discussion of how the concept of levels of abstraction is also relevant for flowcharts as well as structure charts. As we

FIGURE 6-8
Structure Chart Showing Data, Loops, and Decision Point

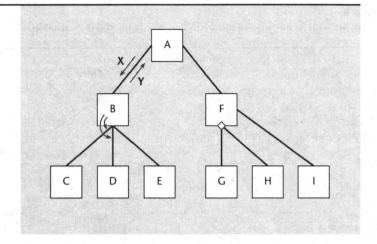

recall from the discussion in the beginning of this chapter on the basic flowchart forms of program structure, a fundamental property of the five basic structures is that each has *one entry* and *one exit*. Based on that property, we may represent a structure either in detail or in summary form. A given block structure may represent a series of interrelated blocks with the same entry and exit point. Figure 6-9 illustrates the property. The rectangular borders in Figure 6-9(a) illustrate how we can use different levels of abstraction depending on our needs. In part (b) one block has been substituted for the entire diagram in part (a). This is the highest level of abstraction. Then in part (c) we represent the entire part (a) structure as a simple selection. Finally, part (d) presents more detail by demonstrating the nested selection structure of part (a).

The one-entry, one-exit property can be used as a powerful tool both when developing a new program and when trying to review or comprehend a program already written. We can deal with the details of the code or we can focus on higher levels of abstraction, as needed.

R E V I E W . . . .

1. The process by which the overall programming task is subdivided into several more specific tasks is called _____ .

   partitioning

2. The type of chart that represents the hierarchical organization of program modules is the _____ .

   structure chart

3. In terms of structure chart representation, the entire program is represented by the [top / bottom] module.

   top

4. Any given module in the structure chart can have [only one / any number of] subordinate module(s).

   any number of

5. Except for the top module, which has no superior module, any module in the structure chart representation has [only one / any number of] superior module(s).

   only one

FIGURE 6-9

Illustration of Levels of Abstraction Based on the One-Entry One-Exit Property

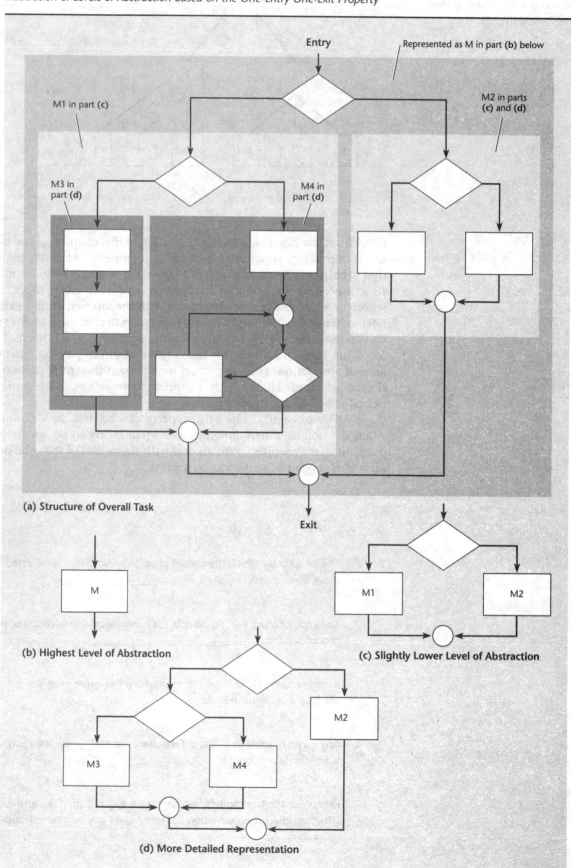

(a) Structure of Overall Task

(b) Highest Level of Abstraction

(c) Slightly Lower Level of Abstraction

(d) More Detailed Representation

6. When a given module is in fact subordinate to more than one superior in terms of program logic, that module is _____ in the structure chart.

                                                              repeated (and shaded)

7. If module C is the superior of module D in a structure chart, this indicates that module C includes in it the PROCEDURE DIVISION command, _____ , in some form.

                                                                        PERFORM D

8. As contrasted to the structure chart, which is based on hierarchical program structure, the type of chart that is based on sequential procedure is the _____ .

                                                                         flowchart

9. A fundamental property of the basic structures is the existence of [only one / several] entry point(s) and [only one / several] exit point(s).

                                                                  only one; only one

. . . .

ALTERNATIVE FORMS OF STRUCTURE CHARTS

The preceding section presented some basic conventions for representing program structure in the form of charts. However, there is no one universal format for drawing such charts; rather, there are several somewhat competing alternative formats. Each alternative encompasses a design methodology that provides a standard set of conventions for representing program structure, data structure, and program code. In a given organization it makes good sense to use one of the alternative formats consistently, so that efficient and clear communication among programming professionals in that organization is achieved. In a general context, such as in this book, it is impractical to attempt the simultaneous use of different diagramming conventions. For this reason a simplified set of formats is used in the text examples, leaving the choice of a specific convention to your preference.

Of the several available diagrammatic conventions for representing program structure, we present a brief overview of two of them: HIPO charts and Warnier-Orr charts.

Hierarchical Input-Process-Output (HIPO) is the set of diagramming conventions developed by IBM that focuses on the inputs, processes, and outputs of programs. Figure 6-10 includes a sample HIPO chart. Figure 6-10(a) is a *Visual Table of Contents (VTOC,* pronounced "vee-tok") diagram that essentially is a hierarchical structure chart very similar to the type used throughout this book. At the lower right corner of each block in the VTOC diagram, a number is included as a reference to an associated HIPO chart. The HIPO chart included in Figure 6-10(b) is for block 1.0, which is the root module representing the entire program. As illustrated in Figure 6-10(b), a HIPO chart consists of three portions, labeled INPUT, PROCESS, and OUTPUT, respectively. As part of the HIPO methodology, a similar chart would be prepared for each of the 12 blocks in the VTOC chart in Figure 6-10(a). Thus HIPO charts provide documented detail for the input, process, and output for each module or function in the program, and therefore can be used as the basis for writing the program code.

Warnier-Orr charts are named after Jean-Dominique Warnier and Ken Orr, who were the principal developers of this approach to representing program structure. Figure 6-11 presents a Warnier-Orr chart corresponding to the structure chart in Figure 6-10(a). The notable characteristic of such charts is that they use *horizontally arranged brackets* rather than vertically placed blocks to represent the

FIGURE 6-10

A Hierarchical Structure Chart and One Associated HIPO Chart

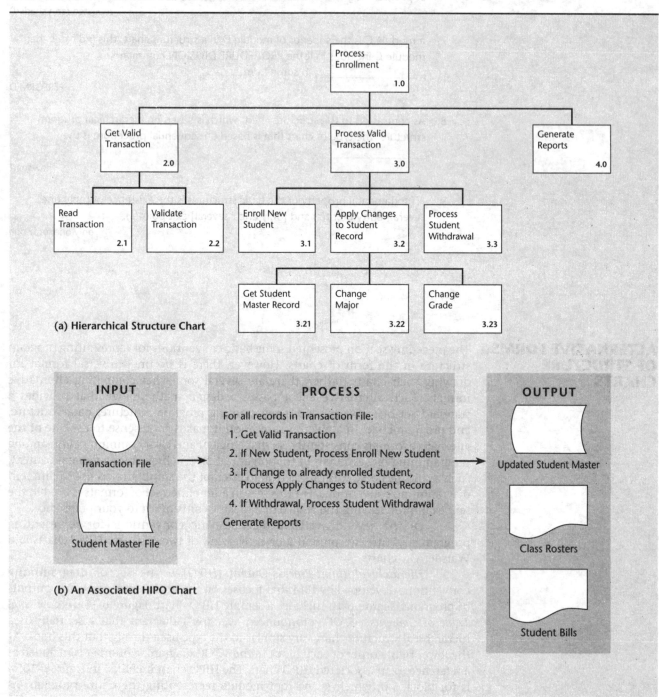

(a) Hierarchical Structure Chart

(b) An Associated HIPO Chart

hierarchical structure of a program. Warnier-Orr charts focus on the hierarchical relationships of the functions to be performed, and, as is the case for HIPO charts, they can be used as the basis for developing the program code. Warnier-Orr charts are generally more compact than corresponding HIPO charts because they incorporate the functions of both the VTOC and HIPO charts into one diagram. However, combining the two types of functions into one chart results in a somewhat more complex diagram.

FIGURE 6-11
Sample Warnier-Orr Chart

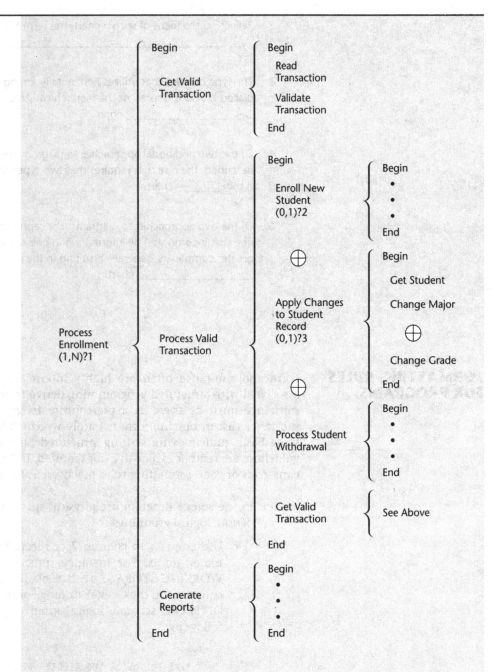

(1,N) means that this process is repeated N times and ?1 is an indication that there is a footnote and it is labeled 1. Warnier-Orr diagrams use footnotes to explain control logic; for this example, footnote 1 might state that the N repetitions are terminated when the end-of-file condition is true. ⊕ is a symbol to indicate the exclusive *or*; for example, either Enroll New Student *or* Apply Changes to Student Record will be executed.

R E V I E W . . . .

1. The type of chart developed by IBM that focuses on the inputs, processes, and outputs of programs is the _____ chart.

HIPO

2. Reflecting the focus of such a chart, the term HIPO stands for

   _____ .

   Hierarchical Input-Process-Output

3. The type of chart that utilizes horizontally arranged brackets rather than vertically placed blocks to represent the hierarchical structure of a program is the _____ chart.

   Warnier-Orr

4. Of the two additional approaches to diagrammatic representation that were described, the one that requires that two types of associated charts be prepared is the _____ chart.

   HIPO

5. Of the two approaches to diagrammatic representation that were discussed, the one that incorporates all information in one rather than two types of charts, with greater complexity generally resulting in the one chart, is the _____ chart.

   Warnier-Orr

·   ·   ·   ·   ·   ·   ·   ·   ·   ·   ·   ·   ·   ·   ·   ·   ·   ·   ·   ·

FORMATTING RULES FOR PROGRAMS

Form and substance often are highly interrelated. A number of the benefits associated with structured programming derive from use of certain forms. Proper substance must be there as a prerequisite to good programming, but proper substance cast in obscure form is hardly worthwhile. In this section we provide some basic guidelines for writing structured programs in readable form. These guidelines are neither exhaustive nor required, but they represent collectively the consensus of good formatting rules practiced in the field.

1. In the source program use physical spacing to enhance visibility and to denote logical groupings.

   - Use asterisks in column 7 of the COBOL coding form to separate major items. For instance, precede each new 01 item in the WORKING-STORAGE with a blank line containing an asterisk in column 7 on the COBOL Coding Form. Similarly, in the PROCEDURE DIVISION, separate logical groups by a comment line, as in the following:

     ```
     *
     *THE FOLLOWING TWO RECORDS DESCRIBE THE REPORT FORMAT
     *
     01  SALES-REP-HEADING.
         05 . . .
     *
     01  SALES-REP-DETAIL
         05 . . .
     ```

   - If there is a series of MOVE statements and then a WRITE, put a blank comment line before the WRITE to block together the MOVEs that perform a common function, as in the following:

     ```
     *
     *THE FOLLOWING STATEMENTS MOVE AND WRITE THE DATA FOR THE
     *SALES REPORT SUMMARY
     ```

```
          *
                MOVE . . .
                MOVE . . .
                MOVE . . .
          *
                WRITE . . .
```

- Use the stroke (/) in column 7 of the COBOL coding form to start a new page. For instance, always begin the DATA DIVISION on a new page and the PROCEDURE DIVISION on a new page. Then within each of these divisions, start a new page when a major logical unit begins. If you have, for example, three 01 heading descriptions and they require about 20 lines of codes, it is much better to start a new page and to precede the program code with a comment such as

```
*THE FOLLOWING THREE ITEMS DESCRIBE THE PAGE HEADERS OF THE
*SALES REPORT.
```

Then the reader can quickly grasp the common element in the items on the page, and can choose either to give attention to the page or to bypass it.

- In the PROCEDURE DIVISION it is a good practice to list a PROGRAM SUMMARY type of module on the first page and, if there is enough space, also to list all its immediate subordinates. If there is not enough space for all the immediate subordinates, then start a new page for each first-level module and, similarly, place all its immediate subordinates on one page.

2. Use vertical alignment of similar items to convey similarity of function.

- Align all PICTURE and VALUE clauses on the same column when possible, especially with respect to each 01-level item. For example:

```
01  A.
    02 B      PIC  9(6).
    02 C      PIC  X(2)      VALUE  'ABC'.
    02 D      PIC  99V9.
    02 E      PIC  99V9.
    02 F      PIC  X(3)      VALUE  'XYZ'.
    02 G      PIC  X(29)     VALUE
              'LONG LITERAL ON SEPARATE LINE'.
```

- Align similar verbs and their operands in the PROCEDURE DIVISION, as in the following:

```
OPEN INPUT   FILE-A
             FILE-B
     OUTPUT  FILE-C
             .
             .
             .
MOVE AMOUNT       TO ED-AMOUNT
MOVE RATE         TO FACTOR
MOVE PREVIOUS-BAL TO TEST-VALUE.
```

- Indent subordinate clauses under the main clause. In the DATA DIVISION, for instance, 88 items should be indented as follows:

```
02  TRANS-CODE        PIC  X.
    88  CHANGE-RATE             VALUE '1'.
    88  CHANGE-BAL              VALUE '2'.
    88  ERROR-CODE              VALUE LOW-VALUES THRU ZERO
                                      3 THRU HIGH-VALUES.
```

In the PROCEDURE DIVISION we can use indentation, as in the following examples:

```
READ SOURCE-FILE RECORD
    AT END . . .
WRITE DISK-FILE RECORD
PERFORM PROCESS-RATE-CHANGE
        UNTIL AMOUNT-OWED > MAX-LIMIT
           OR ERROR-CODE
MOVE LAST-NAME OF TRANSACTION-FILE-REC
  TO LAST-NAME OF REPORT-REC
```

The above illustrations should serve to suggest the various possibilities. There is no reason why one should commit to memory any detailed rules of indentation. Instead, one should develop a general practice and a state of mind to indent to advantage. Within a given organization there may be "standard" indentation rules developed, but petty adherence to any strict set of rules may defeat the main purpose of indentation, which is to facilitate writing readable programs.

3. Use group labels to convey common functions.

   - In the DATA DIVISION it is desirable to group similar items under the same group item. For instance, if four totals are accumulated in a report-generating program, it is preferable to write them under one group name:

```
01  REPORT-TOTALS.
    02  PRODUCT-TOTAL
    02  SALESPERSON-TOTAL
    02  DEPARTMENT-TOTAL
    02  GRAND-TOTAL
```

   - In the PROCEDURE DIVISION, group labels can be written in many ways. As one approach a comment line preceding a group of statements may, in effect, be a group label that explains the common function:

```
*TEST WHETHER GROSS-PAY FALLS WITHIN REASONABLE LIMITS
*
IF  SALARIED-EMPL
    IF  GROSS-PAY-THIS-WEEK > MIN-SAL-LEVEL
    AND GROSS-PAY-THIS-WEEK < MAX-SAL-LEVEL
        PERFORM COMPUTE-NET
    ELSE
        PERFORM UNREASONABLE-SALARY
ELSE . . .
```

Another way of creating a group label is, of course, by the paragraph-name. It should be chosen to convey the function of the paragraph.

- Whenever a series of paragraphs constitute a logical unit, then the SECTION name should be used to give a name to the function of the whole group. (SECTIONs are discussed in Chapter 11, but we mention them here for completeness.) Remember, though, that the end of a section is signaled when another section begins. Thus if there is one section, there must be at least one additional section unless the single section is in the last physical position in the program. In general, instead of using PERFORM A THRU B (see Chapter 7) it is better to give a section name to the paragraphs A through B and then say "PERFORM section-name" instead.

4. Use similar names for similar items.

- In most programs we encounter fields such as Name or Employee-Number that are present in an input file record, an output file record, and a report record. All three records contain similar items, and we should use a naming convention that facilitates recognition of this similarity. One way to approach the nomenclature is to use qualification, which is explained in Chapter 7, as follows:

```
MOVE NAME OF EMPL-SOURCE-FILE
   TO NAME OF PAY-REG-REPORT
MOVE ADDRESS OF EMPL-SOURCE-REC
   TO ADDRESS OF EMPL-NEW-MAST-REC.
```

But qualification requires more extensive writing; therefore programmers avoid qualification in their hurry to complete the program. Actually, the typing effort associated with a programming task is a very small portion of the total programming effort, but programmers tend to place undue weight on the amount of typing involved. Therefore qualification should be considered a good approach to naming similar items and achieving good program documentation.

- Another way of naming similar items is to use a mnemonic prefix or suffix to differentiate the items. For example:

```
NAME-IN     [IN is understood to mean the input file]
NAME-WS     [WS = WORKING-STORAGE]
```

5. Use a numerical prefix to indicate the physical order of paragraphs.

- Structure charts allow for a two-dimensional representation of the program modules and their relationships. However, programs are written in one dimension—top to bottom, or beginning to end. In large programs such a statement as PERFORM GROSS-CALC provides no clue as to where the paragraph GROSS-CALC is located. We may need to scan many pages of listing to find the paragraph. To make it easy to "navigate" through the program, a numerical prefix is assigned as part of a section or paragraph name and serves as the indicator of the physical location of the section or paragraph. For example, inclusion of the numerical prefix in PERFORM 260-GROSS-CALC makes it much easier to find the paragraph-name.

R E V I E W . . . .

1. The purpose of this section has been to present the consensus of rules relating to the _____ of structured COBOL programs.

format

2. Many of the rules are concerned with spacing and indentation, with the objective particularly being to make the programs easier to [read / write].

read

3. The use of group labels in the program and the use of similar data-names for similar items particularly [minimize writing time / enhance readability] for the program.

enhance readability

4. The physical location of paragraphs in a program can be made explicit by assigning a numerical _____ to each paragraph name.

prefix

5. The rules presented in this section [should be followed strictly / are general guidelines] for establishing the format for a COBOL program.

are general guidelines

SUMMARY

This chapter was concerned with the concepts and techniques of structured programming, which is now accepted as being the appropriate method for writing COBOL programs.

We began the chapter with a study of five standard structures that are used in structured programs. Included were the COBOL commands that can be used to implement them. (1) The *sequence structure* represents the successive execution of program statements or modules. (2) The *decision structure* has two forms. The first form is the IF ... ELSE, while in the second form one of the "legs" is null, and no action is taken in that case. (3) In *pretest iteration* (or *do while*) a test is performed *before* any execution of a module. (4) In *posttest iteration* the module is executed first, and then may be executed more times according to the result of each subsequent test. (5) The *case structure* is concerned with the selection of an alternative from among several possible alternative statements or modules.

Partitioning refers to the process of subdividing a large programming task into smaller parts or functions. To achieve partitioning in a programming project, we first establish *program modules,* each of which is a *named* and *well-defined* program segment.

For purposes of designing a good program, a module can be viewed as being a *black box.* That is, we take an abstract point of view and focus on *what* the task is for each module, rather than on *how* the task is carried out. Such modules then can be organized systematically in a hierarchical structure in which there is only one top module. Each module in the resulting *structure chart* can have only one superior, but may have many subordinates.

Whereas a structure chart is based on hierarchical structure, a *flowchart* is based on sequential procedure. Because each of the five basic structures described above has *one entry* and *one exit,* their use in flowcharts permits one to focus on the detail or the summary of individual processes.

Two of the several available diagrammatic conventions for representing program structure were overviewed in this chapter. *Hierarchical Input-Process-Output (HIPO)* was developed by IBM and focuses on the *inputs, processes,* and *outputs* of programs, as the name of the approach indicates. The *Visual Table of Contents (VTOC)* diagram is the hierarchical structure chart used with this approach. In contrast, *Warnier-Orr charts* use horizontally arranged brackets rather than vertically placed blocks to represent the hierarchical structure of a program. Since these two methods are not the only ones available and no method has been accepted as the standard, in this book we use hierarchical structure charts as a simplified diagrammatic representation of programs.

Formatting rules and guidelines used with structured COBOL programs were described and illustrated in the final section of this chapter. Major consideration was given to (1) use of physical spacing in the source program; (2) use of vertical alignment of similar items to convey similarity of function; (3) use of group labels to convey common functions; (4) use of similar names for similar items; and (5) use of numerical prefixes to indicate the physical order of the paragraphs in the program.

EXERCISES

6.1 Demonstrate each of the five fundamental structures for programming in flowchart form and also through COBOL programming examples.

6.2 Figure 6-12 presents a detailed flowchart segment of a program.

FIGURE 6-12
Flowchart for Exercise 6.2

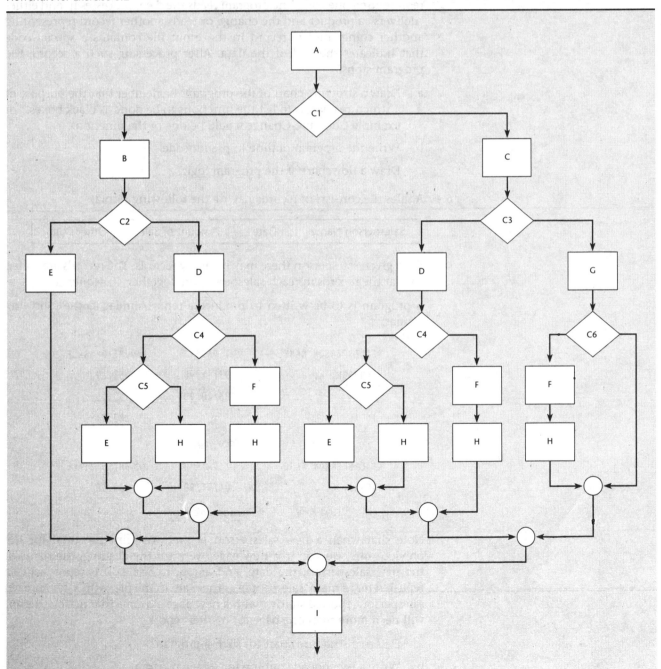

a. Demonstrate your understanding of the concept of levels of abstraction by drawing two revised versions of the flowchart—one at a high and one at an intermediate level of abstraction.

b. Draw a structure chart of the functions included in Figure 6-12. Each rectangular block in the flowchart is assumed to stand for a PERFORMed procedure. For example, the B block in the upper left of the flowchart should be visualized to be the name of a paragraph which is executed if condition C1 is false.

6.3 A program is to be developed to represent the basic logic and function of a vending machine that accepts nickels, dimes, and quarters, dispenses a 30-cent snack, and provides the correct change, if any. Coins other than nickels, dimes, and quarters are rejected. We assume that we want to develop a program that reads data records, with each data record representing one coin. The program reads the data, processes it, and either "delivers" a product and the change or reads another record representing another coin. The last record in the input file contains a special code that indicates the end of the data. After processing such a record, the program stops.

a. Draw a structure chart of the program. Remember that the purpose of a structure chart is to list the functions to be done as black boxes. For example Compute-Change would be one of the functions.

b. Write the program outline in pseudocode.

c. Draw a flowchart of the program logic.

6.4 A sales file consists of records having the following format:

Salesperson Name	Date	Amount of Sale	Other Data

For a given salesperson there may be many records. The records are sorted so that the records for each salesperson are together, in sequence.

A program is to be written to produce a report similar to the following format:

```
SALESPERSON NAME          DATE          AMOUNT OF SALE

JOHNSON, A. J.            03/11/90          132.29

                         03/20/90          150.15

TOTAL                                      282.44
```
                                 (new page)
```
SALESPERSON NAME          DATE          AMOUNT OF SALE

NOWAK, C. J.             04/01/90          300.00
```
                          (etc. for each salesperson)

Note that when a new salesperson begins, we print the total for the previous one, we skip to a new page, we print the heading, the name of the new salesperson, the date, and amount of sale. This report will be repeated for as many salespeople as there are in the file, with sales for each salesperson reported starting with a new page. Assume that no salesperson will need more than one page for his/her report.

a. Design a structure chart for such a program.

b. Write a pseudocode outline for such a program.

Additional
COBOL
Instructions

7

Additional Procedure Division Statements

THE FOUR ARITHMETIC VERBS

THE COMPUTE VERB

ADDITIONAL PERFORM OPTIONS

THE GO TO VERB

THE ACCEPT AND DISPLAY VERBS

QUALIFICATION AND THE MOVE
CORRESPONDING

CHARACTER PROCESSING VERBS

SAMPLE PROGRAM

IN THIS CHAPTER *you will do what the title directly indicates: you will study a variety of PROCEDURE DIVISION statements. The purpose of this chapter is to complete the description of the main verbs that are available in the PROCEDURE DIVISION, as a follow-up to the introduction in Chapter 2.*

An obvious characteristic of COBOL is the rich set of available commands. Unlike many other languages, COBOL consists of many specialized statements, and features within statements.

In this chapter you will study a relatively large number of verbs and the options associated with them. However, you should not expect to master all of the verbs at this point. This chapter is intended to serve as a useful reference as you continue to develop your COBOL programming skills.

THE FOUR ARITHMETIC VERBS

Chapter 4 introduced the *four basic arithmetic verbs:* ADD, SUBTRACT, MULTIPLY, and DIVIDE. Now we complete the discussion of these verbs in greater detail. Figure 7-1 presents the standard formats for the four principal arithmetic verbs. As can be seen in this figure, a variety of statement formats can be written. Rather than discuss every format, we present a number of selected and representative examples to illustrate the format and effect of executing different arithmetic statements. However, before considering the examples, we first discuss two specialized clauses that can be used with arithmetic statements in the following two subsections: the ROUNDED and ON SIZE ERROR clauses.

The ROUNDED Clause

A need frequently exists for *rounding* numeric values. For example, even though prices or rates of interest may be quoted to three or four decimal places, any billing must be rounded to two decimal places, since the smallest monetary unit is the cent. COBOL provides automatic rounding by use of the ROUNDED clause, which can be used with all arithmetic verbs.

Execution of the statement ADD A TO B ROUNDED will result in a rounded number in B. If B were specified as containing two decimal places in a PIC 999V99 description, for example, rounding would be accomplished by adding 0.005 to the result of the addition and truncating the third place. Thus if A had the value 1.286 and B had the value 2.00, ADD A TO B ROUNDED would result in the value 3.29 being stored in B. Therefore, when the remainder that is to be dropped begins with a 5 or higher value, the number is rounded up; otherwise, it is rounded down. If B were specified to contain one place to the right of the decimal (say PIC 999V9), 0.05 is added to the result of the addition, and the second place is truncated.

The ON SIZE ERROR Clause

The case may arise in which an arithmetic result is larger than anticipated, in terms of the number of digit positions available. For example, a person earning $10.00 per hour should have a weekly gross pay well under $999.99. But suppose that by some mistake in the input the computed weekly pay is over $1,000.00. Rather than allow truncation of this figure to occur, such "overflows" can be detected by use of the ON SIZE ERROR clause. For example, assume GROSS has PICTURE 999V99. We can write

```
MULTIPLY RATE BY HOURS GIVING GROSS
    ON SIZE ERROR
        MOVE "GROSS PAY EXCEEDS $999.99" TO ERR-MESSAGE.
```

The ON SIZE ERROR clause is simply a conditional statement that says, if the size of a value does not fit in the field, do whatever is indicated in the statement that follows in that sentence. The statement that follows must be imperative; that is, it cannot be conditional. When ON SIZE ERROR is used and the condition is met, the arithmetic operand intended to receive the result is not altered from its previous value. In other words, it is as if the arithmetic operations had not happened.

In addition to "large" results, the ON SIZE ERROR condition also is met when there is a division by zero. As you may recall from algebra, division by zero is an undefined operation yielding an "infinitely" large quotient.

In COBOL '85 two enhancements have been made that are included as the last two lines in each of the formats presented in Figure 7-1. These are the NOT

FIGURE 7-1

Standard COBOL Formats for the Four Arithmetic Verbs

$$
\underline{ADD} \begin{Bmatrix} \text{identifier -1} \\ \text{literal -1} \end{Bmatrix} \begin{bmatrix} \text{identifier -2} \\ \text{literal -2} \end{bmatrix} \dots \underline{TO} \text{ identifier-m } [\underline{ROUNDED}]
$$

[identifier-n [ROUNDED]] . . . [ON SIZE ERROR imperative-statement-1]

[NOT ON SIZE ERROR imperative-statement-2]

[END-ADD]

$$
ADD \begin{Bmatrix} \text{identifier -1} \\ \text{literal -1} \end{Bmatrix} \begin{bmatrix} \text{identifier -2} \\ \text{literal -2} \end{bmatrix} \begin{bmatrix} \text{identifier -3} \\ \text{literal -3} \end{bmatrix} \dots
$$

GIVING identifier-m [ROUNDED] [identifier-n [ROUNDED]] . . .

[ON SIZE ERROR imperative-statement-1]

[NOT ON SIZE ERROR imperative-statement-2]

[END-ADD]

$$
\underline{SUBTRACT} \begin{Bmatrix} \text{identifier -1} \\ \text{literal -1} \end{Bmatrix} \begin{bmatrix} \text{identifier -2} \\ \text{literal -2} \end{bmatrix} \dots \underline{FROM} \text{ identifier-m } [\underline{ROUNDED}]
$$

[identifier-n [ROUNDED]] . . . [ON SIZE ERROR imperative-statement-1]

[NOT ON SIZE ERROR] imperative-statement-2]

[END-SUBTRACT]

$$
\underline{SUBTRACT} \begin{Bmatrix} \text{identifier -1} \\ \text{literal -1} \end{Bmatrix} \begin{bmatrix} \text{identifier -2} \\ \text{literal -2} \end{bmatrix} \dots \underline{FROM} \begin{Bmatrix} \text{identifier -m} \\ \text{literal -m} \end{Bmatrix}
$$

GIVING identifier-n [ROUNDED] [identifier-o [ROUNDED]] . . .

[ON SIZE ERROR imperative-statement-1]

[NOT ON SIZE ERROR imperative-statement-2]

[END-SUBTRACT]

$$
\underline{MULTIPLY} \begin{Bmatrix} \text{identifier -1} \\ \text{literal -1} \end{Bmatrix} \underline{BY} \text{ identifier-2 } [\underline{ROUNDED}]
$$

[identifier-3 [ROUNDED]] . . . [ON SIZE ERROR imperative-statement-1]

[NOT ON SIZE ERROR imperative-statement-2]

[END-MULTIPLY]

$$
\underline{MULTIPLY} \begin{Bmatrix} \text{identifier -1} \\ \text{literal -1} \end{Bmatrix} \underline{BY} \begin{Bmatrix} \text{identifier -2} \\ \text{literal -2} \end{Bmatrix} \underline{GIVING} \text{ identifier-3 } [\underline{ROUNDED}]
$$

[identifier-4 [ROUNDED]] . . . [ON SIZE ERROR imperative-statement-1]

[NOT ON SIZE ERROR imperative-statement-2]

[END-MULTIPLY]

$$
\underline{DIVIDE} \begin{Bmatrix} \text{identifier -1} \\ \text{literal -1} \end{Bmatrix} \underline{INTO} \text{ identifier-2 } [\underline{ROUNDED}]
$$

[identifier-3 [ROUNDED]] . . . [ON SIZE ERROR imperative-statement-1]

[NOT ON SIZE ERROR imperative-statement-2]

[END-DIVIDE]

$$
\underline{DIVIDE} \begin{Bmatrix} \text{identifier -1} \\ \text{literal -1} \end{Bmatrix} \underline{INTO} \begin{Bmatrix} \text{identifier -2} \\ \text{literal -2} \end{Bmatrix} \underline{GIVING} \text{ identifier-3 } [\underline{ROUNDED}]
$$

[identifier-4 [ROUNDED]] . . . [ON SIZE ERROR imperative-statement-1]

[NOT ON SIZE ERROR imperative-statement-2]

[END-DIVIDE]

<u>DIVIDE</u> $\begin{Bmatrix} \text{identifier -1} \\ \text{literal -1} \end{Bmatrix}$ <u>BY</u> $\begin{Bmatrix} \text{identifier -2} \\ \text{literal -2} \end{Bmatrix}$ <u>GIVING</u> identifier-3 [<u>ROUNDED</u>]

<u>REMAINDER</u> identifier-4 [ON <u>SIZE ERROR</u> imperative-statement-1]

[<u>NOT</u> ON <u>SIZE ERROR</u> imperative-statement-2]

[<u>END-DIVIDE</u>]

<u>DIVIDE</u> $\begin{Bmatrix} \text{identifier -1} \\ \text{literal -1} \end{Bmatrix}$ <u>INTO</u> $\begin{Bmatrix} \text{identifier -2} \\ \text{literal -2} \end{Bmatrix}$ <u>GIVING</u> identifier-3 [<u>ROUNDED</u>]

[identifier-4 [ROUNDED]] . . . [ON <u>SIZE ERROR</u> imperative-statement-1]

[<u>NOT</u> ON <u>SIZE ERROR</u> imperative-statement-2]

[<u>END-DIVIDE</u>]

<u>DIVIDE</u> $\begin{Bmatrix} \text{identifier -1} \\ \text{literal -1} \end{Bmatrix}$ <u>BY</u> $\begin{Bmatrix} \text{identifier -2} \\ \text{literal -2} \end{Bmatrix}$ <u>GIVING</u> identifier-3 [<u>ROUNDED</u>]

<u>REMAINDER</u> identifier-4 [ON <u>SIZE ERROR</u> imperative-statement-1]

[<u>NOT</u> ON <u>SIZE ERROR</u> imperative-statement-2]

[<u>END-DIVIDE</u>]

ON SIZE ERROR clause and the END-verb terminators. Figure 7-2 presents code and corresponding flowcharts for purposes of illustrating and contrasting COBOL '74 and COBOL '85. The flowcharts are intended to show the actual meaning of the program statements. As can be seen in the figure, because the 1974 version does not have the NOT ON SIZE ERROR and END-ADD features, a test flag field (SIZE-ERR-TEST) was used to code the required logic. In contrast, the program code for the 1985 version is much more straightforward.

The ON SIZE ERROR and other conditionals such as the AT END are actually specialized IF statements; in this vein, they apply until a period is encountered. In COBOL '74 the ON SIZE ERROR provides for a course of action when the condition is true, but it does not provide for a course of action when it is false. The 1985 version allows for a symmetrical specification with the ON SIZE ERROR and NOT ON SIZE ERROR dual alternatives, as illustrated in the flowchart in the second column of Figure 7-2.

The END-verb clause provides for termination of the SIZE ERROR conditional statement. Notice that in the example in Figure 7-2, there is no period after the END-ADD, and none is required. As the flowchart illustrates, the MOVE Z TO A is executed regardless of the truth or falsity of the SIZE ERROR condition.

As a final point, let us test our understanding of the difference in the two sample program codes in Figure 7-2. Suppose that in each case the following program statement preceded the code:

```
.
.
W   PIC 9.
.
.
MOVE 3 TO W
MOVE 10 TO X
MOVE 20 TO Y
```

Deliberately, W has been defined with PIC 9 in the DATA DIVISION, which then invariably will result in the SIZE ERROR condition being true in the example

FIGURE 7-2
ON SIZE ERROR Illustration

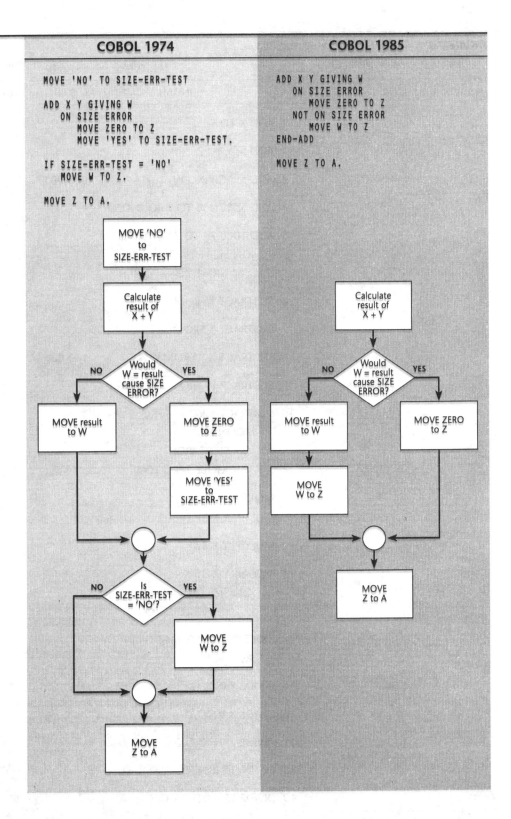

above. What is the value stored in A at the completion of each program version in Figure 7-2? The answer is, A is equal to zero.

Use of the Arithmetic Verbs

Figure 7-3 presents a set of examples involving the use of the arithmetic verbs. Review these examples and note the effects of the various forms of the instructions

FIGURE 7-3
Examples of the Use of Arithmetic Verbs

	W	X	Y	Z
PICTURE:	S999V99	999V99	999V99	999
INITIAL VALUE:	010.0̄0̄	090.00	030.00	040
1. ADD X TO Y			120.00	
2. ADD X, Y TO Z				160
3. ADD 5 Y GIVING W	035.00			
4. ADD X, 12.456 TO Y ROUNDED			132.46	

5. ADD 1000.25 TO Y ROUNDED
    ON SIZE ERROR
        MOVE ZERO TO Z
				000

6. SUBTRACT Y FROM X		060.00		
7. SUBTRACT X FROM Y			060.00	
8. SUBTRACT X Y FROM W	130.0̄0̄			
9. SUBTRACT W FROM X GIVING Y			100.00	

10. SUBTRACT 1260.256 FROM Y
    ROUNDED
    ON SIZE ERROR
        MOVE ZERO TO Z
				000

11. MOVE 10 TO X MULTIPLY X BY Y		010.00	300.00	
12. MULTIPLY X BY Y			700.00	

13. MULTIPLY X BY Y
    ON SIZE ERROR
        MOVE ZERO TO Z
				000

14. MULTIPLY Y BY 0.2453 GIVING X ROUNDED		077.36		
15. DIVIDE Y INTO X		003.00		
16. DIVIDE X INTO Y			000.33	
17. DIVIDE Z INTO 100 GIVING Y			002.50	
18. DIVIDE 12.2 INTO X Y ROUNDED		007.37	002.46	
19. DIVIDE 12.2 INTO Y GIVING Z REMAINDER X		005.60		002
20. DIVIDE Z BY 12.2 GIVING Y ROUNDED REMAINDER X		000.10	003.28	

on the data fields. Negative values are indicated by a negative sign above the rightmost digit of a number, while decimal points are indicated by a caret (∧). In addition, the following paragraphs direct your attention to some particular results.

Example 4 illustrates the effect of the ROUNDED clause. The result of 132.456 has been rounded to 132.46 because Y has two decimal positions.

Example 5 shows the effect of the ON SIZE ERROR clause. Since Y has three positions to the left of the decimal point, the result 1030.25 is too large. Incidentally, if the ON SIZE ERROR had not been used, the result in Y would have been stored as 030.25 due to truncation of the first significant digit.

Example 7 illustrates that a negative result is stored as an absolute value (without sign) if the numeric field does not include the S PICTURE character.

Example 8 illustrates the application of the rule of arithmetic that subtracting from a negative value is equivalent to adding the number to be subtracted to that negative value.

Example 12 illustrates that truncation will occur if the number is larger than the defined field.

Example 18 shows the effects of the absence of ROUNDED in the result in X and the presence of ROUNDED in the result in Y. Incidentally, it is permissible to write DIVIDE 12.2 INTO X ROUNDED Y ROUNDED.

Example 19 illustrates the storage of the integer result in Z (since the PICTURE of Z is integer) and storage of the remainder in X. The remainder is determined as follows. Because the integer quotient is $30.00 / 12.2 = 2$, the remainder is $30.00 - (2 \times 12.2) = 5.6$.

Example 20 shows that the value is stored in the REMAINDER field before the rounding takes place. Thus the unrounded quotient is 3.278, which, if stored in Y, would have been stored unrounded as 3.27. The remainder is, then, $40 - (3.27 \times 12.2) = 0.106$, which is stored (right-truncated) in X as 0.10.

R E V I E W . . . .

1. If the result of an arithmetic operation is 45.4545, rounding to three decimal places will result in the value _____ being placed in a storage location, whereas rounding to two places will result in the value _____ being placed in the storage location.

   45.455; 45.45

2. If the ROUNDED option is not used, 45.4545 reported to three places would result in the value _____ , whereas the value reported to two places would be _____ .

   45.454; 45.45

3. When the number of digits of an arithmetic result is greater than the number defined in the PIC specifications, such an overflow can be signaled by use of the _____ clause.

   ON SIZE ERROR

4. In addition to the availability of the ON SIZE ERROR clause, COBOL '85 provides for a course of action when there is no such error by the _____ clause.

   NOT ON SIZE ERROR

5. In COBOL '85 termination of the SIZE ERROR statement, or processing associated with any verb, is signalled clearly by the _____-verb clause.

   END

6. Complete the following table by entering the numeric result of each arithmetic operation:

	W	X	Y	Z
PICTURE:	99V9	99	99V9	S999.9
INITIAL VALUE:	15.0	10	12.8	100.0

1. ADD W, Y TO X
2. ADD W, Y GIVING X ROUNDED
3. SUBTRACT W FROM Y
4. SUBTRACT W FROM Y GIVING Z
5. MULTIPLY W BY Y
6. MULTIPLY X BY Y GIVING Z
   ROUNDED
7. DIVIDE X INTO Y ON SIZE
   ERROR MOVE ZERO TO X
8. DIVIDE X INTO Y ROUNDED
   REMAINDER Z

1. $X = 37$	5. $Y = 92_\wedge 0$
2. $X = 28$	6. $Z = 128_\wedge 8$
3. $Y = 02_\wedge 2$	7. $Y = 1_\wedge 2$
4. $Z = 002_\wedge \bar{2}$	8. $Y = 1_\wedge 3; Z = 008_\wedge 8$
	$[= 12.8 - (1.2 \times 10)]$

THE COMPUTE VERB

Use of the four arithmetic verbs we have studied thus far is well suited for single arithmetic operations, but suppose it is required that an answer be obtained by use of such a formula as $a = 3b - c + b(d - 2)$. If we were to use the four arithmetic verbs to evaluate this expression, a large number of statements would be required. However, use of the COMPUTE verb along with symbolic arithmetic operators makes it possible to write compact arithmetic statements for mathematical expressions.

Table 7-1 lists the symbols used for the arithmetic operations of addition, subtraction, multiplication, division, and exponentiation. Only the symbols for multiplication and exponentiation are different from the symbols commonly used in mathematics. In addition to the symbols, parentheses can be used to designate the *order of operations;* however, unlike their use in algebra, parentheses never are used to designate multiplication.

TABLE 7-1
The Five Arithmetic Operations in COBOL

+	Addition
–	Subtraction
*	Multiplication
/	Division
**	Exponentiation (raising to a power)

An *arithmetic expression* is formed by the use of arithmetic operators and data-names or literals. At least one space must separate each operator symbol from the preceding and following data-names, with parentheses used to designate or clarify the order of operations. Some examples of arithmetic expressions are shown here.

ALGEBRAIC EXPRESSION	COBOL ARITHMETIC EXPRESSION
$a + b$	A + B
$a - b + (a - 5)c$	A - B + (A - 5) * C
$a^2 - \dfrac{b + c}{2}$	A * *2 - (B + C) / 2

When parentheses are used, the operations within the parentheses are completed first, with order of priority given to the innermost sets, working from left to right in the arithmetic expression. In the absence of parentheses, the arithmetic operations are performed according to the following order of priority:

1. Exponentiation
2. Multiplication and division from left to right in the order written
3. Addition and subtraction from left to right in the order written

Consider the following COBOL examples:

COBOL ARITHMETIC EXPRESSION	ALGEBRAIC EXPRESSION
A + B / C	$a + \dfrac{b}{c}$
(A + B) / C	$\dfrac{a + b}{c}$
A + (B / C)	$a + \dfrac{b}{c}$

The first and third COBOL expressions represent the same algebraic expression. This is so because in the first example the rule that division takes priority over addition applies. Nevertheless, it is good programming practice to include the parentheses in such cases, since it improves documentation.

In addition to the five arithmetic operations, COBOL defines a " + " and a " – " *unary* operator. The operator is simply an instruction to multiply a variable by +1 or –1, respectively. Thus, if we want to multiply variable B times the negative value of variable A, we could use the unary operator as follows:

```
B * (- A)
```

The "–" in the above expression is the unary operator. In this example parentheses are used to avoid having two consecutive arithmetic operators.

Returning to the COMPUTE verb, we note that the general format associated with the use of this verb is

COMPUTE {identifier-1 [ROUNDED]} . . . = arithmetic-expression-1

    [ON SIZE ERROR imperative-statement-1]

    [NOT ON SIZE ERROR imperative-statement-2]

    [END-COMPUTE]

A simple example of using the COMPUTE verb is

```
COMPUTE GROSS = (REGULAR * WAGE) + 1.5 * (OVERTIME * WAGE).
```

An example that includes use of the ROUNDED and ON SIZE ERROR options is

```
COMPUTE GROSS ROUNDED =
    (REGULAR * WAGE) + 1.5 * (OVERTIME * WAGE)
    ON SIZE ERROR
        PERFORM GROSS-TOO-BIG.
```

The NOT ON SIZE ERROR clause and the END-COMPUTE terminator are available only in the 1985 standard. These additional features are used for the same purposes as for the arithmetic verbs, as described in the preceding section of this chapter.

The identifier-1 in the COMPUTE format is the storage field that receives the results. It should be noted that it can be a numeric or numeric edited item. It really corresponds to the GIVING identifier clause in the other arithmetic verbs. All identifiers on the right-hand side, however, must be elementary numeric (nonedited) items.

The arithmetic operators +, –, *, and / correspond to the verbs ADD, SUBTRACT, MULTIPLY, and DIVIDE, respectively. The arithmetic operator ** has no corresponding verb and can be used only with the COMPUTE. Since exponentiation is a general mathematical process, it can be used to extract square roots as well as to raise numbers to various powers. Thus A**2 means a^2, but A**0.5 means $\sqrt{A}$. This facility to extract roots increases the usefulness of the exponentiation operator. In general, however, COBOL has limited computational capabilities. COBOL is used for data processing tasks rather than for computational tasks. Thus logarithmic and trigonometric functions are not available in COBOL, although they commonly are available in languages developed for scientific work.

R E V I E W . . . .

1. As an alternative to the arithmetic verbs, arithmetic operators can be used in conjunction with the _____ verb.

    COMPUTE

2. The arithmetic symbols used with the COMPUTE verb—which indicate the operations addition, subtraction, multiplication, division, and exponentiation— are _____ , _____ , _____ , _____ , and _____ , respectively.

    +, –, *, /, and **

3. The COBOL arithmetic expression corresponding to the algebraic expression $a^2 - 2ac + c^2$ is _____ .

    (A**2) – (2 * A * C) + (C**2) (See further comment in the next review item.)

4. Suppose that all the parentheses included in the above answer were omitted. The algebraic expression that corresponds to the resulting COBOL expression would be _____ .

    $a^2 - 2ac + c^2$ (Discussion continued in the next review item.)

5. Therefore, because of the order in which the arithmetic operations always are performed, no parentheses are required in the COBOL expression just given. However, such parentheses usually are included to improve readability of the program. In the absence of parentheses, the order of priority for the arithmetic operations is such that _____ always is performed first, followed by _____ and _____ , and culminating with _____ and _____ .

    exponentiation; multiplication; division; addition; subtraction

6. Typically, however, the use or nonuse of parentheses *does* make a difference in the way a COBOL arithmetic expression is evaluated. For each of the following COBOL expressions, indicate the equivalent algebraic expression:

COBOL ARITHMETIC EXPRESSION	ALGEBRAIC EXPRESSION
((A + (B * C)) / D)**2	_____
(A + (B * C)) / D**2	_____
A + (B * C) / D**2	_____
A + B * C / D**2	_____

$$\left(\frac{a+bc}{c}\right)^2; \quad \frac{a+bc}{d^2}; \quad a+\frac{bc}{d^2}; \quad a+\frac{bc}{d^2}$$

7. An example of the use of the unary operator in a simple COBOL expression involving multiplication is _____ .

A * (−B) (or other similar example)

8. In the general format associated with the COMPUTE verb, the results of the arithmetic operation are stored in [identifier-1 / arithmetic-expression-1].

identifier-1

. . . .

ADDITIONAL PERFORM OPTIONS

The PERFORM ... TIMES

There are tasks in which a procedure needs to be executed a definite number of times, and in such cases the TIMES option is useful. The format is

PERFORM [procedure -name] $\begin{Bmatrix} \text{integer} \\ \text{identifier} \end{Bmatrix}$ TIMES

[imperative -statement]

[END-PERFORM]

As an example, in accounting applications we sometimes need to form the "sum of the digits" for depreciating an asset over N years, where N is always an integer (whole number). In general, the required sum is $1 + 2 + 3 + ... + (N-1) + N$. Thus, if N = 5, we have $1 + 2 + 3 + 4 + 5 = 15$. In a COBOL program, we can form the sum-of-digits for N, by using the TIMES option, as follows:

```
MOVE ZERO TO SUM-OF-DIGITS
MOVE 1 TO YEAR-COUNTER
PERFORM FORM-SUM N TIMES
   .
   .
   .
FORM-SUM.
   ADD YEAR-COUNTER TO SUM-OF-DIGITS
   ADD 1 TO YEAR-COUNTER.
```

Alternatively, using the in-line PERFORM of COBOL '85, we could write

```
MOVE ZERO TO SUM-OF-DIGITS
MOVE 1 TO YEAR-COUNTER
PERFORM N TIMES
    ADD YEAR-COUNTER TO SUM-OF-DIGITS
    ADD 1 TO YEAR-COUNTER
END-PERFORM.
```

The PERFORM ... THRU

Instead of PERFORMing one procedure, it is possible to reference a series of procedures that are all written in sequence by referencing the first and the last procedure. In general, whenever we have "procedure-name" in a PERFORM format, we can substitute

$$\underline{PERFORM} \quad procedure\text{-}name\text{-}1 \left\{ \begin{array}{l} \underline{THROUGH} \\ \underline{THRU} \end{array} \right\} procedure\text{-}name\text{-}2$$

Consider the following example:

```
PERFORM PROCESS-DETAIL-START THRU PROCESS DETAIL-EXIT
    UNTIL END-OF-FILE = 'YES'.
    .
    .
    .
PROCESS-DETAIL-START.
    ADD . . . .
COMPUTE-SPECIAL-PRICE.
    IF . . .
READ-RECORD.
    READ CUSTOMER-FILE
        AT END MOVE 'YES' TO END-OF-FILE.
PROCESS-DETAIL-EXIT.
    EXIT.
```

The example, in effect, states that the group of paragraphs that begin with the one named PROCESS-DETAIL-START through the one named PROCESS-DETAIL-EXIT are to be executed in sequence, one after another. When the last statement in the last-named paragraph is executed, then program execution returns to the original PERFORM statement. In everyday language the PERFORM ... THRU states

Perform the group of consecutive paragraphs that begins with the first-named paragraph and ends with the second-named paragraph.

With use of the PERFORM ... THRU option, it is common practice to use the specialized EXIT verb to mark the last paragraph in the THRU range. The last paragraph consists of only one statement, the EXIT statement. In effect, the EXIT is a do-nothing, or "no-op" (no-operation) statement. It allows the programmer to identify a place in the program but it does not require any processing. In the above example the only purpose for the EXIT is program documentation: it simply makes it easier for the reader of the program to see that PROCESS-DETAIL-EXIT is the last paragraph in a PERFORM ... THRU range of paragraphs. At other times the EXIT statement is used in conjunction with the GO TO verb, discussed later in this chapter. Briefly, if we want to bypass execution of some paragraph(s) in a range of paragraphs referenced by a PERFORM ... THRU, we could include a statement such as

```
IF some condition is true
    GO TO PROCESS-DETAIL-EXIT.
```

The effect of this code would be to reach the end of the range and return to the original PERFORM ... THRU without executing anything else (recall that EXIT is a no-op type of statement).

Although the THRU option is available, we do not recommend its use except for very special circumstances. The reason is that it relies heavily on the physical position of paragraphs. For instance, in the above example, if the COMPUTE-SPECIAL-PRICE paragraph were moved elsewhere in the program, a most serious error would result.

Instead of using the THRU option, we recommend using one paragraph that, in turn, includes PERFORM commands that make reference to each of the other paragraphs. Using such an approach for the above example, we have

```
        PERFORM PROCESS-CUSTOMER
            UNTIL END-OF-FILE = 'YES'.
            .
            .
            .
    PROCESS-CUSTOMER.
        PERFORM PROCESS-DETAIL
        PERFORM COMPUTE-SPECIAL-PRICE
        PERFORM READ-RECORD.
    PROCESS-DETAIL.
        ADD . . .
    COMPUTE-SPECIAL-PRICE.
        IF . . .
    READ-RECORD.
        READ CUSTOMER-FILE . . .
```

In this revised structure the physical position of paragraphs is irrelevant, and the relationship among the paragraphs is clear.

Alternatively, in COBOL '85 we can use an in-line PERFORM, as follows:

```
    PERFORM UNTIL END-OF-FILE = 'YES'
        PERFORM PROCESS-DETAIL
        PERFORM COMPUTE-SPECIAL-PRICE
        PERFORM READ-RECORD
    END-PERFORM.
```

Nested PERFORM statements

We have already seen examples of *nested PERFORM statements:* one paragraph performs another paragraph, which, in turn, performs another paragraph, and so on. Such nesting is common and useful. In a structure chart it corresponds to blocks at systematically lower levels. However, one important rule is that we cannot have *cyclical (recursive) nesting.* Consider this example:

```
    PAR-A.
        PERFORM PAR-B.
    PAR-B.
        PERFORM PAR-C.
    PAR-C.
        PERFORM PAR-A
        PERFORM PAR-B.
```

Both PERFORM statements in PAR-C are in error; it is not valid to issue a PER-FORM backwards. What will happen if we do? In general, the results are unpredictable, and often are very strange, depending on the particular compiler used. In fact, if a program compiles without errors and then during execution does "strange" things, it may be well worth the effort to check for the possibility of cyclical PERFORM statements.

When the THRU option is exercised, it is possible to have one or more PERFORM statements included in the range of procedure-1 to procedure-2. These are nested PERFORM statements. It is also possible to have PERFORM statements whose range is totally outside the range of the first PERFORM. The following two examples illustrate the two permitted structures:

CORRECT STRUCTURE

```
A.    . . . PERFORM B THRU F.
B.                                        ┌─── B
C.    . . . PERFORM D THRU E.             │
D.                                        │  ┌ D
E.                                        │  └ E
F.                                        └─── F
```

CORRECT STRUCTURE

```
A.    . . . PERFORM B THRU D.
B.                                 ┌─ B
C.    . . . PERFORM M THRU Q.      │        . . . PERFORM M THRU Q.
D.                                 └─ D
G.
M.                                 ┌─ M
I.                                 │
Q.                                 └─ Q
```

Finally, the following example illustrates an incorrect structure:

INCORRECT STRUCTURE

```
A.    . . . PERFORM B THRU E.      ┌── B
B.                                 │ ┌ D
C.    . . . PERFORM D THRU F.      │ │
D.                                 │ │
E.                                 └─┼ E
F.                                   └ F
```

R E V I E W . . . .

1. The format of the PERFORM statement that specifies execution of a procedure a definite number of times is the PERFORM ... _____ .

    TIMES

2. The PERFORM ... THRU format permits the execution of [two / two or more] procedures.

    two or more

3. Suppose that four consecutive paragraphs are to be executed by use of the PERFORM ... THRU command. The PERFORM statement specifically would include reference to [two / four] procedure-names.

    two

4. Because a change in the physical position of paragraphs generally would disrupt the intent of a PERFORM ... THRU command, the use of this format has to be considered as being _____-prone.

    error

5. When a PERFORM statement results in execution of a paragraph that itself contains another PERFORM statement (and so forth), the program structure is described as having a _____ PERFORM structure.

nested

6. The type of nesting of PERFORM statements that is not allowed, and may have unpredictable results upon program execution, is _____ nesting.

cyclical (recursive)

7. The "no-op" type of verb discussed in this section that is always used alone in a paragraph is the _____ verb.

EXIT

8. A common use of the EXIT verb is to indicate the _____ of a PERFORM ... THRU range of paragraphs for documentation purposes.

end (or last paragraph)

THE GO TO VERB

For a long time the GO TO was one of the most frequently used verbs in all programming languages. However, it has been found that its unrestricted use is likely to create difficulty in reading a program and may contribute to the development of error-prone programs. With some minor exceptions in this book we refrain from the use of GO TO. Still, programs written in the first quarter-century of programming history are full of GO TO statements, and the reader should be familiar with this control verb.

GO TO is an unconditional branch to a paragraph or section name (sections are discussed in chapter 11). Consider the following example, which incorporates use of the GO TO:

```
READING-DATA.
    READ EMPLOYEE-FILE
        AT END GO TO WRAP-UP.
    PERFORM PROCESS-EMPLOYEE
    GO TO READING-DATA.
PROCESS-EMPLOYEE.
    .
    .
    .
WRAP-UP.
    PERFORM. . . .
    CLOSE. . .
    STOP RUN.
```

Notice that AT END the program specifies GO TO WRAP-UP, which terminates the program, among other things. If the AT END is not true, PERFORM PROCESS-EMPLOYEE is executed and then execution continues with GO TO READING-DATA. This last GO TO implements an iterative procedure, and it does so by referring to its own paragraph name.

Use of the GO TO in simple programs, such as the above example, seems straightforward and even, perhaps, appealing. However, in programs of typical size and complexity, use of GO TO is likely to cause unnecessary complications in logic. Of course, it should be made very clear that the use of the GO TO in the above example is unstructured code!

1. The COBOL verb that provides the programmer with the capability of achieving unconditional branching in a program without returning to the point of original branching is the _____ .

                                                                        GO TO

2. The GO TO verb has been used in both COBOL and other programming languages. The use of this verb steadily has been [increasing / decreasing] in recent years.

                                                                        decreasing

. . . .

THE ACCEPT AND DISPLAY VERBS

Up to this point we always have discussed input and output in connection with files. Such is the normal use of input and output verbs, but it also is possible to execute input and output in conjunction with storage fields that are not part of any files. This typically is done to permit the input and/or output of short data items to or from devices such as video terminals, the system console, and printers. The verbs that allow such input and output are ACCEPT and DISPLAY.

The ACCEPT Verb

There are two general formats associated with use of the ACCEPT verb. The first format is

FORMAT 1

ACCEPT identifier [FROM mnemonic-name]

This format can be used as in this example:

```
ACCEPT STARTING-CHECK-NO FROM OPERATOR-CONSOLE.
```

As a result of executing this instruction, the computer will input data into the STARTING-CHECK-NO storage field from the device previously defined as OPERATOR-CONSOLE in the SPECIAL-NAMES paragraph of the ENVIRONMENT DIVISION, as in, for instance:

```
ENVIRONMENT DIVISION.
CONFIGURATION SECTION.
SOURCE-COMPUTER.  . . .
OBJECT-COMPUTER.  . . .
SPECIAL-NAMES.
   CONSOLE IS  OPERATOR-CONSOLE.
```

If this device is a keyboard, further program execution is delayed until the operator enters the appropriate input. If the device referenced in the ACCEPT is a file, the next record will be read, and data will be input into STARTING-CHECK-NO.

Data input via ACCEPT is treated as if it were alphanumeric with respect to positioning. Suppose that STARTING-CHECK-NO has been defined with a PICTURE 99999. If ACCEPT is executed with reference to the operator's control terminal and the operator types in 12345, the receiving field will contain 12345. On the other hand, if the operator types 12, the 12 will be stored left-justified in

STARTING-CHECK-NO, followed by three blanks. In general, an entire record is moved from the input device to the identifier specified in ACCEPT. Thus, when we typed 12 above, we were, in effect, transmitting a whole line from the terminal with blanks trailing the 12.

The second general format of ACCEPT is

FORMAT 2

$$\underline{\text{ACCEPT}} \quad \text{identifier} \quad \underline{\text{FROM}} \left\{ \begin{array}{l} \underline{\text{DATE}} \\ \underline{\text{DAY}} \\ \underline{\text{DAY-OF-WEEK}} \\ \underline{\text{TIME}} \end{array} \right\}$$

This format of ACCEPT can be used to move the contents of the COBOL pre-defined fields DATE, DAY, DAY-OF-WEEK, or TIME to a specified identifier. These latter fields are not defined by the programmer but are made available by the compiler. Their implicit definition is

1. DATE   PIC 999999
2. DAY   PIC 99999
3. DAY-OF-WEEK   PIC 9
4. TIME   PIC 99999999

1. The DATE field contains the year, month, and day. Assume that TODAY was defined as follows:

   ```
   02  TODAY.
       03  T-YEAR      PIC 99.
       03  T-MONTH     PIC 99.
       03  T-DAY       PIC 99.
   ```

   The instruction ACCEPT TODAY FROM DATE issued on February 1, 1990, will cause the content of DATE, 900201, to be moved to TODAY.

2. The DAY field contains the year and the day of the year, counting from January 1 as 001 to December 31 as 365 (assuming a nonleap year). Thus, February 1, 1990, would be stored as 90032.

3. The DAY-OF-WEEK yields a one-digit code that corresponds to the days of the week as follows: 1 = Monday, 2 = Tuesday, ..., 7 = Sunday. For example, if we define

   ```
   02  DAY-NAME-CODE  PIC 9.
       88  MONDAY      VALUE 1.
       88  TUESDAY     VALUE 2.
       .
       .
       .
       88  SUNDAY      VALUE 7.
   ```

   Then we can use program statements like the following:

   ```
   ACCEPT DAY-NAME-CODE FROM DAY-OF-WEEK
   IF MONDAY PERFORM MONDAY-ROUTINE.
   IF TUESDAY PERFORM TUESDAY-ROUTINE.
       .
       .
       .
   ```

4. TIME contains hours, minutes, seconds, and hundredths of a second, based on elapsed time after midnight on a 24-hour-clock. Thus, 8:30 p.m. is stored as 20300000. The smallest value of TIME is 00000000, and the largest is 23595999.

The DISPLAY Verb

The general format associated with use of the DISPLAY verb is

$$
\underline{\text{DISPLAY}} \quad \begin{Bmatrix} \text{identifier -1} \\ \text{literal -1} \end{Bmatrix} \begin{bmatrix} \text{, identifier -2} \\ \text{, literal -2} \end{bmatrix} \ldots [\underline{\text{UPON}} \text{ mnemonic-name}]
$$

$$
[\text{WITH } \underline{\text{NO ADVANCING}}]
$$

Notice that DISPLAY can reference a series of identifiers or literals. Thus, we can write

```
DISPLAY
  AMOUNT-A, 'IS A VALUE OUT OF RANGE' UPON OPERATOR-CONSOLE.
```

Execution of this statement will result in the contents of the storage field AMOUNT-A followed by the literal message in the quotation marks being output on the device named OPERATOR-CONSOLE.

In some computer installations ACCEPT and DISPLAY can be used only with devices predefined by the installation itself; thus the device will not be named in the statement. For example, writing ACCEPT CODE-A may be valid and would refer to some specific device in the particular installation, such as the operator's console. Similarly, DISPLAY ERR-MESSAGE-1 may be valid in installations in which the DISPLAY verb is associated automatically with a particular device, such as the operator's console or a specific printer.

A common use of DISPLAY is for program debugging purposes. For instance, if we encounter an error in results associated with a field MEN-TOTAL-SALARY, we may want to DISPLAY the contents of this field each time a value is added to it, as in the following example:

```
DISPLAY
  'MEN-TOTAL-SALARY BEFORE ADDING = '  MEN-TOTAL-SALARY
ADD EMPLOYEE-SALARY TO MEN-TOTAL-SALARY
DISPLAY
  '                    AFTER  ADDING = '  MEN-TOTAL-SALARY
```

As an illustration, the output resulting from execution of the above statements might be:

```
MEN-TOTAL-SALARY BEFORE ADDING = 0125000
                 AFTER  ADDING = 0149250
```

These statements allow the programmer to trace the accumulation of values in the target field and, perhaps, provide a clue as to the cause of the error. We could, of course, use the WRITE verb to do the same thing, but it would require additional specifications and commands. For instance, a WORKING-STORAGE group item consisting of two elementary fields would have to be defined: one field for the explanatory header in the above examples and one for the content of MEN-TOTAL-SALARY. Then we would MOVE and WRITE the appropriate data.

In the 1985 standard a new enhancement of DISPLAY has been introduced that includes the WITH NO ADVANCING option. This option is useful when writing on a video monitor because it prevents the cursor from moving to the next line, which is the normal action after a DISPLAY command.

The ACCEPT and DISPLAY verbs are also used to handle input and output on a video monitor. Cursor positioning, and special print effects such as a message in bold or in blinking mode, are features that we want to be able to program for interactive processing. Unfortunately, there is no standard set of commands in COBOL for programming such features. Still, the subject is discussed in Chapter 22. (The high chapter number does not imply that the topic is advanced. Rather, it is placed toward the end of this book because video monitor programming is different for each compiler or computer system).

R E V I E W . . . .

1. The verb used to input data items not usually part of any file as such is the _____ verb, whereas the verb similarly used for output, often on a CRT terminal or video monitor, is the _____ verb.

    ACCEPT; DISPLAY

2. DATA input by use of the ACCEPT verb is always treated as being [alphabetic / numeric / alphanumeric].

    alphanumeric

3. Because the DISPLAY verb can reference literals as well as identifiers, it can be used to convey certain _____ , as well as data items.

    messages

4. Although the DISPLAY verb has limited use in computer programs for regular data processing applications, it is used frequently in conjunction with the _____ of computer programs.

    debugging

. . . .

QUALIFICATION AND THE MOVE CORRESPONDING

This section covers two related subjects. First, we discuss *qualification,* which allows us the flexibility of defining nonunique data-names in the DATA DIVISION but then using qualifiers as a means of clarifying which data-name we are actually referencing. Second, we discuss the MOVE verb with the CORRESPONDING option, which is also related to the subject of nonunique data-names.

Qualification

Up to this point in the book, we always have indicated that every data-name must be unique in a given program. This requirement will be modified now by introducing the use of qualifiers. A *qualifier* is a data-name of higher hierarchical level than the name it qualifies. The use of qualifiers results in having unique data-names for names that otherwise would not be unique, thus providing more flexibility in the assignment of data-names in the program. The following DATA

DIVISION segment is an example of a case in which qualification would be necessary in the PROCEDURE DIVISION:

```
02  WEEKLY-TOTALS.
    03 TOTAL-HOURS      PIC 99V9.
    03 WAGE-RATE        PIC 99V99.
    03 ...
02  MONTHLY-TOTALS.
    03 TOTAL-HOURS      PIC 999V9.
    03 (etc.)
```

Notice that TOTAL-HOURS seems to be used twice, but with respect to two different items, namely, the total hours for the week and the total hours for the month. If reference were made simply to TOTAL-HOURS, it would not be clear which storage field should be used. However, the use of qualifiers results in unique data-names and could be accomplished as follows in the PROCEDURE DIVISION instructions:

```
MOVE TOTAL-HOURS OF WEEKLY-TOTALS TO ...
MOVE TOTAL-HOURS IN MONTHLY-TOTALS TO ...
```

The OF and IN are equivalent, and use of either word after a data-name serves to signal the use of a qualifier. Since a data-name that is not unique in the program must always be qualified, the use of nonunique names always results in longer statements in the PROCEDURE DIVISION. Despite this disadvantage, qualifiers are often used because they improve documentation. For instance, the statements in the above example make it quite clear that we are working with weekly and monthly hours, respectively.

A common use of qualifiers is with files whose record descriptions have corresponding fields. If an employee has an assigned identification number that is included in the record of each of two files, the following type of instruction can be included in the PROCEDURE DIVISION:

```
IF EMPLOY-NUMBER IN MASTER-RECORD
    IS EQUAL TO EMPLOY-NUMBER IN TRANSACTION-RECORD ...
```

The documentation aspect of the program is enhanced in this example in that it is quite clear what is being compared.

At times qualification requires several qualifiers. Consider the following example:

```
01 OLD-RECORD.                    01 NEW-RECORD.
   02 TODAYS-DATE...                 02 TODAYS-DATE ...
      03 MONTH...                       03 MONTH....
      03 YEAR ...                       03 YEAR ...
   02 LAST-PERIODS-DATE ...          02 LAST-PERIODS-DATE ...
      03 MONTH ...                      03 MONTH ...
      03 YEAR. ...                      03 YEAR. ...
      03 TOTAL ...                      03 TOTAL ...
```

In this example the OLD-RECORD and NEW-RECORD are assumed to be in the same program. Notice that there are four fields named MONTH. Thus a qualifier such as MONTH OF LAST-PERIODS-DATE does not provide a unique reference because there are two such fields, one in the OLD-RECORD and one in the NEW-RECORD. Therefore two qualifiers are needed to reference a unique field, such as

$$\text{MONTH} \begin{Bmatrix} \text{OF} \\ \text{IN} \end{Bmatrix} \text{LAST-PERIODS-DATE} \begin{Bmatrix} \text{OF} \\ \text{IN} \end{Bmatrix} \text{OLD-RECORD}$$

Since the TOTAL field in the preceding program example occurs only once in each record, only a single qualifier is required; therefore TOTAL IN OLD-RECORD is an adequate reference in this case. The use of two qualifiers, such as TOTAL OF LAST-PERIODS-DATE IN OLD-RECORD is acceptable but unnecessary for the purpose of unique identification.

The CORRESPONDING option

The CORRESPONDING option, available for use with MOVE and with the ADD and SUBTRACT arithmetic verbs, simplifies programming in cases in which the same operation is to be performed on one or several identically named pairs of elementary data-names. In this section we discuss the MOVE verb. Use of the CORRESPONDING feature with the ADD and SUBTRACT is rare, so we simply direct you to Appendix B, which presents the complete formats of these verbs.

Let us consider an example. Suppose we have the following two records:

```
01  PAY-RECORD.
    02   GROSS      PIC 9999V99.
    02   NET        PIC 9999V99.
    02   TAXES      PIC 999V99.
01  EDITED-RECORD.
    02   GROSS      PIC ZZZ9.99.
    02   TAXES      PIC ZZ9.99.
    02   NET        PIC ZZZ9.99.
```

If we want to move PAY-RECORD to EDITED-RECORD, we cannot do it in one statement. Writing MOVE PAY-RECORD to EDITED-RECORD would be incorrect, because the order of the fields NET and TAXES is not the same in the two records and because there are edited fields in the receiving record (editing works only when we move an individual elementary field to another elementary edited field). Of course, the move could be accomplished by a separate MOVE statement for each of the three fields; however, the same result can be accomplished more easily by use of the CORRESPONDING option:

```
MOVE CORRESPONDING PAY-RECORD TO EDITED-RECORD.
```

The general format associated with the use of the CORRESPONDING option is

$$\underline{\text{MOVE}} \begin{Bmatrix} \underline{\text{CORRESPONDING}} \\ \underline{\text{CORR}} \end{Bmatrix} \text{identifier-1} \underline{\text{TO}} \text{identifier-2}$$

CORR is the abbreviated form of the option. Unlike the situation in the previous example, the two data-names may contain only some items that correspond, as in the following example:

```
        02  INSPECTION.
            03  TOTAL-QUANTITY . . .
            03  REJECTED . . .
            03  ACCEPTED . . .
            03  QUALITY-RATIO . . .
    01  QUALITY-REPORT.
        02  TOTAL-QUANTITY . . .
        02  QUALITY-RATIO . . .
```

With respect to the above, executing the statement

```
    MOVE CORR INSPECTION TO QUALITY-REPORT
```

will result in the two corresponding fields, TOTAL-QUANTITY and QUALITY-RATIO, being moved.

In order for the CORRESPONDING option to be used, there must be pairs of data items having the same name in two group items, and at least one of the items in each pair must be at the elementary level. (We also now mention some other details for future reference, even though the related subjects are covered in later chapters.) Another rule is that any items that are subordinate to identifier-1 and identifier-2 and have RENAMES, REDEFINES, or OCCURS clauses are ignored in the move. Therefore we cannot use the MOVE CORRESPONDING option to move a table of values, for example. However, the identifier-1 and identifier-2 items themselves may have REDEFINES or OCCURS clauses or may be subordinate to data items with such clauses.

In general, the CORRESPONDING option should be avoided or used sparingly with respect to the MOVE as well as the ADD or SUBTRACT arithmetic verbs. Use of the CORRESPONDING option may result in errors when programs are modified subsequently, as in the case of changing a data-name and not being aware that its other "name-sake" was involved in a CORRESPONDING reference.

R E V I E W . . . .

1. The use of qualifiers makes it possible to use the same data-name for variables that otherwise would have different data-names assigned to them. The main advantage of using qualifiers is that _____ thereby is improved.

                                            documentation (or interpretation of the program, etc.)

2. When a qualifier is used, it always [precedes / follows] the referenced data-name, and its use is signaled by one of two words: _____ or _____ .

                                            follows OF; IN

3. Assume that the record-name for one file is MASTER-RECORD and the record-name of another file is TRANSACTION-RECORD. Both records contain a field called CUSTOMER-NUMBER. To determine that we are dealing with two records of the same customer, we say:

```
    IF CUSTOMER-NUMBER OF _____ IS EQUAL TO
    CUSTOMER-NUMBER OF _____
```

                                            MASTER-RECORD; TRANSACTION-RECORD (either order)

4. A sufficient number of qualifiers must be used to differentiate a particular data field from all other data fields in the program that are identified by the same data-name. Suppose that a qualifier is used with a data-name that is unique and thus requires no qualifier. From the standpoint of programming requirements,

the qualifier is unnecessary [and the program will terminate / but will not affect program execution].

but will not affect program execution
(again, such a qualifier might be used to improve documentation)

5. The abbreviated form of the CORRESPONDING option is _____ . Use of this option in conjunction with the MOVE instruction results in transfer of only the _____ items contained in two records.

CORR; common (or corresponding)

6. When the MOVE CORRESPONDING option is used, an item will be moved if at least one of the items in each pair is at the _____ level and only if the receiving group item has an item with the same [storage capacity / name].

elementary; name

.   .   .   .

CHARACTER PROCESSING VERBS

COBOL includes a number of verbs intended to execute tasks that involve data as *characters* rather than as numeric values. These verbs are specialized and very powerful. We will discuss five such verbs: INITIALIZE, COPY, STRING, UNSTRING, and INSPECT. Then we will present a sample program that illustrates use of these verbs in the following section of this chapter.

The INITIALIZE Verb

This verb is available only in COBOL '85. The INITIALIZE statement provides for a convenient way to move data to selected fields. The most common use of this verb is for setting numeric fields to zero and nonnumeric fields to spaces.

Figure 7-4 presents the general format and some examples of using the INITIALIZE verb. When used without the REPLACING option, spaces are moved to alphabetic, alphanumeric, and alphanumeric edited data items, while zeros are moved to numeric and numeric edited items. When identifier-1 is a group item, as in the first INITIALIZE A example, it is as if we wrote a series of elementary MOVE statements to move either spaces or zeros, depending on the receiving data item category.

When the REPLACING option is used, only items matching the specified category are initialized. Thus the third example in Figure 7-4b illustrates that only D is affected by the INITIALIZE statement.

Overall, we can observe that the INITIALIZE serves as a convenient alternative to the VALUE clause in the DATA DIVISION and the use of MOVE in the PROCEDURE DIVISION.

The COPY Verb

COBOL provides for a library facility. By *library* we mean a collection of COBOL source program elements recorded on tape or disk and accessible by reference to text-names. A text-name is similar to a file name, and it serves as the identifier for one or more preprogrammed COBOL items.

For example, suppose that we have stored the following record description in a source library under the text-name CUST-REC.

```
05  CUST-NO     PIC 9(5).
05  CUST-NAME   PIC X(20).
```

FIGURE 7-4

*Format and Sample Uses of
INITIALIZE*

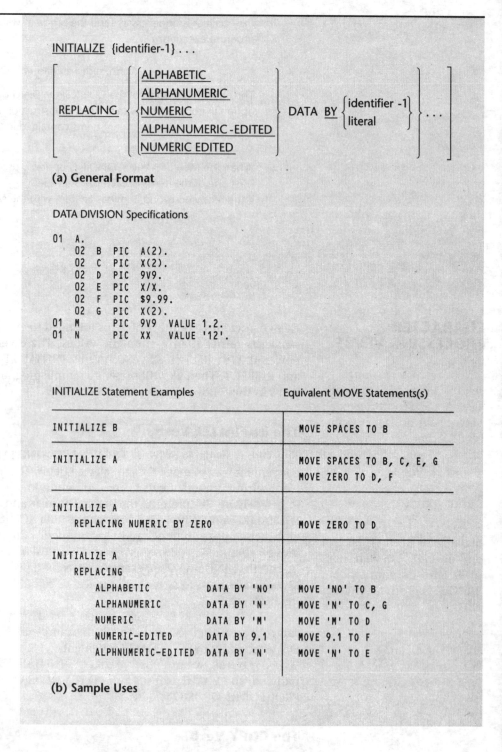

(a) General Format

DATA DIVISION Specifications

```
01  A.
    02  B   PIC  A(2).
    02  C   PIC  X(2).
    02  D   PIC  9V9.
    02  E   PIC  X/X.
    02  F   PIC  $9.99.
    02  G   PIC  X(2).
01  M       PIC  9V9   VALUE 1.2.
01  N       PIC  XX    VALUE '12'.
```

INITIALIZE Statement Examples	Equivalent MOVE Statements(s)
`INITIALIZE B`	`MOVE SPACES TO B`
`INITIALIZE A`	`MOVE SPACES TO B, C, E, G` `MOVE ZERO TO D, F`
`INITIALIZE A` `    REPLACING NUMERIC BY ZERO`	`MOVE ZERO TO D`

`INITIALIZE A`
`    REPLACING`
`        ALPHABETIC          DATA BY 'NO'`
`        ALPHANUMERIC        DATA BY 'N'`
`        NUMERIC             DATA BY 'M'`
`        NUMERIC-EDITED      DATA BY 9.1`
`        ALPHNUMERIC-EDITED  DATA BY 'N'`
	`MOVE 'NO' TO B`
	`MOVE 'N' TO C, G`
	`MOVE 'M' TO D`
	`MOVE 9.1 TO F`
	`MOVE 'N' TO E`

(b) Sample Uses

Then in a program we could write as follows:

```
01  CUSTOMER-RECORD  COPY  CUST-REC.
```

As a result, the program would be compiled as if we had written

```
01  CUSTOMER-RECORD.
    05  CUST-NO     PIC 9(5).
    05  CUST-NAME   PIC X(20).
```

The COPY facility not only saves time for the programmer, but even more importantly, it serves to reduce errors from inconsistent descriptions of the same file data. Commonly, the same file will be used by several programs. In such a case it is very productive to have the description of the file stored in a text library, so that all the programs using that file will copy exactly the same descriptions.

The COPY can be used throughout the COBOL program. For instance, assuming that TEXT-1 refers to specific program elements, we could write

```
SOURCE-COMPUTER.  COPY TEXT-1.
     .
     .
     .

SELECT PRODUCT-FILE COPY TEXT-15.
     .
     .
     .

FD  PRODUCT-FILE COPY TEXT-3.
     .
     .
     .

BILLING-PARAGRAPH.  COPY TEXT-14.
     .
     .
     .
```

In this fashion we need not rewrite those portions of the program that have already been written and stored in the library.

Building the library commonly is done outside the COBOL language by means of JCL (Job Control Language) statements. Use of a library is a very local practice, and we direct the readers to their own computer system for details.

R E V I E W . . . .

1. In effect, the INITIALIZE verb available in the 1985 standard represents a more efficient alternative to the use of the _____ verb.

   MOVE

2. The most common use of this verb is for setting numeric fields to _____ and nonnumeric fields to _____ .

   zero; spaces

3. The verb that makes it possible to reference a precoded program segment from a library of such program segments is the _____ verb.

   COPY

4. When the COPY verb is used to obtain a record description from a library, the record-name used in the program and in the library [must / need not] be the same.

   need not

. . . .

The STRING Verb

The STRING verb is designed to facilitate transfer of data from *several sources into one destination,* while the UNSTRING verb is designed to facilitate transfer of data *from one source to many destinations.* In effect, use of these verbs allows one statement to be used in lieu of multiple uses of the MOVE verb and, possibly, in lieu of some DATA DIVISION entries.

We begin with two examples that illustrate uses of the STRING verb.

Suppose that EDIT-SOC-SEC contains a social security number, including hyphens after the third and fifth digits, as, for instance, '123-45-6789'. We wish to move the social security number to SOC-SEC while also removing the hyphens. The following data description entries are given:

```
01  SOC-SEC               PIC X(9).
01  EDIT-SOC-SEC.
    02  PART-1            PIC 999.
    02  FILLER           PIC X VALUE '-'.
    02  PART-2            PIC 99.
    02  FILLER           PIC X VALUE '-'.
    02  PART-3            PIC 9999.
```

We now use the STRING statement:

```
STRING   PART-1 DELIMITED BY SIZE
         PART-2 DELIMITED BY SIZE
         PART-3 DELIMITED BY SIZE
    INTO    SOC-SEC.
```

The STRING specifies moving the three fields, PART-1, PART-2, and PART-3, and positioning them adjacent to each other. The transfer of data can be thought of as taking place character by character. Thus the data in PART-1 would be transferred into the first three positions of SOC-SEC, the data in PART-2 would be transferred into the next two positions of SOC-SEC, and so on. The DELIMITED BY SIZE clause specifies that the transfer of data from the associated field will stop at (be delimited by) the point when as many characters have been transferred as the size of the source field.

The next example illustrates the availability of other alternatives.

Assume that we want to print a report that lists a company name in columns 5–19, a city name starting with column 26, 1 blank space, and then the ZIP code. The source of data is VENDOR-RECORD:

```
01  VENDOR-RECORD.
    02  COMPANY-NAME          PIC X(15).
    02  STREET                PIC X(40).
    02  CITY-STATE            PIC X(20).
    02  ZIP                   PIC 9(5).
```

The data in CITY-STATE are recorded so that the city-name is followed by a comma, a space, and then the state code, as in LOS ANGELES, CA.

The output record is described as

```
01  OUTPUT-REC PIC X(132).
```

We use the STRING verb as follows:

```
MOVE SPACES TO OUTPUT-REC
MOVE 5 TO STARTING-PLACE.
STRING COMPANY-NAME DELIMITED BY SIZE
       '    ' DELIMITED BY SIZE
       CITY-STATE   DELIMITED BY ','
       SPACE, ZIP   DELIMITED BY SIZE
   INTO OUTPUT-REC
   WITH POINTER STARTING-PLACE.
```

The first MOVE statement clears the output record of any previous contents. The second MOVE sets STARTING-PLACE to a value of 5 so that the beginning of data transfer into OUTPUT-REC will begin in column 5 (WITH POINTER STARTING-PLACE). Of course, STARTING-PLACE is an arbitrary name chosen by the programmer; but it must be an integer field for obvious reasons.

The STRING statement specifies that, in effect, five fields will be transferred: COMPANY-NAME, the 6-byte nonnumeric literal '   ', CITY-STATE, the figurative constant SPACE, and ZIP. Thus, starting with column 5 of OUTPUT-REC, the entire (DELIMITED BY SIZE) COMPANY-NAME is transferred and it is followed by the 6-blank nonnumeric constant to account for columns 20-25. The next data item to be transferred comes from CITY-STATE; this data item is transferred character by character until a comma is encountered (DELIMITED BY ','). We deliberately omitted the state code. Thus if CITY-STATE contained LOS ANGELES, CA, the DELIMITED BY ',' stops the transfer when the comma is encountered. Then we string one blank (SPACE) and then the contents of the ZIP code field. It should be pointed out that use of figurative constants, such as SPACE, ZEROS, or the like, always means one occurrence of the implied character. Thus, we would obtain one blank even if we had used SPACES instead of SPACE.

The general format for the STRING verb is presented in Figure 7-5.

Our two examples have illustrated all but the OVERFLOW option. If the data specified to be transferred are greater than the size of the receiving item (identifier-7) during execution of a STRING statement, then the imperative statement of the OVERFLOW clause is executed. If the optional OVERFLOW is not used and the overflow condition arises, then the STRING operation is discontinued and

FIGURE 7-5

General Format for the STRING Verb

$$\text{STRING} \left\{ \begin{array}{l} \text{identifier -1} \\ \text{literal -1} \end{array} \right\} \left[\begin{array}{l} \text{, identifier -2} \\ \text{, literal -2} \end{array} \right] \ldots \underline{\text{DELIMITED}} \text{ BY} \left\{ \begin{array}{l} \text{identifier -3} \\ \text{literal -3} \\ \underline{\text{SIZE}} \end{array} \right\}$$

$$\left\{ \begin{array}{l} \text{identifier -4} \\ \text{literal -4} \end{array} \right\} \left[\begin{array}{l} \text{, identifier -5} \\ \text{, literal -5} \end{array} \right] \ldots \underline{\text{DELIMITED}} \text{ BY} \left\{ \begin{array}{l} \text{identifier -6} \\ \text{literal -6} \\ \underline{\text{SIZE}} \end{array} \right\} \right\} \ldots$$

<u>INTO</u> identifier-7 [WITH <u>POINTER</u> identifer-8]

[<u>ON OVERFLOW</u> imperative-statement-1]

[<u>NOT</u> ON <u>OVERFLOW</u> imperative-statement-2]

[<u>END-STRING</u>]

the next program statement is executed. During execution, identifier-8, if used, is incremented by 1 as each character is transferred. It is the value of this identifier that is checked in determining an overflow condition. If the identifier-8 option is not used, an implied counter is used to fulfill the same function. When the STRING operation has been completed, the value of identifier-8 is one higher than the number of characters transferred. This feature is used in the sample program at the end of the chapter. The NOT ON OVERFLOW and the END-STRING options apply only to the 1985 standard.

The UNSTRING Verb

The UNSTRING verb, as its name implies, acts in the reverse direction of the STRING verb. The UNSTRING verb facilitates transfer of data from *one source* to *many destinations*. We present two examples to illustrate use of this verb.

Suppose that data are recorded in free form (without predefined fields) as follows:

```
TED S BROWN,4,15,3.52
TINA LORI CHRISTIANSON,1,12,2.50
```

As we can see, name fields are separated by one or more blank spaces; then commas separate the remaining three fields. We would like to move these data fields to a fixed-format record:

```
01  STUDENT-RECORD.
    02   FIRST-NAME          PIC X(15).
    02   MIDDLE-NAME         PIC X(15).
    02   LAST-NAME           PIC X(20).
    02   CLASSIFICATION      PIC 9.
    02   CREDIT-LOAD         PIC 99.
    02   GPA                 PIC XXXX.
```

Assuming that the source data are in

```
01  FREE-FORM-RECORD PIC X(57).
```

we can write

```
UNSTRING FREE-FORM-RECORD
    DELIMITED BY ALL SPACES OR ','
       INTO      FIRST-NAME
                 MIDDLE-NAME
                 LAST-NAME
                 CLASSIFICATION
                 CREDIT-LOAD
                 GPA.
```

The DELIMITED clause above specifies that fields in the source record are separated by one or more blank spaces (ALL SPACES), or single commas (OR ','). In essence, the source record is scanned character by character from left to right. When a blank or a comma appears in FREE-FORM-RECORD, it is assumed that a new field begins. The delimiters in this case are blanks or commas, and they are not included in the data transfer, although the UNSTRING statement does include an option allowing the transfer of delimiters themselves.

When FREE-FORM-RECORD contains

```
TINA LORI CHRISTIANSON,1,12,2.50
```

the receiving fields will contain the following:

```
FIRST-NAME        TINA
MIDDLE-NAME       LORI
LAST-NAME         CHRISTIANSON
CLASSIFICATION    1
CREDIT-LOAD       12
GPA               2.50.
```

Notice that GPA has PIC XXXX. The UNSTRING handles data as characters, not as numeric quantities. Thus the decimal point is considered as a character, not as a numeric decimal.

Consider now a second example that expands on UNSTRING and illustrates combined use of STRING and UNSTRING.

Data records contain numbers in columns 1–6, followed by a name and a header separated from each other by a dollar sign. As in the previous example, a delimiter such as a dollar sign can be used to allow recording of data without adherence to predefined field positions. When data length is highly variable, such free-form data can save a lot of space. Two sample records are as follows:

```
349687INTERNATIONAL TOOLS, INC.$ BALANCE SHEET$
135002ACME CORP.$INCOME STATEMENT$
```

We are interested in printing the company name, centered at column 40 on the top of a new page, followed by the name of the report on the third line, also centered at column 40. Accomplishing this task involves separating the two fields, determining their size, and, on the basis of their size, centering the data with respect to column 40. We also assume that we wish to ascertain that there are indeed two fields available in the relevant part of the source record.

First, we define some data fields:

```
01  FREE-FORM-RECORD      PIC X(46).
01  FIRST-LINE            PIC X(20).
01  SECOND-LINE           PIC X(20).
01  LENGTH-1              PIC 99.
01  LENGTH-2              PIC 99.
01  STARTING-POINT        PIC 99.
01  NO-OF-FIELDS          PIC 9.
01  OUTPUT-RECORD         PIC X(132).
```

Figure 7-6 presents a program segment written to accomplish the desired task. The NO-OF-FIELDS item is used to count the number of fields transferred. Notice its use in the TALLYING clause in the UNSTRING statement. The value 7 is moved to STARTING-POINT because the first 6 columns of FREE-FORM-RECORD contain data that we wish to ignore, as indicated by the clause WITH POINTER STARTING-POINT. Using the $ as a delimiter, we transfer data from the source record into two fields, FIRST-LINE and SECOND-LINE. In the process we obtain a count of the characters moved into each receiving field in LENGTH-1 and LENGTH-2, respectively. The COUNT option provides this length-count. Finally, use of the OVERFLOW specifies execution of PERFORM ERROR-ROUTINE-1 if the data being transferred exceed the size of the receiving field. This could happen in our

FIGURE 7-6

*Example Program Involving the
Use of UNSTRING and STRING*

```
MOVE ZERO TO NO-OF FIELDS
MOVE 7 TO STARTING-POINT
UNSTRING FREE-FORM-RECORD DELIMITED BY '$'
     INTO FIRST-LINE
             COUNT IN LENGTH-1
          SECOND-LINE
             COUNT IN LENGTH-2
     WITH POINTER STARTING-POINT
     TALLYING IN NO-OF-FIELDS
     ON OVERFLOW
          PERFORM ERROR-ROUTINE-1.
   IF NO-OF-FIELDS NOT = 2
     PERFORM ERROR-ROUTINE-2
   ELSE
     PERFORM PRINT-HEADERS.
       .
       .
       .
PRINT-HEADERS.
   COMPUTE LENGTH-1 = 40 - (LENGTH-1 / 2)
   COMPUTE LENGTH-2 = 40 - (LENGTH-2 / 2)
   MOVE SPACES TO OUTPUT-RECORD
   STRING FIRST-LINE DELIMITED BY SIZE
       INTO OUTPUT-RECORD
       WITH POINTER LENGTH-1
   WRITE OUTPUT-RECORD AFTER ADVANCING PAGE
   MOVE SPACES TO OUTPUT RECORD
   STRING SECOND-LINE DELIMITED BY SIZE
       INTO OUTPUT-RECORD
       WITH POINTER LENGTH-2
   WRITE OUTPUT-RECORD AFTER ADVANCING 2 LINES.
```

example if the delimiting dollar sign was missing, or if one field was longer than 20 characters—the size specified for FIRST-LINE and SECOND-LINE.

After the UNSTRING statement, we check to see that we indeed had two fields transferred; if not, we PERFORM ERROR-ROUTINE-2.

The PRINT-HEADERS paragraph computes the starting point of each line to the left of column 40. We divide the length of the field involved by 2 and we subtract this amount from 40. We then use the STRING verb to move the data, using LENGTH-1 as the pointer. Actually, it is the availability of the POINTER option in the STRING verb that makes it capable of achieving what the MOVE verb could not accomplish in this case. After the transfer of the data, we print the record and repeat the process for the next line of printed output.

The general format for the UNSTRING verb is presented in Figure 7-7.

We have illustrated all the options except the DELIMITER IN clause. When used, the clause specifies the identifier to be used to receive the delimiter(s). This option is used if we wish to capture the delimiters themselves for further testing or processing.

FIGURE 7-7

General Format for the UNSTRING Verb

UNSTRING identifier -1 $\left\{ \text{DELIMITED BY [ALL]} \left\{ \begin{matrix} \text{identifier -2} \\ \text{literal -1} \end{matrix} \right\} \right.$

$\left. \left\{ \text{OR [ALL]} \left\{ \begin{matrix} \text{identifier -3} \\ \text{literal -2} \end{matrix} \right\} \right\} \dots \right\}$ INTO identifier -4 [, DELIMITER IN identifier -5]

[, COUNT IN identifier-6] [, identifier-7 [, DELIMITER IN identifier-8]

[, COUNT IN identifier-9] . . . [WITH POINTER identifier-10]

[TALLYING IN identifier-11] [ON OVERFLOW imperative-statement-1]

[NOT ON OVERFLOW imperative-statement-2]

[END-UNSTRING]

R E V I E W . . . .

1. The verb that is used to transfer data from several sources to one destination is the _____ verb.

   STRING

2. The verb that is used to transfer data from one source to many destinations is the _____ verb.

   UNSTRING

3. When the DELIMITED BY SIZE clause is used in conjunction with the STRING verb, transfer of data from the sending field stops when the number of characters that have been transferred equals the size of the [sending / receiving] field.]

   sending (unless the receiving field is shorter than the sending field)

4. If an OVERFLOW clause is not used in conjunction with a STRING verb and an overflow condition occurs, then [the STRING operation / program execution] is terminated.

   the STRING operation

5. Used in conjunction with the UNSTRING verb, the DELIMITED BY clause specifies the basis used to signal the beginning of a new [sending / receiving] field.

   sending

6. The clause that is used if delimiters themselves, such as commas or spaces, are to be transferred to receiving fields during the UNSTRING operation is the _____ clause.

   DELIMITER IN

. . . .

The INSPECT Verb

At times we need to access and manipulate individual characters in a field. One very common use is to edit input data, such as replacing leading blanks by zeros. COBOL provides the INSPECT verb to accomplish such character manipulations.

The INSPECT verb is powerful but a bit complicated. Three formats are available, and these are presented in the format specifications in Appendix B.

Discussion of the complete set of options would exceed the intended scope of this text. We present some examples to illustrate the basic options.

EXAMPLE 1   Suppose we want to replace all leading blanks by leading zeros in a field called TEST. We could write

```
INSPECT TEST REPLACING LEADING ' ' BY '0'.
```

EXAMPLE 2   Suppose we want to replace all blanks (not just leading ones) by zeros in a field called TEST. We could write

```
INSPECT TEST REPLACING ALL ' ' BY '0'.
```

EXAMPLE 3   If we want to replace the first zero by a + , we write

```
INSPECT TEST REPLACING FIRST '0' BY '+'.
```

EXAMPLE 4   Suppose we want to ask the question: How many dollar signs are in TEST? We write

```
INSPECT TEST TALLYING DOLLAR-COUNT FOR ALL '$'.
```

After this instruction is executed, the numeric field DOLLAR-COUNT will contain a value equal to the number of $ in TEST. (DOLLAR-COUNT would have been defined in the DATA DIVISION.)

EXAMPLE 5   Suppose we want to ask the question: How many zero characters are there to the left of the decimal point and how many zeros are there to the right of the decimal point? We write

```
INSPECT TEST TALLYING COUNT-B FOR ALL '0' BEFORE INITIAL '.'
                      COUNT-A FOR ALL '0' AFTER '.'.
```

This instruction would result in COUNT-B containing the number of zeros before the decimal point and COUNT-A containing the number of zeros after the decimal point.

EXAMPLE 6   We want to count the number of dollar signs in TEST and replace all dollar signs after the first one by asterisks. We write

```
INSPECT TEST TALLYING COUNT-A FOR ALL '$'
             REPLACING ALL '$' BY '*' AFTER INITIAL '$'.
```

EXAMPLE 7   We want to ask the question: Assuming that TEST contains a name left-justified, how long is the name? (Unused positions are blank.) We write

```
INSPECT TEST TALLYING COUNT-A FOR CHARACTERS BEFORE INITIAL ' '.
```

EXAMPLE 8   We want to convert all uppercase letters to lowercase. We could write

```
INSPECT TEST REPLACING ALL 'A' BY 'a'
                           'B' BY 'b'
                             .
                             .
                             .
                           'Z' BY 'z'.
```

In some instances the compiler may limit the number of literal pairs used in one INSPECT statement, so that for the example we may need to write two INSPECT statements, say, one for replacing the letters A through M and another one for the letters N through Z.

In COBOL '85 there is an easier way to do the above tests by using the CONVERTING option:

```
INSPECT TEST CONVERTING 'ABCDEFGHIJKLMNOPQRSTUVWXYZ'
                     TO 'abcdefghijklmnopqrstuvwxyz'
```

The above statement specifies to change any "A" to "a", and so on, exactly as the REPLACING ALL statement does at the beginning of this example.

EXAMPLE 9 An integer field, ABC, of six positions may have leading blanks and a sign. We want to move the correct numeric value represented in ABC to S-ABC whose PIC is S9(6). We could write

```
MOVE ZERO TO PLUS-SIGN, MINUS-SIGN
INSPECT ABC
    TALLYING  PLUS-SIGN FOR ALL '+'
              MINUS-SIGN FOR ALL '-'
    REPLACING
              LEADING SPACES BY ZERO
              FIRST '+' BY ZERO
              FIRST '-' BY ZERO.
IF  ABC IS NOT NUMERIC
    PERFORM INCORRECT-DATA
ELSE
    MOVE ABC TO S-ABC
    IF MINUS-SIGN NOT = ZERO
    MULTIPLY -1 BY S-ABC.
```

We initialize two counters, PLUS-SIGN and MINUS-SIGN, to zero and we use them for TALLYING the occurrence of + and –, respectively. Notice, however, that we use REPLACING ... FIRST. In the unlikely event that more than one like sign is present, the statement IF ABC IS NOT NUMERIC would sense the presence of the unconverted extra sign(s). If the field is unsigned or positive, MOVE ABC to S-ABC is sufficient. If the field is negative, however, then MINUS-SIGN would have a nonzero value and we multiply S-ABC by –1 to attain the proper sign. We could also test PLUS-SIGN and MINUS-SIGN to determine how many signs were present, if any.

R E V I E W . . . .

1. Individual characters in a field can be accessed and possibly changed by use of the _____ verb.

    INSPECT

2. Use of the TALLYING option in conjunction with the INSPECT verb makes it possible to _____ designated characters.

    count

3. Use of the REPLACING option in conjunction with the INSPECT verb makes it possible to _____ designated characters.

    change

4. In the 1985 STANDARD, a more efficient way than use of the REPLACING option by which a series of designated characters can be changed is use of the option, _____ .

• •

SAMPLE PROGRAM

We wish to create a file that contains records consisting of persons' names compressed so as to leave the trailing blanks out of each name. We might want to do something like this to save storage space, or to save transmission costs if we are sending the data via telecommunications.

It will be easiest to begin with an example of some input and the desired corresponding output, as presented in Figure 7-8. Observing the sample *output*, we can see that names are written without trailing spaces, with a # serving as a delimiter to separate each name from the next one. If a first name or a middle name is missing, there are two consecutive # symbols. For example, at the end of the first output record, SOTELO THOMAS has no middle name, and WILSON in the third output record has no first name.

The output records are fixed length, in this case 80 characters long. If a complete name does not fit at the end of such a record, we "pad" the end of the output record with * symbols, as shown in the first, third, and fourth sample output records.

FIGURE 7-8

Input and Output for the Sample Program

INPUT FILE

DOAKS	MARY	BETH
LURVEY	ALEXANDER	RALPH
NEWMAN	ANNETTE	MARIE
SOTELO	THOMAS	
ELLIOTT	C	W
RICHARDSON	NICKOLAUS	ANDREW
THOMPSON	PAMELA	ANN
SPENCER	GARY	MARTIN
LIN	CHIN	CHI
RIBBENTROP	RONALD	GENE
WILSON		D
TRAN	TONY	H
WOELFEL	KATHRYN	P
JANES	BEVERLY	EDWARD
MURPHEY	DAN	E

PROGRAM OUTPUT

```
DOAKS#MARY#BETH#LURVEY#ALEXANDER#RALPH#NEWMAN#ANNETTE#MARIE#SOTELO#THOMAS##*****

ELLIOTT#C#W#RICHARDSON#NICKOLAUS#ANDREW#THOMPSON#PAMELA#ANN#SPENCER#GARY#MARTIN#

LIN#CHIN#CHI#RIBBENTROP#RONALD#GENE#WILSON##D#TRAN#TONY#H#WOELFEL#KATHRYN#P#****

JANES#BEVERLY#EDWARD#MURPHEY#DAN#E#**********************************************
```

Figure 7-9 presents a complete program for the task. Notice that the input file (STRING-FILE), contains fields for LAST-NAME, FIRST-NAME, and MIDDLE-NAME, each 15 bytes long. Thus, the longest compressed name could be 48 bytes long when we consider insertion of the delimiting # symbols (two within the name and one at the end of the name). The shortest compressed name could be, conceivably, a person with a single-letter last name and no first and no middle name, in which case the compressed version of the name would be four bytes long.

The logic used in the 200-COMPRESS-DATA paragraph of the sample program STRINGs the full name into a WORKING-STORAGE field named NAME-BUFFER, which has been defined to be 49 bytes in length. We use the WITH

FIGURE 7-9
COBOL Program for the STRING Example

```
*
    IDENTIFICATION DIVISION.
    PROGRAM-ID. STRINGIT.
*
    ENVIRONMENT DIVISION.
*
    CONFIGURATION SECTION.
    SOURCE-COMPUTER. ABC-480.
    OBJECT-COMPUTER. ABC-480.
*
    INPUT-OUTPUT SECTION.
*
    FILE-CONTROL.
        SELECT STRING-FILE ASSIGN TO STRING-DAT.
        SELECT STRING-OUT  ASSIGN TO STRING-RPT.
*
    DATA DIVISION.
*
    FILE SECTION.
*
    FD  STRING-FILE LABEL RECORDS ARE OMITTED
                    RECORD CONTAINS 80 CHARACTERS
                    DATA RECORD IS STRING-RECORD.
    01  STRING-RECORD.
        05 FILLER                           PIC X(4).
        05 LAST-NAME                        PIC X(15).
        05 FIRST-NAME                       PIC X(15).
        05 MIDDLE-NAME                      PIC X(15).
        05 FILLER                           PIC X(31).
*
    FD  STRING-OUT   LABEL RECORDS ARE OMITTED
                     RECORD CONTAINS 80 CHARACTERS
                     DATA RECORD IS STRING-LINE.
    01  STRING-LINE                         PIC X(80).
*
    WORKING-STORAGE SECTION.
*
    01 END-OF-FILE-TEST                     PIC X(3) VALUE "NO".
        88  END-OF-FILE                     VALUE "YES".
*
```

FIGURE 7-9
COBOL Program for the STRING
Example (continued)

```
01 NAME-LENGTH                                      PIC 9(2).
01 STARTING-PT                                      PIC 9(2).
01 SPACE-LEFT                                       PIC 9(2).
01 NAME-BUFFER                                      PIC X(49).
01 STRING-LENGTH                                    PIC 9(2) VALUE 80.
*
PROCEDURE DIVISION.
*
 000-MAIN-ROUTINE.
     OPEN INPUT  STRING-FILE
          OUTPUT STRING-OUT

     PERFORM 100-READ-EXPANDED-REC
     MOVE ALL "*" TO STRING-LINE
     MOVE 1 TO STARTING-PT
     PERFORM 200-COMPRESS-DATA
        UNTIL END-OF-FILE

     WRITE STRING-LINE

     CLOSE STRING-FILE
           STRING-OUT
     STOP RUN.
*
 100-READ-EXPANDED-REC.
     READ STRING-FILE RECORD
        AT END SET END-OF-FILE TO TRUE
*
 200-COMPRESS-DATA.
     MOVE SPACES TO NAME-BUFFER
     MOVE 1 TO NAME-LENGTH
     STRING LAST-NAME DELIMITED BY SPACE
            "#" DELIMITED BY SIZE
            FIRST-NAME DELIMITED BY SPACE
            "#" DELIMITED BY SIZE
            MIDDLE-NAME DELIMITED BY SPACE
            "#" DELIMITED BY SIZE
               INTO NAME-BUFFER
                  WITH POINTER NAME-LENGTH
     END-STRING
*
     SUBTRACT 1 FROM NAME-LENGTH
     COMPUTE SPACE-LEFT = STRING-LENGTH - STARTING-PT + 1
     IF SPACE-LEFT < NAME-LENGTH
         WRITE STRING-LINE
         MOVE ALL "*" TO STRING-LINE
         MOVE 1 TO STARTING-PT
     END-IF
*
     STRING NAME-BUFFER DELIMITED BY SPACE
            INTO STRING-LINE
               WITH POINTER STARTING-PT
     END-STRING
*
     PERFORM 100-READ-EXPANDED-REC.
```

POINTER option in the string operation as a way of determining the length of a compressed name. If a name should happen to be 45 bytes long, the pointer (NAME-LENGTH) will have a value 49. The value 49 is desired based on the following analysis. There will be three # delimiters incorporated in the 45-byte name, which accounts for a value of 48. Then we add 1 to account for the fact that the value of the POINTER field at the end of the STRING operation is one higher than the number of characters transferred, as explained in the earlier section of this chapter on the STRING statement. Thus, the pointer will have a value 1 greater than the length of the compressed name in NAME-BUFFER. For this reason we insert SUBTRACT 1 FROM NAME-LENGTH after the STRING statement.

The COMPUTE SPACE-LEFT statement calculates whether there is room in the current output record for storing the just-compressed name in NAME-BUFFER. Notice that the size of the output record (80 bytes) has been stored in the data-name STRING-LENGTH which was defined in working storage. Thus, if we wanted to change the size of the output records to, say, 132 bytes, all we would have to do is change the VALUE clause for STRING-LENGTH.

If the name in NAME-BUFFER does not fit in the output record, we WRITE STRING-LINE to output the record and then MOVE ALL "∗" TO STRING-LINE to prepare it for the next record. By filling the entire record with asterisks initially, we know that the remaining positions at the end of a partially name-filled record will contain asterisks.

The task is completed by a STRING statement that strings the data in NAME-BUFFER into STRING-LINE WITH POINTER STARTING-PT. The pointer value is equal to 1 plus the ending point of the previous string operation; thus the pointer automatically keeps track of where to begin stringing. Finally, the DELIM- ITED BY SPACE in the last STRING statement is used because at the beginning of the 200-COMPRESS-DATA we have written MOVE SPACES TO NAME-BUFFER, and therefore when a blank space is encountered we have reached the end of the name data in NAME-BUFFER.

One of the exercises at the end of this chapter asks you to do the reverse of the operation in this sample program: to take compressed data and to reformat it into typical, fixed-length fields.

SUMMARY

As indicated in the chapter objectives, the coverage in this chapter was intended to complete the presentation of the main verbs available in COBOL, as a follow-up to the introduction to PROCEDURE DIVISION commands in Chapter 2.

The four basic *arithmetic verbs* that were reviewed and discussed further were the ADD, SUBTRACT, MULTIPLY, and DIVIDE. A variety of examples, in- cluding use of the ROUNDED and ON SIZE ERROR clauses, were considered. The use of the END-verb, available in COBOL '85, also was explained.

The COMPUTE verb makes it possible to write compact arithmetic state- ments for mathematical expressions. The arithmetic operators +, −, ∗, and / corre- spond to the verbs ADD, SUBTRACT, MULTIPLY, and DIVIDE, respectively. The ∗∗ operation provides for exponentiation.

Features associated with the PERFORM verb that were covered in this chapter are the PERFORM ... TIMES and PERFORM ... THRU options, and the use of nested PERFORM statements. The format of the PERFORM statement that specifies execution of a procedure a definite number of times is the PERFORM ... TIMES. Associated with the PERFORM ... THRU, we can use the EXIT statement to mark the end of the THRU range of procedures referenced by such a PERFORM. Because a change in the physical position of paragraphs in the PROCEDURE DIVISION can disrupt the intent of a PERFORM ... THRU command, use of this option is discouraged. A *nested* PERFORM structure is exemplified when a PERFORM statement results in execution of a paragraph that itself contains another PERFORM statement.

The GO TO verb is an *unconditional branch* to a paragraph or section name. Because extensive use of this verb makes a program difficult both to read and to modify, the GO TO verb should be used very sparingly.

The ACCEPT verb is used for input and the DISPLAY verb is used for output for storage fields that are *not* part of any files, usually in conjunction with using such hardware devices as video monitors. Use of the DISPLAY verb is particularly useful for the debugging of COBOL programs.

Two general approaches for handling *nonunique data-items* in the PROCE-DURE DIVISION are by use of *qualification* and use of the CORRESPONDING option with the MOVE verb. The use of qualifiers results in having unique data-names for names that otherwise would not be unique. The presence of a qualifier is signalled by use of either OF or IN after a data-name, such as in MOVE TOTAL-HOURS OF WEEKLY-TOTALS TO ... . To use the CORRESPONDING option with the MOVE verb, there must be pairs of data items having the same name in each of two group items, and at least one of the items must be at the elementary level.

The last major section of the chapter, before the sample program, was concerned with *character processing verbs*. These are verbs that process data as *characters*, rather than as numeric values. The five verbs described were the INITIALIZE, COPY, STRING, UNSTRING, and INSPECT.

The INITIALIZE verb, available only in COBOL '85, is used to set numeric fields to zero and nonnumeric fields to spaces. For such applications, it is a more efficient alternative to the use of the MOVE verb.

The COPY verb makes it possible to reference a program segment from a library of such precoded segments and to copy it into the source program.

The STRING verb facilitates the transfer of data from *several sources* into *one destination*. For example, by use of a STRING command we can specify that three separate data-names and/or nonnumeric literals be moved and positioned adjacent to one another.

The UNSTRING verb facilitates the transfer of data from *one source* to *many destinations*. For example, by use of an UNSTRING command one field can be "split up" and transferred to three different fields.

As indicated by its name, the general purpose of the INSPECT verb is to access, and possibly change, individual characters in a data field. A number of options make the INSPECT verb useful for data editing.

The sample program in the final section of this chapter focuses particularly on the use of the STRING verb and some of its options.

EXERCISES

7.1 Assume the following DATA DIVISION entries:

```
01  A.
    02  X.
        03  Y.
    02  W.
        03  Y.
01  B.
    02  X.
        03  Y.
    02  W.
        03  Y.
```

Write PROCEDURE DIVISION statement(s) to move the last elementary item in A to the first elementary item in B.

7.2 Write a COBOL program to compute depreciation schedules, using the sum-of-the-digits method of depreciation. The sum-of-the-digits method works as follows: Suppose that you have an asset of original value $1,000.00 to be depreciated over 3 years. The following table shows the nature of the calculations involved:

YEAR	DEPRECIATION RATE	DEPRECIATION
1	$\dfrac{3}{1+2+3} = \dfrac{3}{6}$	$1,000 \times \dfrac{3}{6} = 500.00$
2	$\dfrac{2}{1+2+3} = \dfrac{2}{6}$	$1,000 \times \dfrac{2}{6} = 333.33$
3	$\dfrac{1}{1+2+3} = \dfrac{1}{6}$	$1,000 \times \dfrac{1}{6} = 166.67$

Notice that the depreciation rate varies from year to year, but that the rate is applied to the same (original) asset dollar value. The rate consists of a denominator that is the sum of the digits from 1 up to the number of years over which the asset is to be depreciated. To test your understanding of the concept, compute the denominator value for five years. The answer is 15. The numerator of the depreciation rate varies from the number of years over which depreciation is to be taken down to 1, in steps of 1. Thus, for a five-year depreciation schedule the numerator values are 5, 4, 3, 2, 1.

Input: This is in the form of a set of records with the following data format:

COLUMNS	CONTENT
1-5	Asset number
6-14	Original asset value in dollars and cents
15-16	Blank
17-18	Number of years over which the asset is to be depreciated
19-80	Blank

Output: This should be on a new page for each asset and should have approximately the following format:

ASSET 12345   ORIGINAL VALUE: $1,000.00

YEAR	DEPRECIATION	ACCUMULATED DEPRECIATION	BOOK VALUE
1	$ 500.00	$ 500.00	$ 500.00
2	333.33	833.33	166.67
3	166.67	1,000.00	0.00

Note: In order always to show a final accumulated depreciation equal to the original value, as well as a final book value equal to zero, the depreciation of the last year is to be computed as follows:

Last year depreciation = original value – accumulated depreciation

Write and run a COBOL program to produce the desired output. Use as test data those shown in the preceding description.

7.3   The data processing objective of this program is to compute and print the
      monthly schedule of payments resulting from a credit purchase. Given
      the amount of the credit purchase and the number of monthly payments
      planned, the amount of the monthly payment is computed as follows:

$$\text{Payment due} \quad = \quad \frac{\text{amount of credit purchase}}{\text{number of payments}} + 0.015 \text{ of unpaid balance}$$

Of course, this formula presumes an interest charge of 0.015 per month
on the unpaid balance in the account. For example, suppose that a
customer has purchased an item valued at \$1,200.00 and is going to pay
for it over a 12-month period. The payment due at the end of the first
month is

$$\text{Payment due} \quad = \quad \frac{\$1,200.00}{12} + 0.015 \ (\$1,200.00)$$

$$= \$100.00 + 0.015 \ (\$1,200.00) = \$100.00 + \$18.00 = \$118.00$$

Similarly, for the second month the payment is

$$\text{Payment due} \quad = \quad \frac{\$1,200.00}{12} + 0.015 \ (\$1,100.00)$$

$$= \$100.00 + 0.015 \ (\$1,100.00) = \$100.00 + \$16.50 = \$116.50$$

The monthly payment consists of a constant element, which is the original amount of the credit purchase divided by the number of monthly
payments, and a variable element, which is the monthly interest charge
on the unpaid balance. With each monthly payment, the unpaid balance
is decreased by the amount of the constant element.

The desired output for this program is illustrated in Figure 7-10. This case
involves a credit transaction of \$4,291.50. It is assumed that the letterhead
is preprinted, but that the name and address, all column headings, and
the numeric values will be printed as the result of program execution.
Since the column headings are always the same, in practice these headings
also would be preprinted on the form. However, in our example we will
print the headings to illustrate how this can be accomplished through the
use of COBOL. For each monthly payment, the numeric information
provided is the amount of the monthly interest charge, the total payment
due that month, and the unpaid balance remaining after that month.
Note also that the spacing of the computer printout is designed for use
with a window envelope, thereby eliminating the need for separate
addressing of envelopes.

Program input: This will consist of a file, with one record per customer.
The record format and the layout of these data is as follows:

COLUMNS	CONTENT
1–20	Customer's name
21–45	Number and street
46–70	City, state, and ZIP code
71–78	Amount of credit purchase
79–80	Number of monthly payments

Write a COBOL program to accomplish the task we have described. Use
the input for Figure 7-10 as test data for your program, and compare your
output with the output in this figure.

FIGURE 7-10
Desired Form of Output for Exercise 7.3

ABC COMPANY
5000 East Camelback Road
Phoenix, Arizona 85033

ALBERT ROBINSON
3150 NORTH ST.
TEMPE, AZ 85282

Fold here

```
                      SCHEDULE OF PAYMENTS
                   ORIGINAL AMOUNT $4,291.50

       MONTH       INTEREST      TOTAL PAYMENT  UNPAID BALANCE

         1          64.37           422.00        3,933.87
         2          59.00           416.63        3,576.25
         3          53.46           411.27        3,218.62
         4          48.27           405.90        2,861.00
         5          42.91           400.54        2,503.37
         6          37.55           395.18        2,145.75
         7          32.18           389.81        1,788.12
         8          26.82           384.45        1,430.50
         9          21.45           379.08        1,072.87
        10          16.09           373.72          714.25
        11          10.72           368.35          357.62
        12           5.36           362.99             .00
```

Envelope

ABC COMPANY
5000 East Camelback Road
Phoenix, Arizona 85033

Window

```
ALBERT ROBINSON
3150 NORTH ST.
TEMPE, AZ  85282
```

7.4 A file contains data about the inventory of a company. Each inventory item is identified by a unique item number. The file is sorted on item number. There are three types of records in the file. A balance record contains the amount in inventory as of the last time the data were processed. A receipt record contains the amount of a shipment received. An issue record contains the amount sold. For each shipment received and each sale made, a separate record is created. We wish to read the records, process the data, produce an inventory report on the printer, and produce a set of new balance records.

Input is as follows:

COLUMN	CONTENT
1–5	Item number
6–20	Part name (on balance records only)
21	Type code
	1 = balance
	2 = receipt
	3 = issue
22–25	Quantity

(*Note:* The records in the input file have been sorted on item number. For each item the balance record precedes the receipt and issue records.)

Sample input is as follows:

```
01212TRANSFORMER    12350
01212               26000
01212               30150
01212               33050
01212               31600
01515GEAR TRAIN     11000
01515               30600
02010METAL PLATE    14000
```

Sample output: The printer output resulting from the previously given sample input is

```
ITEM NUMBER   PART NAME      PREVIOUS BALANCE   NEW BALANCE
01212         TRANSFORMER         2350             3550
01515         GEAR TRAIN          1000              400
02010         METAL PLATE         4000             4000
```

The balance records resulting from the sample input are

```
01212TRANSFORMER    103550
01515GEAR TRAIN     100400
02010METAL PLATE    104000
```

These balance records serve as input to the next program run, along with the receipt and issue records created between processing runs.

Write and run a COBOL program to accomplish the desired result. Assume all data are correct.

7.5 A file contains customer names in free form. Each record in that file consists of a field of 45 bytes containing the name, and a FILLER field of 35 bytes.

The last name is written first, followed by a comma, followed by the first name or initial, followed by a comma, and finally followed by the middle name or initial. Write a program to read data from that file and print the data in the following fixed format:

- Columns 11–30   Last name
- Columns 32–45   First name
- Columns 47–60   Middle name

Print the data under suitable headings and use the following test data:

```
BROWN,AL,GEORGE
GARCIA,P.,K.
LONGNAME,VALERIE,GEORGIA
```

7.6   Write a program to reverse the action of the sample program in this chapter. The input file will consist of compressed records, each record 80 bytes long and containing names separated by # symbols, as described in the explanation of the sample program.

The output will be a file containing names in fixed-length fields:

- Columns 1–15   Last name
- Columns 16–30   First name
- Columns 31–45   Middle name

If a name (middle or first) is missing, the corresponding field in the output file will contain blanks.

8 More About Conditional Statements

THE IF STATEMENT AND NESTED
    CONDITIONS

THE CONTINUE STATEMENT

CLASS CONDITIONS

THE SIGN CONDITION

SWITCH-STATUS CONDITIONS

COMPOUND CONDITIONS

THE EVALUATE STATEMENT

THE GO TO ... DEPENDING ON
    STATEMENT

VERB-RELATED CONDITIONS

SAMPLE PROGRAM USING COBOL '85

A S YOU MAY RECALL, *a number of features relating to conditional expressions and conditional statements were described in Chapter 5. In the present chapter you will review some of the points covered in that earlier chapter, and expand your study of conditional statements.*

You will begin with a review of the concept of nested conditional statements and extend its applications to more complex cases. Then you will study some types of conditions that expand on your knowledge of relational conditions and condition-name conditions from Chapter 5. These additional conditions are class conditions, sign conditions, and switch-status conditions. You will also review and expand on the subject of compound conditions that was introduced in Chapter 5. The CONTINUE verb, which can help to handle compound conditionals in some instances, will be included in your study.

Following the coverage of conditional statements, you will continue with the EVALUATE statement, available only in COBOL '85. This verb empowers you to write well-structured and easily understood case structures. Then you will study the GO TO ... DEPENDING statement, which provides yet another alternative for programming case structures.

A final sample program illustrates some of the COBOL '85 features and their impact on conditional statements within a complete program.

THE IF STATEMENT AND NESTED CONDITIONS

We begin with a review of the general format of the IF statement presented in Figure 8-1. As you may recall, in this format condition-1 is either a simple or compound conditional expression. Statement-1 and statement-2 represent either an imperative or a conditional statement optionally preceded by an imperative statement. The ELSE NEXT SENTENCE phrase may be omitted if it immediately precedes the terminal period of the sentence. The END-IF is the scope terminator. If the END-IF, available only in COBOL '85, is specified, then the ELSE NEXT SENTENCE must not be specified. Also, COBOL '85 provides the CONTINUE statement (discussed in the next section of this chapter), which can be used in lieu of NEXT SENTENCE for the null side of an IF statement.

When statement-1 and/or statement-2 in the IF statement format are conditional statements, then a nested conditional exists. Nested conditions can be quite extensive. Figure 8-2(a) illustrates an extensively nested condition in flowchart form. At first glance it appears that the flowchart is rather easily comprehensible. However, a flowchart is a good learning tool, but not a good programming tool, because flowcharts are difficult to modify. Figure 8-2(b) presents the corresponding program in both COBOL '74 and COBOL '85. The 1974 version does not include the END-IF scope terminator. As a result, we used duplicate code for the PERFORM G and PERFORM B statements. That is, we had to repeat PERFORM G three times because procedure G is to be executed unconditionally on C3, and the END-IF is not available.

Use of the END-IF scope terminator in the 1985 version helps to block off and identify related units of code in Figure 8-2(b). Still, as the levels of nesting are increased, it becomes difficult to follow the logic of the program. Figure 8-3 illustrates a deeply nested structure that would be very difficult to comprehend without a pictorial aid such as a flowchart. But rather than creating diagrammatic aids to cope with such complexity, our objective should be to reduce the complexity and thereby make the program logic more understandable and easier to code. One effective way of reducing program complexity is to decompose a complex structure into simpler but interrelated modules. Figure 8-4 illustrates one possible decomposition of the nested structure in Figure 8-3. At the top of the figure, we have summarized the entire logic into an abbreviated structure consisting of one IF statement and two modules, M1 and M2. (You may want to review the concept of levels of abstraction, covered in Chapter 6.) Each of the two M modules can be referenced by a PERFORM statement, as follows:

```
IF  C1

    PERFORM M1

ELSE

    PERFORM M2.
```

FIGURE 8-1
General Format for the IF Statement

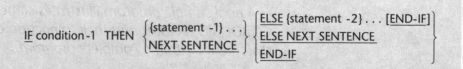

FIGURE 8-2

Illustration of Deeply Nested Program Structure

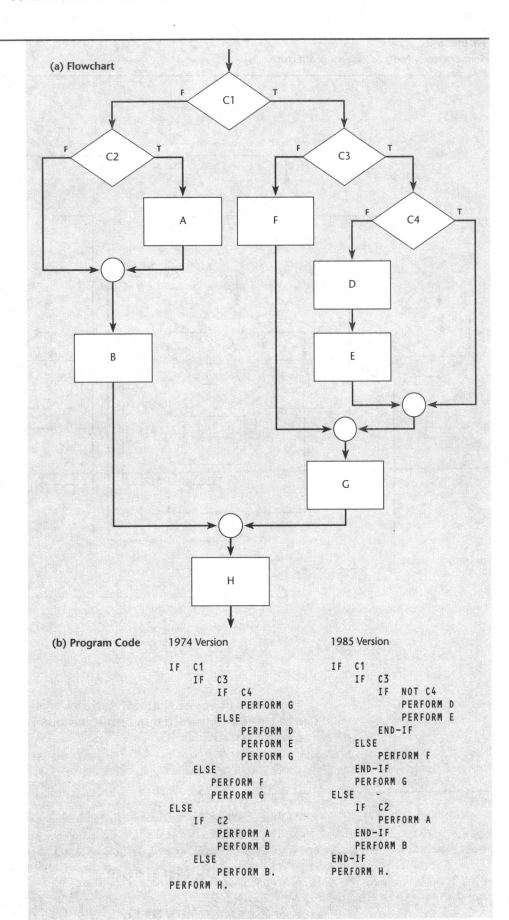

(a) Flowchart

(b) Program Code

1974 Version

```
IF  C1
    IF  C3
        IF  C4
            PERFORM G
        ELSE
            PERFORM D
            PERFORM E
            PERFORM G
    ELSE
        PERFORM F
        PERFORM G
ELSE
    IF  C2
        PERFORM A
        PERFORM B
    ELSE
        PERFORM B.
PERFORM H.
```

1985 Version

```
IF  C1
    IF  C3
        IF  NOT C4
            PERFORM D
            PERFORM E
        END-IF
    ELSE
        PERFORM F
    END-IF
    PERFORM G
ELSE
    IF  C2
        PERFORM A
    END-IF
    PERFORM B
END-IF
PERFORM H.
```

FIGURE 8-3
Sample Deeply Nested Conditional Structure

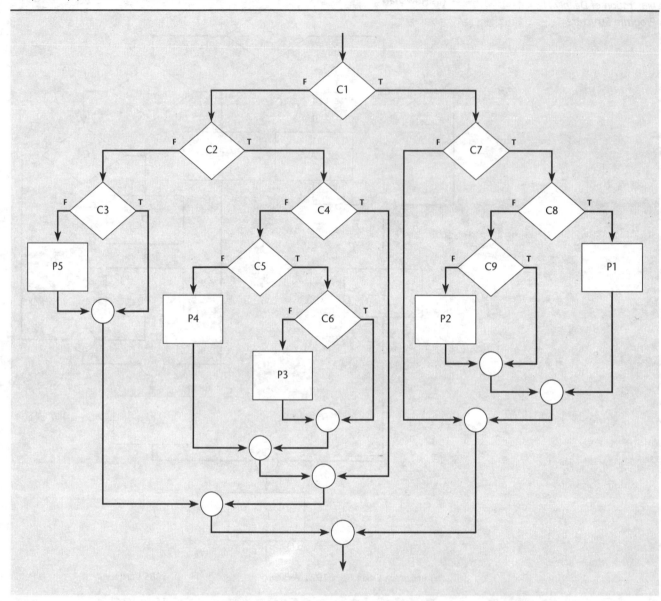

The flowchart for module M1 includes a reference to module M3, which is detailed in the lower left flowchart segment in Figure 8-4. Thus the corresponding code for M1 would be

```
M1.
    IF  C2
        PERFORM M3
    ELSE
        IF  C3
            NEXT SENTENCE
        ELSE
            PERFORM P5.
```

FIGURE 8-4
Decomposition of a Deeply Nested Conditional Structure

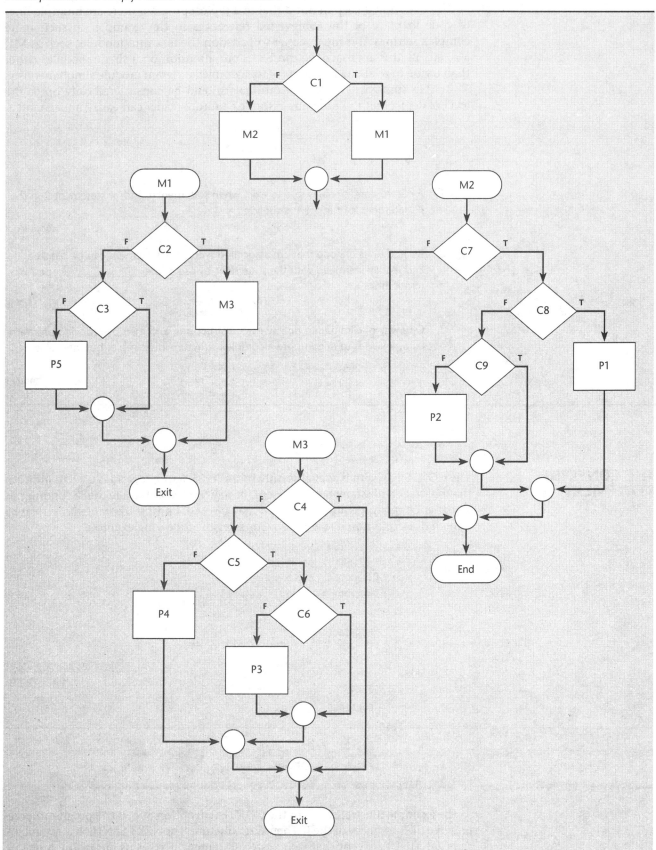

In this particular example we have used simplified and brief references, such as PERFORM P5, which may cause us to wonder if decomposition is worth the bother. We should keep in mind that in a typical program there are multiple lines of code in place of the abbreviated references in the example. In such more complex settings, it is much easier to partition the task into modules such as M1, M2, etc. By this approach we can focus our attention on a single module, rather than trying to relate to all aspects of the complex program module simultaneously.

In summary, nested conditionals should be constructed only up to the level of depth that the program author or a future reader can easily understand.

R E V I E W . . . .

1. A nested conditional is said to exist when statement-1 and/or statement-2 in the IF statement format are themselves _____

conditional

2. Related units of code that are associated with an IF statement can be blocked and readily identified with the statement by use of the _____ scope terminator.

END-IF

3. One way of eliminating deeply nested structures, and thereby reducing program complexity, is to decompose a complex structure into simpler but interrelated _____ .

modules

. . . .

THE CONTINUE STATEMENT

The CONTINUE verb is available only in the 1985 standard, and is used to indicate that no executable statement is present. It may be used anywhere that a conditional statement or an imperative statement may be used. Its most likely use is in the null branch of a conditional statement. Consider the following example:

```
IF  C1
    IF  C2
        PERFORM P-1
    ELSE
        CONTINUE
    END-IF
ELSE
    IF  C3
        CONTINUE
    ELSE
        PERFORM P-2
    END-IF
END-IF.
```

As the example illustrates, use of the CONTINUE option allows the programmer to preserve the symmetry of the If-Then-Else structure. The NEXT SENTENCE resembles the CONTINUE, except that in a nested statement it takes us out of the range of the entire IF statement. Thus, instead of using the CONTINUE in the above example, suppose we had written the following program segment:

```
IF C1
    IF  C2
        PERFORM P-1
    ELSE
        NEXT SENTENCE
    END-IF
END-IF
    .
    .
    .
```

In this case, when C2 is false, program execution will continue with the statement following the second END-IF. Thus the CONTINUE can play a very useful role in nested conditional statements.

In terms of function, CONTINUE is a "no-op" type of instruction, just like the EXIT discussed in Chapter 7. However, the EXIT has more specialized requirements: it must be used as the only statement in a paragraph, and therefore, is not an alternative to the CONTINUE in conditional statements.

Another convenient use of CONTINUE is to form "do-nothing" paragraphs, marking the end of a section or the last paragraph in a PERFORM procedure-1 THRU procedure-n series of paragraphs. In such cases the CONTINUE serves as an alternative to using the EXIT command.

R E V I E W . . . .

1. The verb that can be used to indicate that no executable statement is present is the _____ verb.

   CONTINUE

2. The CONTINUE statement [is / is not] a "no-op" type of statement and [must / need not] be the only statement in a paragraph.

   is; need not

3. When the CONTINUE statement is the only statement in a paragraph, a "do-nothing" paragraph has been formed. The usual function for such a paragraph is to mark the _____ of a section or series of paragraphs.

   end

. . . .

CLASS CONDITIONS

The use of a class condition test makes it possible to determine whether contents of a data field are *numeric, alphabetic, alphabetic lowercase,* or *alphabetic uppercase*. Further, by use of a combination of such conditionals, we also can determine if the field contains *alphanumeric data*. The general format for the class condition test is

identifier -1 is [NOT] $\begin{cases} \text{NUMERIC} \\ \text{ALPHABETIC} \\ \text{ALPHABETIC - LOWER} \\ \text{ALPHABETIC - UPPER} \\ \text{class -name} \end{cases}$

The two options dealing with the lowercase and uppercase aspect of alphabetic data are available only in the 1985 standard.

As an example, we can write statements like

```
IF  SALARY IS NUMERIC
     PERFORM PROCESS-PAY
ELSE
     PERFORM NON-NUMERIC-DATA-ERROR.
```

In general, the class condition test is useful as a check to determine if data fields contain the types of data as defined in the DATA DIVISION: numeric, alphabetic, or alphanumeric. The tests for NUMERIC and ALPHABETIC are straightforward, such as these:

```
IF AMOUNT IS NUMERIC ...
IF NAME IS NOT ALPHABETIC ...
```

In effect, the first statement directly tests the appropriateness of the content in the numeric field called AMOUNT, whereas the second statement tests for inappropriateness of the content in the alphabetic field called NAME.

The identifier being tested can be described as *numeric* (with the 9, V, and possibly S PIC characters), *alphanumeric* (with X characters in the PIC description), or *alphabetic* (with A characters in the PIC string). A data field is considered to be numeric if it contains only the digits 0–9, with or without an operational sign. Alphabetic items, on the other hand, consist of the letters A–Z and/or blanks. It is not valid to perform a NUMERIC class test on an alphabetic field or an ALPHABETIC class test on a numeric field. Thus, suppose we have the following DATA DIVISION specifications:

```
AMOUNT      PIC   9(4)V99.
NAME        PIC   A(15).
```

It would be improper to write

```
IF AMOUNT IS ALPHABETIC ...
```
        or
```
IF NAME IS NUMERIC ...
```

Instead, the AMOUNT field in the above example can be tested to determine if the content is, in fact, NUMERIC or if it is NOT NUMERIC. Similarly, the NAME field

TABLE 8-1
Valid Uses of the Class Condition Test for Different Kinds of Fields

FIELD CLASS	VALID TEST
Numeric	NUMERIC, NOT NUMERIC
Alphabetic	ALPHABETIC, NOT ALPHABETIC
Alphanumeric	NUMERIC, NOT NUMERIC, ALPHABETIC, NOT ALPHABETIC

can be tested only to determine if the content is ALPHABETIC or NOT ALPHABETIC.

A common case of a numeric field not containing numeric data involves reading a field from a record that contains one or more blanks. Specifying the PICTURE with 9s does not guarantee that the field will contain numeric digits. Table 8-1 summarizes the valid uses of the class condition test for different kinds of fields. Note that any of the condition tests may be used with an alphanumeric field.

Since an alphanumeric field can have both alphabetic and numeric content, the alphanumeric content can be ascertained indirectly by determining that the content is not entirely numeric and that it is not entirely alphabetic, as follows:

```
IF  FIELD-A IS NOT NUMERIC
   IF  FIELD-A IS NOT ALPHABETIC
      PERFORM ALPHA-NUM-PAR ...
```

For later reference we mention here that the class condition test cannot be used with numeric items whose USAGE has been declared COMPUTATIONAL. Thus the usage must be explicitly or implicitly DISPLAY. The COMPUTATIONAL and DISPLAY clauses are discussed in Chapter 16.

The ALPHABETIC-LOWER and ALPHABETIC-UPPER are new with the 1985 standard and provide a way of testing the content of a nonnumeric field for the presence of lowercase and uppercase alphabetic characters, respectively. Although data fields may contain lowercase letters, programs written in COBOL '74 themselves must be written in uppercase, except for the nonnumeric literals. For example, the following statements are valid:

```
02 NAME-FIELD PIC X(8) VALUE 'John Doe.'
MOVE 'incompatible codes' TO ERR-MESSAGE.
```

In COBOL '85 we can also use lowercase letters in the COBOL program itself to specify nonreserved words, as in the following:

```
MOVE last-name-in TO last-name-out
PERFORM 250-Report-Detail
   UNTIL  salesperson-no NOT = previous-salesperson-no.
```

Also, many compilers allow reserved COBOL words to be in lowercase.

Because of the multitude of existing programs written in uppercase code, in this book we have chosen *not* to use the 1985 option of using lowercase letters in the program samples.

The fifth class condition in the general format for class conditions at the beginning of this section, *class-name,* can be used for a user-defined class. Such a class can be defined in the SPECIAL-NAMES paragraph of the ENVIRONMENT DIVISION. The user defines a set of characters, assigns them a class-name, and then can refer to that class-name to test whether it is true or false that a data item consists exclusively of the characters identified in the definition of the class-name. Here is an example:

```
ENVIRONMENT DIVISION.
CONFIGURATION SECTION.
SOURCE-COMPUTER.  ABC-480.
OBJECT-COMPUTER.  ABC-480.
```

```
SPECIAL-NAMES.
    CLASS  SPOKEN-NUMERIC
      IS  '0' THRU '9'
                'o', 'O'.  (These are the lowercase and uppercase letter "o")
```

In the above example SPOKEN-NUMERIC is defined as the set of 10 numeric digits and the letter "o", to allow for the use of "o" as an alternate to zero, such as in "the course number is three-o-two" (perhaps as heard and interpreted by a speech-recognition data-input device). In the PROCEDURE DIVISION we now write

```
IF STREET-NUMBER IS SPOKEN-NUMERIC ...
```

The condition is true if STREET-NUMBER contains only the characters in the defined set SPOKEN-NUMERIC, which consists of the 10 digits and the letter "o", as defined above.

R E V I E W . . . .

1. The purpose of a class condition test is to determine if the actual content of a storage field is _____ , _____ , or _____ .

   numeric; alphabetic; alphanumeric

2. Suppose that a field named VENDOR has been defined as an alphabetic field in the DATA DIVISION, with PICTURE A(12). If we wish to check for the possibility that numeric data have been entered into this field, we could do so by the following statement:

   IF VENDOR IS _____

   NOT ALPHABETIC

3. Suppose that a field named ADDRESS has been defined as an alphanumeric field in the DATA DIVISION. If we wish to PERFORM PAR-A when the content of the field is, in fact, alphanumeric, we can do so by the following statement:

   _____

   _____

   _____

   IF ADDRESS IS NOT NUMERIC
IF ADDRESS IS NOT ALPHABETIC
PERFORM PAR-A

4. In the 1985 standard the content of a nonnumeric field can be tested for the presence of lowercase and uppercase alphabetic characters by the respective keywords _____ and _____ .

   ALPHABETIC-LOWER; ALPHABETIC-UPPER

5. In COBOL '85 we can use lowercase letters in the program itself to specify _____ words.

   nonreserved

6. The clause in the SPECIAL-NAMES paragraph that can be used to define a set of characters and to assign a class-name to them is the _____ clause.

   CLASS

. . . .

THE SIGN CONDITION

The sign condition determines whether or not the algebraic value of an identifier or arithmetic expression is greater than, less than, or equal to zero. The general format for the sign condition is

$$\underline{IF} \left\{ \begin{array}{l} \text{identifer} \\ \text{arithmetic -expression} \end{array} \right\} \text{IS [\underline{NOT}]} \left\{ \begin{array}{l} \underline{POSITIVE} \\ \underline{NEGATIVE} \\ \underline{ZERO} \end{array} \right\} \ldots$$

The subject of the condition must be a numeric field or an arithmetic expression. If the value contained in the field is greater than zero, it is POSITIVE; if the value is equal to zero, it is ZERO; and if it is less than zero, it is NEGATIVE.

As was true for the class condition test, the sign condition is used frequently to check on the appropriateness of data. For example, if an inventory value cannot be negative by definition, the presence of a negative value can be detected using the sign condition test, such as in IF INV-QUANTITY IS NEGATIVE. This is a bit more convenient than the equivalent relational test, IF INV-QUANTITY < ZERO. As can be seen by the above two examples, the sign test provides a minor improvement in documentation. By the way, this is a good point to recall that, in order for a field to contain a negative value, it must have been defined with an S character in its PIC string. Also, note that the + and – editing characters do *not* signify algebraic values, since they are not operational signs.

SWITCH-STATUS CONDITIONS

The implementor of a compiler may define certain "switches" and give them associated names. Then such switches can be set as being "on" or "off" at program execution time through the operating system, and the executing program can include a test to determine the status of the switch.

The implementor-name and the ON and OFF values associated with each switch are specified in the SPECIAL-NAMES paragraph of the ENVIRONMENT DIVISION. The following example serves to illustrate such a specification:

```
ENVIRONMENT DIVISION.
CONFIGURATION SECTION.
SOURCE-COMPUTER.  ABC-480.
OBJECT-COMPUTER.  ABC-480.
SPECIAL-NAMES.
    UPSI-0 ON  STATUS IS END-OF-MONTH
           OFF STATUS IS NOT-END-OF-MONTH.
```

The example above defines an external switch by the implementor-name UPSI-0. It is to be referenced by the condition-names END-OF-MONTH and NOT-END-OF-MONTH as corresponding to the ON and OFF status, respectively. The switch is set by an action external to the COBOL program, usually through the operating system. The definition could be applied in the following PROCEDURE DIVISION segment:

```
IF  END-OF-MONTH
    PERFORM CLOSE-THE-BOOKS
ELSE
    PERFORM DAILY-PROCESSING.
```

In essence, the above program segment says: If the external switch called UPSI-0 is ON at the time of program execution, do one thing; if it is OFF, do another thing. The program can then "sense" the operating environment at the time of program execution and take the appropriate action. It is clear that this is not a feature used in a student environment, but in keeping with the "comprehensive" nature of this book, we present the feature for your future reference.

R E V I E W . . . .

1. The sign condition can be used to test for three specific types of conditions in regard to the content held in a particular field: whether it is positive, _____ , or _____ .

negative; zero

2. The subject of the sign condition must be a _____ field or expression.

numeric

3. As indicated by its name, the purpose of a switch-status conditional is to determine if a switch is in an _____ or _____ condition.

ON; OFF

4. The implementor-names and the ON and OFF values associated with each such switch are specified in the _____ paragraph of the ENVIRONMENT DIVISION.

SPECIAL-NAMES

. . . .

COMPOUND CONDITIONS

The subject of compound conditions was introduced in Chapter 5. Here we review and expand on the subject. A *compound condition* is formed by combining two or more simple and/or compound conditions with the logical connectors AND, OR, or NOT. The word *OR* means *either or both*, while *AND* means *both*. Consider the following statement:

```
IF  AMT-DUE IS POSITIVE AND DAYS-OVERDUE > 30
      PERFORM PAR-A.
```

The instruction indicates that the program should execute PAR-A when *both* AMT-DUE is positive and DAYS-OVERDUE exceeds 30.

On the other hand, consider the following statement:

```
IF  AMT-DUE IS POSITIVE OR DAYS-OVERDUE > 30
      PERFORM PAR-A.
```

In this case PAR-A will be executed when *either* AMT-DUE is positive or DAYS-OVERDUE exceeds 30.

Parentheses can be and are used to clarify the meaning of a compound condition. For example, consider the following:

```
IF  ((KODE = 2) OR (KODE = 3)) AND (BALANCE-CODE = 1)
      MOVE SPACES TO ERROR-MESSAGE
      PERFORM OLD-ITEM-2.
```

In this example the condition is true if KODE is equal to 2 or 3 *and* BALANCE-CODE is equal to 1.

In the absence of parentheses the order of precedence (priority) in execution is NOT, AND, and OR. Thus

```
IF  A > B OR NOT C = 10 AND D < K
```

is equivalent to

```
IF  A > B OR ((NOT C = 10) AND D < K)
```

With reference to the examples above, it is obvious that omission of parentheses may result in unnecessarily greater difficulty in understanding a compound conditional expression.

A compound condition can also be abbreviated by omitting the subject of the relation condition or by omitting both the subject and the relational operator in any relational condition except the first. The format for the abbreviated combined relation condition is

$$\text{relation -condition} \left\{ \left\{ \frac{\text{AND}}{\text{OR}} \right\} \underline{[\text{NOT}]} \text{ [relational operator] object} \right\} \ldots$$

Presented below are some relational examples in both expanded and abbreviated form:

- Expanded
  ```
  (A NOT = B) OR (A NOT = C)
  ```
- Abbreviated
  ```
  A NOT = B OR C
  ```

- Expanded
  ```
  ((A > B) and (A NOT < C)) OR (A NOT < D)
  ```
- Abbreviated
  ```
  A > B AND NOT < C OR D
  ```

- Expanded
  ```
  (NOT (A = B)) OR (A = C)
  ```
- Abbreviated
  ```
  NOT A = B OR C
  ```

- Expanded
  ```
  NOT ((((A NOT > B) AND (A NOT > C)) AND (NOT (A NOT > D))))
  ```
- Abbreviated
  ```
  NOT (A NOT > B AND C AND NOT D)
  ```

Brevity of expression may or may not be desirable, depending on the conditional expression. For instance, in the last example above, the multiple parentheses in the expanded version are somewhat confusing, and the abbreviated version is easier to understand. In the immediately preceding example, however, the expanded version is less likely to be misinterpreted than is the abbreviated version.

The above examples use abstract data-names to provide a concise presentation of the subject. Using more conventional data-names, the very last example above could be

```
IF  NOT (INCOME NOT > MEDIAN-INCOME
                 AND COLLEGE-LIMIT
                 AND NOT SCHOLARSHIP-LEVEL)
```

In ordinary language we would say: the condition is true if all three of the following are false:

income is greater than the value in median-income

income is greater than the value in college-limit

income is not greater than the value in scholarship-level

If you feel that these examples seem confusing, you are justified in your reaction. In many cases, however, it is the nature of the task that requires complex logical tests. Also, previously written programs often use "clever" conditional tests that are unnecessarily complex, and you will need to understand their meaning even if you personally would not have chosen to write such expressions. Programmers can improve documentation by not using unnecessarily complicated expressions. For instance compare the following equivalent pairs:

```
IF  A  NOT >  B                   IF  A  <=  B
                          or  IF  A  < B  OR  A = B

IF  NOT (A NOT  >  B)              IF  A  >  B
```

The equivalent statements on the right are easier to understand.

R E V I E W . . . .

1. In contrast to the use of simple conditionals, a combination of tests can be included in one statement by the use of _____ conditionals.

   compound

2. The use of a compound conditional requires the use of one of the logical operators: _____ , _____ , or _____ .

   OR; NOT; AND

3. When the logical operator OR is used in a compound conditional test, the presence of [either/ both / either or both] of the conditional states constitutes a true condition.

   either or both

4. When the logical operator AND is used in a compound conditional test, the presence of [either / both / either or both] of the conditional states constitutes a true condition.

   both

5. Generally, the abbreviated form of a compound conditional requires [more / fewer] parentheses and is [easier / more difficult] to interpret in terms of meaning.

   fewer; easier

. . . .

THE EVALUATE STATEMENT

The EVALUATE verb, available only in COBOL '85, provides a powerful and convenient way of implementing the "case" structure in structured programming. Use of the EVALUATE statement eliminates the need to use complicated nested IF statements and allows the programmer to express conditional logic in a well-documented manner. The general format of the statement is presented in Figure 8-5.

As the general format indicates, there are many options available in using the EVALUATE statement, hence its power and flexibility. Let us begin by considering the following simple example:

```
EVALUATE TRANSACTION-CODE
    WHEN 1     PERFORM P-A
    WHEN 2     PERFORM P-B
    WHEN 3     PERFORM P-C
    WHEN OTHER PERFORM P-D.
```

The above statement says to "evaluate" TRANSACTION-CODE and if it is equal to 1, to PERFORM P-A; if it is equal to 2, to PERFORM P-B, and so on. If TRANSACTION-CODE is not 1, 2, or 3, then it is to PERFORM P-D. TRANSACTION-CODE is the

FIGURE 8-5
Format of the EVALUATE Statement

```
           { identifier-1 }       [      { identifier-2 } ]
           { literal-1    }       [      { literal-2    } ]
EVALUATE   { expression-1 }       [ ALSO { expression-2 } ] ...
           { TRUE         }       [      { TRUE         } ]
           { FALSE        }       [      { FALSE        } ]

{{WHEN
 { ANY                                                                        }
 { condition-1                                                                }
 { TRUE                                                                       }
 { FALSE                                                                      }
 {        { identifier-3            } [ { THROUGH } { identifier-4            } ] }
 { [NOT]  { literal-3               } [ {         } { literal-4               } ] }
 {        { arithmetic-expression-1 } [ { THRU    } { arithmetic-expression-2 } ] }

 [        { ANY                                                                         }     ]
 [        { condition-2                                                                 }     ]
 [        { TRUE                                                                        }     ]
 [ ALSO   { FALSE                                                                       } ... ] ...
 [        {        { identifier-5            } [ { THROUGH } { identifier-6            } ] }     ]
 [        { [NOT]  { literal-5               } [ {         } { literal-6               } ] }     ]
 [        {        { arithmetic-expression-3 } [ { THRU    } { arithmetic-expression-4 } ] }     ]

 imperative-statement-1} ...
[WHEN OTHER imperative-statement-2]
[END-EVALUATE]
```

evaluation subject, and as we shall explain below, multiple evaluation subjects may be included in an EVALUATE statement.

The literals 1, 2, and 3 and the keyword OTHER that follow each WHEN in the above example are the evaluation *objects.* Again, as explained below, there may be a single object or multiple objects associated with each WHEN. Execution of an EVALUATE statement involves evaluating each subject with respect to each corresponding object for each of the WHEN statements. Evaluation means substituting each subject and each object with one of the following:

TRUE or FALSE	a. if these very keywords are written as a subject or object
	b. if the subject/object is a condition
A value (numeric or alphanumeric)	a. if the subject/object is a literal or an identifier
	b. if the subject/object is an arithmetic expression
A range of values (numeric or alphanumeric)	if the object is written with the THROUGH or THRU option

The evaluation subject(s) and the corresponding object(s) are compared for each WHEN statement. If they match, then the imperative statement that follows the WHEN is executed. If no such statement immediately follows the WHEN, then the next encountered imperative statement associated with a subsequent WHEN is the one executed, as will be illustrated later in this section in Figure 8-10.

We now illustrate the uses of the EVALUATE command by a series of sample applications.

Figure 8-6 presents a sample case structure that is implemented in Figure 8-7 by use of an EVALUATE statement. Figure 8-8 represents the EVALUATE

FIGURE 8-6
Sample Case Structure

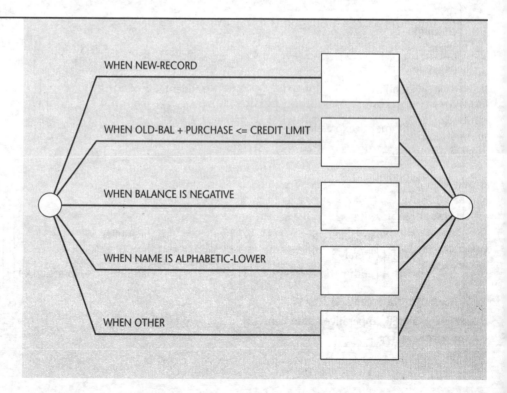

FIGURE 8-7

Sample EVALUATE Statement

```
EVALUATE TRUE                                The evaluation subject is "TRUE".

    WHEN NEW-RECORD                          NEW-RECORD is a condition-name and is the first
                                             evaluation object. If the condition NEW-RECORD is true
        PERFORM P-1                          then P-1 is executed and A is MOVED to B and
                                             program control continues with execution of P-6.
        MOVE A TO B

    WHEN OLD-BAL + PURCHASE <= CREDIT LIMIT  The second evaluation object is a relational condition.
                                             If it is true, then P-2 is executed and program control
        PERFORM P-2                          continues with execution of P-6.

    WHEN BALANCE IS NEGATIVE

        PERFORM P-3

        IF  X > Y
                                             The third evaluation object is a sign condition. If it is
            THEN                             true, P-3 is executed, followed by the conditional
                                             statement and then program control continues with
                MOVE P TO Q                  execution of P-6.

            ELSE

                MOVE R TO Q

        END-IF

    WHEN NAME IS ALPHABETIC-LOWER            The fourth evaluation object is a class condition. If it is
                                             true then P-4 is executed and program control
        PERFORM P-4                          continues with P-6.

    WHEN OTHER                               If none of the above four evaluation objects were
                                             TRUE, then P-5 is executed and program control
        PERFORM P-5                          continues with P-6.

END-EVALUATE

PERFORM P-6
```

statement in flowchart form in order to focus on the chronological order of execution of the commands. Finally, Figure 8-9 presents an equivalent nested IF coding of the same logic, so that this approach can be contrasted with the EVALUATE code in Figure 8-7.

Figure 8-10 illustrates use of the EVALUATE statement with multiple subjects and objects. There are three evaluation subjects: TRUE, TRUE, and FALSE; therefore, each WHEN (except a WHEN OTHER) must have three evaluation

FIGURE 8-8

*Flowchart Representation of
Sample EVALUATE Statement*

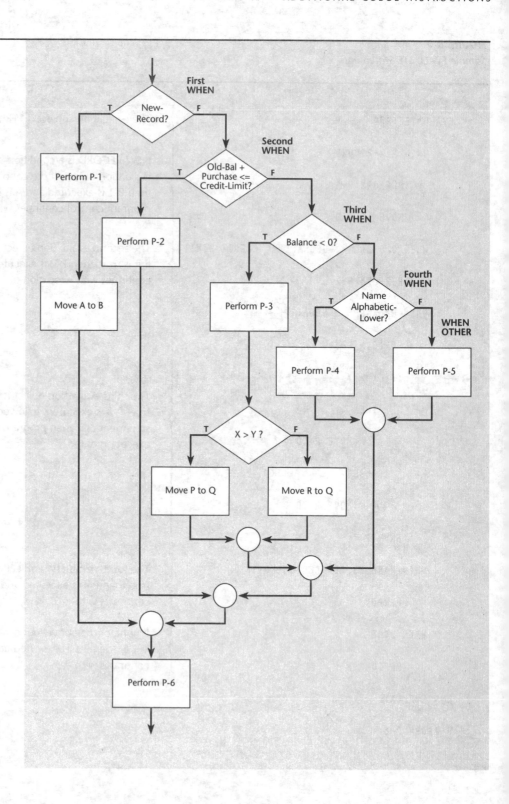

objects, although some may include the null ANY, which satisfies any comparison. Notice that the third and fourth WHEN "share" the PERFORM P-C imperative statement. If either of these two WHEN statements is satisfied, P-C is executed.

Figure 8-11 illustrates the incorporation of the EVALUATE verb in a conditional statement and omission of the optional WHEN OTHER clause. Notice the third evaluation subject, which is an arithmetic expression: BALANCE + (PRICE * QUANTITY) < CREDIT-LIMIT.

FIGURE 8-9
Nested IF Alternative to Sample EVALUATE Statement

```
IF  NEW-RECORD
    THEN
         PERFORM P-1
         MOVE A TO B
    ELSE
         IF  OLD-BAL + PURCHASE <= CREDIT-LIMIT
             THEN
                  PERFORM P-2
             ELSE
                  IF  BALANCE IS NEGATIVE
                      THEN
                           PERFORM P-3
                           IF  X > Y
                               THEN
                                   MOVE P TO Q
                               ELSE
                                   MOVE R TO Q
                           END-IF
                      ELSE
                           IF  NAME IS ALPHABETIC-LOWER
                               THEN
                                   PERFORM P-4
                               ELSE
                                   PERFORM P-5
                           END-IF
                  END-IF
         END-IF
END-IF
PERFORM P-6.
```

FIGURE 8-10
Additional Sample EVALUATE Illustration

EVALUATE	TRUE	ALSO	TRUE	ALSO	FALSE
WHEN	ACCOUNTANT **PERFORM P-A**	ALSO	EXPERIENCED	ALSO	WILLING-TO-TRAVEL
WHEN	ACCOUNTANT **PERFORM P-B**	ALSO	INEXPERIENCED	ALSO	WANTS-TO-STAY-PUT
WHEN	COMPUTER-SCIENTIST	ALSO	ANY	ALSO	UNDERPAID
WHEN	SYSTEM-ANALYST **PERFORM P-C**	ALSO	EXPERIENCED	ALSO	ANY
WHEN	EXPERIENCED **PERFORM P-D**	ALSO	ANY	ALSO	ANY

FIGURE 8-11

Sample EVALUATE as Part of a Conditional Statement

```
IF  A = B
    THEN
        EVALUATE TRUE   ALSO     BALANCE  ALSO  BALANCE + (PRICE * QUANTITY) < CREDIT-LIMIT
            WHEN EXCELLENT       ALSO                     ANY              ALSO          ANY
                 PERFORM P-1
            WHEN AVERAGE         ALSO  LOW-BAL  THRU MEDIUM-BAL           ALSO          ANY
                 PERFORM P-2
            WHEN MARGINAL        ALSO  LOW-BAL  THRU HIGH-BAL             ALSO          TRUE
                 PERFORM P-3
            WHEN DAYS-SINCE-LAST-PMT < LATE-LIMIT  ALSO  ANY             ALSO          TRUE
                 PERFORM P-4
        END-EVALUATE
    ELSE
        PERFORM P-A
END-IF
```

As the final example of using the EVALUATE statement, Figure 8-12 presents a decision table that shows two fields, YEAR-CODE and LETTER-GRADE. There are four alternative actions specified, depending on the joint values of the two fields. For instance, when YEAR-CODE has a value of 4, then the procedure called PROC-3 is executed regardless of the value of LETTER-GRADE. Figure 8-12 also includes an EVALUATE statement to implement the decision table. For example, the first WHEN clause is interpreted as follows:

If the value of YEAR-CODE is 1 thru 2 and the value of LETTER-GRADE is A thru C, then PERFORM PROC-1.

The ANY option in the third WHEN in Figure 8-12 specifies that any value of LETTER-GRADE fulfills the evaluation criterion for this WHEN conditional. Finally, the WHEN OTHER refers to both the YEAR-CODE and LETTER-CODE; it is equivalent to saying

Any combination of values of YEAR-CODE and LETTER-GRADE other than the ones specified in the previous WHEN statements.

THE GO TO ... DEPENDING ON STATEMENT

This is a specialized version of the GO TO verb introduced in Chapter 7. It is a conditional statement designed to implement a case structure. However, it is limited to only certain situations. The general format is

GO TO {procedure-name-1} . . . DEPENDING ON identifier-1

An example of using this format is

```
GO TO WEEKLY-REPORT
      MONTHLY-REPORT
      QUARTERLY-REPORT
DEPENDING ON PERIOD-FLAG.
```

FIGURE 8-12

Sample Use of the EVALUATE Verb

CONDITION		ACTION
YEAR-CODE	LETTER-GRADE	
1 or 2	A, B, or C	Execute PROC-1
3	A or B	Execute PROC-2
4	any	Execute PROC-3
any other	any	Execute PROC-4

```
EVALUATE YEAR-CODE  ALSO  LETTER-GRADE
    WHEN 1 THRU 2  ALSO  'A' THRU 'C'  PERFORM PROC-1
    WHEN 3         ALSO  'A' THRU 'B'  PERFORM PROC-2
    WHEN 4         ALSO  ANY           PERFORM PROC-3
    WHEN OTHER PERFORM PROC-4
END-EVALUATE
```

This example says to check the value of PERIOD-FLAG (identifier-1 in the format) and if the value is equal to 1, to GO TO the paragraph named WEEKLY-REPORT; if the value of PERIOD-FLAG is equal to 2, to GO TO MONTHLY-REPORT; and if it is equal to 3, to GO TO QUARTERLY-REPORT. Thus the statement is the equivalent of a series of mutually exclusive branching instructions.

A special feature, and a limitation, is that the identifier used in the statement must have values of 1, or 2, or 3, and so on. Then we can specify an implied GO TO statement corresponding to each of these consecutive values. Thus there must be as many procedure-names written as the possible values of identifier-1. If, however, the identifier has a value outside the implied range of values, then the program bypasses this GO TO, and execution continues with the next statement in the program. For example, if PERIOD-FLAG, above, had a value other than 1, 2, or 3, then the whole GO TO ... DEPENDING would be bypassed.

Although it may seem that the statement includes some very restrictive requirements, it is not unusual to have situations where these restrictions apply. For instance, suppose that student records in a college contain a field that serves as a code for the year of studies, such that 1 = freshman, 2 = sophomore, 3 = junior, and 4 = senior. This is typical of many situations where a code is used and the range of values assigned to the code is 1, 2, etc.

We now illustrate use of the application of the GO TO ... DEPENDING statement as a means of implementing case structures. We also take the opportunity to use the example to put together four alternative ways that a case structure can be implemented. Figure 8-13 consists of four parts and illustrates the implementation of the required case structure by use of the (a) EVALUATE statement; (b) nested IF; (c) GO TO ... DEPENDING; and (d) simple conditionals with GO TOs. In the example we assume that we have a field, YEAR-OF-STUDIES, which contains values in the range 1–4, indicating freshman through senior. In each of the four cases we want to execute a specialized procedure, such as FROSH-PAR. If the value in YEAR-OF-STUDIES is not within the valid range, we want to execute ERROR-PAR.

The sample code in parts (a) and (b) of Figure 8-13 is routine. Part (c) shows the use of the GO TO ... DEPENDING. Notice that we have made the effort

FIGURE 8-13

Alternative COBOL Implementations of Case Structure

```
EVALUATE TRUE
      WHEN     FRESHMAN      PERFORM    FROSH-PAR
      WHEN     SOPHOMORE     PERFORM    SOPH-PAR
      WHEN     JUNIOR        PERFORM    JUNIOR-PAR
      WHEN     SENIOR        PERFORM    SENIOR-PAR
      WHEN     OTHER         PERFORM    ERROR-PAR
END-EVALUATE
```

(a) Case Implementation using the EVALUATE Statement (ANSI 1985)

```
IF  FRESHMAN
      PERFORM FROSH-PAR
ELSE
      IF  SOPHOMORE
          PERFORM SOPH-PAR
      ELSE
          IF  JUNIOR
              PERFORM JUNIOR-PAR
          ELSE
              IF  SENIOR
                  PERFORM SENIOR-PAR
              ELSE
                  PERFORM ERROR-PAR
```

(b) Case Implementation using Nested IF Statements

to preserve the one-entry, one-exit concept of structured programming even while using GO TO statements. The initial GO TO ... DEPENDING branches to one of four paragraphs implementing the case structure. However, at the end of each of those four paragraphs, we have included a GO TO EXIT-PAR statement which brings program flow to one converging point so that there is a common exit.

In the ENTRY-PAR paragraph, notice the very last line following the DEPENDING ON YEAR-OF-STUDIES. It consists of the statement GO TO ERROR-PAR. If YEAR-OF-STUDIES does not contain a value in the range 1–4, the program will not have branched to any of the four named procedures. Instead, execution will bypass the GO TO ... DEPENDING statement and will "fall through" to the unconditional GO TO statement. Thus the counterpart of the OTHER option in the EVALUATE statement is the statement following the GO TO ... DEPENDING.

For completeness Figure 8-13 also illustrates use of simple conditionals with the GO TO statement in part (d) of the figure. Again, we have used GO TO EXIT-PAR for all cases to force convergence of program control flow to one exit point. As a final remark about the example in Figure 8-13(d), we should mention that we could have used nested IF with GO TOs just as well, but we chose to use simple IF statements. This choice would have been even more appropriate if the number of alternatives was large and we did not want to write a very deeply nested IF.

FIGURE 8-13

Alternative COBOL
Implementations of Case Structure
(continued)

```
02   YEAR-OF-STUDIES   PIC 9.
     88   FRESHMAN      VALUE 1.
     88   SOPHOMORE     VALUE 2.
     88   JUNIOR        VALUE 3.
     88   SENIOR        VALUE 4.
ENTRY-PAR.
     GO TO FROSH-PAR
           SOPH-PAR
           JUNIOR-PAR
           SENIOR-PAR
     DEPENDING ON YEAR-OPF-STUDIES.
     GO TO ERROR-PAR.


FROSH-PAR.
     --------------------
     --------------------
     GO TO EXIT-PAR.


SOPH-PAR.
     --------------------
     --------------------
     GO TO EXIT-PAR.


JUNIOR-PAR.
     --------------------
     --------------------
     GO TO EXIT-PAR.


SENIOR-PAR.
     --------------------
     --------------------
     GO TO EXIT-PAR.


ERROR-PAR
     --------------------
     --------------------
     GO TO EXIT-PAR.


EXIT-PAR.
```

(Notice that values start with 1 and are consecutive—a requirement for correct use of the GO TO . . . DEPENDING ON statement.)

(In case EXIT-PAR is not physically contiguous.)

(This is the converging point for all cases, so that the one-entry, one-exit structure is preserved and GO TOs are in control.)

(c) Case Implementation using GO TO . . . DEPENDING ON . . . .

FIGURE 8-13
Alternative COBOL Implementations of Case Structure (continued)

```
        IF  FRESHMAN
            PERFORM FROSH-PAR
            GO TO EXIT-PAR.


        IF  SOPHOMORE
            PERFORM SOPH-PAR
            GO TO EXIT-PAR.


        IF  JUNIOR
            PERFORM JUNIOR-PAR
            GO TO EXIT-PAR.


        IF  SENIOR
            PERFORM SENIOR-PAR
            GO TO EXIT-PAR.


        PERFORM ERROR-PAR
        GO TO EXIT-PAR.              (In case EXIT-Par is not physically contiguous.)


    EXIT-PAR.          (This is the converging point for all cases, so that the one-entry,
                       one-exit structure is preserved and GO TOs are in control.)
```

(d) Case Implementation using Simple Conditionals and GO TO

VERB-RELATED CONDITIONS

Several verbs in COBOL contain "built-in" conditionals. These are summarized in Table 8-2 along with the verb or verbs with which each of these conditionals is associated. Many of the verbs shown in Table 8-2 will be discussed in subsequent chapters. However, we have included them in this chapter for future reference since the subject falls naturally under the topic of conditional statements. COBOL uses such specialized conditionals to serve as special-purpose "if" statements, in contrast with the general-purpose IF.

R E V I E W . . . .

1. A powerful and convenient way of implementing the "case" type of program structure in COBOL '85 is provided by use of the _____ statement.

    EVALUATE

2. For each of the WHEN statements, execution of an EVALUATE verb involves evaluating each _____ with respect to its corresponding _____ .

    subject; object

3. The conditional GO TO verb that can be used in either COBOL '74 or COBOL '85 to implement the "case" type of program structure is the GO TO ... _____ verb.

    DEPENDING (or DEPENDING ON)

TABLE 8-2
Specialized Conditionals Related to Control Verbs

CONDITIONAL	RELATED VERB
AT <u>END</u>	READ, SEARCH
[<u>NOT</u>] AT <u>END</u>	READ
[<u>NOT</u>] AT $\begin{Bmatrix} \text{END-OF-PAGE} \\ \text{EOP} \end{Bmatrix}$	WRITE
[<u>NOT</u>] <u>INVALID</u> KEY	DELETE, READ, REWRITE, START, WRITE
[<u>NOT</u>] ON <u>EXCEPTION</u>	CALL
[<u>NOT</u>] ON <u>OVERFLOW</u>	STRING, UNSTRING
[<u>NOT</u>] ON <u>SIZE ERROR</u>	ADD, COMPUTE, DIVIDE, MULTIPLY, SUBTRACT
<u>UNTIL</u>	PERFORM
<u>WHEN</u>	EVALUATE, SEARCH

4. The [NOT] ON OVERFLOW and [NOT] ON SIZE ERROR conditionals are examples of _____-related conditionals.

verb

5. In its effect, a verb-related conditional serves as a special "_____" statement.

if

· · · · · · · · · · · · · · · · · · ·

SAMPLE PROGRAM USING COBOL '85

We conclude the chapter by presenting a revised version of the sample program in Figure 4-8 in Chapter 4. The revised program is presented in Figure 8-14. It includes use of selected COBOL '85 features, such as the in-line PERFORM, SET condition-name, and NOT AT END, and the scope terminators END-IF, END-READ, and END-PERFORM. The cumulative effect of these features is to allow us to write the entire PROCEDURE DIVISION as one paragraph. This particular occurrence is incidental to this case. Still, the general effect of using scope terminators is to enable COBOL '85 programs to reduce the number of paragraphs without impacting the self-documentation and clarity of the programs.

SUMMARY

The purpose of this chapter was to review and expand your knowledge of the use of conditional statements in COBOL.

The IF command is the fundamental type of conditional statement. A *nested* conditional is said to exist when statement-1 or statement-2 in the general format are themselves conditional statements. Use of the END-IF scope terminator in COBOL '85 helps to block off and identify units of code in a nested design. The CONTINUE verb, also available only in COBOL '85, is used to indicate that no

FIGURE 8-14

Sample Program Using COBOL '85

```
    PROCEDURE DIVISION.
*
    000-MAIN-ROUTINE.
        OPEN INPUT  EMPLOYEE-FILE
             OUTPUT REPORT-FILE.
*
* PRINT REPORT HEADINGS
        WRITE PRINT-LINE FROM HEADING-1 AFTER ADVANCING PAGE
        WRITE PRINT-LINE FROM HEADING-2 AFTER 2 LINES
        MOVE SPACES TO PRINT-LINE
        WRITE PRINT-LINE AFTER 2 LINES
*
* PROCESS AND PRINT EACH RECORD
        PERFORM UNTIL END-OF-EMPLOYEE-FILE
            READ EMPLOYEE-FILE
                AT  END
                    MOVE "YES" TO END-OF-FILE-TEST
                NOT AT  END
                    IF  MALE
                        MOVE EMPLOYEE-SALARY TO REPORT-MEN-SALARY
                        MOVE ZERO TO REPORT-WOMEN-SALARY
                        ADD 1 TO NO-OF-MEN
                        ADD EMPLOYEE-SALARY TO MEN-TOTAL-SALARY
                    ELSE
                        IF  FEMALE
                            MOVE EMPLOYEE-SALARY TO REPORT-WOMEN-SALARY
                            MOVE ZERO TO REPORT-MEN-SALARY
                            ADD 1 TO NO-OF-WOMEN
                            ADD EMPLOYEE-SALARY TO WOMEN-TOTAL-SALARY
                        ELSE
                            MOVE ALL "*" TO REPORT-ERROR-CODE
                        END-IF
                    END-IF
                    MOVE EMPLOYEE-NAME TO REPORT-EMPL-NAME
                    WRITE PRINT-LINE FROM REPORT-DETAIL-LINE BEFORE
                        ADVANCING 1 LINE
                    MOVE SPACES TO REPORT-DETAIL-LINE
            END-READ
        END-PERFORM
*
* PRINT REPORT FOOTINGS
        MOVE MEN-TOTAL-SALARY TO REPORT-TOT-MEN-SALARY
        MOVE WOMEN-TOTAL-SALARY TO REPORT-TOT-WOMEN-SALARY
        WRITE PRINT-LINE FROM REPORT-TOTAL-LINE AFTER 3 LINES
*
        DIVIDE NO-OF-MEN INTO MEN-TOTAL-SALARY
            GIVING REPORT-AVG-MEN-SALARY
        DIVIDE NO-OF-WOMEN INTO WOMEN-TOTAL-SALARY
            GIVING REPORT-AVG-WOMEN-SALARY
*
        WRITE PRINT-LINE FROM REPORT-AVERAGES-LINE AFTER 2 LINES
*
        CLOSE EMPLOYEE-FILE
              REPORT-FILE
*
        STOP RUN.
```

executable statement is present, and thereby also helps to block off and identify units of code.

The use of a *class condition test* makes it possible to determine whether the contents of a data field are *numeric, alphabetic, alphabetic lowercase, alphabetic uppercase, alphanumeric,* or belong to a user-defined class. The main purpose for such tests is to ascertain that the designated data classes in fact contain the types of data as defined in the DATA DIVISION or the SPECIAL-NAMES paragraph of the ENVIRONMENT DIVISION. On the other hand, the *sign condition test* is used to determine whether the content in a numeric data field or the value of an arithmetic expression is *positive, negative,* or *zero.* The purpose of a *switch-status conditional* is to test for the status of an "on" or "off' switch. The implementor-names and the ON and OFF values associated with each such switch are specified in the SPECIAL-NAMES paragraph of the ENVIRONMENT DIVISION.

A *compound condition* is formed by combining two or more simple and/or compound conditionals with the logical connectors AND, OR, or NOT. Parentheses are often used to clarify the meaning of compound conditions. A compound condition can be abbreviated by omitting the subject, or both the subject and relational operator, in any relational condition except the first one in the expression. As illustrated by a number of examples, the abbreviated version generally requires fewer parentheses.

The EVALUATE verb, available only in COBOL '85, is particularly useful for implementation of the *case* type of program structure. This is the type of structure that provides for the execution of one of *several* alternatives. The GO TO … DEPENDING statement, available in both COBOL versions, also can be used to implement the "case" structure. However, it is more limited in its applications than is the EVALUATE verb. Examples of implementing the "case" structure by several different approaches were given in the chapter.

Finally, *verb-related conditionals* were briefly overviewed. These are verbs that contain "built-in" conditionals, such as the AT END and [NOT] ON SIZE ERROR verbs.

EXERCISES

8.1   An input field has been defined as

```
03 IN-FIELD PICTURE X(10).
```

Two other fields in WORKING-STORAGE have been defined as

```
01 AMOUNT PICTURE 9(10).

01 NAME   PICTURE A(10).
```

We wish to test the content of IN-FIELD and, if it contains a number, to store it in AMOUNT; if it contains a name, to store it in NAME; and if a mixture of characters, to execute a paragraph called ERRORS.

a.   Write PROCEDURE DIVISION statements to accomplish this task.

b.   Suppose that if the IN-FIELD contains a number, it is actually in dollars and cents. What would you do to make the number available in dollars and cents instead of as an integer?

8.2.   We want to write a program to "edit" input data. In this context, editing means to check the data for accuracy and compliance with certain rules.

The data are in the following file:

```
FD  EMPLOYEE-FILE     LABEL RECORDS STANDARD
                      RECORD CONTAINS 80 CHARACTERS
                      DATA RECORD IS EMPLOYEE-RECORD.
01  EMPLOYEE-RECORD.
    02  EMPL-NAME           PIC X(15).
    02  EMPL-NO             PIC 9(4).
    02  PAY-CODE            PIC X.
        88  SALARIED        VALUE 'S'.
        88  HOURLY          VALUE 'H'.
        88  VALID-PAY-CODE  VALUE 'H', 'S'.
        88  ERROR-PAY-CODE  VALUE ... (You insert the value.)
    02  PAY-RATE            PIC 9(4)V99.
    02  FILLER              PIC X(54)
        .
        .
        .

WORKING-STORAGE SECTION.
01  PAY-LIMITS.
    02  MINIMUM-SALARY  PIC 9(4)V99 VALUE 940.00.
    02  MAXIMUM-SALARY  PIC 9(4)V99 VALUE 6800.00.
    02  MINIMUM-WAGE    PIC 9(2)V99 VALUE 5.50.
    02  MAXIMUM-WAGE    PIC 9(2)V99 VALUE 18.99.
```

We want to read the data and screen them for the kinds of errors implied by the above data definitions and by the sample output in Figure 8-15. As you can see in the sample output, if a record contains one or more errors, the record itself is printed, followed by the appropriate error messages.

Write a program to do this data editing task, and use the sample input in Figure 8-15 as test data.

FIGURE 8-15

Sample Input and Output for
Exercise 8.2

INPUT FILE

```
BROWN,R.K.              1234S156035
DAVIS,M.O.              5246H250603
GARCIA,L.A.             3345H000676
HARRISON,P.N            21005000700
MARTIN,A.C.             5123S12000
MARTINEZ,P.M.           4433S800000
PETERSON,R.A.           6161H0001256
                        8990H000600
```

PROGRAM OUTPUT

```
                        INPUT DATA ERROR LISTING
                   (RECORD PRECEDES ITS ERROR MESSAGES)

BROWN,R.K.      1234S156035
                UNREASONABLE PAY RATE FOR HOURLY EMPLOYEE

DAVIS,M.O.      5246H250603
                UNREASONABLE PAY RATE FOR HOURLY EMPLOYEE

HARRISON,P.N    21005000700
                PAY CODE IS NEITHER S NOR H

MARTIN,A.C.     5123S12000
                PAY RATE CONTAINS NON-NUMERIC CHARACTERS
                UNREASONABLE PAY RATE FOR HOURLY EMPLOYEE

MARTINEZ,P.M.   4433S800000
                UNREASONABLE PAY RATE FOR SALARIED EMPLOYEE

PETERSON,R.A.   6161H0001256
                UNREASONABLE PAY RATE FOR HOURLY EMPLOYEE

                8990H000600
                EMPLOYEE NAME IS MISSING
```

9

Control Break Processing for Reports

THE GENERAL STRUCTURE OF REPORTS

CONTROL BREAKS IN REPORT WRITING

LOGIC OF REPORT PROGRAMS

A SIMPLE REPORT PROGRAM

A MORE ADVANCED EXAMPLE

THE WRITE VERB WITH THE LINAGE CLAUSE

IN THIS CHAPTER *you will develop a basic level of expertise for producing reports. A report may consist of a* **report heading**, *the* **report body**, *and a* **report footing.** *The report body then is made up of pages, and you will learn what distinct types of parts can be included on each page from the standpoint of required programming. Then you will consider the topic of* **control breaks** *in programming for reports, and the general logical structure that applies to most such programs.*

Following this overall study of the topic, you will then be "walked through" two examples of preparing reports with control breaks: one relatively simple and the other more advanced. Your study will conclude with some specialized options in the WRITE verb that facilitate report generation.

THE GENERAL STRUCTURE OF REPORTS

Report output is a common and important purpose associated with the use of computers in business. People use computer data through reports. A *report* is a formatted collection of data recorded either as printed output or on a display screen.

Figure 9-1 presents the general structure of a report. There may be a *report heading* at the beginning of the report, which may contain such information as the report title, the date, the name of the person who prepared the report, intended recipients of the report, and the like. Then the *report body* consists of one or more pages. A page is a formatted collection of lines. Usually, pages are defined on the basis of some physical characteristics of the output medium. For instance, printed reports are usually printed on paper that is 11 inches in vertical length, while display-screen reports tend to be equal in vertical length to the size of the screen (about 24 lines). A page is subdivided into five parts, or types of report groups: a *page heading, control heading(s), report detail lines, control footing(s),* and a *page footing.*

A *page heading* is included to enhance the readability of long reports by including such information as page numbers and column headings. The report data are included in *detail lines* of one or more formats. A *control heading* is used to introduce a new category of data, such as a new department or a new salesperson. A *control footing* typically is used to summarize the data presented in the preceding group of detail lines, such as the total sales for the salesperson whose detail sales were just reported. Finally, the end of each page may include a *page footing* that contains summary data for the page or simply serves as an alternate page-numbering position (unless page numbers were included in the page heading).

After all pages have been presented, a *report footing* may be included to designate the end of the report and to provide summary data about the report as a whole.

FIGURE 9-1

General Report Structure

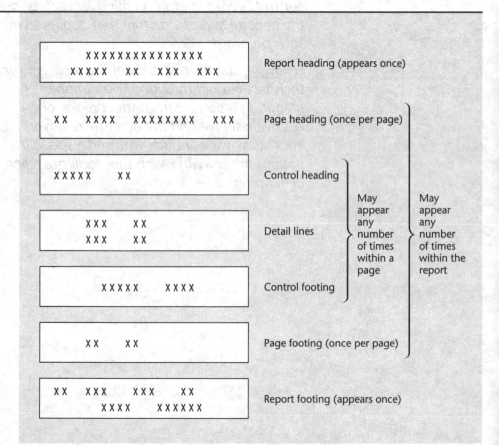

Figure 9-2 illustrates most of these report group types by means of a brief example. In the output the report heading consists of the first two lines. It is assumed that it appears only once at the beginning of the report. The indicated line serving as page heading consists of column headings to help the reader interpret the meaning of the report data. The control heading in this example is very simple, but nevertheless, distinct. When the report shows sales data for a new product number, the product number is listed; it is not repeated on every line, thus making the report easy to read. The fact that we do something distinctive when a new group of data is reported constitutes the control heading in this case.

The detail lines show the amount of individual sales transactions for each product. In the example we have two transactions for the first product and three for the second one. Notice that the control heading in this example (the line with the product number) happens to include the detail data (sales amount) for the first detail line. This need not be the case, but often it is so.

The control footing consists of the total sales for each product. In a less simple report, the control footing would typically include additional data. Finally, Figure 9-2 illustrates the idea of a report footing by means of the last line showing the grand total of sales figures for the report.

Report generation is characterized by common logical program procedures. Because of the common characteristics and the frequent need for report programs, a large number of report writer program products have been developed. These proprietary report writers are of two types. One type uses a specialized language that the programmer can use to compose a report-generating program. Such specialized languages are, of course, nonstandard and are unique to each program product. Many are "user-friendly" languages that can be used by "layman" users with just a few hours of training. A second type of report writer is the parameter-driven report writer. The program requires specifications about headings, totals, etc., as parameters, and then uses these to generate the desired report.

In the context of COBOL programming many report-generating programs are coded in the usual fashion. However, a special *report writer feature,* which facilitates report programming and also has the property of being standardized, is available. This COBOL feature is a language type of report writer. In essence, the report writer feature is a specialized language embedded in the

FIGURE 9-2
Sample Report Groups

```
              ACME CORPORATION                    Report Heading
          SALES REPORT FOR JULY, 1990


     PRODUCT NO.   SALES AMOUNT   TOTAL SALES     Page heading


        123          125.27                       Control heading
                     100.00                       Detail line
                                    $225.27        Control footing
        345           50.00
                     110.25
                      10.09

                                    $170.34
     GRAND TOTAL                    $395.61        Report footing
```

COBOL framework for use in report-generating programs. The report writer is described in Chapter 24.

R E V I E W . . . .

1. In general, a report may consist of a report heading, a report body, and a report
    _____.

    footing

2. The report body is normally subdivided into _____.

    pages

3. Of the subdivisions in a page of a report, the type of heading that introduces a
    new category of data is the _____ heading.

    control

4. Data that have been presented in the preceding group of data lines are
    summarized in the control _____.

    footing

5. With respect to commercially available report writer programs, one type is based
    on the use of specialized _____ while the second type requires
    specification of _____ for the desired report.

    languages; parameters

6. The COBOL feature that facilitates the programming of report-generating
    programs, is called the _____ feature.

    report writer

. . . .

CONTROL BREAKS IN REPORT WRITING

Most reports pertain to data that are associated with categories that bear a hierarchical relation to each other. Very often the categories correspond to organizational departments or groupings. For instance, suppose that we are producing a report listing student enrollment for a college. We have students enrolled in a course section, sections belonging to a course, courses belonging to a department, and departments belonging to a college. Suppose that we are interested in having the enrollment reported in a way that makes these relationships meaningful. To achieve this objective, we designate that each course section begin on a new page with a heading, that there be a heading for each course, and that there be a heading for each department. Further, we designate that total enrollment be reported for each section, for each course, for each department, and for the entire college.

In the above example we would say that we have three control breaks: *course section, course,* and *department.* We speak of department as the *major* control, course as the *intermediate* control, and section as the *minor* control. Of course, we may have more than three control levels. Regardless of the number of control levels, each level is subordinate to its superior and all are subordinates to one control level—the major control. In other words, control levels are nested in a hierarchical structure so that the report groups are clearly related.

As the report is being produced, we want to break the report routine whenever a new course section, a new course, or a new department begins. The control is based on the content of the fields that designate the course section, course, and department. We would expect that the report program logic would check the course section, for instance; and, if it changed value, we would want to print the total enrollment for the course section just listed. But it may be that the section did not change (say, section 1 of a one-section course), but the course changed from CIS-302 to CIS-402. The report program then also must be checking the course designation to capture the change. A similar checking procedure is required for department designation. In simple terms, as the report is being produced, the program has to be checking for a new department, a new course, and a new course section.

The highest level of control break is called the *final control,* which is, of course, nonrecurring. In essence, it is a means of controlling the report action when all the detail data have been processed. In the above student registration example, a final control break would occur when the last course section in the last course of the last department in the college had been processed. At that point the final control might involve reporting the enrollment for the entire college.

A point that relates to the control breaks is the fact that they are used to present control headings and control footings. As we explained at the beginning of the chapter, a *control heading* is a report group (one or more lines of output) that is presented when a control break occurs. For example, a control heading specified for the department field could be used to print the department name and start a new page. As the name implies, a *control footing* is a report group that is presented at the end of a group and before the next category begins. In our example, at the end of each course we might desire a control footing to write the accumulated total enrollment of all the sections in that course. Typically, control footings are used for accumulating and reporting totals, while control headings are used for printing headers.

It should be noted that the control fields and the sort order of the input file are related. In our example we would expect that the data have been sorted by student within section, by section within course, by course within department, and by department within the college. This sorting would be appropriate to establishing control breaks that treat department as a more inclusive control than course, course as more inclusive than section, and so forth.

R E V I E W . . . .

1. When control breaks are used in conjunction with a report program, the category that is at the highest hierarchical level compared with the other categories is termed the _____ control.

    major

2. In addition to the major control breaks, other levels of such breaks are the _____ and _____ controls.

    intermediate; minor

3. When all the report detail data have been processed, the last break is associated with the output of grand totals for all of the categories and is called the _____ control break.

    final

4. A heading (or footing) that is printed just before (or just after) a data group that is associated with a control break is called a _____ heading (or footing).

    control

. . . .

FIGURE 9-3

Sample Report Logic Flowchart for
Three Control Breaks

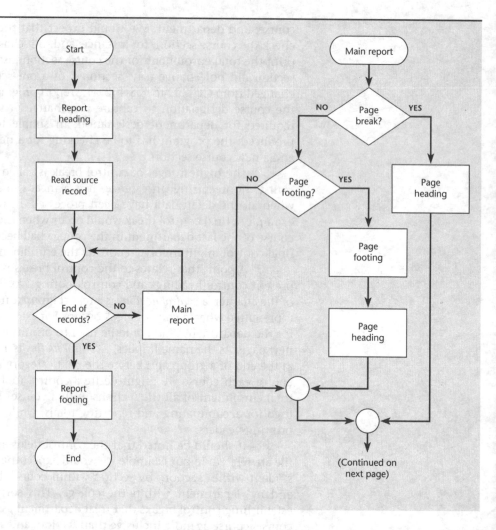

LOGIC OF REPORT PROGRAMS

The logical structure of report-generating programs tends to be similar regardless of the specific characteristics of the individual report. Figure 9-3 outlines this general logic in flowchart form. The figure is based on a report with three control breaks that are associated with the three fields: Dept., Month, and Part. Although the flowchart references these three control breaks, it is easy to see that it applies in concept to any report program with three levels of control breaks. Also, if we have a different number of control breaks, the flowchart can be easily adapted to that need.

In the flowchart of Figure 9-3, notice that a test for page break is made first. A condition of needing to start a new page is similar to the condition of a control heading or control footing: we need to pause the report routine and do something special. In the logic of a report program the page break case is hierarchically superior to the other control groups. If it is time to start a new page, we need to take care of that situation regardless of whether we do or do not have a new department, or a new month, etc.

Further studying the flowchart in Figure 9-3, notice that we test for Dept. break first, for Month next, and for Part last. We can assume that these represent the major, intermediate, and minor control levels, respectively. Thus if the program logic is "looking" at data for a new Dept., there is no need to know if it is a new Month or new Part; it is time to process a control footing for Dept., regardless.

FIGURE 9-3
*Sample Report Logic Flowchart for
Three Control Breaks (continued)*

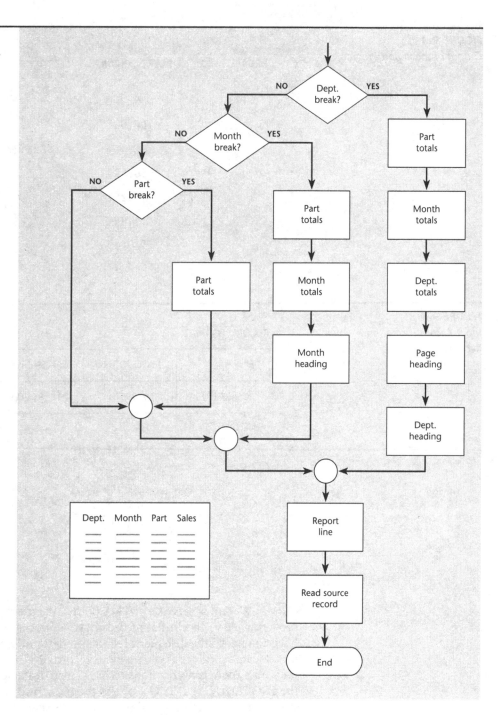

A SIMPLE REPORT PROGRAM

We present first a simple report program that illustrates many of the general concepts about report writing without being overwhelming in detail. Then we present a more advanced example in the next section of this chapter.

The objective of this program is to read records in a file and produce a report such as that shown in Figure 9-4. The input records are sorted so that all records pertaining to a given product are grouped together. The input records have the format and sample input presented in Figure 9-5.

Figure 9-6 presents a structure chart for the program, while Figure 9-7 is the corresponding COBOL program itself.

FIGURE 9-4

Output of the Report Program

```
     PRODUCT NO.    SALES AMOUNT    TOTAL SALES

         123           125.27
                       100.00
                                       $225.27

         345            50.50
                       110.25
                        10.09          $170.84
```

FIGURE 9-5

Input Record Format and Sample Records

RECORD FORMAT

FILLER	PRODUCT-NO	SALES-AMOUNT	FILLER
PIC X(15)	PIC 999	PIC 9(4)V99	PIC X(56)

SAMPLE INPUT

```
123012527
123010000
345005050
345011025
345001009
```

We can observe several key points that are typical of such report-generating programs. First, the initial record that is input is treated separately. Whereas we have to check all subsequent records to determine whether the current record is for the same product as the previous record, this is not the case for the first record, for which there is no previous record. The 010-PROCESS-FIRST-SALES-RECORD in the PROCEDURE DIVISION of the program, and the corresponding block in the structure chart, are designed to handle this special case.

After the first record has been processed, the remaining records are handled by the logic in 050-PROCESS-RECORD, which tests for a control break first by the statement IF PRODUCT-NUMBER = PREVIOUS-PRODUCT-NUMBER. The typical detail line is handled in 060-PROCESS-REPORT-LINE, while the case of a control break is handled in the 070-PROCESS-NEW-RECORD. The latter paragraph presents a control footing that, in this case, is simply the MOVE PRODUCT-TOTAL TO TOTAL-SALES-OUT statement followed by printing the control footing through execution of 040-PRINT-LINE. Then the control heading for the new product is handled by executing the 030-PRINT-NEW-PRODUCT-LINE.

Notice that all the actual printing is handled through the 040-PRINT-LINE procedure. Having one single printing point gives us easy control over the printing

FIGURE 9-6

Structure Chart for the Report Program

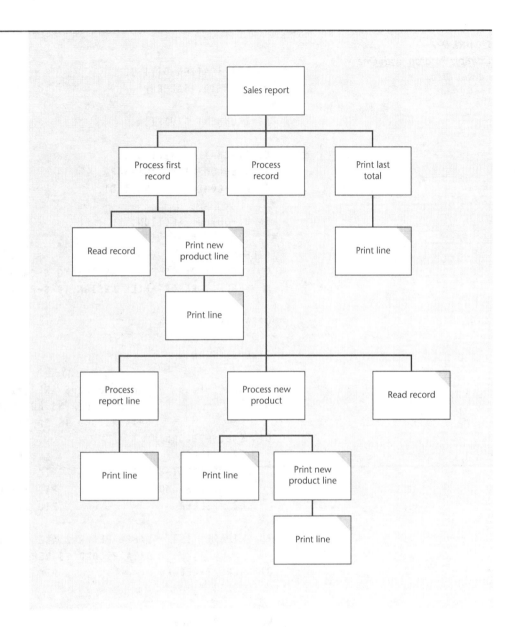

of a page heading at the top of each page. As we are about to print a report line, we check to see if we should be starting a new report page, in which case we should print a page heading. In the structure chart for the program, in Figure 9-6, Print Line is a module that is subordinate to five different modules. The reason for the repeated use of this module is that the page-heading logic is included in this module; therefore, it involves more than just printing a line. In a report-oriented program it is always best to do the printing in one module, rather than dispersing this function throughout the program. Report formats often need to be changed, and it is much easier to change one cohesive module than to attempt changing scattered statements throughout the program. In the program we assume that each page will consist of 25 lines, and we have defined a constant, PAGE-SIZE, in the WORKING-STORAGE SECTION for this value. Should we want to generate the report with a different number of lines per page, all we would have to do is change the VALUE clause of PAGE-SIZE.

As a final point in discussing the sample program, notice that the last input record is handled as another special case. After the AT END is true, we

FIGURE 9-7

Example Program with One
Control Break

```
IDENTIFICATION DIVISION.
PROGRAM-ID. SALEREP1.
*
ENVIRONMENT DIVISION.
*
CONFIGURATION SECTION.
SOURCE-COMPUTER. IBM-3081.
OBJECT-COMPUTER. IBM-3081.
*
INPUT-OUTPUT SECTION.
*
FILE-CONTROL.
    SELECT SALES-FILE  ASSIGN TO S-CARDS.
    SELECT REPORT-FILE ASSIGN TO S-PRINTER.
*
DATA DIVISION.
*
FILE SECTION.
*
FD  SALES-FILE      LABEL RECORDS ARE OMITTED
                    RECORD CONTAINS 80 CHARACTERS
                    DATA RECORD IS SALES-RECORD.
01  SALES-RECORD.
    02  FILLER               PIC X(15).
    02  PRODUCT-NUMBER       PIC 9(3).
    02  SALES-AMOUNT         PIC 9(4)V99.
    02  FILLER               PIC X(56).
*
FD  REPORT-FILE     LABEL RECORDS ARE OMITTED
                    DATA RECORD IS REPORT-RECORD.
01  REPORT-RECORD            PIC X(132).
*


WORKING-STORAGE SECTION.
*
01  PREVIOUS-VALUES.
    02  PREVIOUS-PRODUCT-NUMBER PIC 9(3).
*
01  END-OF-FILE-INDICATOR    PIC XXX    VALUE 'NO'.
    88 END-OF-FILE                      VALUE 'YES'.
    88 NOT-END-OF-FILE                  VALUE 'NO'.
*
01  PAGE-SIZE                PIC 99     VALUE 25.
*
01  PAGE-LINE-COUNTER        PIC 99     VALUE 25.
*
01  PRODUCT-TOTAL            PIC 9(5)V99 VALUE ZERO.
*
```

FIGURE 9-7
Example Program with One
Control Break (continued)

```
01  REPORT-HEADING.
    02 FILLER                   PIC X(10) VALUE SPACES.
    02 FILLER                   PIC X(11) VALUE 'PRODUCT NO.'.
    02 FILLER                   PIC X(3)  VALUE SPACES.
    02 FILLER                   PIC X(12) VALUE 'SALES AMOUNT'.
    02 FILLER                   PIC X(4)  VALUE SPACES.
    02 FILLER                   PIC X(11) VALUE 'TOTAL SALES'.
*
01  REPORT-LINE.
    02 FILLER                   PIC X(14) VALUE SPACES.
    02 PRODUCT-NUMBER-OUT       PIC 999.
    02 FILLER                   PIC X(9)  VALUE SPACES.
    02 SALES-AMOUNT-OUT         PIC Z,ZZ9.99.
    02 FILLER                   PIC X(7)  VALUE SPACES.
    02 TOTAL-SALES-OUT          PIC $$$,$$9.99.
*

PROCEDURE DIVISION.
*
000-PROGRAM-SUMMARY.
    OPEN INPUT SALES-FILE
        OUTPUT REPORT-FILE.
*
    PERFORM 010-PROCESS-FIRST-SALES-RECORD.
*
    PERFORM 050-PROCESS-RECORD
        UNTIL END-OF-FILE.
*
    PERFORM 080-PRINT-LAST-TOTAL.
*
    CLOSE SALES-FILE
        REPORT-FILE.
*
    STOP RUN.
*
010-PROCESS-FIRST-SALES-RECORD.
    PERFORM 020-READ-SALES-RECORD.
*
    IF NOT-END-OF-FILE
        MOVE PRODUCT-NUMBER TO PREVIOUS-PRODUCT-NUMBER
        MOVE SALES-AMOUNT TO PRODUCT-TOTAL
        PERFORM 030-PRINT-NEW-PRODUCT-LINE
        PERFORM 020-READ-SALES-RECORD
    END-IF.
*
020-READ-SALES-RECORD.
    READ SALES-FILE RECORD
        AT END SET END-OF-FILE TO TRUE.
*
```

FIGURE 9-7

*Example Program with One
Control Break (continued)*

```
030-PRINT-NEW-PRODUCT-LINE.
    MOVE SPACES TO REPORT-LINE
    MOVE PRODUCT-NUMBER TO PRODUCT-NUMBER-OUT
    MOVE SALES-AMOUNT TO SALES-AMOUNT-OUT
*
    PERFORM 040-PRINT-LINE.
*
040-PRINT-LINE.
    IF PAGE-LINE-COUNTER = PAGE-SIZE
        WRITE REPORT-RECORD FROM REPORT-HEADING
                AFTER ADVANCING PAGE
        MOVE SPACES TO REPORT-RECORD
        WRITE REPORT-RECORD AFTER ADVANCING 1 LINE
        MOVE 2 TO PAGE-LINE-COUNTER
    END-IF
*
    WRITE REPORT-RECORD FROM REPORT-LINE
        AFTER ADVANCING 1 LINE
*
    ADD 1 TO PAGE-LINE-COUNTER.
*
050-PROCESS-RECORD.
    IF PRODUCT-NUMBER = PREVIOUS-PRODUCT-NUMBER
        PERFORM 060-PROCESS-REPORT-LINE
    ELSE
        PERFORM 070-PROCESS-NEW-RECORD
    END-IF
*
    ADD SALES-AMOUNT TO PRODUCT-TOTAL
*
    PERFORM 020-READ-SALES-RECORD.
*
060-PROCESS-REPORT-LINE.
    MOVE SPACES TO REPORT-LINE
    MOVE SALES-AMOUNT TO SALES-AMOUNT-OUT
*
    PERFORM 040-PRINT-LINE.
*
070-PROCESS-NEW-RECORD.
    MOVE SPACES TO REPORT-LINE
    MOVE PRODUCT-TOTAL TO TOTAL-SALES-OUT
    PERFORM 040-PRINT-LINE
*
    MOVE ZERO TO PRODUCT-TOTAL
*
    PERFORM 030-PRINT-NEW-PRODUCT-LINE
*
    MOVE PRODUCT-NUMBER TO PREVIOUS-PRODUCT-NUMBER.
*
080-PRINT-LAST-TOTAL.
    MOVE SPACES TO REPORT-LINE
    MOVE PRODUCT-TOTAL TO TOTAL-SALES-OUT
    PERFORM 040-PRINT-LINE.
*
```

PERFORM 080-PRINT-LAST-TOTAL. This is another case of having a control break, but it is different from having a new product number. When the last record has been read in, we want to execute the control footing logic to show the total for the previous product, as usual. But there is no need to show the control heading for the next product, because there is no next product. Thus, the logic in 070-PROCESS-NEW-RECORD would not be correct, and we have developed, instead, the 080-PRINT-LAST-TOTAL procedure to handle this special case.

In a report program it is natural to distinguish three cases: the first record, the last record, and the ones between. Each of these types requires special processing. In our case we developed three distinct paragraphs to handle these three cases. An alternate approach would be to combine the processing of more than one of these cases in the same physical paragraph. For instance, we could have written this:

```
070-PROCESS-NEW-RECORD.
    MOVE SPACES TO REPORT-LINE
    MOVE PRODUCT-TOTAL TO TOTAL-SALES-OUT
    PERFORM 040-PRINT-LINE
    IF  END-OF-FILE
        NEXT SENTENCE
    ELSE
        MOVE ZERO TO PRODUCT-TOTAL
        PERFORM 030-PRINT-NEW-PRODUCT-LINE
        MOVE PRODUCT-NUMBER TO PREVIOUS-PRODUCT-NUMBER.
```

In this alternative code we have used the end-of-file condition to differentiate the processing of the last versus the "middle" records. It is easy to see that we could take a similar approach with the special case of the first record. We could set a flag at the beginning of the program:

```
01  FIRST-TIME-FLAG  PIC X  VALUE 'Y'.
    88  FIRST-RECORD  VALUE 'Y'.
```

Then we could modify the 050-PROCESS-RECORD paragraph as follows:

```
050-PROCESS-RECORD.
    IF  NOT FIRST-RECORD
        IF  PRODUCT-NUMBER = PREVIOUS-PRODUCT-NUMBER
            PERFORM 060-PROCESS-REPORT-LINE
        ELSE
            PERFORM 070-PROCESS-NEW-RECORD
        END-IF
        ADD SALES-AMOUNT TO PRODUCT-TOTAL
        PERFORM 020-READ-SALES-RECORD
    ELSE
following is the case of the first record
            MOVE 'N' TO FIRST-TIME-FLAG
            MOVE PRODUCT-NUMBER TO PREVIOUS-PRODUCT-NUMBER
            MOVE SALES-AMOUNT TO PRODUCT-TOTAL
            PERFORM 030-PRINT-NEW-PRODUCT-LINE
            PERFORM 020-READ-SALES-RECORD.
```

In the above illustration we have used the 1985 version END-IF scope terminator to delimit the second nested IF. In the 1974 version either we would have to repeat the two lines now following the END-IF and place them in front of the first ELSE, or we would set up a separate paragraph (which defeats the very point of the illustration about using one paragraph for multiple functions).

Although programmers differ in their preferences, we certainly advocate using distinct physical procedures/paragraphs for distinct functions. Use of flags, etc., complicates the logic for both the original program writer and the subsequent reader.

A MORE ADVANCED EXAMPLE

We now consider a revised version of the previous task that involves a report with *two* control breaks: Salesman Name and Product No. We have modified the source data file for the simple example in the previous section by including a SALESMAN-NAME instead of the FILLER in the first 15 bytes:

```
01   SALES-RECORD.
     SALESMAN-NAME          PIC X(15).
     PRODUCT-NUMBER         PIC 9(3).
     SALES-AMOUNT           PIC 9(4)V99.
     FILLER                 PIC X(56).
```

We want to report sales by salesman as well as by product number. Figure 9-8 presents the output resulting from the following input:

```
ADAMSON, JOHN   123012527
ADAMSON, JOHN   123010000
ADAMSON, JOHN   345005000
ADAMSON, JOHN   345011025
ADAMSON, JOHN   345001029
ROSELLE, LINDA  123400000
WILLIAMS, MARY  123020000
WILLIAMS, MARY  123050000
WILLIAMS, MARY  123030000
WILLIAMS, MARY  123112500
```

Notice in Figure 9-8 that we have two control footings, one for the product and one for the salesman. Additionally, each footing includes an explanatory message and repeats the Product Number or Salesman Number for easier reading. There is a report heading and also a report footing that shows the total sales for the report.

Before considering the details of this program, we first consider a simplified structure chart for such a two-level control break program in Figure 9-9. The first sales record is handled as a special case, as discussed in the previous example. Then, in the main repeating module that processes sales records, we determine the control break level and we identify three possibilities: no control break, a control break due to a new product, or a control break due to a new salesman. Separate modules have been designed for product footing, product heading, salesman footing, and salesman heading. Finally, a "print line" module and its subordinates are common to many modules. Figure 9-10 presents simplified pseudocode for the two-level program. It is easy to extrapolate this approach to programs with additional control levels. We would simply have more control heading and footing groups.

Figure 9-11 presents the structure chart for the specific example program. The sample program that corresponds to the structure chart in Figure 9-11 is presented in Figure 9-12.

FIGURE 9-8

Sample Output for a Program with
Two Control Breaks

```
                    SALES REPORT FOR ACME CORPORATION

      SALESMAN NAME      PRODUCT NO.     SALES AMOUNT     TOTAL SALES

      ADAMSON, JOHN      123                 125.27
                                             100.00

          * TOTAL FOR PRODUCT  123                          $225.27

      ADAMSON, JOHN      345                  50.00
                                             110.25
                                              10.29

          * TOTAL FOR PRODUCT  345                          $170.54

         ** TOTAL FOR SALESMAN    ADAMSON, JOHN             $395.81

      ROSELLE, LINDA     123               4,000.00

          * TOTAL FOR PRODUCT  123                        $4,000.00

         ** TOTAL FOR SALESMAN    ROSELLE, LINDA          $4,000.00

      WILLIAMS, MARY     123                 200.00
                                             500.00


      ---------- (page break here) ----------


      SALESMAN NAME      PRODUCT NO.     SALES AMOUNT     TOTAL SALES

      WILLIAMS, MARY     123                 300.00
                                           1,125.00

          * TOTAL FOR PRODUCT  123                        $2,125.00

         ** TOTAL FOR SALESMAN    WILLIAMS, MARY          $2,125.00

           *** TOTAL SALES FOR REPORT                     $6,520.81
```

Reviewing Figure 9-11, notice the module labeled 030-DETERMINE-CNTRL-BRK-LEVEL. What was the basis for including this module in the chart? We asked the question: "What is needed in order to select execution of particular control headings and footings?" We then realized that their execution is dependent on the particular control break. So we concluded that a module is needed to do the task of "sorting out" the control break situation.

FIGURE 9-9
Structure Chart for Two-Level Control Break Logic

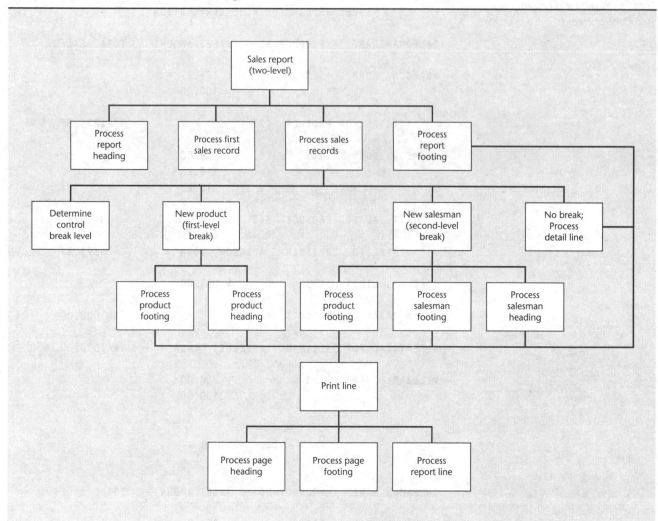

The 100-PRINT-LINE module(s) in Figure 9-11 do not show subordinates, unlike the counterpart in the more abstract case in Figure 9-9. Since no page footing is needed in this case, and since the page heading is a minor task, we chose to combine these functions in one module. However, should we later need to add more elaborate page heading and/or page footing functions, it would be easy to make such additions both to the chart and to the program.

As in the case of the simple program in the preceding section of this chapter, we have designed specialized modules for the first, the in-between, and the last records: 010-PRINT-REPORT-HEADING, 015-PROCESS-FIRST-SALES-RECORD, 020-PROCESS-SALES-RECORDS, and 110-END-OF-REPORT-FOOTING. The last of these three paragraphs combines the processing of the last record and the report footing. Because these are simple and related functions, we combined them in the same paragraph. If the report footing were more extensive, we would want to create a distinct module for processing the last record and another one for the report footing.

Let's discuss some points in the 020-PROCESS-SALES-RECORDS procedure of the program in Figure 9-12. First, we PERFORM 030-DETERMINE-CNTRL-BRK-

FIGURE 9-10

Pseudocode for Two-Level Report Program

```
Two-Level Report Program with Control Breaks

PERFORM
    Open Input and Output Files
    Print Report Headings
    Process First Input Record
    PERFORM  UNTIL End of Input File
        If No Control Break
            Then Process Detail Line
        Else
            If Second-Level (Product) Control Break
                Then   Process Second-Level (Product) Footing
                       Process Second-Level (Product) Heading
            Else
                Process Second-Level (Product) Footing
                Process First-Level (Salesman) Footing
                Process First-Level (Salesman) Heading
            End-If
        End-If
    END-PERFORM
    Process Report Footing
END-PERFORM
```

LEVEL, which is designed to "decide" what type of control break there is, if any. In this program there are two control fields, SALESMAN-NAME and PRODUCT-NUMBER. By having a distinct module, it is easy to see that we can expand the logic to accommodate any number of control break levels. Then the 020 paragraph of the program continues with

```
EVALUATE TRUE
    WHEN NO-BREAK        PERFORM 080-PRINT-DETAIL-LINE
    WHEN PRODUCT-BREAK   PERFORM 022-NEW-PRODUCT
    WHEN SALESMAN-BREAK  PERFORM 025-NEW-SALESMAN
END-EVALUATE
```

In both the 022-NEW-PRODUCT and 025-NEW SALESMAN, we first perform 070-PRINT-PRODUCT-FOOTING. Since PRODUCT-NUMBER is the minor level, if we do have any control break, we need to process the product control footing regardless of the specific control break. In other words, we want to show the sales total for the previous product if there is either a new salesman or a new product.

To see this point better, suppose that we have *three* levels: Department, Salesman, and Product, with Department being the highest level. We could write

FIGURE 9-11

Structure Chart for Sample Report Program

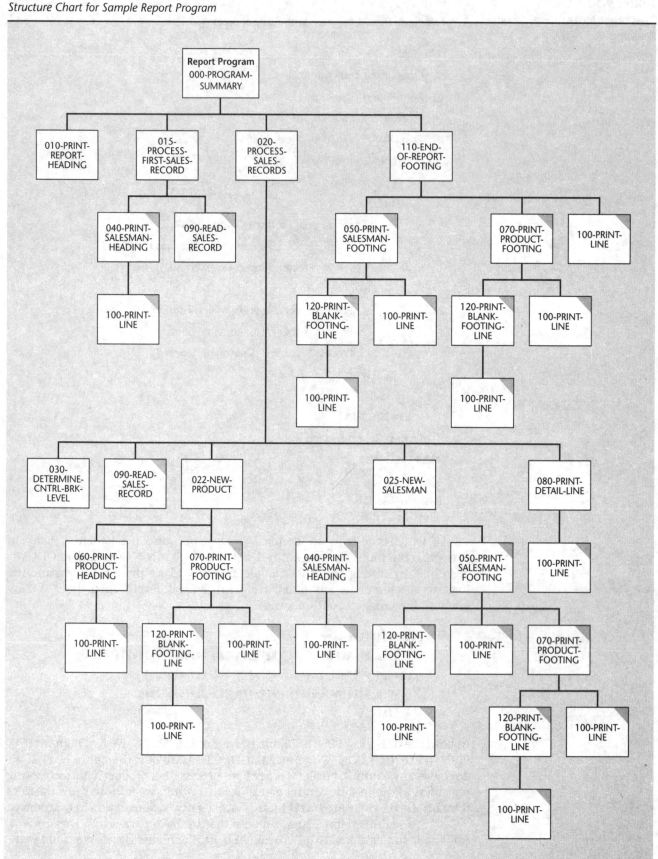

FIGURE 9-12

Example Program with Two Control Breaks

```
       IDENTIFICATION DIVISION.
       PROGRAM-ID. CTRLBRK.
      *
       ENVIRONMENT DIVISION.
      *
       CONFIGURATION SECTION.
       SOURCE-COMPUTER. ABC-490.
       OBJECT-COMPUTER. ABC-490.
      *
       INPUT-OUTPUT SECTION.
      *
       FILE-CONTROL.
           SELECT SALES-FILE   ASSIGN TO CTRLBRK.IN.
           SELECT REPORT-FILE   ASSIGN TO CTRLBRK.OUT.
      *
       DATA DIVISION.
      *
       FILE SECTION.
      *
       FD   SALES-FILE     LABEL RECORDS ARE OMITTED
                           RECORD CONTAINS 80 CHARACTERS
                           DATA RECORD IS SALES-RECORD.
       01 SALES-RECORD.
           02 SALESMAN-NAME         PIC X(15).
           02 PRODUCT-NUMBER        PIC 9(3).
           02 SALES-AMOUNT          PIC 9(4)V99.
           02 FILLER                PIC X(56).
      *
       FD   REPORT-FILE    LABEL RECORDS ARE OMITTED
                           DATA RECORD IS REPORT-RECORD.
       01   REPORT-RECORD           PIC X(132).
      *
       WORKING-STORAGE SECTION.
      *
       01   PREVIOUS-VALUES.
           02  PREVIOUS-SALESMAN-NAME PIC X(15).
           02  PREVIOUS-PRODUCT-NUMBER PIC 9(3).
      *
       01 PROGRAM-FLAGS.
           02  END-OF-FILE-INDICATOR  PIC XXX     VALUE 'NO'.
               88 END-OF-FILE                     VALUE IS 'YES'.
      *
           02  CONTROL-BREAK-LEVEL    PIC 9.
               88 NO-BREAK                         VALUE ZERO.
               88 PRODUCT-BREAK                    VALUE 1.
               88 SALESMAN-BREAK                   VALUE 2.
      *
           02  FOOTING-INDICATOR      PIC XXX     VALUE 'NO'.
               88  NO-FOOTING                      VALUE 'NO'.
               88  YES-FOOTING                     VALUE 'YES'.
      *
       01  PAGE-SIZE                  PIC 99      VALUE 25.
       01  PAGE-LINE-COUNTER          PIC 99      VALUE 25.
```

FIGURE 9-12

Example Program with Two
Control Breaks (continued)

```
*
 01  PAGE-HEADING.
     02  FILLER                  PIC X(10)    VALUE SPACE.
     02  FILLER                  PIC X(13)
             VALUE 'SALESMAN NAME'.
     02  FILLER                  PIC X(4)     VALUE SPACES.
     02  FILLER                  PIC X(11)
             VALUE 'PRODUCT NO.'.
     02  FILLER                  PIC X(3)     VALUE SPACES.
     02  FILLER                  PIC X(12)
             VALUE 'SALES AMOUNT'.
     02  FILLER                  PIC X(4)     VALUE SPACES.
     02  FILLER                  PIC X(11)
             VALUE 'TOTAL SALES'.
*
 01  REPORT-HEADING.
     02  FILLER                  PIC X(20)    VALUE SPACES.
     02  FILLER                  PIC X(33)    VALUE
             "SALES REPORT FOR ACME CORPORATION".
*
 01  REPORT-LINE.
     02  FILLER                  PIC X(10)    VALUE SPACES.
     02  SALESMAN-NAME-OUT       PIC X(15).
     02  FILLER                  PIC X(2)     VALUE SPACES.
     02  PRODUCT-NUMBER-OUT      PIC 999.
     02  FILLER                  PIC X(11)    VALUE SPACES.
     02  SALES-AMOUNT-OUT        PIC Z,ZZ9.99.
     02  FILLER                  PIC X(8)     VALUE SPACES.
     02  TOTAL-SALES-OUT         PIC $$$,$$9.99.
*
 01  SALESMAN-FOOTING.
     02  FILLER                  PIC X(12)    VALUE SPACES.
     02  FILLER                  PIC X(24)
                 VALUE '** TOTAL FOR SALESMAN '.
     02  SALESMAN-NAME-FOOTING   PIC X(15).
     02  FILLER                  PIC X(3)     VALUE SPACES.
     02  TOTAL-SALESMAN-FOOTING  PIC $$,$$$,$$9.99.
*
 01  PRODUCT-FOOTING.
     02  FILLER                  PIC X(14)    VALUE SPACES.
     02  FILLER                  PIC X(21)
                 VALUE '*TOTAL FOR PRODUCT '.
     02  PRODUCT-NUMBER-FOOTING  PIC 999.
     02  FILLER                  PIC X(16)    VALUE SPACES.
     02  TOTAL-PRODUCT-FOOTING   PIC $$,$$$,$$9.99.
*
 01  REPORT-FOOTING.
     02  FILLER                  PIC X(18)    VALUE SPACES.
     02  FILLER                  PIC X(26)
                 VALUE '*** TOTAL SALES FOR REPORT'.
     02  FILLER                  PIC X(10)    VALUE SPACES.
     02  TOTAL-REPORT-FOOTING    PIC $$,$$$,$$9.99.
```

FIGURE 9-12

Example Program with Two
Control Breaks (continued)

```
*
 01  SALES-TOTALS.
     02  PRODUCT-TOTAL-SALES    PIC 9(6)V99 VALUE ZERO.
     02  SALESMAN-TOTAL-SALES   PIC 9(6)V99 VALUE ZERO.
     02  REPORT-TOTAL-SALES     PIC 9(7)V99 VALUE ZERO.
*
 PROCEDURE DIVISION.
*
 000-PROGRAM-SUMMARY.
     OPEN  INPUT   SALES-FILE
     OPEN  OUTPUT  REPORT-FILE
*
     PERFORM 010-PRINT-REPORT-HEADING
*
     PERFORM 015-PROCESS-FIRST-SALES-RECORD
*
     PERFORM 020-PROCESS-SALES-RECORDS
             UNTIL END-OF-FILE
*
     PERFORM 110-END-OF-REPORT-FOOTING
*
     CLOSE SALES-FILE
           REPORT-FILE
*
     STOP RUN.
*
 010-PRINT-REPORT-HEADING.
     MOVE REPORT-HEADING TO REPORT-RECORD
     WRITE REPORT-RECORD AFTER ADVANCING PAGE
     MOVE PAGE-HEADING TO REPORT-RECORD
     WRITE REPORT-RECORD AFTER ADVANCING 2 LINES
     MOVE SPACES TO REPORT-RECORD
     WRITE REPORT-RECORD AFTER ADVANCING 1 LINE
     MOVE 4 TO PAGE-LINE-COUNTER.
*
 015-PROCESS-FIRST-SALES-RECORD.
     PERFORM 090-READ-SALES-RECORD
     IF NOT END-OF-FILE
         MOVE SALESMAN-NAME TO PREVIOUS-SALESMAN-NAME
         MOVE PRODUCT-NUMBER TO PREVIOUS-PRODUCT-NUMBER
         PERFORM 040-PRINT-SALESMAN-HEADING
         PERFORM 090-READ-SALES-RECORD.
*
 020-PROCESS-SALES-RECORDS.
*
     PERFORM 030-DETERMINE-CNTRL-BRK-LEVEL
*
     EVALUATE TRUE
         WHEN NO-BREAK        PERFORM 080-PRINT-DETAIL-LINE
         WHEN PRODUCT-BREAK   PERFORM 022-NEW-PRODUCT
         WHEN SALESMAN-BREAK  PERFORM 025-NEW-SALESMAN
     END-EVALUATE
```

FIGURE 9-12

Example Program with Two
Control Breaks (continued)

```
*
  PERFORM 090-READ-SALES-RECORD.
*
  022-NEW-PRODUCT.
      PERFORM 070-PRINT-PRODUCT-FOOTING
      PERFORM 060-PRINT-PRODUCT-HEADING.
*
  025-NEW-SALESMAN.
      PERFORM 070-PRINT-PRODUCT-FOOTING
      PERFORM 050-PRINT-SALESMAN-FOOTING
      PERFORM 040-PRINT-SALESMAN-HEADING.
*
  030-DETERMINE-CNTRL-BRK-LEVEL.
      IF  SALESMAN-NAME NOT = PREVIOUS-SALESMAN-NAME
          SET SALESMAN-BREAK TO TRUE
      ELSE
          IF  PRODUCT-NUMBER NOT = PREVIOUS-PRODUCT-NUMBER
              SET PRODUCT-BREAK TO TRUE
          ELSE
              SET NO-BREAK TO TRUE.
*
  040-PRINT-SALESMAN-HEADING.
      MOVE SPACES TO REPORT-LINE
      MOVE SALESMAN-NAME TO SALESMAN-NAME-OUT
      MOVE PRODUCT-NUMBER TO PRODUCT-NUMBER-OUT
      MOVE SALES-AMOUNT TO SALES-AMOUNT-OUT
      PERFORM 100-PRINT-LINE
      ADD SALES-AMOUNT TO PRODUCT-TOTAL-SALES.
*
  050-PRINT-SALESMAN-FOOTING.
      MOVE PREVIOUS-SALESMAN-NAME TO SALESMAN-NAME-FOOTING
      MOVE SALESMAN-TOTAL-SALES TO TOTAL-SALESMAN-FOOTING
      MOVE SALESMAN-FOOTING TO REPORT-LINE
      MOVE 'YES' TO FOOTING-INDICATOR
      PERFORM 100-PRINT-LINE
      MOVE 'NO' TO FOOTING-INDICATOR
      PERFORM 120-PRINT-BLANK-FOOTING-LINE
      ADD SALESMAN-TOTAL-SALES TO REPORT-TOTAL-SALES
      MOVE ZERO TO SALESMAN-TOTAL-SALES
*
      MOVE SALESMAN-NAME TO PREVIOUS-SALESMAN-NAME
      MOVE PRODUCT-NUMBER TO PREVIOUS-PRODUCT-NUMBER.
*
  060-PRINT-PRODUCT-HEADING.
      MOVE SPACES TO REPORT-LINE
      MOVE SALESMAN-NAME TO SALESMAN-NAME-OUT
      MOVE PRODUCT-NUMBER TO PRODUCT-NUMBER-OUT
      MOVE SALES-AMOUNT TO SALES-AMOUNT-OUT
      PERFORM 100-PRINT-LINE
      ADD SALES-AMOUNT TO PRODUCT-TOTAL-SALES.
*
```

FIGURE 9-12

*Example Program with Two
Control Breaks (continued)*

```
070-PRINT-PRODUCT-FOOTING.
    PERFORM 120-PRINT-BLANK-FOOTING-LINE
    MOVE PREVIOUS-PRODUCT-NUMBER TO PRODUCT-NUMBER-FOOTING
    MOVE PRODUCT-TOTAL-SALES TO TOTAL-PRODUCT-FOOTING
    MOVE PRODUCT-FOOTING TO REPORT-LINE
    MOVE 'YES' TO FOOTING-INDICATOR
    PERFORM 100-PRINT-LINE
    MOVE 'NO' TO FOOTING-INDICATOR
    PERFORM 120-PRINT-BLANK-FOOTING-LINE
    ADD PRODUCT-TOTAL-SALES TO SALESMAN-TOTAL-SALES
    MOVE ZERO TO PRODUCT-TOTAL-SALES
*
    MOVE PRODUCT-NUMBER TO PREVIOUS-PRODUCT-NUMBER.
*
080-PRINT-DETAIL-LINE.
    MOVE SPACES TO REPORT-LINE
    MOVE SALES-AMOUNT TO SALES-AMOUNT-OUT
    PERFORM 100-PRINT-LINE
    ADD SALES-AMOUNT TO PRODUCT-TOTAL-SALES.
*
090-READ-SALES-RECORD.
    READ SALES-FILE RECORD
        AT END SET END-OF-FILE TO TRUE.
*
100-PRINT-LINE.
    IF  PAGE-LINE-COUNTER > PAGE-SIZE OR
        PAGE-LINE-COUNTER = PAGE-SIZE
        WRITE REPORT-RECORD FROM PAGE-HEADING
            AFTER ADVANCING PAGE
        MOVE SPACES TO REPORT-RECORD
        WRITE REPORT-RECORD AFTER ADVANCING 1
        MOVE 2 TO PAGE-LINE-COUNTER
*
        IF  NO-FOOTING
            MOVE SALESMAN-NAME TO SALESMAN-NAME-OUT
            MOVE PRODUCT-NUMBER TO PRODUCT-NUMBER-OUT.
*
    WRITE REPORT-RECORD FROM REPORT-LINE
        AFTER ADVANCING 1
    ADD 1 TO PAGE-LINE-COUNTER.
*
110-END-OF-REPORT-FOOTING.
    PERFORM 070-PRINT-PRODUCT-FOOTING
    PERFORM 050-PRINT-SALESMAN-FOOTING
    MOVE REPORT-TOTAL-SALES TO TOTAL-REPORT-FOOTING
    MOVE REPORT-FOOTING TO REPORT-LINE
    MOVE 'YES' TO FOOTING-INDICATOR
    PERFORM 100-PRINT-LINE.
*
120-PRINT-BLANK-FOOTING-LINE.
    IF  PAGE-LINE-COUNTER < PAGE-SIZE
        MOVE SPACES TO REPORT-LINE
        PERFORM 100-PRINT-LINE.
```

the following type of logic (using nested IF, instead of EVALUATE, just to show that either approach can be used):

```
IF Department-break
      perform Product control footing
      perform Salesman control footing
      perform Department control footing
      perform Department control heading
ELSE
      IF Salesman-break
            perform Product control footing
            perform Salesman control footing
            perform Salesman control heading
      ELSE
            IF Product-break
                  perform Product control footing
                  perform Product control heading
```

Continuing with the 020-PROCESS-SALES-RECORDS paragraph in Figure 9-12, notice the use of the EVALUATE statement to select the appropriate case to execute: detail, product heading, or salesman heading. Of course, if we were using the 1974 standard, we would have used simple or nested IF statements in lieu of the EVALUATE. Also, we could use GO TO ... DEPENDING ON CONTROL-BREAK-LEVEL. However, either we would need to have defined the values of CONTROL-BREAK-LEVEL to be 1, 2, and 3 instead of 0, 1, and 2, or, alternatively, we could increment the value of that field by 1 just before the GO TO ... was executed.

Another feature in the sample program in Figure 9-12 is the handling of page breaks. The 100-PRINT-LINE paragraph uses a field called PAGE-LINE-COUNTER to keep track of the number of lines printed so far, and compares it to PAGE-SIZE, which contains the number of desired lines per page. After printing a control footing, we want to double-space. However, when the footing is the last line on the page we do not want to print a blank line, because it would be printed on the next page. The 120-PRINT-BLANK-FOOTING-LINE paragraph serves the purpose of controlling for such a case.

When we have a page break, we want to repeat the SALESMAN-NAME and the PRODUCT-NUMBER values at the top of the new page. For this reason, in the two footing paragraphs (050 and 070) we use a FOOTING-INDICATOR field as a flag to tell 100-PRINT-LINE that we are printing a control footing and it must not print the salesman name and the product number when there is a page break. Thus, 100-PRINT-LINE contains the following statement:

```
IF  NO-FOOTING
    MOVE SALESMAN-NAME TO SALESMAN-NAME-OUT
    MOVE PRODUCT-NUMBER TO PRODUCT-NUMBER-OUT.
```

As you review some of these detailed points in the sample program, it is likely that you wonder whether there could have been a simpler way to code these printer-spacing details. In particular, one might wonder if having a single point for printing all output (100-PRINT-LINE) does not make things more complex than they have to be. Our answer to such questions is that for a relatively simple program such as the current example, it might be easier to distribute the printing function throughout the program. However, the program structure that we have used is robust. It can be used with more complex program tasks without major modifications to the basic logical structure of the sample program. Thus, we suggest that you use this sample program as a generalized prototype for writing report programs with control breaks.

THE WRITE VERB WITH THE LINAGE CLAUSE

We conclude the chapter with discussion of some specialized options in the WRITE statement that facilitate report generation. Figure 9-13 presents the expanded format for the WRITE verb. We observe the AT END-OF-PAGE conditional statement. When specified, a check is made to determine if the END-OF-PAGE (abbreviated EOP) condition is met. If it is, then the imperative statement is executed.

The END-OF-PAGE condition is defined by means of the LINAGE clause in the DATA DIVISION, which has the format presented in Figure 9-14. Let us consider an example. We want to produce a report with the following format:

LINE NUMBER	CONTENTS
1–5	Not used
6	The page heading
7–56	The body of the report
57–59	The page totals
60–66	Not used

We could proceed as follows:

```
DATA DIVISION.
  .
  .
  .
FD  PRINT-FILE LABEL RECORD OMITTED
               DATA RECORD IS PRINT-REC
               LINAGE IS 54 LINES
                 WITH FOOTING AT 51
                 LINES AT TOP 5
                 LINES AT BOTTOM 7.
```

The page will consist of 66 lines, which is the sum of the values referenced in each phrase except for the FOOTING phrase (54 + 5 + 7 = 66). Five lines are unused at the top (lines 1–5), and 7 at the bottom (lines 60–66).

FIGURE 9-13
General Format for the WRITE Verb

```
WRITE record-name   [FROM identifier-1]
 [ {BEFORE}             { {identifer-2} [LINE ] } ]
 [ {AFTER }  ADVANCING  { {integer    } [LINES] } ]
 [                      { mnemonic-name         } ]
 [                      { PAGE                  } ]
 [AT {END-OF-PAGE} imperative-statement-1]
 [   {EOP        }                       ]
 [NOT AT {END-OF-PAGE} imperative-statement-1]
 [       {EOP        }                       ]
[END-WRITE]
```

FIGURE 9-14
General Format for the LINAGE Clause

```
LINAGE IS {data-name-1} LINES   [WITH FOOTING AT {data-name-2}]
          {integer-1  }         [                {integer-2  }]

[LINES AT TOP {data-name-3}]    [LINES AT BOTTOM {data-name-4}]
[             {integer-3  }]    [                {integer-4  }]
```

In the PROCEDURE DIVISION the statement

```
WRITE PRINT-REC FROM TOP-HEADER
      AFTER ADVANCING PAGE
```

will cause printing of the content of TOP-HEADER on line 6 because now PAGE is associated with line 6, since LINES AT TOP 5 means that 5 lines will be left blank at the top of the page. (TOP-HEADER in this example is assumed to contain the desired header.)

Now consider the following commands, assumed to be executed iteratively under control of a PERFORM . . . UNTIL or other such statement:

```
WRITE PRINT-REC FROM BODY-OF-REPORT-LINE
      AFTER ADVANCING 1 LINE
      AT END-OF-PAGE PERFORM TOTALS.
             .
             .
             .
TOTALS.
      WRITE PRINT-REC FROM TOTALS-LINE
            AFTER ADVANCING 3 LINES
      WRITE PRINT-REC FROM TOP-HEADER
            AFTER ADVANCING PAGE.
```

With reference to the above, we will keep printing data from BODY-OF-REPORT-LINE until we have reached line 56 (51 + 5), which is defined as the footing: WITH FOOTING AT 51. At that point the END-OF-PAGE condition will hold, and we will PERFORM TOTALS, in which we print data on line 59 (triple-spacing) and then skip to the next page (line 6 of the next page) to print the page header TOP-HEADER.

A special counter is used whenever LINAGE is specified. It is called LINAGE-COUNTER, a COBOL reserved word. It is set to 1 when a print file is opened or when an ADVANCING PAGE is encountered. Afterward, the counter is automatically incremented the appropriate number of lines implied in each WRITE statement. When LINAGE-COUNTER is equal to the value of the FOOTING phrase, then an END-OF-PAGE condition occurs. The LINAGE-COUNTER may not be modified by the program, but it may be accessed. Thus, it is legitimate to write IF LINAGE-COUNTER = 25 PERFORM MID-PAGE ROUTINE, for example.

It can be seen that this version of the WRITE statement can be used to automate the process of counting lines in a report program and testing for the end of the page. In the two sample programs in this chapter we defined a field to which we added a number equal to the number of lines printed in each case. Then we kept comparing the value of that line-counter field to the page length, to determine if it was the end of the page.

The LINAGE clause, the reserved field LINAGE-COUNTER, and the AT END-OF-PAGE test of the WRITE statement can be used for similar purposes. There are, in fact, some advantages to using these options. For instance, if instead of defining the LINAGE values, we define data-names containing the same values and then use them accordingly, we may need to write some additional statements. For example, if we want to begin the page heading on line 6, as in the above example, we could have defined TOP-LINES with a VALUE of 5 and then have written

```
MOVE SPACES TO PRINT-LINE
WRITE PRINT-LINE AFTER ADVANCING PAGE
```

```
WRITE PRINT-LINE FROM PAGE-HEADER
    AFTER ADVANCING TOP-LINES.
```

As the above example illustrates, we cannot write in one statement to advance to the top of a new page *and* to skip a given number of lines. We must use two WRITE commands, one to position the printer to the top of a new page by printing a blank line there, and another WRITE to print the desired data after skipping a number of lines. We conclude by observing that although there are some advantages to the WRITE and LINAGE options, they are relatively minor.

R E V I E W . . . .

1. When an END-OF-PAGE (EOP) condition is specified in conjunction with a WRITE statement, then the description of the number of lines and their use has to be defined in a(n) _____ clause in the DATA DIVISION.

   LINAGE

2. The special counter that is a reserved word and is used implicitly whenever the LINAGE option is specified is the _____.

   LINAGE-COUNTER

3. Assume the following page specifications:

```
LINAGE IS 25 LINES
    WITH FOOTING AT 21
        LINES AT TOP 2
        LINES AT BOTTOM 3
```

   Fill in the missing numbers in the following page mock-up:

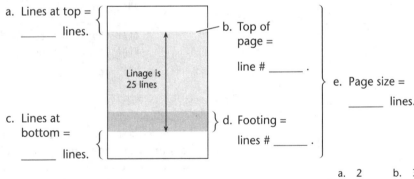

a. Lines at top = _____ lines.

b. Top of page = line # _____ .

c. Lines at bottom = _____ lines.

d. Footing = lines # _____ .

e. Page size = _____ lines.

   a. 2   b. 3
   c. 3   d. 23 to 27
   e. 24 + 2 + 3 = 30

. . . .

SUMMARY

This chapter was concerned with the knowledge that you need to write COBOL programs for producing reports.

In terms of overall structure, a report may contain a *report heading, report body,* and *report footing.* The report body consists of one or more pages, each of which is a formatted collection of lines. A page contains five types of report groups: *page heading, control heading(s), report detail lines, control footing(s),* and *page footing.*

Control breaks in report writing are associated with the hierarchical categories of data in a report. For example, a report of vehicle registrations by city, county, and state would involve three control breaks. State would be the *major* control, county would be the *intermediate* control, and city would be the *minor* control, which follows the hierarchical structure of the data.

A general logical structure in flowchart form was presented in Figure 9-3 for the case of three control breaks. This flowchart can be easily adapted for use with any other number of control breaks as well.

Two example programs for producing reports were described in detail in this chapter. The "simple" program involves one control break, while the "more advanced" program involves two control breaks.

The last section of this chapter described specialized options in the WRITE statement when the LINAGE clause has been used in a data description. This included the END-OF-PAGE option and use of the LINAGE-COUNTER.

EXERCISES

9.1 Student registration records have the following format:

```
01  STUD-REC.
    05  DEPT-NO        PIC XXX.
    05  COURSE-NO      PIC X(7).
    05  SECTION-NO     PIC X.
    05  STUD-NAME      PIC X(20).
```

We want to read the records in the file and produce a report such as the following example:

```
DEPARTMENT NUMBER: ACC   COURSE NUMBER: MIS-101   SECTION: 1
-------------------------------------------------------------
        STUDENT NAME
ANDERSON, ROSE ANN
BROWN, LORI BETH
CRAWFORD, CHRIS L.
DONALD, DON DANIEL

    TOTAL STUDENTS IN SECTION:  4

                        Section page  2
                        Report  page  9
```

Each course section must begin on a new page. For the assignment, assume that each page has room for up to six students. The total enrollment for each section is shown on the last page only. Notice that at the bottom of each page we print the section page number as well as the report page number.

Write a program to produce such a report.

9.2 Revise the sample program in Figure 9-12 so that a third control break is included. Each record includes a department name in columns 25–34, as well as the salesperson name in columns 1–15, the product number in columns 16–18, and the sales amount in columns 19–24.

Assume that department is the major control break. In other words, salespersons are grouped within departments, and products are grouped under salespersons. Include a page number at the bottom of each page.

Figure 9-15 shows sample input and the corresponding 3-page output. Draw a structure chart and write a complete program.

FIGURE 9-15
Sample Input and Output for Exercise 9.2

INPUT FILE

```
ADAMSON, JOHN   123012527DEPRTMENT1
ADAMSON, JOHN   123010000DEPRTMENT1
ADAMSON, JOHN   345005000DEPRTMENT1
ADAMSON, JOHN   345011025DEPRTMENT1
ADAMSON, JOHN   345001029DEPRTMENT1
ROSELLE, LINDA  123400000DEPRTMENT1
WILLIAMS, MARY  123020000DEPRTMENT1
WILLIAMS, MARY  123050000DEPRTMENT1
WILLIAMS, MARY  123030000DEPRTMENT1
WILLIAMS, MARY  123112500DEPRTMENT1
ADAMSON, JOHN   123012527DEPRTMENT2
ADAMSON, JOHN   123010000DEPRTMENT2
ADAMSON, JOHN   345005000DEPRTMENT3
ADAMSON, JOHN   345011025DEPRTMENT3
ADAMSON, JOHN   345001029DEPRTMENT3
ROSELLE, LINDA  123400000DEPRTMENT3
WILLIAMS, MARY  123020000DEPRTMENT3
WILLIAMS, MARY  123050000DEPRTMENT3
WILLIAMS, MARY  123030000DEPRTMENT3
WILLIAMS, MARY  123112500DEPRTMENT3
```

PROGRAM OUTPUT

```
DEPT. NAME     SALESMAN NAME     PRODUCT NO.     SALES AMOUNT     TOTAL SALES

DEPRTMENT1     ADAMSON, JOHN     123                  125.27
                                                      100.00

               * TOTAL FOR PRODUCT  123                               $225.27

               ADAMSON, JOHN     345                   50.00
                                                      110.25
                                                       10.29

               * TOTAL FOR PRODUCT  345                               $170.54

            ** TOTAL FOR SALESMAN   ADAMSON, JOHN                     $395.81

               ROSELLE, LINDA    123                4,000.00

               * TOTAL FOR PRODUCT  123                             $4,000.00

            ** TOTAL FOR SALESMAN   ROSELLE, LINDA                  $4,000.00

               WILLIAMS, MARY    123                  200.00
                                                      500.00
                                                      300.00
                                                    1,125.00

          ---------- (page break here) ----------
```

FIGURE 9-15
Sample Input and Output for Exercise 9.2 (continued)

DEPT. NAME	SALESMAN NAME	PRODUCT NO.	SALES AMOUNT	TOTAL SALES
	* TOTAL FOR PRODUCT 123			$2,125.00
	** TOTAL FOR SALESMAN WILLIAMS, MARY			$2,125.00
	*** TOTAL FOR DEPARTMENT DEPRTMENT1			$6,520.81
DEPRTMENT2	ADAMSON, JOHN	123	125.27	
			100.00	
	* TOTAL FOR PRODUCT 123			$225.27
	** TOTAL FOR SALESMAN ADAMSON, JOHN			$225.27
	*** TOTAL FOR DEPARTMENT DEPRTMENT2			$225.27
DEPRTMENT3	ADAMSON, JOHN	345	50.00	
			110.25	
			10.29	
	* TOTAL FOR PRODUCT 345			$170.54
	** TOTAL FOR SALESMAN ADAMSON, JOHN			$170.54

---------- (page break here) -----------

DEPT. NAME	SALESMAN NAME	PRODUCT NO.	SALES AMOUNT	TOTAL SALES
DEPRTMENT3	ROSELLE, LINDA	123	4,000.00	
	* TOTAL FOR PRODUCT 123			$4,000.00
	** TOTAL FOR SALESMAN ROSELLE, LINDA			$4,000.00
	WILLIAMS, MARY	123	200.00	
			500.00	
			300.00	
			1,125.00	
	*** TOTAL FOR DEPARTMENT DEPRTMENT3			$4,170.54
	* TOTAL FOR PRODUCT 123			$2,125.00
	** TOTAL FOR SALESMAN WILLIAMS, MARY			$2,125.00
	*** TOTAL SALES FOR REPORT			$10,916.62

9.3 A file contains data pertaining to student grades. Each record consists of the following:

```
01  STUDENT-RECORD.
    05  NAME      PIC X(15).
    05  COURSE    PIC X(7).
    05  CREDITS   PIC 9.
    05  GRADE     PIC X.
```

For each student we want to produce a semester grade report illustrated in the following example:

```
                    SEMESTER GRADE REPORT
        NAME            COURSE-NO   CREDITS     GRADE       G.P.A
        ANDERSON, A. J. CIS-200        3          A
                        ACC-101        4          B
                        CSC-200        3          B
                        ART-111        2          C
                                                            3.08
```

The grade point average (G.P.A.) is computed by assigning the following point values to letter grades: A = 4, B = 3, C = 2, D = 1, E = 0. We multiply credits times the numeric grade, sum the total products, and divide by the total number of credits.

The report for each student begins on a new page.

Write a program to produce such a report.

10

Sequential File Processing

FILE ORGANIZATION

FILE STORAGE DEVICES

FILE LABELS

COBOL INSTRUCTIONS FOR
    SEQUENTIAL FILES

THE FILE-CONTROL SPECIFICATION

THE FILE DESCRIPTION ENTRY

THE OPEN AND CLOSE VERBS

THE READ, WRITE, AND REWRITE
    VERBS

SAMPLE PROGRAM TO CREATE A
    SEQUENTIAL FILE

SEQUENTIAL FILE UPDATING

SAMPLE SEQUENTIAL FILE UPDATE
    PROGRAM

I **N THIS CHAPTER** *you will learn how to create and update sequential files. For such files the records are written and accessed in a serial order.*

Often, the storage device that is used dictates the method of file storage. For example, sequential file storage must be used for data stored on magnetic tape. Therefore a discussion of such devices and their storage characteristics is included early in this chapter.

You will then study the COBOL instructions that are associated with sequential files. This will include the FILE-CONTROL specification in the ENVIRONMENT DIVISION, the file description entry in the DATA DIVISION, and use of specialized verbs in the PROCEDURE DIVISION.

Finally, you will study a sample program to create a sequential file, and another sample program to update a sequential file.

FILE ORGANIZATION

The concept of *file organization* refers to the manner in which data records are arranged on a file-storage medium. There are three principal methods of file organization in COBOL: sequential, indexed, and relative.

In a *sequential file* the records are written in a serial order and are accessed (read) in the same order as written. The serial order is chronological and need not be in any particular logical sequence, such as according to account number. Files assigned to printers and magnetic tape drives are always organized as sequential files. On the other hand, files stored on magnetic disk and other direct access storage devices may be sequential, indexed, or relative files.

Although the language does not require it, sequential files on tape or disk most commonly are sorted so that the records are in some logical sequential order. For instance, if we have a customer file, we might choose to sort the records on the basis of customer number. Then, if customer numbers are unique, each successive record read from the file should have a higher customer number than the one before. This practice of sorting the records is convenient when processing "batch" jobs, such as payroll. In such jobs, we sort the "transaction" data, such as time cards, in the same order as the employee payroll file. Then we process the time cards by reading the two files from beginning to end without the need to go back and forth looking for employee records in random order.

Indexed file organization means that an index has been created so that records can be located directly without accessing them in sequence. We describe this file organization method in Chapter 20. *Relative* file organization means that the file is stored in such a way that each record can be accessed directly by means of its relative position in the file. Such positions are the first, second, third, etc., record in the file. This method is covered in Chapter 21.

R E V I E W . . . .

1. The manner in which data records are arranged on a file-storage medium is referred to as file _____ .

    organization

2. The type of file for which the records are written in a serial order and for which the records must be accessed in the same order as written is the _____ file organization.

    sequential

3. The type of file for which the records have been read and stored in a serial order, but for which access can be direct, is the _____ file organization.

    indexed

4. The type of file for which records are both stored and accessed directly according to the relative position of the record is the _____ file organization.

    relative

5. If a file is assigned to a printer or magnetic tape drive, it must be organized as a(n) _____ file.

    sequential

6. A file that can be organized by any of the three methods described in this section is one for which the records are stored on magnetic _____ .

    disk

FILE STORAGE DEVICES

While the characteristics of the data processing task dictate which method of file organization is preferred, the storage device that is used determines which methods are possible. As related to file organization, it is useful to distinguish two main categories of storage devices: *magnetic tape* and *direct access storage devices* (DASD, pronounced das-dee). The latter category refers mainly to magnetic disk, but it also includes other direct access storage devices, such as cartridge systems. As indicated in the preceding section, only the sequential file organization can be used for files stored on magnetic tape, whereas any method of file organization can be used for files stored on direct access storage devices.

The *magnetic tape unit* is the specialized input-output device used for reading and writing magnetic tapes. As illustrated in Figure 10-1, it includes two

FIGURE 10-1
*IBM 3420 Magnetic Tape Drive
(IBM Corporation)*

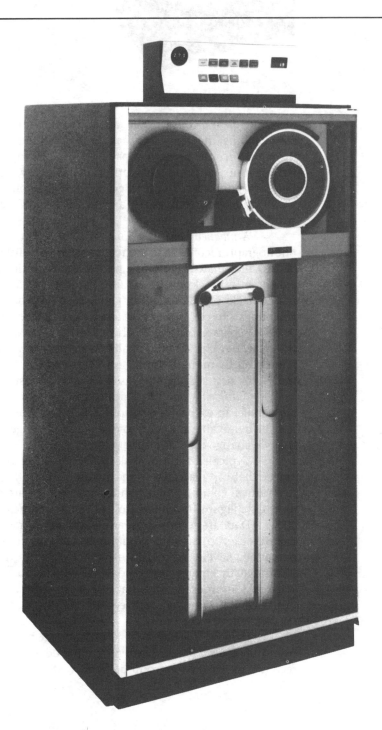

FIGURE 10-2

Magnetic Disk Storage Device and Schematic Representation of Tracks on a Disk Surface (IBM Corporation)

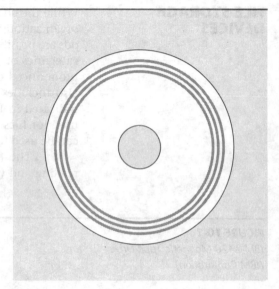

reels. The *file reel* contains the tape to be read or to be written on, and the *machine reel* contains the tape that has already been processed. The tape is threaded through a *read-write head* capable of performing the functions of reading and writing; thus, the tape transport unit works very much like a home tape recorder. Use of magnetic tape in cartridges is becoming common. These cartridges resemble VCR or audio cassette tapes, and the two reels are less evident in the enclosed structure of the cartridge.

A *magnetic disk* is a magnetically sensitive circular surface resembling a phonograph record. Data are recorded on this disk surface in designated circular bands called *tracks*. Figure 10-2 portrays a magnetic disk storage device and includes a diagram of tracks on the surface of a disk. There may be up to several hundred usable tracks on the surface of a magnetic disk, depending on the size of the unit. Each track can contain a few thousand characters around its circular length. Each track is separate from the others, and all tracks have the same capacity, even though the circles become smaller as we move away from the periphery. Tracks are referenced in numeric order from 0 up to the last track. Thus, if we have 200 tracks, the first is designated as track 000 and last as track 199.

A *disk pack* refers to a group of disks stacked on a vertical spindle. The disks are parallel to each other but physically separated from one another. Such packs may be removable as a unit, so that we can change disk packs for the same reasons that we change reels of magnetic tape.

Typically, for each disk surface in a disk pack there is a *read-write head*—a device that can read data from or write data on the surface. These heads are fixed to a vertical column and can move as a unit toward or away from the center of the disk pack. Figure 10-3 illustrates the read-write head mechanism.

Data are recorded on any magnetic storage device in the form of *blocks*. Each block consists of a grouping of data written (or read) in one continuous operation. Several formats are possible for the data included in the block, as illustrated in Figures 10-4 and 10-5, which illustrate blocks on magnetic tape. The *gap* is an unused space that serves as a separator between blocks. Disk files do not need the same gap between blocks due to the more precise nature of the hardware device.

Data records handled in a program are called *logical records,* as distinguished from the *physical records* written on a file device such as a tape or disk. A physical record is defined as a group of bytes written or read in one I/O (input-output)

FIGURE 10-3

Disk Access Mechanism (IBM Corporation)

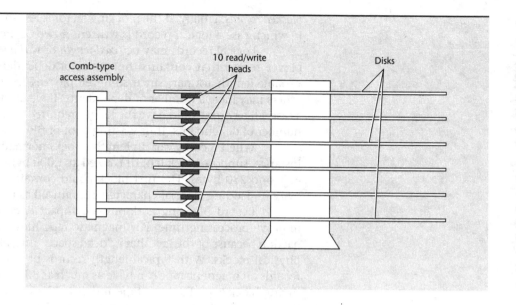

FIGURE 10-4

Tape Recording Format Containing One Record Per Block

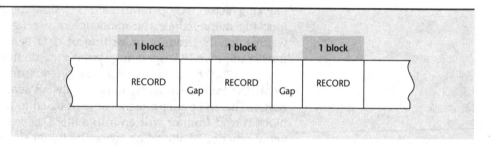

FIGURE 10-5

Tape Recording Format Containing Four Records Per Block

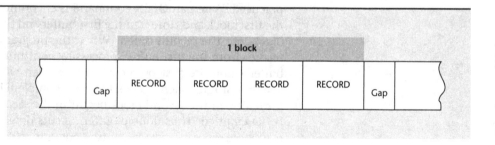

operation. The physical and logical records are related to each other in various ways:

- They may be identical.

- A physical record may consist of several complete logical records.

- A physical record may consist of a portion of one logical record or may consist of a mixture of several complete and partial logical records. (These possibilities are uncommon in practice, however.)

The term *block* often is used as being synonymous with physical record, while the term *blocking factor* denotes the number of logical records per block. When the blocking factor is 1, the physical and logical records are equivalent, and we often refer to them as *unblocked records*. When the blocking factor is greater than 1, then a block contains several logical records, and we refer to them as *blocked records.* Finally, if the blocking factor is less than 1, we have *spanned records,* in which case a logical record is written in two or more physical records.

Logical records may be *fixed-length* or *variable-length.* For example, an employee record that contains the names of dependents would be a candidate for variable-length format, since some employees may have no dependents while others may have a number of dependents. If we used fixed-length records in such a case, all records would have the length required for the record with the maximum number of dependents, thus wasting a lot of file storage.

When records vary in length, blocks normally would contain *padding.* For instance, suppose block length is fixed at 1,000 bytes and we have records of 300, 450, and 280 bytes. The first block could contain the first two records and 250 bytes of padding (special characters recognized as not being data).

Record blocking is done to compact data in file storage media and to improve processing time. For magnetic tape files, blocking results in data compaction because of the fact that a "dead space" interblock gap is necessary between physical blocks. With typical-length records of a few hundred bytes, unblocked records on magnetic tape can have as much as 80 to 90 percent of the tape devoted to interblock gaps. For both tape and disk, blocking also improves processing time because the number of physical read and write operations is reduced by the blocking factor. I/O operations are very slow compared to central processing, and blocking helps reduce the incidence of a program being "I/O-bound," that is, waiting for the reading or writing of data before processing can continue. To further improve I/O, operating systems use double-buffering, as described below.

A *buffer* is a storage space. Data read from a file medium are always stored in an I/O buffer; similarly, data are always sent to the file device from an I/O buffer. This I/O buffer must be at least equal to the block size, so that a complete block is read from or written into a file. *Double-buffering* refers to the nearly universal practice of allocating twice the buffer size needed to store a block of data from a given file. If the file is an input file, anticipatory double-buffering is practiced. When an OPEN command is encountered, the system proceeds to read the first block and store it in the first buffer and then continues reading the second block into the second buffer. When the program has read and processed all the records from the first buffer, processing continues with the records in the second buffer while the first buffer is being refilled with the third block of data. In a similar fashion, when a block has been completed in one buffer for an output file, formation of the second block begins in the second buffer while the first buffer is being emptied. Thus double-buffering cuts down on the waiting period between read-write operations. Of course, one can see that the advantage of double-buffering is enhanced as the blocking factor is increased. However, as the block size increases, so does the amount of central storage needed for the program.

In addition to the number of records contained in each block, the *size* of each record is also of importance. In using magnetic storage, the record size is not restricted to any particular limit. The records can be as long as is suitable for the applications involved. In the case of disk files, the track size is a natural upper limit on the block size. Furthermore, the records can be either fixed or variable in length. Just as record size can be variable, so can the number of records per block. Overall, then, we can have fixed-length or variable-length records and fixed-length or variable-length blocks. Variable-length records and blocks are discussed in Chapter 17.

R E V I E W . . . .

1.   The magnetic tape unit requires the use of two reels when it is used: the machine reel and the file reel. The reel that contains the tape to be written on or read is

the _____ reel. The reel that contains the tape that already has been processed is the _____ reel.

file; machine

2. A group of magnetic disks stacked on a vertical shaft in a parallel fashion is called a(n) _____ .

disk pack

3. A grouping of data that is written on a magnetic storage device in one continuous operation, and that may include one or more records, is called a _____ .

block

4. In addition to the number of records contained in each block, block size also is determined by the length of each record. Whereas both the record size and the block size can be fixed, variable size is possible [only for records / only for blocks / also for both records and blocks].

also for both records and blocks

5. The type of record that is defined as a group of bytes written or read in one I/O operation is the _____ record.

physical

6. In contrast to physical records, the data records handled in a program are called _____ records.

logical

7. The term "block" is another name for a [logical / physical] record.

physical

8. The blocking factor represents the number of _____ per block.

logical records

9. When the records are described as being "unblocked," then by definition the blocking factor has the value _____ .

1

10. The logical records in a program may be fixed-length or variable-length. If fixed-length blocks are used with variable-length records, then each block can be restricted to an integer number of records by filling in the unused portion of the block with _____ .

padding

11. In terms of actual practice, records are most often [fixed / variable] in length and [blocked / unblocked].

fixed; blocked

12. Principal advantages of record blocking are that it results in data compaction and a reduction in the physical read and write operations, thereby also reducing processing _____ .

time

13. In addition to using blocking, the practice associated with defining the buffer size that further reduces the time devoted to I/O operations is called _____

double-buffering

14. Given a particular number of records all of the same length and given that blocking is used, the larger the block size, the [smaller / larger] is the total physical file size for magnetic tape files.

smaller

FILE LABELS

Each magnetic file, such as a reel of tape or a disk pack, is identified by two means. Externally, an adhesive label is attached so that the human operator can identify the contents of the file by reading this label. In addition, magnetic labels are included with the file itself. In general, two types of magnetic labels are used: the header label and the trailer label.

As implied by the name, a *header label* is located at the beginning of the file. This label contains such information as

- File identification: in terms of a file name or a file number

- Retention period: the date prior to which the file cannot be overwritten

- Creation date: the date the file was established

- Sequence number: the sequence number for a multivolume file that consists of several volumes (reels or disk packs).

The header label not only serves as a means of verifying the correct identity of an input file but also is used as a means of preventing inadvertent overwriting as explained below.

The *trailer label* is a record written as the last record on the file. Typically, it contains the same information as the header label, but in addition it contains a block count, which is a count of the number of data blocks written on the file.

The trailer label differs depending on whether a file is a single-volume or a multivolume file. If it is a single-volume file, the trailer is as described above. If it is a multivolume file, the trailer label of each volume indicates the volume (reel or disk pack) number as well.

As far as label processing is concerned, we can differentiate the processing on the basis of whether a file is opened for *output* or *input*.

When a file is used in the output mode, the three main actions are OPEN, WRITE, and CLOSE. The following general operations take place with respect to label processing:

- When the file is OPENed for OUTPUT, the beginning label is checked for the field that contains the expiration date of the previously written file. If the expiration date has not yet been reached, then the label processing results in some appropriate diagnostic message and prevention of the output function. Thus, a file is protected from inadvertent overwriting. If the expiration date indicates that the previous file can be overwritten, then the header label of the new file is written.

- WRITE operations proceed normally until the physical end of the file is reached. If the file is on magnetic tape and it is to be continued on another reel, a trailer label is written indicating that this is the end of the reel and not the end of the file. Then the operator is notified to make the next reel available by replacing the present reel with a "fresh" reel on the same tape drive or by providing for continuation on another drive. A beginning-volume label and a header label are then inserted before the next record block is written on the new reel. Thus three label records are written between the last data record on the first reel and the first data record on the new reel: the trailer label on the previous volume, a beginning-volume label, and a header label on the next volume.

- If the file is stored on magnetic disk and it is to continue on another disk, the actions parallel those of tape. However, in the case of a disk file, the physical end of the file may be reached without it being the end of the volume. For example, we may have allocated cylinders 21 to 80 to the file, but the file now requires more than 60 cylinders. In such a case the operating system will issue a diagnostic message to the operator and the job will be abnormally terminated (although some operating systems may expand file size automatically).

- When a CLOSE file command is carried out, the resulting operation is the writing of a trailer label at the end of the file. As records are written into the file, their number typically is accumulated by the label-processing routine, and this "block count" is written as a field in the trailer label. When the file is used as input on future occasions, the counting is repeated, and the new count is compared to the count in the trailer label to ascertain that all the records in the file have been read by the time the trailer label is processed. In a sequential input file we must have read all of the records in the file if we are at the end of the file.

When a file is used in the INPUT mode, the three main actions are OPEN, READ, and CLOSE. The following general operations take place with respect to label processing:

- When the file is OPENed for INPUT, the beginning labels are read to ascertain that the file identification provided in the job control statements agrees with the information in the label record.

- The READ operation proceeds normally until the trailer label is reached. If the label signifies the end of the file, then the operating system communicates this information to the program (recall READ ... AT END ...) and aborts the program if a further attempt is made to read from the file. If the file is a multivolume file, the end-of-volume label will signify such a condition and will result in reading and processing the volume and file header labels on the next volume. Of course, the label-processing routine will check to see that the correct sequence of volumes is presented.

- When an INPUT file is CLOSEd, the trailer label is processed to verify that all records have been read. If the file is on tape, the reel is normally rewound as a result of closing the file. In rare instances it is desirable to read a file in reverse order, in which case an "open reverse" command may be issued after a suitable "close with no rewind" command. The trailer label then acts as a header label.

In general, label processing involves a number of specialized functions having to do with proper identification of data files and ensuring the data integrity in such files. As stated earlier, it is a function governed by localized conventions and procedures, and the programmer has to obtain specific instructions from the particular installation.

R E V I E W . . . .

1. Magnetic files are identified by two general types of labels: _____ labels for human use and _____ labels for machine use.

    external, magnetic

2. Magnetic labels used with files are of two types. The label included at the beginning of a file is called the _____ label, while the label at the end of the file is called the _____ label.

    header; trailer

3. For a multivolume file, both the header and trailer labels include a
_____ number.

sequence

4. For a file used in the output mode, the three main actions (COBOL verbs) are
_____ , _____ , and _____ .

OPEN; WRITE; CLOSE

5. For a file used in the input mode, the three main actions (COBOL verbs) are
_____ , _____ , and _____ .

OPEN; READ; CLOSE

6. The specific procedures associated with label processing [have generally been
standardized / are governed by localized conventions].

are governed by localized conventions

· ·

COBOL INSTRUCTIONS FOR SEQUENTIAL FILES

A number of COBOL instructions have been designed for use with sequential file processing. In the following sections we present most of the common options. Additional features are discussed in Chapter 17. We then conclude the chapter with two sample programs that illustrate the application of such instructions in some typical tasks.

THE FILE-CONTROL SPECIFICATION

For sequential files the FILE-CONTROL specification in the ENVIRONMENT DIVISION has the format presented in Figure 10-6.

The OPTIONAL specification is used for files that may or may not be present. For example, we could have a file on which we output end-of-month reports only when it is the end of the month. In a program using such a file we would specify the file as OPTIONAL and we include some test in the PROCEDURE DIVISION to determine whether the file is used.

OPTIONAL files must be OPENed in the INPUT, I-O, or EXTEND modes (the latter two modes are discussed later in this chapter).

In the ASSIGN statement, *implementor-name-1* refers to the way each particular operating system designates files. Such designation varies. For example, for IBM mainframes the designation consists of a so-called data-set definition name, which is associated with a corresponding job control language statement, as in this example:

```
SELECT STUDENT-FILE ASSIGN TO STUFILE
        .
        .
        .
//STUFILE DD DSN=  ...  etc.        (This is a JCL statement,
                                     not a COBOL statement.)
```

In the 1985 standard a file can be ASSIGNed to literal-1 in Figure 10-6, which may be a file name. For example, for a diskette file on the "B:" drive of a personal computer we could have

```
SELECT STUDENT-FILE ASSIGN TO "B:STUDENT.DAT".
```

The ORGANIZATION clause is optional for sequential files. When it is omitted, as has been done in this book up to now, the specification defaults to

FIGURE 10-6
FILE-CONTROL Format for
Sequential Files

```
FILE-CONTROL.

    SELECT [OPTIONAL] file-name

        ASSIGN TO  { implementor-name-1 }  ...
                   { literal-1           }

    [ [ORGANIZATION IS] SEQUENTIAL ]

    [                        { data-name-1 }  ]
    [ PADDING CHARACTER IS   { literal-2   }  ]

    [                      { STANDARD-1          }  ]
    [ RECORD DELIMITER IS  { implementor-name-2  }  ]

    [ACCESS MODE IS SEQUENTIAL ]

    [FILE STATUS IS data-name-2]
```

ORGANIZATION IS SEQUENTIAL. As one might guess, with indexed and relative files their organization is declared to be INDEXED and RELATIVE, respectively, as will be illustrated in later chapters.

The PADDING CHARACTER option available in COBOL '85 allows the programmer to specify the character to be used to fill the remainder of a partially filled block. If a block is 6000 bytes long and the records require 200 bytes each, there could be 30 records per block. If the total number of records in the file is 125, the last block would contain 5 data records, and the remaining $(30 - 5) \times 200 = 5000$ bytes would be "padded" with the specified characters.

Both data-name-1 and literal-2 must be one character long. When a PADDING option is not specified, then the padding character is the default character used by that particular operating system.

The RECORD DELIMITER is a 1985 feature that allows the programmer to specify either the standard or a specific alternative method for delimiting variable-length records. Such a method is used to determine the length of each record when records are variable. Variable-length records are discussed in Chapter 17.

The optional ACCESS MODE clause serves mainly a documentation role in the case of sequential files, since SEQUENTIAL is the default case even if the clause is not used. However, for indexed and relative files the clause has a more important role.

The final optional clause, FILE STATUS IS, has to do with exception processing during input or output operations. When executing an I/O operation, there may be exceptions. For example, we may have attempted to close an unopened file, and the like.

As a case in point, consider the AT END clause associated with the READ statement. Its purpose is to provide for specific processing when a particular exception occurs during input, namely, when an end-of-file condition occurs. Other I/O verbs, such as OPEN, WRITE, and CLOSE, do not have clauses paralleling the AT END feature of READ. Yet it is important for the programmer to be able to test for exceptions and treat them under control of program logic. For example, if we attempt to open a file and for some reason the command is not successfully completed, we should be able to recognize the exceptional condition and be able to continue with appropriate processing.

The FILE STATUS clause designates a field into which a code is placed after each I/O statement execution (such as OPEN, CLOSE, READ, WRITE, REWRITE). Let us consider an example:

```
SELECT CUSTOMER-FILE ASSIGN TO file-name
       ORGANIZATION IS SEQUENTIAL
       ACCESS MODE IS SEQUENTIAL
       FILE STATUS IS CUST-FILE-IO-STATUS.
       .
       .
       .

WORKING-STORAGE SECTION.
       .
       .
       .

01 CUST-FILE-IO-STATUS PIC X(2).
```

Notice that we chose CUST-FILE-IO-STATUS as the data-name for a two-byte field in WORKING-STORAGE. As each input/output command involving CUSTOMER-FILE is executed, the operating system places a two-byte code in the designated field. Figure 10-7 presents these codes and their meaning.

The FILE STATUS field can then be tested to ascertain the outcome of an I/O operation. For example, we may have

```
OPEN INPUT CUSTOMER-FILE
IF  CUST-FILE-IO-STATUS = "00"
   PERFORM READ-CUSTOMER
ELSE
       IF  CUST-FILE-IO-STATUS = "10"
           PERFORM NO-MORE-CUSTOMERS
       ELSE
           PERFORM ERROR-ROUTINE.
```

The first IF statement checks to determine if the OPEN command was executed successfully (see Figure 10-7 for the meaning of the codes), while the second IF statement checks for the end-of-file condition.

This approach of using the FILE STATUS feature enables the programmer to have better control over exception processing. The program can test for specific exception conditions and take the appropriate action.

R E V I E W . . . .

1. In the FILE-CONTROL statement the specification that is included for files that may or may not be present is the _____ specification.

   OPTIONAL

2. The implementor-name-1 in the ASSIGN statement designates a file according to the method of the particular _____ system being used.

   operating

3. When the ORGANIZATION clause is omitted in the FILE-CONTROL statement, program execution defaults to ORGANIZATION IS _____ .

   SEQUENTIAL

FIGURE 10-7
File Status Codes and Their Meanings

I-O STATUS CODE	EXPLANATION
00	Successful execution.
04	A record whose length is inconsistent with the record description for the file that has been read.
05	Attempt to OPEN a file that is not available.
07	The file storage device is not magnetic tape, yet a CLOSE or OPEN involved a corresponding NO REWIND, REEL, FOR REMOVAL phrase.
10	End-of-file condition.
15	Attempt to read an optional file which is not present.
16	A READ statement was executed while the at end condition is true (attempt to read past the end of the file).
30	A permanent error exists; no further information is available.
34	An attempt is made to write beyond the boundaries of the file.
35	Attempt to OPEN as INPUT, I-O, or EXTEND a nonoptional file.
37	Attempt to OPEN a file that should be on mass storage but is not.
38	Attempt to OPEN a file that has been CLOSED with LOCK.
39	Error during OPEN execution, due to inconsistency between the file description and the actual file.
41	Attempt to OPEN a file that is already opened.
42	Attempt to CLOSE a file that is not open.
43	A successful READ did not precede execution of the current REWRITE command.
44	A boundary violation due to attempt to WRITE or REWRITE a record of improper length.
46	Attempt to READ the next nonexistent record.
47	Attempt to READ from a file not open in INPUT or I-O mode.
48	Attempt to WRITE on a file not open in OUTPUT or EXTEND mode.
49	Attempt to REWRITE on a file not open in I-O mode.
9X	An error condition defined by the particular system in use.

4. The clause available in the 1985 version by which the character that is to be used to fill the remainder of a partially filled block can be specified is the
_____ clause.

PADDING CHARACTER

5. If the optional ACCESS MODE clause is used, the only mode available in the clause is SEQUENTIAL. If the clause is not used, the default mode is the
_____ mode.

SEQUENTIAL

6. The optional clause that makes it possible to test for exceptional conditions during program execution and thereby achieve better program control and the processing of exceptional conditions is the _____ IS clause.

FILE STATUS

. . . .

THE FILE DESCRIPTION ENTRY

Figure 10-8 presents the general format of the file description entry used for sequential files in the DATA DIVISION.

FD marks the beginning of a file description entry and is followed immediately by the name of the file. The name of the file already has been declared in the SELECT statement of the ENVIRONMENT DIVISION, where it was assigned to a hardware device.

If records are grouped together, the BLOCK CONTAINS clause is used. If each record constitutes one block, the clause may be omitted or the equivalent BLOCK CONTAINS 1 RECORD can be used. When a block contains several records, then the clause must be used. Typically, this clause is used with the RECORDS option. In such a case it references the number of records per block. For example, if we have

```
FD PAYROLL-FILE BLOCK CONTAINS 10 RECORDS
```

each block will contain 10 records.

Because of the widespread use of IBM systems, we now mention the common convention in such environments, which is to use

```
BLOCK CONTAINS 0 RECORDS
```

Zero records per block is not a logical statement. However, it is a special convention that states that the blocking factor for this file will be specified in the accompanying JCL statements. Thus the same program can be executed with files of different blocking factors, thereby introducing flexibility at the time of program execution.

The VARYING clause is used to specify variable-length records, as will be discussed in Chapter 17.

The LABEL RECORDS clause is required for all files in the 1974 version but is optional in the 1985 standard. The OMITTED option indicates that the file either has no beginning or ending label (as is the case with printer files), or they are ignored if they exist. If the STANDARD option is used, it is understood to be the standard label for the particular computer installation. As we mentioned earlier, the label record contains data that identify the file, and obviously each file is identified uniquely. There are two basic ways of saying what the label contents should be. By the first approach this information is communicated through

FIGURE 10-8
Format for a FILE DESCRIPTION Entry

```
FD file-name

   [ BLOCK CONTAINS [ integer-1 TO ] integer-2 { RECORDS    } ]
                                               { CHARACTERS }

   [        { CONTAINS integer-3 CHARACTERS                                          } ]
   [        { IS VARYING IN SIZE [ [FROM integer-4] [TO integer-5] CHARACTERS ]      } ]
   [ RECORD {           [DEPENDING on data-name-1]                                   } ]
   [        { CONTAINS integer-6 TO integer-7 CHARACTERS                             } ]

   [ LABEL { RECORD IS    } { STANDARD } ]
   [       { RECORDS ARE  } { OMITTED  } ]

   [ VALUE OF { implementor-name-1 IS { data-name-2 } } ... ]
   [          {                       { literal-1   } }     ]

   [ DATA { RECORD IS    } { data-name-3 } ... ]
   [      { RECORDS ARE  }                      ]
```

program control statements submitted with the COBOL program. In other words, this information is not communicated, strictly speaking, in the COBOL program language. Another way of communicating the contents of label records is by use of the VALUE OF clause in Figure 10-8. For example, we could have this for a particular case:

```
FD  PAYROLL-FILE BLOCK CONTAINS 10 RECORDS
                 LABEL RECORDS ARE STANDARD
                 VALUE OF IDENTIFICATION IS "A2359"
                 RETENTION-PERIOD IS 090
                 DATA RECORD IS PAY-REC.
```

The words IDENTIFICATION and RETENTION-PERIOD above are meaningful in a particular installation, and indicate that the STANDARD label contains a field called IDENTIFICATION, whose content should be A2359. When the file is opened, the field is checked to ascertain that A2359 is there (to check that the correct file is mounted). The RETENTION-PERIOD field implies that this file cannot be written on until 90 days have elapsed. Of course, other similar fields are used in the VALUE clause for more complete label specification, depending on the conventions at each computer system.

The VALUE clause has been marked as being obsolete in the 1985 version. This means that it should not be used in new programs and that it will he deleted in a future version of COBOL. The "obsolete" category allows for a transitional period so that "old" features can be phased out of the language. The VALUE clause is not in common use. Most implementors provide means external to COBOL for specifying file label contents.

The DATA RECORD clause is optional and identifies the name of the record(s) in the file. A file may contain more than one type of record as will be discussed in Chapter 16. For example:

```
DATA RECORDS ARE CHARGE-REC
                 PAY-REC.
```

In the above example, there are two records in the file.

The DATA RECORD clause mainly serves a documentation role, since it is followed immediately by the data record names and the 01 level-number.

As a way of summarizing the discussion in this section, the following are examples of file descriptions in the DATA DIVISION:

```
FD PAYROLL-FILE BLOCK CONTAINS 10 RECORDS
                RECORD CONTAINS 80 CHARACTERS
                LABEL RECORDS ARE OMITTED
                DATA RECORD IS SAMPLE-REC.

   FD FILE-A     BLOCK CONTAINS 600 CHARACTERS
                 LABEL RECORD IS STANDARD
                 VALUE OF IDENTIFICATION IS "A1-2B"
                 DATA RECORD IS REC.

   FD FILE-B     LABEL RECORDS OMITTED
                 DATA RECORD IS SIMPLE-REC.

   FD FILE-85    (this is a minimum specification for COBOL '85)
```

R E V I E W . . . .

1. With reference to the sample file descriptions just given, the names of the four files are _____ , _____ , _____ , and _____ , respectively.

   PAYROLL-FILE; FILE-A; FILE-B; FILE-85

2. The file description just given in which each block contains one record is the [first / second / third] description. The file description in which the record size may be variable is the [first / second / third] description.

   third; second

3. The file description that includes a label record is the [first / second / third] description. The file description that includes the optional VALUE OF clause is the [first / second / third] description.

   second; second

. . . .

THE OPEN AND CLOSE VERBS

The OPEN verb initiates processing of a file and performs appropriate label processing. If the file is to be used as output, when the file is opened, the existing label is checked to ascertain that the previous file can be overwritten by the new one. If so, the new header label is written on the file. Similarly, if the file is opened for input, its label is read and checked for proper identification.

If an error condition arises as a result of such label processing, either it is reported by the operating system, which normally terminates the program, or it is handled by the program itself through use of the FILE STATUS feature discussed earlier in this chapter.

The OPEN verb has the following format:

$$\text{OPEN} \begin{cases} \underline{\text{INPUT}} & \text{file-name} \; [\,\text{with} \; \underline{\text{NO REWIND}}\,] \\ \underline{\text{OUTPUT}} & \text{file-name} \; [\,\text{with} \; \underline{\text{NO REWIND}}\,] \\ \underline{\text{I-O}} & \text{file-name} \\ \underline{\text{EXTEND}} & \text{file-name} \end{cases}$$

In the general format the INPUT and OUTPUT modes contain the NO REWIND option that can be used with magnetic tape files. Absence of the NO REWIND implies that the reel should be rewound, if necessary, so that it is at its beginning. If the NO REWIND is used, it is assumed that a previous CLOSE ... WITH NO REWIND has resulted in the multifile tape being positioned at the beginning of the next desired file (by being at the end of the previous file that was just closed).

The I-O option can be used only for disk or other DASD (direct access storage device) files. It allows the program to both input from and output on the file. It is used if we want to change a record that we have just read. With tape files, however, we cannot rewrite a record that we have just read in.

The EXTEND option positions the file after its last record. It can be used to add new records at the end of the file and is really a special case of the OUTPUT mode option.

Correct use of input-output verbs depends on the option, or mode, used in the OPEN statement. Table 10-1 summarizes this relationship, with an X designating each permissible combination. For instance, if the INPUT mode option is used, then the READ verb can be used, but the WRITE and REWRITE verbs cannot be used.

The CLOSE verb has the following expanded format:

$$\underline{\text{CLOSE}} \; \text{file-name} \; \left[\begin{cases} \underline{\text{REEL}} \\ \underline{\text{UNIT}} \end{cases} \begin{bmatrix} \text{WITH} \; \underline{\text{NO REWIND}} \\ \text{FOR} \; \underline{\text{REMOVAL}} \end{bmatrix} \\ \text{WITH} \begin{cases} \underline{\text{NO REWIND}} \\ \underline{\text{LOCK}} \end{cases} \right] \; \dots$$

Prior to closing, a file must have been opened. "CLOSE file-name" results in end-of-file procedures. If label records have not been omitted, a trailer label is written; and if a tape file, the tape is rewound automatically.

TABLE 1

Permissible Combinations of OPEN Mode Options and Input-Output Verbs

STATEMENT:	OPEN MODE			
	INPUT	OUTPUT	I/O	EXTEND
READ	X		X	
WRITE		X		X
REWRITE			X	

With tape files, if the option CLOSE file-name REEL is used, this results in closing that reel but not the file as such. The file itself still will be in an open status. The common circumstance under which the REEL option is used is in the case of multireel files, when the processing of a particular reel for a file may have been completed but other reels for the file still might remain to be processed. If we are using disk files, then the term UNIT is used instead of REEL. The NO REWIND option prevents the rewinding that otherwise is caused automatically by the CLOSE verb. As also explained in connection with the OPEN statement above, one circumstance in which the user would not want to rewind the tape is when a second file subsequently is to be read from or written on the same tape reel. When the LOCK option is used instead of the NO REWIND, the file is locked and can be reopened only by restarting the program. The LOCK option serves as protection against accidentally opening and misusing a file whose data have already been processed. The FOR REMOVAL option is used to allow the operator to intervene, remove the reel or disk unit (at least logically), and replace it with another reel. The specific procedure that should take place in conjunction with using the FOR REMOVAL option is not defined by COBOL; rather, it is determined by the implementor.

R E V I E W . . . .

1. Processing of a file is initiated by the use of the _____ verb.

    OPEN

2. If the READ verb is to be used subsequent to a file being opened, then the INPUT mode option should be included in the OPEN statement. Similarly, if the WRITE verb is to be used then the _____ mode option should be included in the OPEN statement.

    OUTPUT (or EXTEND)

3. End-of-file procedures are specified by use of the _____ verb.

    CLOSE

4. The option of the OPEN verb that enables us to rewrite a disk record that has been read is the _____ option.

    I-O

5. The option in the closing routine that serves to protect the file from use (and misuse) is the [NO REWIND / LOCK] option, whereas the option that permits further use of the reel is the [NO REWIND / LOCK] option.

    LOCK; NO REWIND

. . . .

THE READ, WRITE, AND REWRITE VERBS

The format for the READ verb is

    READ file-name-1 [NEXT] [INTO identifier-1]

        [AT END imperative-statement-1]

        [NOT AT END imperative-statement-1]

    [END-READ]

This is the same format as we have encountered before, with one small exception: the NEXT option. This option is available only in COBOL '85. The NEXT option serves mainly a documentary role for sequential files, but it has a much more important role in indexed and relative files, as explained in later chapters.

The AT END clause is optional. In its place we can use the FILE STATUS feature to check whether an end-of-file (as well as any other) condition has occurred while reading. However, some compilers require the AT END specification for all sequential files.

If a file was designated as OPTIONAL in the SELECT statement and the file is not present, the AT END condition occurs when the first READ is executed. As Table 10-1 indicates, a READ is valid when a file has been opened as INPUT or I-O.

The NOT AT END and the END-READ options apply to the 1985 standard only.

The relevant WRITE format for a sequential file is

WRITE   record -name   [FROM identifier]

$$[\text{NOT}] \text{ AT } \begin{Bmatrix} \text{END-OF-PAGE} \\ \text{EOP} \end{Bmatrix} \text{ imperative -statement}$$

[END-WRITE]

As discussed in Chapter 9, the END-OF-PAGE option is meaningful only for files assigned to a printer device. Also, the END-WRITE is a 1985-only feature.

As Table 10-1 indicates, the file must be opened as either OUTPUT or EXTEND if the WRITE verb is to be used.

If a BLOCK CONTAINS clause was used in the file description, the system will control automatically the operations needed to form an appropriate block prior to a physical write of the block itself. The programmer need not be concerned about the blocking operation.

The REWRITE statement is a specialized instruction for direct access storage files. Its format is

REWRITE record-name [FROM identifier]

To update a sequential file on disk, we may use "OPEN I-O file-name." Then, after issuing a READ command that accesses the record to be updated, we use the REWRITE verb to replace the updated record in the same file instead of WRITE on a different file. With magnetic tape files, we must read a record from one file and MOVE and write the updated record on a new file.

It should be noted that REWRITE can be used only to update an existing file. If we are creating a new file, we must use the WRITE verb.

R E V I E W . . . .

1. If the OPEN verb is to be used, the file must be opened in the _____ or _____ mode.

    INPUT; I-O

2. If the WRITE verb is to be used, the file must be opened in the _____ or _____ mode.

    OUTPUT; EXTEND

3. The verb that is used to update an existing file is the _____ verb. To use this verb, the file must be opened in the _____ mode.

    REWRITE; I-O

SAMPLE PROGRAM TO CREATE A SEQUENTIAL FILE

Figure 10-9 illustrates the process of creating a sequential file on magnetic tape or disk. The source records are assumed to be in CUST-SOURCE-FILE. The new file will be CUST-MAST-FILE and is defined so that BLOCK CONTAINS 5 RECORDS.

The PROCEDURE DIVISION illustrates use of the file status feature after the OPEN OUTPUT CUST-MAST-FILE statement. CUST-FILE-STATUS was declared to be the FILE STATUS for this file in the SELECT statement of the ENVIRONMENT DIVISION. Recall from the earlier discussion of file status that a "00" value means that the I/O operation (OPEN in this case) was successful. If after the OPEN statement CUST-FILE-STATUS does not contain a "00" value, then we PERFORM 400-I-O-EXCEPTION, which prints an explanatory error message containing the file status value and sets the ABEND (abnormal end) condition-name condition to true, so that the program will terminate.

If the OPEN command is successfully executed, then we execute the 100-CREATE-MASTER which controls the execution of 200-READ-SOURCE. In the latter paragraph we check the file status after the READ statement. A value of "10" indicates an end-of-file condition, as you can verify by reviewing Figure 10-7, which lists the file status values and their meanings. If the file status is not "10" and it is not "00", then, again, we execute 400-I-O-EXCEPTION.

Each record read in is checked in 300-CHECK-WRITE-READ for sequence on a field called CUST-NO in columns 1–5. If a record is not in ascending sequence, it is listed on the printer for visual review. In this manner we know that after the new file has been created, the records are in sequence in ascending order of the CUST-NO field.

Figure 10-10 shows sample input and output from execution of the sample program in Figure 10-9. Notice that the sample input contained one sequence error, which was reported in the error file.

Figure 10-11 presents the same program using features from the 1985 standard. We have used two paragraphs, 000-CREATE-MASTER and 100-I-O-EXCEPTION. The capability of using the in-line PERFORM and END-IF scope terminators allows us to consolidate the logic into fewer paragraphs. This is

FIGURE 10-9

Program to Create a Sequential File

```
IDENTIFICATION DIVISION.
PROGRAM-ID. CREATE-FILE.
*
ENVIRONMENT DIVISION.
*
CONFIGURATION SECTION.
SOURCE-COMPUTER. ABC-490.
OBJECT-COMPUTER. ABC-490.
*
INPUT-OUTPUT SECTION.
FILE-CONTROL.
    SELECT CUST-MAST-FILE ASSIGN TO MASTOUT.
*
    SELECT CUST-SOURCE-FILE    ASSIGN TO SOURCE
        FILE STATUS IS CUST-FILE-STATUS.
*
    SELECT ERROR-FILE          ASSIGN TO PRINTER.
*
```

FIGURE 10-9

*Program to Create a Sequential
File (continued)*

```
DATA DIVISION.
*
FILE SECTION.
*
FD  CUST-MAST-FILE
    LABEL RECORDS ARE STANDARD
    BLOCK CONTAINS 5 RECORDS
    DATA RECORD IS CUST-MAST-REC.
01  CUST-MAST-REC            PIC X(75).
*
FD  CUST-SOURCE-FILE
    LABEL RECORDS OMITTED
    DATA RECORD IS CUST-SOURCE-REC.
01  CUST-SOURCE-REC.
    02  CUST-NO              PIC 9(5).
    02  CUST-NAME            PIC X(20).
    02  CUST-ADDRESS         PIC X(50).
    02  FILLER               PIC X(5).
*
FD  ERROR-FILE
    LABEL RECORDS ARE OMITTED
    DATA RECORD IS ERROR-REC.
01  ERROR-REC                PIC X(132).
*
WORKING-STORAGE SECTION.
*
01  END-OF-FILE-INDICATOR    PIC XXX   VALUE 'NO'.
    88  END-OF-FILE                    VALUE 'YES'.
*
01  CUST-FILE-STATUS         PIC XX.
*
01  PREVIOUS-CUST-NO         PIC 9(5)  VALUE ZERO.
*
01  SEQ-ERROR-MESSAGE.
    02  FILLER               PIC X     VALUE SPACE.
    02  FILLER               PIC X(13) VALUE
            'ERROR RECORD:'.
    02  RECORD-OUT           PIC X(75).
*
01  I-O-ERROR-MESSAGE.
    02  FILLER               PIC X(25) VALUE
            'CUST-MASTER I/O EXCEPTION'.
    02  FILLER               PIC X(16) VALUE
            ' FILE STATUS = '.
    02  ERR-MESS-FILE-STATUS PIC XX.
*
01  JOB-TERMINATOR           PIC XXX   VALUE 'NO'.
    88  ABEND                          VALUE 'YES'.
*
*
```

FIGURE 10-9

Program to Create a Sequential
File (continued)

```
/
  PROCEDURE DIVISION.
*
  000-MAIN-ROUTINE.
      OPEN INPUT CUST-SOURCE-FILE
           OUTPUT ERROR-FILE.
*
      OPEN OUTPUT CUST-MAST-FILE.
*
      IF  CUST-FILE-STATUS = '00'
          PERFORM 100-CREATE-MASTER
      ELSE
          PERFORM 400-I-O-EXCEPTION.
*
      CLOSE CUST-SOURCE-FILE
      ERROR-FILE
      CUST-MAST-FILE.
*
      STOP RUN.
*
  100-CREATE-MASTER.
*
      PERFORM 200-READ-SOURCE
*
      PERFORM 300-CHECK-WRITE-READ
          UNTIL END-OF-FILE
              OR ABEND.
*
  200-READ-SOURCE.
      READ CUST-SOURCE-FILE RECORD
      IF  CUST-FILE-STATUS = '10'
          MOVE 'YES' TO END-OF-FILE-INDICATOR
      ELSE
          IF CUST-FILE-STATUS NOT = '00'
          PERFORM 400-I-O-EXCEPTION.
*
  300-CHECK-WRITE-READ.
      IF  CUST-NO NOT > PREVIOUS-CUST-NO
          MOVE CUST-SOURCE-REC TO RECORD-OUT
          WRITE ERROR-REC FROM SEQ-ERROR-MESSAGE AFTER 2
      ELSE
          WRITE CUST-MAST-REC FROM CUST-SOURCE-REC
          MOVE CUST-NO TO PREVIOUS-CUST-NO.
*
      PERFORM 200-READ-SOURCE.
*
  400-I-O-EXCEPTION.
      MOVE CUST-FILE-STATUS TO ERR-MESS-FILE-STATUS
      WRITE ERROR-REC FROM I-O-ERROR-MESSAGE AFTER 1
      MOVE 'YES' TO JOB-TERMINATOR.
```

FIGURE 10-10

Sample Input and Output for the Program in Figure 10-9

CUSTOMER SOURCE FILE

```
11111NAME-1                  ADDRESS-1
22222NAME-2                  ADDRESS-2
33333NAME-3                  ADDRESS-3
44444NAME-4                  ADDRESS-4
10000SEQUENCE ERROR
55555NAME-5                  ADDRESS-5
60000NAME-6                  ADDRESS-6
```

CUSTOMER MASTER FILE

```
11111NAME-1                  ADDRESS-1
22222NAME-2                  ADDRESS-2
33333NAME-3                  ADDRESS-3
44444NAME-4                  ADDRESS-4
55555NAME-5                  ADDRESS-5
60000NAME-6                  ADDRESS-6
```

ERROR FILE

```
ERROR RECORD:10000SEQUENCE ERROR
```

FIGURE 10-11

Program to Create a Sequential File Using COBOL '85

```
IDENTIFICATION DIVISION.
PROGRAM-ID. CREATE-FILE-85.
*
ENVIRONMENT DIVISION.
INPUT-OUTPUT SECTION.
FILE-CONTROL.
    SELECT CUST-MAST-FILE      ASSIGN TO MASTOUT.
*
    SELECT CUST-SOURCE-FILE    ASSIGN TO SOURCE-FILE
            FILE STATUS IS CUST-FILE-STATUS.
*
    SELECT ERROR-FILE          ASSIGN TO PRINTER.
*
DATA DIVISION.
*
FILE SECTION.
FD  CUST-MAST-FILE    LABEL RECORDS ARE STANDARD
                      BLOCK CONTAINS 5 RECORDS.
01  CUST-MAST-REC             PIC X(75).
*
```

FIGURE 10-11
*Program to Create a Sequential
File Using COBOL '85 (continued)*

```
FD   CUST-SOURCE-FILE LABEL RECORDS OMITTED.
01   CUST-SOURCE-REC.
     02   CUST-NO               PIC 9(5).
     02   CUST-NAME             PIC X(20).
     02   CUST-ADDRESS          PIC X(50).
     02   FILLER                PIC X(5).
*
FD   ERROR-FILE       LABEL RECORDS ARE OMITTED.
01   ERROR-REC                  PIC X(132).
*
WORKING-STORAGE SECTION.
*
01   END-OF-FILE-INDICATOR      PIC XXX    VALUE 'NO'.
     88   END-OF-FILE                      VALUE 'YES'.
*
01   CUST-FILE-STATUS           PIC XX.
*
01   PREVIOUS-CUST-NO           PIC 9(5)   VALUE ZERO.
*
01   SEQ-ERROR-MESSAGE.
     02   FILLER                PIC X      VALUE SPACE.
     02   FILLER                PIC X(13) VALUE
                'ERROR RECORD:'.
     02   RECORD-OUT            PIC X(75).
*
01   I-O-ERROR-MESSAGE.
     02   FILLER                PIC X(25) VALUE
                'CUST-MASTER I/O EXCEPTION'.
     02   FILLER                PIC X(16) VALUE
                ' FILE STATUS = '.
     02   ERR-MESS-FILE-STATUS    PIC XX.
*
01   JOB-TERMINATOR             PIC XXX    VALUE 'NO'.
     88   ABEND                            VALUE 'YES'.
*
/
PROCEDURE DIVISION.
*
000-CREATE-MASTER.
*
     OPEN INPUT  CUST-SOURCE-FILE
         OUTPUT ERROR-FILE
                 CUST-MAST-FILE
*
     IF  CUST-FILE-STATUS NOT = '00'
         PERFORM 100-I-O-EXCEPTION
         SET ABEND TO TRUE
     END-IF
*
     PERFORM UNTIL END-OF-FILE  OR ABEND
*
```

FIGURE 10-11

Program to Create a Sequential File Using COBOL '85 (continued)

```
                    READ CUST-SOURCE-FILE RECORD
                    IF  CUST-FILE-STATUS = '10'
                        SET END-OF-FILE TO TRUE
                    ELSE
                        IF  CUST-FILE-STATUS NOT = '00'
                            PERFORM 100-I-O-EXCEPTION
                        ELSE
                            IF  CUST-NO NOT > PREVIOUS-CUST-NO
                                MOVE CUST-SOURCE-REC TO RECORD-OUT
                                WRITE ERROR-REC FROM SEQ-ERROR-MESSAGE
                                      AFTER ADVANCING 2 LINES
                            ELSE
                                WRITE CUST-MAST-REC FROM CUST-SOURCE-REC
                                MOVE CUST-NO TO PREVIOUS-CUST-NO
                            END-IF
                        END-IF
                    END-IF
    *
                END-PERFORM
    *
                CLOSE CUST-SOURCE-FILE
                      ERROR-FILE
                      CUST-MAST-FILE
    *
                STOP RUN.
    *
            100-I-O-EXCEPTION.
                MOVE CUST-FILE-STATUS TO ERR-MESS-FILE-STATUS
                WRITE ERROR-REC FROM I-O-ERROR-MESSAGE AFTER 1
                SET ABEND TO TRUE.
```

especially appealing when the logic of a module, or a whole PROCEDURE DIVISION in this case, can fit on one page; we can easily scan the logic up-and-down, without needing to jump from one paragraph to another. Of course, the exceptionally small size of this program is not representative.

SEQUENTIAL FILE UPDATING

Files on magnetic tape or disk are maintained or updated to reflect changes that take place. We speak of *master* and *transaction* files as being involved in the updating process.

A *master* file contains reference data that reflect the cumulative status as of a point in time. For example, a payroll master file would contain data on each employee, such as name, address, pay rate, year-to-date earnings, and so forth.

A *transaction* file contains records that either reflect events or indicate changes to the master file. For example, a transaction record at a bank might be a deposit made or a check written. Other examples of transactions would be the addition of a new customer to the master file, deletion of a former customer's record, or a change of the customer's address.

File *updating* involves processing the transaction file against the master file. Figure 10-12 illustrates the general procedure involved in updating magnetic tape and disk files. Beginning with the top of the figure, we assume that the

FIGURE 10-12

*Procedure Used for Updating a
Sequential File*

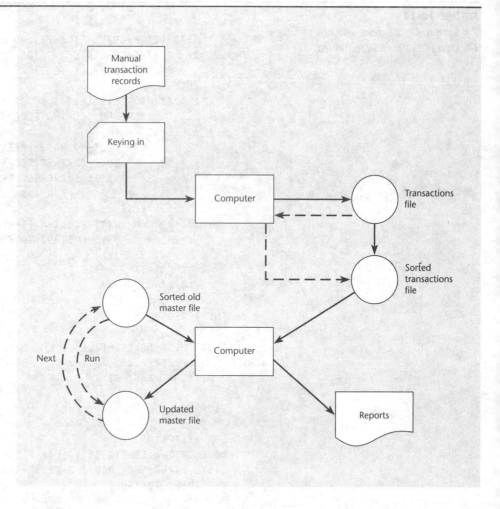

FIGURE 10-12

*Procedure Used for Updating a
Sequential File*

transactions originally were recorded manually and then were keyed in and transferred onto a magnetic tape or disk file. The old master file then is processed against the sorted transactions file to produce the updated master file. In addition, related reports might be produced on the printer.

As indicated by the dashed lines in Figure 10-12, what is now the updated master file becomes the old master file in the next update run, and the old master file from the first run will be used for entry of the updated master file on the next update run. This is known as a parent/child file relationship. However, the procedure we have described results in each case in destruction of the file for the period preceding the one being updated. If we want to have more historical backup, we could use a third file in this procedure, giving rise to a grandparent/parent/child relationship.

To update a master file, both the master file and the transaction file must be sorted on the same basis. Typically, they are sorted according to part number, account number, employee number, or the like.

In the case of a master file stored on disk, it is not necessary to create a new file. We could REWRITE each updated record in its original location. However, we should realize that doing so eliminates our backup capability. If something went wrong in the previous update run, we would not find it easy to reconstruct the file and rerun the update program. Thus, even with disk storage it often is preferable to create a new master file. Also, we cannot add new records to a sequential file unless we create a new, updated file. New records cannot be "squeezed in" between existing records.

R E V I E W . . . .

1. The file that contains cumulative data as of a point in time is called the
    _____ file.

    master

2. The file that contains records that reflect required changes to the master file is
    the _____ file.

    transaction

3. In the process of updating, the updated master file becomes the _____
    master file in the next update run.

    old

4. An existing master file can be updated directly, rather than by creating a new
    master file, when the existing file is stored on [tape / disk].

    disk

. . . .

SAMPLE SEQUENTIAL FILE UPDATE PROGRAM

We illustrate the general logic involved in a sequential file update by means of a simple example.

Master records consist of a customer number, a customer name, and an address. Transaction records consist of a customer number, a transaction code, a name field, and an address field. The transactions are of three general types: changing the content of a specified customer's master record, adding a new customer record, and deleting a customer record. The "change" transactions are of two types: change name and change address. In more complex tasks, there may be a large number of types of transactions. However, whether we have two types or ten, the programming logic is similar. Another point is that we may have several transaction records corresponding to one master record. In our simple example we could have both a change of name and a change of address for a given customer.

A structure chart for the program is presented in Figure 10-13, a complete program listing is included in Figure 10-14, and sample input and output are shown in Figure 10-15.

The main function involved is to process a transaction record against a master record. The 000-MAIN-LOGIC paragraph in Figure 10-14 begins with an OPEN command for the four files involved. Then we execute what is called a "primal read" to read the first record from each file:

```
PERFORM 010-READ-TRANS
PERFORM 020-READ-MASTER
```

At any point in the program logic we are in a position of having a record read from the master and transaction files. We repeatedly execute the 030-COMPARE-M-TO-T procedure to find out which of the three cases we have: the master record customer number is equal to, less than, or greater than the transaction record. We need to discuss each of these cases individually. However, first let us consider the 010 and 020 paragraphs that read the two input files.

To make sure that both files are in sequence, the 010-READ-TRANS and 020-READ-MASTER paragraphs perform appropriate sequence checking. In each case we save the value of the respective previous record and store it in PREVIOUS-TRANS-NO and PREVIOUS-MAST-NO, both of which were initialized with a VALUE ZERO. In the case of the transaction file a sequence error is indicated when a new

FIGURE 10-13
Structure Chart for the Update Program

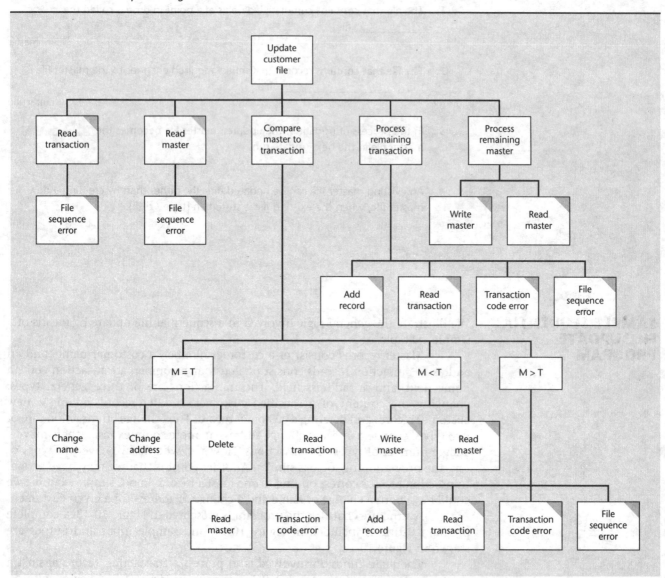

transaction record is smaller than the previous record. If it is equal, it simply means that we have a second, third, and so forth, transaction for the same customer. For the master file an out-of-sequence condition exists if the new record read does not have a customer number value greater than the one before it, since we cannot have two master records with the same customer number.

In the 020-READ-MASTER, notice that we READ OLD-CUST-MASTER RECORD INTO NEW-MAST-REC, thereby storing a copy of the record read into the record area of the new master. The purpose of this action will become clear as we continue with our explanation.

In 040-M-EQUALS-T when a master record is equal to a transaction record, we execute one of four possible cases: 070-NAME-CHANGE, 080-ADDRESS-CHANGE, 090-DELETION, or 130-TRANS-CODE-ERROR. Use of the EVALUATE statement from the 1985 standard is appropriate here, but we stay with the nested IF because there are so many existing programs before the 1985 standard, and if anything, the EVALUATE is easier to understand.

FIGURE 10-14

Program to Update a Sequential
File

```
IDENTIFICATION DIVISION.
PROGRAM-ID.  SIMPLUPD.
*
ENVIRONMENT DIVISION.
*
CONFIGURATION SECTION.
SOURCE-COMPUTER. ABC-480.
OBJECT-COMPUTER. ABC-480.
*
INPUT-OUTPUT SECTION.
*
FILE-CONTROL.
    SELECT OLD-CUST-MASTER ASSIGN TO A
            ORGANIZATION IS SEQUENTIAL
            ACCESS MODE IS SEQUENTIAL.
    SELECT NEW-CUST-MASTER ASSIGN TO B
            ORGANIZATION IS SEQUENTIAL
            ACCESS MODE IS SEQUENTIAL.
    SELECT TRANS-FILE ASSIGN TO CARDS.
    SELECT REPORT-FILE ASSIGN TO PRINTER.
/
DATA DIVISION.
*
FILE SECTION.
*
FD  OLD-CUST-MASTER
    LABEL RECORDS ARE STANDARD
    BLOCK CONTAINS 5 RECORDS
    DATA RECORD IS OLD-MAST-REC.
*
01  OLD-MAST-REC.
    02  CUST-NO             PIC X(5).
    02  CUST-NAME           PIC X(20).
    02  CUST-ADDRESS        PIC X(50).
*
FD  NEW-CUST-MASTER
    LABEL RECORDS ARE STANDARD
    BLOCK CONTAINS 5 RECORDS
    DATA RECORD IS NEW-MAST-REC.
*
01  NEW-MAST-REC.
    02  CUST-NO             PIC X(5).
    02  CUST-NAME           PIC X(20).
    02  CUST-ADDRESS        PIC X(50).
*
FD  TRANS-FILE
    LABEL RECORDS OMITTED
    DATA RECORD IS TRANS-REC.
*
```

FIGURE 10-14

Program to Update a Sequential File (continued)

```
01  TRANS-REC.
    02  CUST-NO              PIC X(5).
    02  TRANS-CODE           PIC 9.
        88  NEW-NAME         VALUE 1.
        88  NEW-ADDRESS      VALUE 2.
        88  NEW-RECORD       VALUE 3.
        88  DELETE-RECORD    VALUE 4.
        88  ERROR-TRANSACTION VALUES ZERO, 5 THRU 9.
    02  CUST-NAME            PIC X(20).
    02  CUST-ADDRESS         PIC X(50).
    02  FILLER               PIC X(4).
*
 FD  REPORT-FILE
     LABEL RECORDS OMITTED
     DATA RECORD REPORT-REC.
*
 01  REPORT-REC              PIC X(132).
*
/
 WORKING-STORAGE SECTION.
*
 01  END-OF-FILE-SWITCHES.
     02  END-OF-TRANS-SWITCH  PIC XXX VALUE 'NO'.
         88  TRANS-ENDED      VALUE 'YES'.
     02  END-OF-MASTER-SWITCH PIC XXX VALUE 'NO'.
         88  MASTER-ENDED     VALUE 'YES'.
*
 01  TERMINATION-SWITCH       PIC XXX VALUE 'NO'.
         88  TERMINAL-ERROR   VALUE 'YES'.
*
 01  PREVIOUS-REC-VALUES.
     02  PREVIOUS-TRANS-NO    PIC 9(5) VALUE ZEROS.
     02  PREVIOUS-MAST-NO     PIC 9(5) VALUE ZEROS.
*
 01  ERROR-MESSAGE-RECORD.
     02  FILLER               PIC X VALUE SPACE.
     02  MESSAGE-FIELD        PIC X(75).
*
 01  PREVIOUS-VALUES-OUT.
     02  FILLER               PIC X VALUE SPACE.
     02  FILLER               PIC X(18)
                              VALUE 'PREVIOUS TRANS NO'.
     02  TRANS-NO-OUT         PIC 9(5).
     02  FILLER               PIC X(3) VALUE SPACES.
     02  FILLER               PIC X(17) VALUE
                              'PREVIOUS MAST NO'.
     02  MAST-NO-OUT          PIC 9(5).
/
```

FIGURE 10-14

Program to Update a Sequential
File (continued)

```
*
   PROCEDURE DIVISION.
*
   000-MAIN-LOGIC.
       OPEN INPUT  OLD-CUST-MASTER
                   TRANS-FILE
            OUTPUT NEW-CUST-MASTER
                   REPORT-FILE.
*
       PERFORM 010-READ-TRANS
       PERFORM 020-READ-MASTER
*
       PERFORM 030-COMPARE-M-TO-T UNTIL TRANS-ENDED
                                     OR MASTER-ENDED
                                     OR TERMINAL-ERROR.
*
       CLOSE OLD-CUST-MASTER
             NEW-CUST-MASTER
             TRANS-FILE
             REPORT-FILE
*
       STOP RUN.
*
   010-READ-TRANS.
       READ TRANS-FILE RECORD
            AT END MOVE 'YES' TO END-OF-TRANS-SWITCH
            MOVE HIGH-VALUES TO CUST-NO OF TRANS-REC.
*
       IF  TRANS-ENDED
           NEXT SENTENCE
       ELSE
           IF  CUST-NO OF TRANS-REC < PREVIOUS-TRANS-NO
               MOVE 'TRANSACTION FILE OUT OF SEQUENCE'
                               TO MESSAGE-FIELD
               PERFORM 120-FILE-SEQUENCE-ERROR
           ELSE
               MOVE CUST-NO OF TRANS-REC TO PREVIOUS-TRANS-NO.
*
   020-READ-MASTER.
       READ OLD-CUST-MASTER RECORD INTO NEW-MAST-REC
            AT END MOVE 'YES' TO END-OF-MASTER-SWITCH
                   MOVE HIGH-VALUES TO CUST-NO OF OLD-MAST-REC.
*
       IF  MASTER-ENDED
           NEXT SENTENCE
       ELSE
           IF CUST-NO OF OLD-MAST-REC NOT > PREVIOUS-MAST-NO
               MOVE 'MASTER FILE OUT OF SEQUENCE' TO MESSAGE-FIELD
               PERFORM 120-FILE-SEQUENCE-ERROR
           ELSE
               MOVE CUST-NO OF OLD-MAST-REC TO PREVIOUS-MAST-NO.
*
```

FIGURE 10-14

Program to Update a Sequential
File (continued)

```
        030-COMPARE-M-TO-T.
            IF  CUST-NO OF TRANS-REC = CUST-NO OF OLD-MAST-REC
                PERFORM 040-M-EQUALS-T
            ELSE
                IF  CUST-NO OF TRANS-REC > CUST-NO OF OLD-MAST-REC
                    PERFORM 050-M-LESS-THAN-T
                ELSE
                    PERFORM 060-M-GREATER-THAN-T.
        *
        040-M-EQUALS-T.
            IF  NEW-NAME
                PERFORM 070-NAME-CHANGE
            ELSE
                IF  NEW-ADDRESS
                    PERFORM 080-ADDRESS-CHANGE
                ELSE
                    IF  DELETE-RECORD
                        PERFORM 090-DELETION
                    ELSE
                        PERFORM 130-TRANS-CODE-ERROR.
        *
            PERFORM 010-READ-TRANS.
        *
        050-M-LESS-THAN-T.
            PERFORM 110-WRITE-MASTER
            PERFORM 020-READ-MASTER.
        *
        060-M-GREATER-THAN-T.
            IF  NEW-RECORD
                PERFORM 100-ADD-RECORD
                PERFORM 010-READ-TRANS
            ELSE
                IF  ERROR-TRANSACTION
                    PERFORM 130-TRANS-CODE-ERROR
                    PERFORM 101-READ-TRANS
                ELSE
                    MOVE 'FILES OUT OF SEQUENCE' TO MESSAGE-FIELD
                    PERFORM 120-FILE-SEQUENCE-ERROR.
        *
        070-NAME-CHANGE.
            MOVE CUST-NAME OF TRANS-REC TO CUST-NAME OF NEW-MAST-REC.
        *
        080-ADDRESS-CHANGE.
            MOVE CUST-ADDRESS OF TRANS-REC
                    TO CUST-ADDRESS OF NEW-MAST-REC.
        *
        090-DELETION.
            PERFORM 020-READ-MASTER.
        *
        100-ADD-RECORD.
            MOVE CUST-NO OF TRANS-REC TO CUST-NO OF NEW-MAST-REC
            MOVE CUST-NAME OF TRANS-REC TO CUST-NAME OF NEW-MAST-REC
            MOVE CUST-ADDRESS OF TRANS-REC
                    TO CUST-ADDRESS OF NEW-MAST-REC.
        *
```

FIGURE 10-14

Program to Update a Sequential
File (continued)

```
        PERFORM 110-WRITE-MASTER
*
    IF  NOT MASTER-ENDED
        MOVE OLD-MAST-REC TO NEW-MAST-REC.
*
* THE ABOVE MOVE RESTORES THE CONTENTS OF NEW-MAST-REC
* WHICH WERE DESTROYED BY THE NEW RECORD JUST ADDED.
* RECALL THAT IN READ-MASTER PARAGRAPH AS EACH OLD-MAST-REC
* IS READ IN IT IS MOVED INTO NEW-MAST-REC.
*
 110-WRITE-MASTER.
    WRITE REPORT-REC FROM NEW-MAST-REC
                AFTER ADVANCING 1 LINE
*
    WRITE NEW-MAST-REC.
*
 120-FILE-SEQUENCE-ERROR.
    WRITE REPORT-REC FROM ERROR-MESSAGE-RECORD
                AFTER ADVANCING PAGE.
*
    MOVE 'TRANSACTION RECORD AT TIME OF ERROR'
                TO MESSAGE-FIELD
    WRITE REPORT-REC FROM ERROR-MESSAGE-RECORD
                AFTER ADVANCING 2 LINES
    MOVE TRANS-REC TO MESSAGE-FIELD
    WRITE REPORT-REC FROM ERROR-MESSAGE-RECORD
                AFTER ADVANCING 2 LINES
*
    MOVE 'MASTER RECORD AT TIME OF ERROR'
                TO MESSAGE-FIELD
    WRITE REPORT-REC FROM ERROR-MESSAGE-RECORD
                AFTER ADVANCING 2 LINES
    MOVE OLD-MAST-REC TO MESSAGE-FIELD
    WRITE REPORT-REC FROM ERROR-MESSAGE-RECORD
                AFTER ADVANCING 2 LINES
*
    MOVE PREVIOUS-TRANS-NO TO TRANS-NO-OUT
    MOVE PREVIOUS-MAST-NO TO MAST-NO-OUT
    WRITE REPORT-REC FROM PREVIOUS-VALUES-OUT
*
    MOVE 'YES' TO TERMINATION-SWITCH.
*
 130-TRANS-CODE-ERROR.
    MOVE SPACES TO REPORT-REC
    WRITE REPORT-REC
                AFTER ADVANCING 1 LINE
    MOVE 'THE FOLLOWING RECORD CONTAINS A CODE ERROR'
                TO MESSAGE-FIELD
    WRITE REPORT-REC
                AFTER ADVANCING 1 LINE
    WRITE REPORT-REC FROM TRANS-REC
                AFTER ADVANCING 1 LINE
    MOVE SPACES TO REPORT-REC
    WRITE REPORT-REC
                AFTER ADVANCING 1 LINE.
```

FIGURE 10-15

Sample Input and Output for the Update Program in Figure 10-14

INPUT TRANSACTION FILE

```
222221NEW-NAME
234563NEW-CUSTOMER          ADDRESS OF NEW
4000032ND-NEW-CUSTOMER      ADDRESS OF 2ND NEW
444444 DELETE EXAMPLE
555555WRONG CODE EXAMPLE
555554                      NEW ADDRESS
543211 SEQ ERROR
666663 3RD NEW
```

OLD CUSTOMER MASTER FILE

```
11111NAME-1                 ADDRESS-1
22222NAME-2                 ADDRESS-2
33333NAME-3                 ADDRESS-3
44444NAME-4                 ADDRESS-4
55555NAME-5                 ADDRESS-5
60000NAME-6
```

NEW CUSTOMER MASTER

```
11111NAME-1                 ADDRESS-1
22222NEW-NAME               ADDRESS-2
23456NEW-CUSTOMER           ADDRESS OF NEW
33333NAME-3                 ADDRESS-3
400002ND-NEW-CUSTOMER       ADDRESS OF 2ND NEW
```

ERROR REPORT OUTPUT

```
555555WRONG CODE EXAMPLE

 TRANSACTION FILE OUT OF SEQUENCE
 TRANSACTION RECORD AT TIME OF ERROR
 543211 SEQ ERROR
 MASTER RECORD AT TIME OF ERROR
 60000NAME-6
 PREVIOUS TRANS NO 55555  PREVIOUS MAST NO 60000
```

If the master record is less than the transaction record, then we execute 050-M-LESS-THAN-T in which we first PERFORM 110-WRITE-MASTER. The latter paragraph writes the new master record on the printer first and then writes it onto the new master file. At this point we should emphasize that a WRITE instruction is destructive. After the WRITE NEW-MAST-REC command, for instance, the data in NEW-MAST-REC are unavailable. The basic reason is that while an output record is being "sent" to the file, the operating system defines a new space in memory to refer to the record, and the contents of that space are "garbage," that is they are dependent on what happened to be in that place in memory at that moment in time. Thus, if in 110-WRITE-MASTER we were to reverse the order of the two WRITE statements, the data in REPORT-REC would come as a surprise, since they would be unpredictable.

Returning to the content of the 050-M-LESS-THAN-T paragraph in Figure 10-14, we can better understand its purpose by considering the following simple example:

TRANSACTION	MASTER
10 change name	10
10 change address	15
20 change address	20

Customer 10 has two transactions. When we compare the first transaction to the master we find them to be equal. We process the first transaction, which changes the name in the copy of the 10 master record in the new master record (recall that when we read a master record, we also make a copy of it in the new master record). We read the second transaction, which changes the address of the 10 new master record. When we read the third transaction, we have the case of the master record (10) being less than the transaction record (20). As indicated in 050-M-LESS-THAN-T, at that point we write the already updated 10 master record into the new master file and PERFORM 020-READ-MASTER, which results in customer 15 being read in. In this case when we compare the two records, the master (15) is less than the transaction (20). Again we write the new master record to its file, but in this case it is simply a copy of the original record, since there have been no updates to the record of customer 15. Thus, the logic in 050-M-LESS-THAN-T is based on the premise that NEW-MAST-REC already holds the appropriate content.

If the master record is higher than the transaction record, then it must be an "add" transaction to be valid. The 100-ADD-RECORD paragraph handles the addition of new records. Consider an example set of data:

TRANSACTION	MASTER
10 change	10
12 add new	15
20 change	20

When transaction 12 is read in, the program takes the path to 050-M-LESS-THAN-T, where we write the updated record for customer 10 and we read the next master, record 15. Now the program executes 060-M-GREATER-THAN-T since 15 is greater that 12. Since transaction 12 is an add transaction, we execute 100-ADD-RECORD, in which the data in the transaction record are MOVEd to the NEW-MAST-REC and written onto the new master file. However, when the master record for customer 15 was read in, it was also copied (READ ... INTO) in NEW-MAST-REC, and the process for creating the new record for customer 12 erased the data for customer 15 in NEW-MAST-REC. Thus the statement

```
IF NOT MASTER-ENDED
    MOVE OLD-MAST-REC TO NEW-MAST-REC
```

in 100-ADD-RECORD will restore the data for customer 15 in NEW-MAST-REC.

Observing the main iteration instruction in 000-MAIN-LOGIC, we see

```
PERFORM 030-COMPARE-M-TO-T
    UNTIL TRANS-ENDED AND MASTER-ENDED
        OR TERMINAL-ERROR.
```

Then, in the 010 and 020 paragraphs, when either the transaction or old master file is at the end, we make the TRANS-ENDED and MASTER-ENDED conditions true, and we MOVE HIGH-VALUES TO the respective CUST-NO. Consider these two cases:

TRANS.	MASTER	TRANS.	MASTER
10	10	10	10
20	eof	eof	20
30			30
eof			eof
(a)		(b)	

The "eof" represents the last (end of file) record. In case (a) the old master file's last record is for customer 10. The transactions for customers 20 and 30 would be add types, unless they were errors. In case (b) the transaction file ends before the old master, and the records for customers 20 and 30 will need to be copied unchanged onto the updated new master file. When transaction 20 is read in case (a), the 050-M-LESS-THAN-T is executed, which writes the updated record for customer 10; and through PERFORM 020-READ-MASTER the end-of-file record is read, and we MOVE HIGH-VALUES TO CUST-NO OF OLD-MAST-REC. From that point on, 060-M-GREATER-THAN-T will be executed, since HIGH-VALUES is always greater than any customer-number value in the transaction record. However, when the eof record is read from the transaction file, then the compound TRANS-ENDED AND MASTER-ENDED condition is true, and the PERFORM in 000-MAIN-LOGIC will terminate the iteration. Before the eof record is read from the transaction file in case (a), however, the comparison of 30 to the HIGH-VALUES contained in the customer-number field of the old master record will have caused 060-M-GREATER-THAN-T to execute, and record 30 will have been added to the new file. You are asked to trace processing of the records in case (b) on your own.

Two kinds of error messages are produced in the sample program in Figure 10-14. The first one is generated in 120-FILE-SEQUENCE-ERROR when the files are found to be out of sequence. We then terminate the program, printing first the records involved and then the immediately preceding records, for reference. It is not always necessary to terminate the program, but in this case it seems the reasonable thing to do. The second type of error has to do with incorrect transaction codes, and it is processed in 130-TRANS-CODE-ERROR. When such errors occur, we write an error message on a separate file, which we assume also is ASSIGNed to the printer device.

The printed output for this program is a simple listing of the updated file. Generally, there would be a list of updated, new, and deleted records printed, rather than the complete file. Exercise 10.2 at the end of this chapter asks for such a modification to the program.

The sample program in Figure 10-14 hopefully is sufficiently self-documenting that you should be able to follow it. This program can be used as the basis for most sequential updating programs, because the basic logic of all such programs is very similar. Chapter 17 presents an expanded discussion and further examples of processing sequential files.

SUMMARY

The three principal methods of file organization in COBOL are the *sequential, indexed,* and *relative.* In this chapter we focused on sequential file processing, in which records are written and accessed in a serial order.

The storage device that is used often determines which methods of file organization are possible. If the storage device is *magnetic tape,* then sequential file organization must be used. In the chapter, characteristics of magnetic tape and *magnetic disk* were considered.

Data are recorded on any magnetic storage device in the form of *blocks.* The *blocking factor* denotes the number of *logical* (as contrasted to *physical*) records included in each block. Some of the factors that need to be considered in enhancing storage efficiency, and therefore reducing processing time, are *padding, buffering, double-buffering,* and the use of *fixed-length* or *variable-length* records.

In the FILE-CONTROL paragraph of the ENVIRONMENT DIVISION, a sequential file organization is designated either by ORGANIZATION IS SEQUENTIAL, or by omitting this option, in which case the default is the SEQUENTIAL choice. The use of other options in the FILE-CONTROL paragraph as they relate to sequential files also was described.

In the DATA DIVISION the FD entry is followed immediately by the file name that was declared in the ENVIRONMENT DIVISION, where it was assigned to a hardware device. Again, the various options in the file description entry as they relate to sequential files were described.

Processing of a file is initiated by use of the OPEN verb in the PROCEDURE DIVISION, while end-of-file procedures are specified by use of the CLOSE verb. The READ, with its available options, is used with respect to *file input.* The WRITE, with its available options, is used with respect to *file output.* The REWRITE can be used with respect to *updating* an existing disk file. Exceptions or errors can be identified by use of the FILE STATUS feature, which results in a two-digit code that identifies the status of each input or output operation. The programmer can test the contents of that field and decide on the next program sequence.

In general, updating a sequential file involves processing a *transaction file* against a *master file* and generating a *new master file* as backup.

The chapter concluded with detailed discussion of two sample COBOL programs: one for *creating* a sequential file, and the other for *updating* an established sequential file.

EXERCISES

10.1 Modify the sample update program in Figure 10-14 so that transaction error records are saved on a tape or disk file and are printed after the update process has been completed. In a process chart form, we should have this:

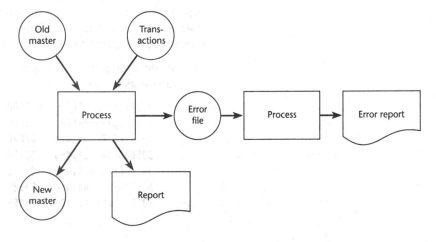

10.2 Modify the sample update program in Figure 10-14 so that during the update process only those master records that were in some way altered are output on the printer. Where appropriate, show both the old and the new record for visual reference and comparison. If a record is added or deleted, however, only one master record is relevant. The report should have the following format:

```
                        Changes to Customer Master
                              MM/DD/YR

        RECORD                                  ACTION

        OLD: xxxxxxxxxxxxx                       CHANGED ADDRESS
        NEW: xxxxxxxxxxxxx

        NEW: xxxxxxxxxxxxx                       NEW RECORD ADDED
        OLD: xxxxxxxxxxxxx                       DELETED RECORD
        OLD: xxxxxxxxxxxxx                       CHANGED NAME
        NEW: xxxxxxxxxxxxx
```

10.3 A company maintains inventory data on a master file sorted on part number. Each record contains the following types of data for each item held in inventory:

FIELD	SIZE
Part number	5 numeric positions
Part name	15 alphanumeric positions
Quantity	5 numeric positions

For the sake of simplicity, there are two types of transactions: receipts and issues. Each transaction has the following format:

FIELD	SIZE
Part number	5 numeric positions
Transaction code 1 = receipt 2 = issue	1 numeric position
Quantity	5 numeric positions

Batches of transaction records are accumulated and then processed to update the master file and to print a report that lists each part number, name, previous quantity balance, and new balance. When the transaction code is 1, the quantity is added; if the code is 2, the quantity is subtracted.

a. Write a program to create the master file. Sample input for the master tape is as follows:

```
035611/2 HP EL MOTOR02000
10513TRANSFORMER    08000
30561GEAR TRAIN-A   07890
30562GEAR TRAIN-B   10250
30564GEAR TRAIN-C   04650
30579GEAR TRAIN-G   08529
40100STEEL PLATE-1A 06099
```

```
40110STEEL PLATE-2A 00852
40120STEEL PLATE-3A 00996
40130STEEL PLATE-4A 01250
40140STEEL PLATE-5B 02899
40150STEEL PLATE-3C 08192
51000BRASS FTNGS-A  12695
51020BRASS FTNGS-B  08569
51030BRASS FTNGS-C  09992
60256BALL BEARING-A201695
60257BALL BEARING-A302561
60258BALL BEARING-A410883
60259BALL BEARING-A513429
60260BALL BEARING-A608866
60261BALL BEARING-A706219
```

b. Write a program to update the master file, given a set of transaction records. The program should perform a sequence check to ascertain that the transaction input records are in the same sequence as the master records. It is possible that some items may have no corresponding transactions, but no transactions are present for items not on the master file. Sample input for transactions is as follows (the master file input is the same as shown in part (a):

```
10513200200
10513110000
30562200500
30562200800
30562200900
30564108000
40100112000
40100204000
40100203000
40140110000
51030200200
51030200965
60261200600
60261200500
60261200900
60261104000
```

Sample output is presented in Figure 10-16 on the following page.

FIGURE 10-16

Sample Output for Exercise 10.3

ITEM NUMBER	PART NAME	PREVIOUS BALANCE	NEW BALANCE
03561	1/2 HP EL MOTOR	2000	2000
10513	TRANSFORMER	8000	17800
30561	GEAR TRAIN-A	7890	7890
30562	GEAR TRAIN-B	10250	8050
30564	GEAR TRAIN-C	4650	12650
30579	GEAR TRAIN-G	8529	8529
40100	STEEL PLATE-1A	6099	11099
40110	STEEL PLATE-2A	0852	0852
40120	STEEL PLATE-3A	0996	0996
40130	STEEL PLATE-4A	1250	1250
40140	STEEL PLATE-5B	2899	12899
40150	STEEL PLATE-3C	8192	8192
51000	BRASS FTNGS-A	12695	12685
51020	BRASS FTNGS-B	8569	8569
51030	BRASS FTNGS-C	9992	8827
60256	BALL BEARING-A2	1695	1695
60257	BALL BEARING-A3	2561	2561
60258	BALL BEARING-A4	10883	10883
60259	BALL BEARING-A5	13429	13429
60260	BALL BEARING-A6	8866	8866
60261	BALL BEARING-A7	6219	8219

11 Sorting and Merging Sequential Files

INTRODUCTION

THE COBOL SORT FEATURE

DATA DIVISION FORMAT
   SPECIFICATIONS

PROCEDURE DIVISION FORMAT
   SPECIFICATIONS

FILE MERGING IN COBOL

THE PURPOSE OF THIS CHAPTER *is to learn how to use the COBOL sort feature to sort data in a sequential file according to a desired sequence. In addition, you will study the related operation of merging two or more presorted files to form one combined file.*

You will begin by studying some general concepts about file sorting. You will then observe the use of the specialized COBOL statements that are used for sorting by means of two example programs. This will be followed by detailed consideration of the formats in the DATA DIVISION and the PROCEDURE DIVISION for the specialized statements.

The chapter concludes with a general discussion of file merging, and the COBOL specialized instructions for file merging.

INTRODUCTION

In our description of sequential file processing in the preceding chapter, it was evident that sequential files must be sorted in sequence. In file updating, the master file and the transaction file must both have been sorted in the same order. The basis for the sequence is dependent on the situation. For example, in the processing of sales transactions, we may sort the data in the order of customer number. Then we may want to use the same transaction data to update the inventory master file. So next we sort the transaction file in the order of product number to match the sequence of the product inventory master. In addition, we may need reports organized by salesperson, by date, and by geographic area. It should be rather evident that sorting is a very common activity.

Sorting files is so common and so important in business applications of the computer that people have devoted special efforts to devise efficient ways of sorting. When a company acquires a computer, invariably it will acquire indispensable software, such as the operating system, one or more programming language compilers, and a number of "utility" programs. *Utilities* are programs designed to do general-purpose tasks that are not specific to a single application. Typical utilities include programs to create files (catalog their given name in the system table of files, allocate disk space, etc.); to copy a file from, say, magnetic tape to disk; and to sort or merge files. Sorting and merging are so interrelated that the name "sort-merge" is the common way of referring to such a utility program.

Usually the computer hardware vendor will supply a basic set of utilities, including sort-merge, along with the operating system. However, many companies have devised more efficient ways of sorting, and they sell their programs as software products. There are a number of such "proprietary" sorting programs on the market, and their exact method of sorting is the very value of their product. So file sorting can be done in a variety of ways, and the details of each proprietary method are trade secrets. Still, there are many sorting algorithms in the public domain, and it can be presumed that all sort programs use the same basic principles. Where they differ is in critical details.

Basically, all sort routines proceed along these general lines:

- Read a group of records into the central memory of the computer and sort the records in that group using the high speed of the central memory. However, the file is much larger than the central memory, so we can read and sort internally only a relatively small set of records.

- Write the sorted group of records out to a file (disk or tape).

- Read another group of records, sort them internally, and write them out to another file. Keep repeating this process, writing sorted groups of records to two or several files, until all the initial records have been so processed.

- Next, there will be a phase of repeated merging of the sorted groups. The reasons for needing possibly several merging operations require more detailed explanation than is warranted by our intended scope of coverage at this time. Suffice it to say that merging is used to eventually combine the sorted groups into one sorted file. Thus, merging and sorting are related operations in practice.

Sorting is frequently done as a separate program step. A file containing the data is input into a sort utility program, and a sorted file is created that can then be used as input to a COBOL program for further processing. Another approach is to do the sorting or merging operation as part of a COBOL program, not as a separate program. In this chapter we concentrate on the latter approach, that of using COBOL itself for sorting and merging files.

THE COBOL SORT FEATURE

Since file sorting is such a common need, the COBOL language incorporates a sort feature that makes it possible to accomplish this operation with minimal programming. The programmer need not be concerned with the details of any sort algorithm in using this feature, but may simply specify the files to be sorted, the sort key (or keys) to be used, and any special procedures for the handling of files before or after the sort. We illustrate here the COBOL sort feature by means of two examples.

Example 1

Assume that we have a sequential file with the following record description in the DATA DIVISION:

```
01   INPUT-RECORD.
     02   ACCOUNT-NUMBER        PICTURE 9(8).
     02   NAME                  PICTURE X(20).
     02   TRANSACTION-DATE.
          03  DAY-OF-YEAR       PICTURE 999.
          03  YEAR             PICTURE 99.
     02   OTHER-DATA           PICTURE X(47).
```

Suppose we wish to sort the file in *ascending sequence* according to AC-COUNT-NUMBER and in *descending sequence* according to YEAR. That is, for each account, all records are to be arranged from the most recent to the least recent YEAR. Also assume that the sorted file is to be called SORTED-FILE. The sorting process can be portrayed as involving three files, INPUT-FILE, SORT-FILE, and SORTED-FILE, as follows:

Because the sorting procedure is preprogrammed, you need not be concerned about the detail of the SORT-FILE. In concept, SORT-FILE represents a preprogrammed file whose description has been embedded in the sorting routine. As the above diagram illustrates, data from the INPUT-FILE are transferred to the SORT-FILE where they are sorted, and the sorted data are then output onto the SORTED-FILE (these specific file names are, of course, arbitrary choices).

The SORT-FILE is a conceptual file that may involve several physical files. Typically, the sort routine uses several sequential files to execute the sort. Since the sort routine is automated, however, the COBOL programmer describes the file as if it were one physical file, and it is through JCL statements that we describe the physical structure of the file.

Figure 11-1 presents the COBOL program that can be used to sort the file described in this example problem, including sample input and output. In the ENVIRONMENT DIVISION three files are identified in the SELECT statements. Notice that SORT-FILE has been ASSIGNed as if it were one physical file.

In the DATA DIVISION the INPUT-FILE is described in the usual fashion. However, the SORT-FILE is introduced with the special SD level indicator (which stands for Sort Descriptor). The SD level indicator specifies that this is a file to be used in conjunction with the sort routine. Notice that there is no LABEL clause given for such a file.

As far as the record description for the SORT-FILE is concerned, it is just like any other such description. We used the same description as we used for the

FIGURE 11-1
*SORT Program for Example 1,
Including Sample Input and
Output*

```
IDENTIFICATION DIVISION.
PROGRAM-ID. SORT1.
*
* THIS PROGRAM ILLUSTRATES SORTING A SEQUENTIAL
* FILE CALLED INPUT-FILE AND MAKING THE SORTED FILE
* AVAILABLE IN SORTED-FILE.
*
ENVIRONMENT DIVISION.
*
CONFIGURATION SECTION.
SOURCE-COMPUTER. ABC-480.
OBJECT-COMPUTER. ABC-480.
*
INPUT-OUTPUT SECTION.
FILE-CONTROL.
    SELECT INPUT-FILE  ASSIGN TO CARD.
    SELECT SORT-FILE   ASSIGN TO SORTWK.
    SELECT SORTED-FILE ASSIGN TO PRINTER.
*
DATA DIVISION.
*
FILE SECTION.
FD  INPUT-FILE LABEL RECORD OMITTED
             DATA RECORD IS INPUT-RECORD.
*
01  INPUT-RECORD.
    02  ACCOUNT-NUMBER     PIC 9(8).
    02  NAME               PIC X(20).
    02  TRANSACTION-DATE.
        03  DAY-OF-YEAR    PIC 999.
        03  YEAR           PIC 99.
    02  OTHER-DATA         PIC X(47).
*
SD  SORT-FILE DATA RECORD IS SORT-RECORD.
*
01  SORT-RECORD.
    02  ACCOUNT-NUMBER     PIC 9(8).
    02  NAME               PIC X(20).
    02  TRANSACTION-DATE.
        03  DAY-OF-YEAR    PIC 999.
        03  YEAR           PIC 99.
    02  OTHER-DATA         PIC X(47).
*
FD  SORTED-FILE LABEL RECORD OMITTED
             DATA RECORD IS SORTED-RECORD.
*
01  SORTED-RECORD         PIC X(80).
*
```

FIGURE 11-1

SORT Program for Example 1, Including Sample Input and Output (continued)

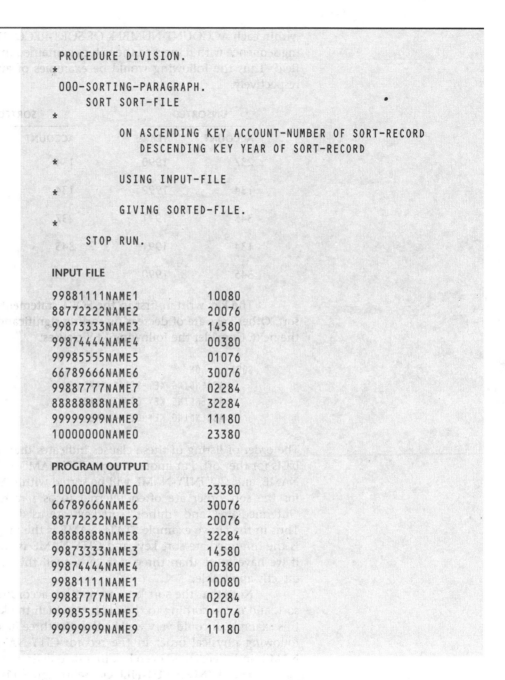

```
      PROCEDURE DIVISION.
*
      000-SORTING-PARAGRAPH.
          SORT SORT-FILE
*
              ON ASCENDING KEY ACCOUNT-NUMBER OF SORT-RECORD
                 DESCENDING KEY YEAR OF SORT-RECORD
*
              USING INPUT-FILE
*
              GIVING SORTED-FILE.
*
          STOP RUN.

      INPUT FILE

      99881111NAME1          10080
      88772222NAME2          20076
      99873333NAME3          14580
      99874444NAME4          00380
      99985555NAME5          01076
      66789666NAME6          30076
      99887777NAME7          02284
      88888888NAME8          32284
      99999999NAME9          11180
      10000000NAME0          23380

      PROGRAM OUTPUT

      10000000NAME0          23380
      66789666NAME6          30076
      88772222NAME2          20076
      88888888NAME8          32284
      99873333NAME3          14580
      99874444NAME4          00380
      99881111NAME1          10080
      99887777NAME7          02284
      99985555NAME5          01076
      99999999NAME9          11180
```

INPUT-FILE, and qualification is used to differentiate between the two records in the SORT statement (ACCOUNT-NUMBER OF SORT-RECORD).

Finally, the SORTED-FILE record has been described as one field of 80 characters to illustrate one possible variation. Since the program is concerned only with the sorting of the file, there is no need to describe the specific fields in the records that constitute this file.

The relevant PROCEDURE DIVISION is simple and consists of just one paragraph. The SORT verb is very powerful in that the programmer need only specify the sort keys and the source and destination of the file records. The statement SORT SORT-FILE identifies the name of the file to be sorted—which should be the same file introduced by an SD entry in the DATA DIVISION. The ASCENDING KEY ACCOUNT-NUMBER OF SORT-RECORD clause specifies that the file is to be sorted in ascending ACCOUNT-NUMBER OF SORT-RECORD sequence. The DESCENDING KEY YEAR OF SORT-RECORD clause specifies that, within each ACCOUNT-NUMBER OF SORT-RECORD, we wish to sort in descending sequence with respect to the values contained in the YEAR OF SORT-RECORD field. Thus the following would be examples of an unsorted and a sorted file, respectively:

UNSORTED		SORTED	
ACCOUNT	YEAR	ACCOUNT	YEAR
237	1990	134	1992
134	1992	134	1991
345	1991	237	1990
134	1991	345	1991
345	1990	345	1990

The key written first in the SORT statement is the principal basis for the sort. Other keys are of decreasing sorting significance as we proceed from one to the next. Consider the following KEY clauses:

```
SORT ... ON
      ASCENDING KEY STATE-NAME
      ASCENDING KEY COUNTY-NAME
      ASCENDING KEY CITY-NAME
```

The order of listing of these clauses indicates that STATE-NAME is the principal basis for the sort. Put another way, CITY-NAME will be sorted within COUNTY-NAME, and COUNTY-NAME will be sorted within STATE-NAME. The fields used for the sort order are often referred to as *sort keys,* and the terms "major," "intermediate," and "minor" sort keys are used to describe multiple sort keys. Thus in the above example STATE-NAME is the major sort key, COUNTY-NAME is the intermediate sort key, and CITY-NAME is the minor sort key. Of course, if we have more than three sort keys, then this three-level terminology is not directly applicable.

Note that the sort keys are written according to the desired order of the sort, and not according to the order in which the keys appear in the record. For this example, it could very well be that the three fields used as sort keys are in the following physical order in the record: CITY-NAME, STATE-NAME, COUNTY-NAME, and there could even be other field definitions intervening between them.

The USING INPUT-FILE clause in Figure 11-1 specifies the file that is the source of the records, while the GIVING SORTED-FILE clause simply specifies the file on which the sort output is to be recorded. Finally, note that in the present example the programmer does not OPEN or CLOSE any of the three files involved. The use of the SORT verb automatically takes care of such procedures.

In the above example the whole function of the PROCEDURE DIVISION is to sort a file. This need not be the case. The SORT is simply one of the COBOL verbs and, as such, it comprises only one statement in the program. The following example illustrates the point:

```
IF  TIME-TO-SORT
    PERFORM ROUTINE-A
    SORT CUST-SORT-FILE
        ON ASCENDING KEY NAME
        USING CUSTOMER-SOURCE-FILE
```

```
            GIVING CUSTOMER-SORTED-FILE
        PERFORM ROUTINE-B
    ELSE
        PERFORM ROUTINE-C.
```

Example 2

We now illustrate use of the COBOL sort feature with a more complex data processing task. Suppose we want to read a set of records, add a field to each record to indicate its original sequential order, sort the file, store the sorted file, and print the sorted file. Figure 11-2 presents the COBOL program designed to accomplish this task, including sample input and output. Notice that there are four files, called INPUT-FILE, SORT-FILE, SORTED-FILE, and PRINT-FILE. DATA DIVISION entries follow the usual format, except for the use of SD to identify SORT-FILE as the sort file, as was the case in the preceding example. In the present example the WORKING-STORAGE SECTION is used to form the SEQUENCE-NUMBER.

Figure 11-3 presents the program logic in flowchart form. Comparing the SORT statement in the PROCEDURE DIVISION in Figure 11-2 with the flowchart, notice that even though the SORT statement is one statement in form, it consists of three executable steps in function. These three steps are

1. Execute the section identified by INPUT PROCEDURE IS.

2. Execute the SORT itself.

3. Execute the section identified by OUTPUT PROCEDURE IS.

In the PROCEDURE DIVISION we first specify that we wish to sort the SORT-FILE on ASCENDING KEY NAME OF SORT-RECORD. Thus the NAME field is the sort key. INPUT PROCEDURE IS 100-READING-SEQUENCING indicates that records will become available to the SORT-FILE according to instructions contained in a section called 100-READING-SEQUENCING. A *section* is a group of paragraphs that can be referenced as a group. To declare the beginning of a section, we give it a name followed by the keyword SECTION and a period. In the example in Figure 11-2 we can see 100-READING-SEQUENCING SECTION.

The first paragraph in the 100-READING-SEQUENCING SECTION, called 110-INPUT-SET-UP, serves to open the INPUT-FILE as input. Then we enter a loop involving the 130-SEQ-RELEASE paragraph. Each record is read, and in each case a four-digit sequence number is assigned to the field called DATA-TO-BE-INSERTED:

```
ADD 1 TO SEQUENCE-NUMBER
MOVE SEQUENCE-NUMBER TO DATA-TO-BE-INSERTED.
```

Then we use the RELEASE SORT-RECORD FROM INPUT-RECORD statement. This simply says to move the contents of INPUT-RECORD to SORT-RECORD and then to write the SORT-RECORD on its file. The RELEASE command can be thought of as a specialized form of the WRITE instruction. If we are writing a record into a file that has been declared with SD rather than the usual FD descriptor, we use the specialized RELEASE verb to do the "write" function. Of course, we use RELEASE only in a section referenced with the INPUT PROCEDURE of the SORT statement. So the analogy between RELEASE and WRITE exists, but they cannot be used interchangeably.

The loop terminates when the last record is read, at which point the program branches to 140-END-OF-INPUT-SECTION, after INPUT-FILE is closed. The 140-END-OF-INPUT-SECTION paragraph is the last paragraph of the 100-READING-SEQUENCING SECTION, and is indicated by the EXIT verb. Recall that

FIGURE 11-2

*Sort Program for Example 2,
Including Sample Input and
Output*

```
*
     IDENTIFICATION DIVISION.
     PROGRAM-ID. SORT2.
*
     ENVIRONMENT DIVISION.
*
     CONFIGURATION SECTION.
     SOURCE-COMPUTER. ABC-480.
     OBJECT-COMPUTER. ABC-980.
*
     INPUT-OUTPUT SECTION.
*
     FILE-CONTROL.
         SELECT INPUT-FILE ASSIGN TO CARDS.
*
         SELECT SORT-FILE ASSIGN TO SORTWK.
*
         SELECT SORTED-FILE ASSIGN TO SORTOUT.
*
         SELECT PRINT-FILE ASSIGN TO PRINTER.
*
     DATA DIVISION.
     FILE SECTION.
*
     FD  INPUT-FILE LABEL RECORD OMITTED
         DATA RECORD IS INPUT-RECORD.
     01  INPUT-RECORD.
         02  FILLER                 PIC X(10).
         02  NAME                   PIC X(15).
         02  FILLER                 PIC X(51).
         02  DATA-TO-BE-INSERTED    PIC 9999.
*
     SD  SORT-FILE DATA RECORD IS SORT-RECORD.
     01  SORT-RECORD.
         02  FILLER                 PIC X(10).
         02  NAME                   PIC X(15).
         02  FILLER                 PIC X(55).
*
     FD  SORTED-FILE LABEL RECORD STANDARD
         BLOCK CONTAINS 77 RECORDS
         DATA RECORD IS SORTED-RECORD.
*
     01  SORTED-RECORD              PIC X(80).
*
     FD  PRINT-FILE LABEL RECORD OMITTED
         DATA RECORD IS PRINT-LINE.
*
     01  PRINT-LINE                 PIC X(132).
*
     WORKING-STORAGE SECTION.
*
     01  END-OF-DATA               PIC XXX.
*
```

FIGURE 11-2

*Sort Program for Example 2,
Including Sample Input and
Output (continued)*

```
01   SEQUENCE-NUMBER              PIC 9(4) VALUE ZEROS.
*
PROCEDURE DIVISION.
*
000-MAIN-SORT-ROUTINE.
    MOVE ZERO TO SEQUENCE-NUMBER.
*
    SORT SORT-FILE ASCENDING KEY NAME OF SORT-RECORD
*
        INPUT  PROCEDURE IS 100-READING-SEQUENCING
*
        OUTPUT PROCEDURE IS 200-RETURNING-PRINTING.
STOP RUN.
*
100-READING-SEQUENCING SECTION.
110-INPUT-SET-UP.
    OPEN INPUT INPUT-FILE.
    MOVE 'NO' TO END-OF-DATA.
*
    PERFORM 120-READ-DATA
*
    PERFORM 130-SEQ-RELEASE
        UNTIL END-OF-DATA = 'YES'
    CLOSE INPUT-FILE
    GO TO 140-END-OF-INPUT-SECTION.
*
120-READ-DATA.
    READ INPUT-FILE RECORD
        AT END MOVE 'YES' TO END-OF-DATA.
*
130-SEQ-RELEASE.
    ADD 1 TO SEQUENCE-NUMBER.
    MOVE SEQUENCE-NUMBER TO DATA-TO-BE-INSERTED.
*
    RELEASE SORT-RECORD FROM INPUT-RECORD.
*
    PERFORM 120-READ-DATA.
*
140-END-OF-INPUT-SECTION.
    EXIT.
*
200-RETURNING-PRINTING SECTION.
210-OUTPUT-SET-UP.
    OPEN OUTPUT SORTED-FILE
               PRINT-FILE
    MOVE 'NO' TO END-OF-DATA
*
    PERFORM 220-RETURN-DATA
*
    PERFORM 230-WRITE-DATA
        UNTIL END-OF-DATA ='YES'.
    CLOSE SORTED-FILE PRINT-FILE
    GO TO 240-END-OF-OUTPUT-SECTION.
```

```
*
 220-RETURN-DATA.
     RETURN SORT-FILE RECORD INTO SORTED-RECORD
            AT END MOVE 'YES' TO END-OF-DATA.
*
 230-WRITE-DATA.
     WRITE PRINT-LINE FROM SORTED-RECORD
     WRITE SORTED-RECORD.
*
     PERFORM 220-RETURN-DATA.
*
 240-END-OF-OUTPUT-SECTION.
     EXIT.
```

INPUT FILE

```
NAME-1
NAME-2
NAME-3
ANDERSON
JOHNSON
SMITH
ADAMS
LILAC
BROWN
```

PROGRAM OUTPUT

```
ADAMS                  0007
ANDERSON               0004
BROWN                  0009
JOHNSON                0005
LILAC                  0008
NAME-1                 0001
NAME-2                 0002
NAME-3                 0003
SMITH                  0006
```

the execution of the 100-READING-SEQUENCING SECTION was initiated by execution of the INPUT PROCEDURE statement in the SORT statement. In fact, the INPUT PROCEDURE statement has the same effect as if we had written PERFORM 100-READING-SEQUENCING. Program execution branches to that section, and, when it is completed, the next statement is executed. The next statement in the present example is the sorting operation itself, as illustrated in the flowchart of Figure 11-3, which depicts the chronological order of execution.

After the sorting has been completed, the statement executed next is OUTPUT PROCEDURE IS 200-RETURNING-PRINTING. Thus program execution proceeds to the 200-RETURNING-PRINTING SECTION.

The first paragraph of the 200-RETURNING-PRINTING SECTION is the 210-OUTPUT-SET-UP, which opens two output files. Then we PERFORM

FIGURE 11-3
Flowchart Representation of
Sample SORT Program

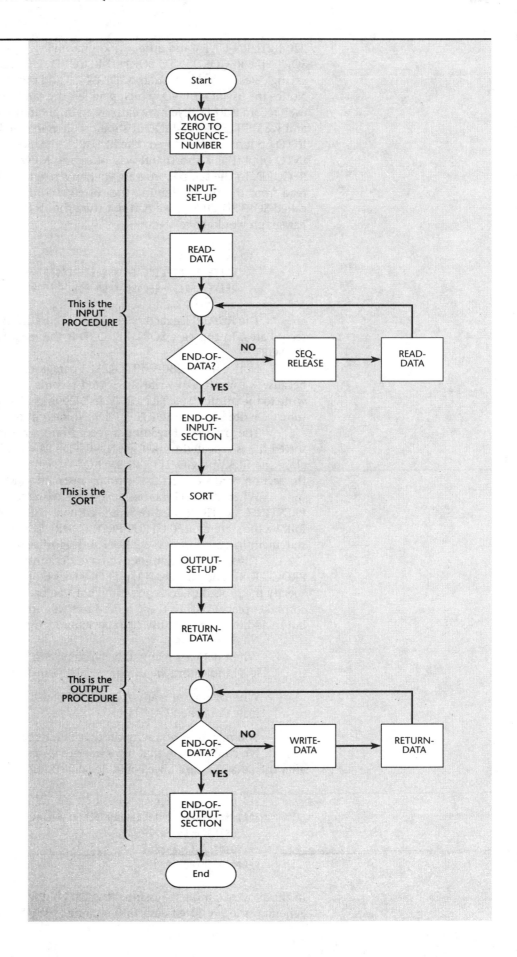

220-RETURN-DATA and enter a loop involving 230-WRITE-DATA. The RETURN SORT-FILE RECORD INTO SORTED-RECORD statement is simply a special form of saying, "Read a record from the SORT-FILE and move it to the SORTED-RECORD." Notice the use of AT END, which parallels the same clause in the READ verb. After each record is RETURNed, we employ an implicit move (FROM SORTED-RECORD) and we WRITE PRINT-LINE. It should be emphasized that use of the RETURN ... INTO option is not required. The RETURN, just like the READ, allows for use of the INTO option as a shorthand way of saying MOVE SORT-RECORD TO SORTED-RECORD. In the sample program we happened to choose to so move each record read from the file containing the sorted records to the record of a file that we called SORTED-FILE. If we had not used the INTO option, the 230-WRITE-DATA paragraph would have been:

```
230-WRITE-DATA.
    WRITE PRINT-LINE FROM SORT-RECORD
    WRITE SORTED-RECORD FROM SORT-RECORD.
```

The RETURN, exactly like the READ, transfers a record from the file to the record area. In this case SORT-RECORD is the record area for the file involved in the SORT.

Notice in the 230-WRITE-DATA paragraph that we WRITE twice. This is so because we wanted to write the sorted records onto two files. The first time we write to the printer (WRITE PRINT-LINE FROM SORTED-RECORD), and the second time we write onto the SORTED-FILE, which will be the sorted file.

The process of reading a record and writing it on the printer and the sorted file is repeated until the END-OF-DATA = 'YES' condition holds. Then we close the files and GO TO 240-END-OF-OUTPUT-SECTION, which is the end of the section, and we execute the no-op instruction EXIT.

When the EXIT has been executed, we have finished the 200-RETURNING-PRINTING SECTION, and program control then returns to the statement that follows the statement, OUTPUT PROCEDURE IS 200-RETURNING-PRINTING. The statement in question is STOP RUN and signifies the logical end of the program.

Thus, in this example we have demonstrated that, by using the INPUT PROCEDURE and the OUTPUT PROCEDURE options of the SORT verb, we can specify the procedure to be executed both before the sort takes place and after the sort takes place. Within these procedures we can execute any COBOL statements, but in addition we must use two specialized I/O verbs:

1. When data are ready to be written onto the sort file (the one with the SD level indicator), we use the RELEASE instead of the WRITE verb.

2. When data are ready to be read from the sort file, we use the RETURN instead of the READ verb.

You may question why the SORT statement was written with this second format. We could reason that if we want to execute some procedure before and/or after the data are sorted, we could do something like the following:

```
PERFORM INPUT-PROC
SORT file-name-1 ASCENDING KEY key-name
    USING file-name-2
    GIVING file-name-3
PERFORM OUTPUT-PROC.
```

In the above example we assume that INPUT-PROC executes some procedure that generates the presorted data in file-name-2. We SORT ... USING file-name-2 and obtain the sorted output in file-name-3 (GIVING file-name-3). Then the OUTPUT-PROC can execute whatever procedure we want to do with the sorted output.

The above approach is correct, but it has the disadvantage that it will consume more I/O processing time than the use of the INPUT PROCEDURE and OUTPUT PROCEDURE options included in Figure 11-2. In the above approach we read the input file once in INPUT-PROC and then read it a second time during the USING file-name-2 routine. Also, the sorted data are read and possibly written twice, once during the GIVING phase, and a second time during the OUTPUT-PROC. In summary, the example in Figure 11-2 has the advantage that the INPUT PROCEDURE is executed while the data are being transferred from the source file to the sort file. Similarly, the OUTPUT PROCEDURE is executed while the data are transferred from the sort file.

We should also point out that we can mix these options, as in

```
SORT ...
    USING file-name
    OUTPUT PROCEDURE IS procedure-name.
```

In this example we combined USING and OUTPUT PROCEDURE. The fourth, and last, alternative would be to use INPUT PROCEDURE and GIVING.

R E V I E W . . . .

1. The COBOL language feature by which a file can be sorted without having to write a sorting algorithm as such is called the COBOL _____ feature.

sort

2. In order to use the sort feature, the programmer must specify the _____ to be sorted and the _____ to be used as the basis for the sort.

file; key (or keys)

3. If a file is to be sorted on the basis of more than one key, the key that is written [first / last] is the principal basis for the sort.

first

4. In the second example problem in this section two options of the SORT verb were used to branch to other parts of the program to perform required processing tasks. These were the _____ and _____ options of the SORT verb.

INPUT PROCEDURE; OUTPUT PROCEDURE

. . . .

DATA DIVISION FORMAT SPECIFICATIONS

In the DATA DIVISION the relevant format associated with use of the sort feature is presented in Figure 11-4.

The level indicator SD identifies the beginning of a sort file sort description. Notice that, other than the SD, the file description has the usual format, except that there is no LABEL RECORD nor BLOCK CONTAINS option. Whether or not any blocking is possible or desirable is determined automatically by the preprogrammed sort routine.

The first two options of the RECORD clause are applicable only in the 1985 version of COBOL. The RECORD CONTAINS integer-1 CHARACTERS specifies fixed-length records, while the RECORD IS VARYING IN SIZE ... specifies

FIGURE 11-4
SORT File Description Entry

SD file-name-1

$$
\left[\underline{RECORD} \left\{ \begin{array}{l} \text{CONTAINS integer -1 CHARACTERS} \\ \text{IS } \underline{\text{VARYING}} \text{ IN SIZE} \\ \quad [\text{ [FROM integer -2] } [\underline{\text{TO}} \text{ integer -3] CHARACTERS]} \\ \quad [\text{ [} \underline{\text{DEPENDING}} \text{ on data-name-1]} \\ \text{CONTAINS [integer -4 } \underline{\text{TO}} \text{] integer -5 CHARACTERS} \end{array} \right\} \right]
$$

$$
\left[\underline{DATA} \left\{ \begin{array}{l} \underline{\text{RECORD}} \text{ IS} \\ \underline{\text{RECORDS}} \text{ ARE} \end{array} \right\} \{ \text{data-name-2} \} \ldots \right]
$$

variable-length records. In the 1974 version of the language, variable-length records are specified by RECORD CONTAINS integer-4 to integer-5 CHARACTERS.

Note that in Figure 11-4 both the RECORD and the DATA clauses are optional. Usually the function of the RECORD clause is embedded in the sort routine itself, while the DATA clause is always optional.

PROCEDURE DIVISION FORMAT SPECIFICATIONS

The SORT verb is the basic verb in the COBOL sort feature. The format is presented in Figure 11-5.

The verb SORT always is required. File-name-1 is the file designated in an SD entry in the DATA DIVISION. At least one KEY must be specified. If more than one sort key is used and several are ascending (or descending), they can be written in the following form:

```
SORT file-name ON ASCENDING KEY ACCOUNT, NAME, YEAR
                   DESCENDING KEY AMOUNT, REGION.
```

Here we have specified an ascending sort by ACCOUNT, by NAME within AC-COUNT, and by YEAR within NAME. Or, we could have used the word ASCEND-ING (or DESCENDING) in conjunction with each KEY, as follows:

```
SORT file-name ON ASCENDING KEY ACCOUNT
                 ON ASCENDING KEY NAME (etc.)
```

The COLLATING SEQUENCE clause is a seldom used one that allows the programmer to specify whether the data in the file to be sorted are to be ordered according to a special "alphabet" or collating sequence. Chapter 16 provides some additional discussion on the subject of alphabet-names.

The WITH DUPLICATES IN ORDER clause can be used to specify that if there are records with duplicate sort-keys, they should be kept in their original order with respect to each other. Thus, if the source file contains ten records whose name-field contains SMITH, these ten records will be in their original order relative to each other.

The INPUT PROCEDURE and the OUTPUT PROCEDURE options refer to a *section-name* in the 1974 standard. In the 1985 standard they can be paragraph-names *or* section-names, thus allowing for greater flexibility. In the example in Figure 11-2 we used the section choice, and as a result we had to use the GO TO verb to reach the end-paragraph in the section. The 1985 version allows us to eliminate the END-OF-INPUT-SECTION and the END-OF-OUTPUT-SECTION types

FIGURE 11-5
The SORT Statement

```
SORT file-name-1

    { ON { ASCENDING  } KEY {data-name-1}... }...
         { DESCENDING }

    [COLLATING SEQUENCE IS alphabet-name-1]

    [WITH DUPLICATES IN ORDER]

    { INPUT PROCEDURE IS { section-name-1   } [ { THROUGH } { section-name-2   } ] }
                         { procedure-name-1 }   { THRU    } { procedure-name-2 }
      USING [file-name-2]...

    { OUTPUT PROCEDURE IS { section-name-3   } [ { THROUGH } { section-name-4   } ] }
                          { procedure-name-3 }   { THRU    } { procedure-name-4 }
      GIVING [file-name-3]...
```

of paragraphs as well as the two GO TO statements in Figure 11-2. In the 1974 version the only way to avoid use of GO TO is to make all paragraphs as sections.

The THRU option is used to specify a *range* of paragraphs.

The section or paragraph referenced by the INPUT PROCEDURE specifies the processing tasks to be performed prior to the sort, while OUTPUT PROCEDURE specifies the processing to be done after the sorting has been completed and the sorted data are in the file referenced in the SORT statement.

If the INPUT PROCEDURE is used, the verb RELEASE must be used somewhere in that procedure. If the OUTPUT PROCEDURE is used, the verb RETURN must be used somewhere in that procedure. The USING file-name-2 option in Figure 11-5 is used when records are made available to the sort from file-name-2 without any processing. The GIVING file-name-3 option specifies that the sorted file is to be recorded on file-name-3.

The RELEASE Verb

The general format of the RELEASE IS

> RELEASE record-name [FROM identifier]

The RELEASE verb can be used only in a procedure referenced by the INPUT PROCEDURE. The record-name in this format refers to a record in the sort file. If the FROM option is used, it resembles the WRITE ... FROM. The effect is to move the contents of identifier to the record-name and then to RELEASE. In effect, RELEASE is a specialized form of the WRITE verb.

The RETURN Verb

The RETURN verb, which is used in conjunction with the OUTPUT PROCEDURE of the SORT verb, has the format presented in Figure 11-6.

The RETURN verb has the effect of a READ verb. The file-name is the name of the sort file. When the INTO option is used, the effect is the same as execution

FIGURE 11-6
The RETURN Statement

RETURN file-name-1 RECORD [INTO identifier]

AT END imperative-statement-1

[NOT AT END imperative-statement-2]

[END-RETURN]

of the two statements RETURN file-name and MOVE record-name TO identifier. The AT END clause is required.

Note that the NOT AT END and the END-RETURN options in the RETURN statement are available only in the 1985 standard. These options can be used for handling conditionals more easily. For example, we could modify the 200-RETURNING-PRINTING SECTION of Figure 11-2 as follows (including omission of the SECTION requirement):

```
            .
            .
            .
        OUTPUT PROCEDURE IS 200-RETURNING-PRINTING
            .
            .
            .
    200-RETURNING-PRINTING.
        OPEN OUTPUT SORTED-FILE
                   PRINT-FILE
        MOVE 'NO' TO END-OF-DATA
        PERFORM 220-RETURN-DATA
            UNTIL END OF DATA = 'YES'.
        CLOSE SORTED-FILE
              PRINT-FILE.
    220-RETURN-DATA.
        RETURN SORT-FILE RECORD INTO SORTED-RECORD
            AT END
                MOVE 'YES' TO END-OF-DATA
            NOT AT END
                WRITE PRINT-LINE FROM SORTED-RECORD
                WRITE SORTED-RECORD
        END-RETURN.
```

Notice that OUTPUT PROCEDURE makes reference to a paragraph, thus avoiding the need to use a GO TO statement to reach the end of the section, as in Figure 11-2. Also, the END-RETURN is not necessary. However, if we wanted to execute a statement regardless of the outcome of the AT END condition test, we would need to use the END-RETURN scope terminator so that the statement(s) that follow the END-RETURN are executed unconditionally.

R E V I E W . . . .

1. In the DATA DIVISION the file to be sorted is identified by the level indicator _____.

2. The option of specifying a variable-length record depending on a data-name in the sort description is available only in the [1974 version / 1985 version] of COBOL.

1985 version

3. If the INPUT PROCEDURE option is used in conjunction with the SORT verb, designated processing is performed [before / after] the sort, and the verb _____ must be used somewhere in the procedure.

before; RELEASE

4. If the OUTPUT PROCEDURE option is used in conjunction with the SORT verb, designated processing is performed [before / after] the sort, and the verb _____ must be used somewhere in the procedure.

after; RETURN

5. In COBOL '74 the subject of INPUT PROCEDURE and OUTPUT PROCEDURE must be a section-name. In COBOL '85 it can be either a section-name or a _____.

paragraph-name

6. The RELEASE verb can be considered a specialized form of the _____ verb, while the RETURN verb can be considered a form of the _____ verb.

WRITE; READ

7. In order to handle conditionals more easily, the NOT AT END and the END-RETURN options can be used in a RETURN statement that utilizes the [1974 version / 1985 version] of COBOL.

1985 version

. . . .

FILE MERGING

Essentially, *merging* refers to the process by which two or more sorted files are combined to form one file. Merging is often a required step in the process of sorting. Merging is also often used simply to combine two or more presorted files. For example, the sales transactions in a department store might be processed on a daily basis, thus creating a daily sales tape sorted by item number. Then, at the end of each week it may be desirable to merge the several daily tapes to form a weekly sales tape for batch processing use. The procedure of combining the several daily tapes to form one weekly tape exemplifies the merging process.

The simplest case of merging is the one in which there are two sorted files A and B, and they are merged to form one file. The process consists of reading a record from each input file, comparing the two records, and writing the "smaller" of the two onto the output file, based on a reference, or "sort key," field. Then another record is read from the file that supplied the last smaller record, and the comparison is repeated. To illustrate the procedure, consider these two input files:

File A: 12   15   22
File B: 13   14   20   30

Merging these two files involves initially reading records 12 and 13, one from each file. The smaller record, 12, is written onto the output file C, and another record is read from file A. Next, records 15 and 13 are being compared. The 13 record is written onto C and the 14 record is read in from B. The 14 record goes to C and the

20 record is read. The process continues until all records have been read in from both files, forming the merged file C:

File C: 12 13 14 15 20 22 30.

Suppose, however, that *five* daily transaction files are to be merged to form one weekly file. In such a case the process of merging requires a more complex logic. In each comparison five records are involved, one from each respective daily file, and the smallest of the five is to be written on the output file. The flowchart in Figure 11-7 indicates the essential logic of the comparisons that are required to find the smallest record. In this figure, A, B, C, D, and E are the five records from the five input files. File F is the output file. Notice that the process described in Figure 11-7 ignores end-of-file conditions to keep the illustration simple.

When merging multiple files on magnetic tape, the number of tape drives available is an important factor. In general, we prefer to use all available drives, since merging is more efficient with a greater number of tape drives. Still, when the number of files is larger than the number of tape drives, we may have to choose the right merging sequence to avoid unnecessary processing. For example, suppose that we have 12 files to be merged. These files are identified by the letters A through L in Figure 11-8. If four tape drive units are available, three units would be used for input and one would be used for output. As illustrated in Figure 11-8, in such a case we could merge A, B, and C to form file 1, D, E, and F to form file 2, and G, H, and I to form file 3. Next we could merge files J and K to form file 4. Then files 3, 4, and L can be merged to form file 5, and finally, files 1, 2, and 5 can be merged to form file 6.

An alternative way of merging the 12 files, which is not as efficient, would be to merge files J, K, and L to form one file, as illustrated in Figure 11-9. Notice, however, that this alternative merging procedure would take longer to accomplish. To see this, let us count the number of file passes that are required by each approach. By *file pass* we mean the process of inputting and merging the contents of a file with the contents of one or more other files. Thus, by the procedure portrayed in Figure 11-9, the formation of files 1, 2, 3, and 4 requires 3 file passes each. The formation of file 5 requires 9 file passes because the contents of 9 original input files are involved. Similarly, the formation of file 6 requires 12 file passes. Thus, in total 33 file passes are required to merge the files by the procedure portrayed in Figure 11-9.

However, by the procedure portrayed in Figure 11-8 only 29 file passes are required. As it happens, given the 12 input files and four tape units, the 29 file passes associated with the procedure in Figure 11-8 is the optimum result. A computational procedure, or algorithm, is available to determine the optimum merge configuration, given the number of files to be merged and the tape units available. The algorithm is included in most merge program packages, so that its application is automatic without the user having to determine the optimum merging routine for each situation.

Frequently, the files to be merged are not stored on magnetic tape. Rather, it may be that designated disk areas constitute files. In such a case the limitation of the number of available input-output units does not apply and the need to merge, say, 20 files could conceivably be accomplished by one merge operation.

R E V I E W . . . .

1. When two or more sequential files are combined to form one sequential file, the process is called _____.

merging

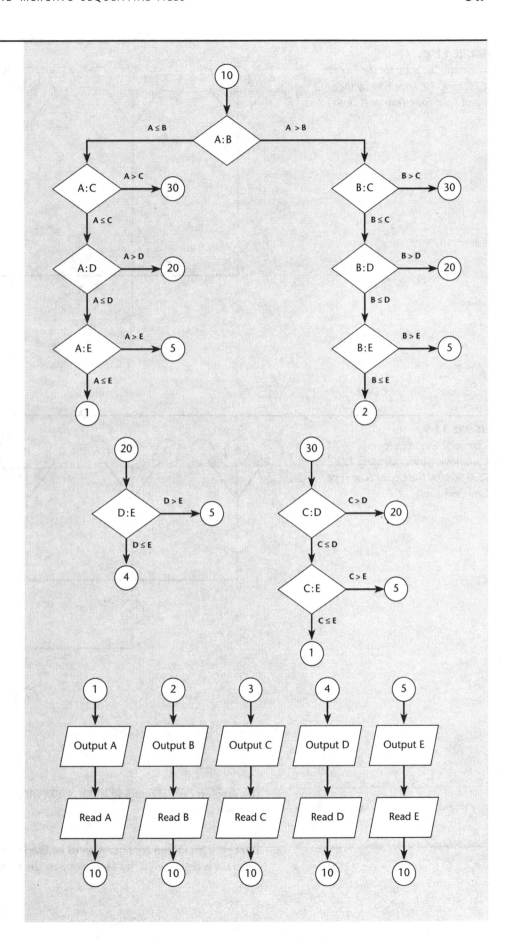

FIGURE 11-7
Flowchart for the Process of Merging Five Files

FIGURE 11-8

Schematic Diagram for the Process of Merging 12 Tape Files by the Use of Four Tape Transport Units

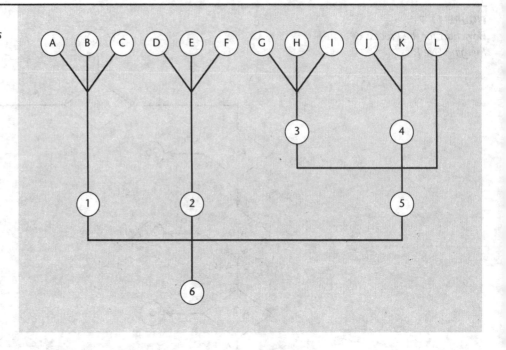

FIGURE 11-9

Schematic Diagram for an Alternative Way of Merging 12 Tape Files by the Use of Four Tape Transport Units

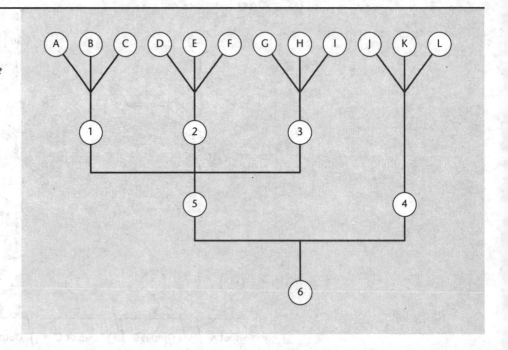

2. The simplest case of merging is the one in which _____ (number) files are merged.

                                                                                          two

3. The optimum merge configuration to be used in merging several tape files generally is determined [by each user / by the merge program package].

                                                                 by the merge program package

FILE MERGING IN COBOL

Merging is implemented in COBOL as a very-high-level language feature, in the form of the MERGE statement.

Let us consider an example. A business firm generates a sales history file at the end of the quarter. Each record in the file contains a department number and a product number, as well as many other fields. This quarterly file is sorted, with department number being the major sort key and product number being the minor sort key. At the end of the year we are interested in merging the four quarterly sales history files into one. Figure 11-10 presents an outline of the

FIGURE 11-10

Outline for a MERGE Program

```
FD   FIRST-QUARTER LABEL RECORDS STANDARD
                    DATA RECORD   SALES-HISTORY.
01   SALES-HISTORY.
     02 DEPT-NO              PIC 999.
     02 PROD-NO              PIC 99999.
     .
     .
     .
FD   SECOND-QUARTER...
     .
     .
     .
FD   THIRD-QUARTER...
     .
     .
     .
FD   FOURTH-QUARTER...
     .
     .
     .
FD   YEARLY LABEL RECORDS STANDARD
             DATA RECORD   CUMULATIVE-SALES.
01   CUMULATIVE-SALES.
     02  DEPT-NO            PIC 999.
     02  PROD-NO            PIC 99999.
     .
     .
     .
SD   MERGE-FILE DATA RECORD  MERGE-RECORD.
01   MERGE-RECORD.
     02  DEPARTMENT         PIC 999.
     02  PRODUCT            PIC 99999.
     .
     .
PROCEDURE DIVISION.
     .
     .
     .
     MERGE MERGE-FILE    ON ASCENDING KEY DEPARTMENT
                         ON ASCENDING KEY PRODUCT
         USING FIRST-QUARTER, SECOND-QUARTER,
               THIRD-QUARTER, FOURTH-QUARTER
         GIVING YEARLY.
```

relevant parts of the program. Four files are introduced with an FD entry, one for each quarter. The fifth FD entry is for the output file. Then the SD introduces the file to be used for the merge, which in this example is called MERGE-FILE. Notice that the data record description for this file corresponds to the record description of the four quarterly files. The MERGE statement in the PROCEDURE DIVISION references the SD file and specifies that the merge will proceed on the basis of DEPARTMENT being the major key and PRODUCT being the minor key. As is the case with the SORT verb, the keys decrease in significance in the order written. The ASCENDING option specifies that the next record of each of the four quarterly files will be examined; and the record sent to the output file next is the one that has the highest department number, or the highest product number if the department numbers are equal. If all four records have identical department and product values, then the records will be sent to the output file in the order in which the file names are written in the merge statement.

The USING clause specifies the files to be merged, which are the input files. These files must be closed at the time of merging. Opening is carried out by the MERGE statement implicitly.

The GIVING clause specifies the output file. This file will contain the combined set of the four quarterly files. This new file will be in the same sort order as the quarterly files. Note that in order for the merge process to take place correctly, the input files must be in the sort order indicated by the KEY specifications.

The general format of the MERGE statement is presented in Figure 11-11.

The OUTPUT PROCEDURE option parallels the one available with the SORT verb. A RETURN statement is used within the output procedure to make merged records available for processing, just as is the case with SORT. Unlike SORT, MERGE does not include any INPUT PROCEDURE options; thus the input files must be in proper form for merging before a MERGE instruction is executed.

R E V I E W . . . .

1. The COBOL language feature by which monthly summaries of transactions can be combined to create an annual summary is the _____ statement.

                                                                                     MERGE

FIGURE 11-11
The MERGE Statement

MERGE file-name-1

$$\left\{ ON \left\{ \begin{array}{l} \underline{ASCENDING} \\ \underline{DESCENDING} \end{array} \right\} \underline{KEY} \{data\text{-}name\text{-}1\} \ldots \right\} \ldots$$

[COLLATING SEQUENCE IS alphabet-name-1]

USING file-name-2 {file-name-3} . . .

$$\left\{ \underline{OUTPUT\ PROCEDURE}\ IS \left\{ \begin{array}{l} section\text{-}name\text{-}1 \\ procedure\text{-}name\text{-}1 \end{array} \right\} \left[\left\{ \begin{array}{l} \underline{THROUGH} \\ \underline{THRU} \end{array} \right\} \left\{ \begin{array}{l} section\text{-}name\text{-}2 \\ procedure\text{-}name\text{-}2 \end{array} \right\} \right] \right\}$$

GIVING {file-name-4} . . .

2. If 12 monthly summaries are to be combined to form an annual summary, then in addition to the one SD entry, the number of FD entries required in the associated MERGE program is _____ (number).

13

3. In order for the merge process to take place correctly, it [is / is not] necessary that each input file be in the exact sort order indicated by the KEY specifications.

is

. . . .

SUMMARY

This chapter covered the general concepts and specialized COBOL statements for sorting and merging sequential files. The requirement that sequential files be sorted is pervasive. For example, it is the basis by which different types of reports, such as "by product" as contrasted to "by region" can be produced.

In the COBOL *sort feature,* the sorting procedure is preprogrammed. In the ENVIRONMENT DIVISION the source file, the file used for the sort, and the output file are assigned to hardware devices in the FILE-CONTROL paragraph of the INPUT-OUTPUT SECTION. In the DATA DIVISION the source and output files are described in the usual fashion, while the sort file is introduced with the special SD level indicator. In the PROCEDURE DIVISION the SORT verb incorporates the sort keys and the source and destination of the file records. The sort key written first is the principal basis for the sort (*major* key). Other keys are referred to as being *intermediate* and *minor* sort keys.

Two complete examples of sorting sequential files were presented. In the first a file was sorted in ascending sequence according to ACCOUNT-NUMBER and in descending order according to YEAR. In the second example the INPUT PROCEDURE and OUTPUT PROCEDURE options of the SORT verb were used to branch to other parts of the program to perform required processing tasks.

Following the above examples, detailed attention was given to the specific format specifications of the COBOL sort-associated statements. In the DATA DIVISION this included consideration of the options associated with the RECORD clause. In the PROCEDURE DIVISION this included consideration of the SORT statement and its options, and then of the RELEASE and RETURN verbs.

File merging is the process by which two or more sorted files are combined to form one file. Of course, the greater the number of files, the more complex is the merging operation. The MERGE verb is the specialized COBOL verb that is used for merging presorted sequential files. The example in the chapter showed how this verb can be used to merge four quarterly sales history files for the purpose of producing one cumulative sales file for the entire year.

EXERCISES

11.1 A sort file has been defined as SORT-FILE, and, in part, its DATA DIVISION entries include

```
02   DEPT-CODE          PIC X(3).
02   COURSE-NUMBER      PIC 99.
02   STUDENT-NAME       PIC X(6).
```

Using the following data, write a SORT statement that could cause the sorted data shown. The original data come from SOURCE-FILE, and we want to have the sorted data in SORTED-FILE. Be sure to specify which are the major, intermediate, and minor sort keys.

ORIGINAL DATA	SORTED DATA
CIS20BILL	MGT10BRENDA
CIS30LINDA	QBA10JILL
QBA10BRENDA	CIS20MARY
CIS30XAVIER	CIS20JOHN
MGT10JILL	CIS20BILL
CIS20JOHN	CIS30XAVIER
CIS20MARY	CIS30LINDA

11.2 A file contains data about students and has the following record format:

```
FIRST-NAME   PIC   X(10).
LAST-NAME    PIC   X(15).
YEAR         PIC   X(2).
MAJOR        PIC   X(3).
GPA          PIC   9V99.
```

Write a program to sort the file so that student records are in order by year of studies (YEAR) within major field of study (MAJOR) and in descending order of GPA. In addition, the sorted file must have a different format from the original file: the FIRST-NAME and LAST-NAME fields must be reversed:

```
LAST-NAME    PIC   X(15).
FIRST-NAME   PIC   X(10).
YEAR         PIC   X(2).
MAJOR        PIC   X(3).
GPA          PIC   9V99.
```

The sorted file is to be saved as a separate file as shown below:

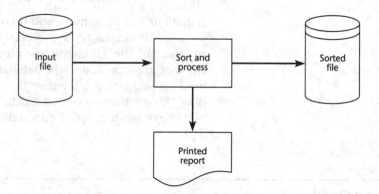

It is also desired to produce a report from the newly sorted file as presented in Figure 11-12. Use the sample data given in Figure 11-13 on page 354 as input for your program.

11.3 Using any data file available, write a program incorporating the COBOL sort feature to sort a file. For example, you could modify any of the exercises at the end of Chapter 10 to sort the master file or the transaction file in the required order.

FIGURE 11-12

Report Format for Exercise 11.2

```
MAJOR FIELD: XXX      (New page for each new field)

STUDENT NAME        YEAR      GPA       AVG. GPA

   L1      F1        FR       3.40
   L2      F2        FR       2.00
   L3      F3        FR       1.90
                                          2.43
   L4      F4        SO
                      .
                      .
                      .
                     JR
                      .
                      .
                      .
                     SR
                      .
                      .
                      .

AVG. GPA FOR XXX MAJOR FIELD = 9.99
```

11.4 Consider the following to be the contents of the four quarterly files discussed in the merging example in this chapter. Show the content of the output file.

FIRST QUARTER	SECOND QUARTER	THIRD QUARTER	FOURTH QUARTER
345 12345	123 00112	345 56111	931 00001
345 25936	987 56111		999 99999
619 01110			

11.5 Using any two sorted data files, write a program incorporating the MERGE feature to combine the two files into one file.

FIGURE 11-13

Sample Input Data for
Exercise 11.2

MAURICE	HOLLMAN	03CIS273
ADAM	LENHARDT	01ACC205
ROBERT	HAYWOOD	04MKT312
ALLAN	TEEGARDEN	05MGT400
JAMES	NORVELL	02F1N302
ROGER	WHITTIER	02F1N395
MARGARET	AKIN	05ACC295
CHRIS	NORTON	01ACC271
JIM	BEECHER	01CIS240
TOD	FORBES	03MGT362
FLOYD	MCNEELY	04ACC314
MICHAEL	DERKS	04MGT268
DEAN	WERNER	01MKT250
CORDELIA	MONTGOMERY	04MKT400
MAGGIE	WILSON	03F1N254
JACK	HOLT	02ACC267
LEONARD	LESMEISTER	02MGT332
DONALD	FAUBERT	04ACC348
WILLARD	FICKER	01F1N257
EDWARD	EASTON	03MKT260
MICHAEL	VOLRICH	02C1S378
RITA	SOLANO	02ACC400
BRYON	ELLIS	01F1N285
FRANCIS	QUIGLEY	04C1S395
CORNELIUS	CLAXTON	03F1N215
HERBERT	SCHAEFER	03MGT400
ROSELLA	MCGOWEN	04MKT390
LAURA	HOFSTATTER	03CIS268
GORDON	PETRIE	01FIN240
TRACY	ZIMMERMAN	03ACC272
EVELYN	RAGSDALE	02FIN278
SIDNEY	KRAMER	01MKT179
GIBSON	GORMAN	02MKT349
LINDSEY	YOUNGBLOOD	03MGT311
STANLEY	FORRESTER	04CIS329
ROBERT	UPDIKE	04FIN268
LESTER	CROWLEY	03ACC287
ELWOOD	ISAAC	01F1N305
MORRIS	JACOBY	02CIS298
JESSIE	LANGFORD	04MGT205
MERRILL	ORMSBEE	03CIS400

12

Single-Level Table Handling

INTRODUCTION

SUBSCRIPTING AND THE OCCURS CLAUSE

READING VALUES INTO A TABLE

ENTERING CONSTANT VALUES INTO A TABLE

THE PERFORM VERB AND TABLE HANDLING

SAMPLE PROGRAM I—FORECASTING

SAMPLE PROGRAM II—PRINTER GRAPHIC OUTPUT

I N THIS CHAPTER *you will learn the basic concepts and methods for processing tables of data. First you will study the specialized COBOL instructions that are used for defining tables and for manipulating data in such tables. Then two sample programs will be presented to provide illustrations of table handling.*

The function of the first program is to output a monthly sales forecast for the next several months. The function of the second program is to present graphic output in the form of a bar chart, using table-processing techniques.

INTRODUCTION

A table, like a file, is a collection of logically related entries. Examples are tax rates for different municipalities in a metropolitan area, commission rates for different product classes, and income tax rates for different levels of income and numbers of dependents. Such data are normally short enough to be placed in central storage and thus constitute a table. Table handling is fundamental to data processing. COBOL recognizes this fact and includes specialized instructions for table definition and manipulation.

SUBSCRIPTING AND THE OCCURS CLAUSE

A great deal of the documentation in COBOL derives from the use of appropriate data-names, that is, names that provide a direct clue to the type of data contained in the named storage location. There are situations, however, when practicality dictates that we dispense with the use of such names. For example, suppose we are processing data on the average income per household in each of the 50 states in the United States. If we chose to name the average income for each state uniquely, we could have such data names as ALABAMA-INCOME, ALASKA-INCOME, and so on, for a total of 50 names. It is easy to imagine the problems that this practice would cause. For example, 50 MOVE statements would be required before the results could be printed.

The use of tables and subscripts is a programming feature that is particularly useful in such situations. A *table* is simply a set of values stored in consecutive storage locations and assigned one data-name. Reference to specific entries in the table is made by the use of the one name along with a subscript that identifies the location of the particular entry. Entries in a *single-level,* or *one-dimensional,* table are numbered sequentially 1, 2, 3, ... , on to the last. Thus, in our example of the average household income for the 50 states, imagine that we have a table of 50 entries. If the entries are arranged alphabetically and we wish to reference the average income for the third state, Arizona, the subscript will have a value of 3. Similarly, the subscripts for the last two states, Wisconsin and Wyoming, will be 49 and 50, respectively. Use of the OCCURS clause in conjunction with the PICTURE clause enables the programmer to set up tables so that reference can be made to entire tables or individual values in tables by means of subscripts. A DATA DIVISION entry involving an OCCURS clause includes the data-name assigned to the table, the number of levels or dimensions, the number of entries in each level, and the field characteristics of the entries.

A *level* or *dimension* (the terms are synonymous) in a table refers to a category of data. For instance, if a table contains sales data for each of five departments as one dimension and for the 12 months of the year as the other dimension, we have a two-dimensional table: the first level being department, and the second level being month. In this chapter we consider single-level tables only, such as the one for the average household income in the 50 states; in Chapter 18 we discuss two-level and higher-level tables.

Assume that the data for average income is contained in a WORKING-STORAGE table, although it could be a FILE SECTION table just as well. Thus we have

```
WORKING-STORAGE SECTION.
      .
      .
      .
   01   STATE-INCOME-TABLE.
        02  AVERAGE-INCOME OCCURS 50 TIMES
                          PICTURE 9(6)V99.
```

The OCCURS 50 TIMES clause sets up a table in storage that has the conceptual structure portrayed in Figure 12-1. The 01 group-name STATE-INCOME-TABLE

FIGURE 12-1

Conceptual Structure of a Table of
Average Income by State

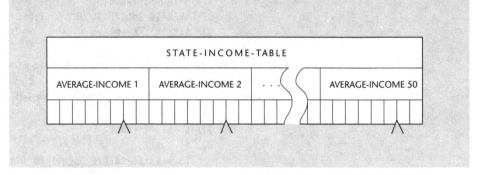

includes the entire set of 50 elementary data items that are defined at the 02 level. Execution of the statement

```
MOVE STATE-INCOME-TABLE TO FIELD-X
```

will result in the entire table of 50 fields being moved.

To reference a single field or entry in the table, a subscript is included in parentheses. For instance, the 12th occurrence of the average income value is referenced as follows:

```
MOVE AVERAGE-INCOME (12) TO ....
```

The subscript may be a variable instead of a constant, but it always must be a positive integer (whole number) with a value greater than zero. To illustrate the need for a subscript that is a variable, consider the following example. Suppose that source records have the following layout:

```
01  STATE-REC.
      02  STATE-NUMBER     PIC 99.
      02  INCOME           PIC 9(6)V99.
```

The value in columns 1–2 is a number assigned to each state signifying its alphabetical order. The value in columns 3–10 is the average household income for that state. The following statement can be used to insert the income value in the appropriate place in the table after the record has been read:

```
MOVE INCOME TO AVERAGE-INCOME (STATE-NUMBER).
```

As a result of this statement, if the state number were 49, the income value would be inserted in the forty-ninth entry of the average-income table.

The OCCURS clause can be written with any level-number item, except the 01 level. In other words, we cannot have a table of records. Of course, that is not a significant restriction, since we can use any level-number in the range 02 to 49, but it is a rule of the language that must be obeyed. Thus the minimum table definition will consist of two lines, as in

```
01  TABLE-GROUP-ITEM.
      02  TABLE OCCURS 10 TIMES PIC XXX.
```

The OCCURS clause need not be used alone in a record definition; other reference entries may be included as well. For example, the record might have been structured as follows:

```
01  STATE-INCOME-TABLE.
    02  AVERAGE-INCOME OCCURS 50 TIMES        PIC 9(6)V99.
    02  NATIONAL-AVERAGE                      PIC 9(6)V99.
```

Notice, however, that the all-encompassing group name STATE-INCOME-TABLE now refers to more than the table of 50 entries. If we want to make specific reference to the entire table of 50 entries, we will have to write something like this:

```
01  STATE-INCOME-TABLE.
    02  AV-TABLE.
        03  AVERAGE-INCOME OCCURS 50 TIMES
                              PIC 9(6)V99.
    02  NATIONAL-AVERAGE  PIC 9(6)V99.
```

As a further illustration of a single-level table, assume that we want to include the names of the states along with their corresponding average-income values:

```
01  STATE-INCOME-TABLE.
    02  NAME-INCOME OCCURS 50 TIMES.
        03  NAME         PIC X(12).
        03  INCOME       PIC 9(6)V99.
```

The OCCURS 50 TIMES clause sets up a table in storage that has the structure portrayed in Figure 12-2. Each NAME-INCOME is a group item consisting of the two elementary items NAME and INCOME. STATE-INCOME-TABLE refers to the entire table of 100 fields.

If we write NAME (1), we are referring to a storage field of 12 positions, whereas INCOME (1) refers to an 8-position field. If we write NAME-INCOME (1), we are referring to a storage field of 20 positions. Thus, when an OCCURS clause defines a table at the group level, either the group item or each of its subordinates may be subscripted. In the above example NAME-INCOME is the group item with the OCCURS clause, specifying that we want to define a table of 50 STATE-INCOME items. Since each STATE-INCOME is subdivided into two fields (NAME and INCOME), we must use a subscript to reference one of the 50 name values or one of the 50 income values.

A point to be made clear is that in the above example we have a *single-level table*. Each entry in the table happens to consist of two fields, but this is still a table of one level or category, the STATE-INCOME category. To have a two-level table, we need multiple occurrences nested within multiple occurrences. For example, if

FIGURE 12-2

Structure of a Table of Average Income that Includes State Names

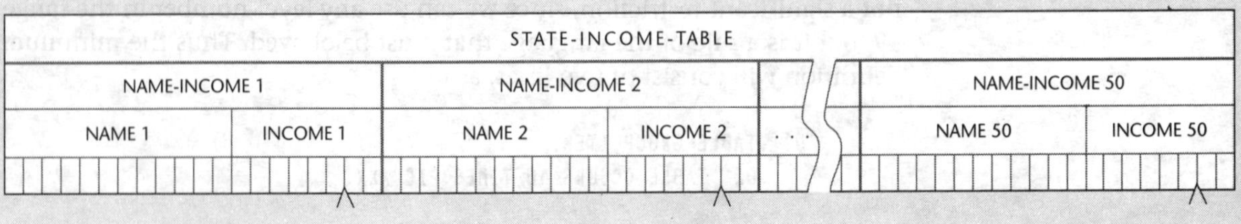

we had a table of 50 names and for each name we had, say, 12 monthly income values, then we would have a two-level table. Again, tables involving more than one level are the subject of Chapter 18.

R E V I E W . . . .

1. The programmer can set up tables by using the _____ clause in the DATA DIVISION.

   OCCURS

2. The OCCURS clause indicates the maximum number of _____ in the table.

   entries

3. Suppose a STATE-POPULATION-TABLE is to include the population figures for 50 states in alphabetical order. Complete the description below by writing the appropriate OCCURS clause. Assume that the PICTURE for POPULATION is 9(8).

   ```
   01 STATE-POPULATION-TABLE.
   ```
   _____

   ```
      02 POPULATION OCCURS 50 TIMES
                 PIC 9(8).
   ```

4. Suppose that both the state names and the population figures are read in and we wish to set up a STATE-POPULATION record such that the 50 state names are located first as a table, followed by the 50 population figures. Complete the following description, assuming that the PICTURE for NAME is X(12).

   ```
   01 STATE-POPULATION.
   ```
   _____

   _____

   ```
      02 NAME OCCURS 50 TIMES PIC X(12).
      02 POPULATION OCCURS 50 TIMES PIC 9(8).
   ```

5. The STATE-POPULATION record set up in the preceding question will have a total of _____ (number) fields.

   100

6. For the table in #4, above, suppose we wish to obtain data about Wyoming, which is the 50th state alphabetically. If we make reference to POPULATION (50), the storage field includes the [state name / state population / both state name and population].

   state population

7. For the record in #4, suppose we make reference to NAME-POPULATION (50). The storage field referenced is [the state name and population for Wyoming / one that has not been defined].

   one that has not been defined

8. The STATE-POPULATION description in #4 is an example of a [single-level / two-level] table.

   single-level

. . . .

READING VALUES INTO A TABLE

Let us suppose that we have defined a tax table to contain 10 deduction rates, thus:

```
01  TAX-TABLE.
    02 TAX-RATE OCCURS 10 TIMES    PIC V999.
```

We want to read in 10 values from a source file and store them in the above table. Assume that the source file is called RATE-FILE, and that the specific field containing the rate is called RATE. We will use a data-name, N, to specify the subscript value. Initially, we want to read the first record and store the value of RATE in the first cell of the TAX-TABLE. Then we want to increase the value of N and repeat the process, storing each newly read value in the Nth place of TAX-TABLE. The following PROCEDURE DIVISION entries can accomplish the rate-reading objective.

```
        MOVE 'NO' TO DATA-END
        MOVE 1 TO N
        PERFORM TABLE-READ UNTIL N > 10 OR DATA-END = 'YES'.
                    .
                    .
                    .
    TABLE-READ.
        READ RATE-FILE RECORD AT END MOVE 'YES' TO DATA-END.
        IF DATA-END = 'YES'
            PERFORM NOT-ENOUGH-DATA
        ELSE
            MOVE RATE TO TAX-RATE (N)
            ADD 1 TO N.
    NOT-ENOUGH-DATA.
                (etc.)
```

Notice that we account for the possibility of fewer than 10 records in the input file, in which case we execute an error routine called NOT-ENOUGH-DATA.

ENTERING CONSTANT VALUES INTO A TABLE

It is often desirable to build tables that contain specified constant values. One way to accomplish this objective was illustrated in the example we just reviewed. We define the table by using the OCCURS clause in the DATA DIVISION and then read in the desired values through suitable PROCEDURE DIVISION instructions. This approach generally is used when there are a large number of constant values to be entered into the table or the values could change from time to time and we do not want to recompile the program every time the data changes. For small tables of constant values other approaches, as described in the following subsections, are commonly used.

Use of the REDEFINES Clause

Suppose that we want to have a table that contains the names of the 12 months of the year, so that we can reference these names by use of the table name and a subscript. For instance, we may want to reference the fifth month or the twelfth month, and so on. Using numeric values to reference the months is desirable, because arithmetic can be performed with numeric values. For instance, if we are on the sixth month and we want to reference the next month, we can simply add

1 to 6 and then make reference to the resulting month. The following example illustrates the common way of accomplishing this task:

```
01  MONTH-TABLE.
    02   FILLER    PICTURE X(9)   VALUE 'JANUARY  '.
    02   FILLER    PICTURE X(9)   VALUE 'FEBRUARY '.
    02   FILLER    PICTURE X(9)   VALUE 'MARCH    '.
    02   FILLER    PICTURE X(9)   VALUE 'APRIL    '.
    02   FILLER    PICTURE X(9)   VALUE 'MAY      '.
    02   FILLER    PICTURE X(9)   VALUE 'JUNE     '.
    02   FILLER    PICTURE X(9)   VALUE 'JULY     '.
    02   FILLER    PICTURE X(9)   VALUE 'AUGUST   '.
    02   FILLER    PICTURE X(9)   VALUE 'SEPTEMBER'.
    02   FILLER    PICTURE X(9)   VALUE 'OCTOBER  '.
    02   FILLER    PICTURE X(9)   VALUE 'NOVEMBER '.
    02   FILLER    PICTURE X(9)   VALUE 'DECEMBER '.
01  MONTHS REDEFINES MONTH-TABLE.
    02   MONTH PICTURE X(9) OCCURS 12 TIMES.
```

Notice that the record MONTH-TABLE consists of 12 equal-sized fields, with each field containing the name of a month. The VALUE clause is used to assign the constant (nonnumeric literal) values. The record called MONTHS is described by the use of the REDEFINES clause. MONTHS simply is an alternate definition of MONTH-TABLE. Thus both MONTHS and MONTH-TABLE are synonyms for the same storage area. The subject of REDEFINES is further discussed in Chapter 16. Here we use it for a limited, specific purpose. The data-name MONTH-TABLE is a field of 108 (12 x 9 = 108) bytes. Instead of the 12 FILLER definitions, we could have defined one long FILLER 108 bytes in size and given it a long literal value, as in

```
... VALUE 'JANUARY   FEBRUARY MARCH     APRIL ...'
```

Instead of such a long literal, we chose to divide the record into 12 fields corresponding to the twelve months.

MONTHS is also a field of the same 108 bytes because it is simply another name redefining the same field. But MONTHS has been subdivided into the table called MONTH, which OCCURS 12 TIMES and has a PIC of X(9). Therefore each of the PIC X(9) FILLER fields corresponds to one of the 12 table entries. Each entry can be referenced by the use of MONTH and a subscript. Thus, executing the instruction MOVE MONTH (3) TO PRINT-AREA WRITE PRINT-AREA results in the word MARCH being printed. A practical example is given later in this chapter, using the table of months.

Use of the VALUE Clause

Another approach that is available in both the 1974 and the 1985 versions of COBOL permits the entry of different constants into the different table positions. The technique involves use of the VALUE clause at a level superior to the OCCURS clause, as illustrated in the following example:

```
01  ALPHABET-TABLE  VALUE 'ABCDEFGHIJKLMNOPQRSTUVWXYZ'.
    02  LETTER OCCURS 26 TIMES PIC X.
```

By using the VALUE clause at the 01 level in the example above, we built a table of 26 cells, each cell containing a different letter of the alphabet.

If we want to fill a table with the same constant in all positions, there is a difference between the 1974 and 1985 standards. In the 1974 version of COBOL we *cannot* use the OCCURS and VALUE clauses to enter the same constant into all of the positions. However, in the 1985 version we can write

```
01  SAMPLE-TABLE.
    02  TABLE-CELL OCCURS 100 TIMES
                PIC 9(5)V99
                VALUE ZERO.
```

When the above program segment is compiled, each of the 100 fields in the table is set to zero. In the 1974 version, typically we would utilize the approach below, using the MOVE verb.

Use of the MOVE Verb

Another way of entering either the same or different constants into the various positions of a table is to reference the superior level of the OCCURS clause in an appropriate MOVE statement. For example, we could write

```
01  SAMPLE-TABLE.
    02  TABLE-CELL OCCURS 100 TIMES
                PIC 9(5)V99.
                  .
                  .
                  .
    MOVE ZEROS TO SAMPLE-TABLE.
```

The MOVE statement fills the 700-byte SAMPLE-TABLE field with zeros. As a result, each of the 7-byte TABLE-CELL fields will also contain zero values.

Also, we can use the COBOL '85 INITIALIZE option:

```
INITIALIZE SAMPLE-TABLE.
```

The INITIALIZE would insert zeros into all numeric fields comprising the table.

As a final example of moving data to the group level, we could rewrite the alphabet example as

```
01  ALPHABET-TABLE.
    02  LETTER OCCURS 26 TIMES PIC X.
                  .
                  .
                  .
    MOVE 'ABCDEFGHIJKLMNOPQRSTUVWXYZ' TO ALPHABET-TABLE.
```

As a result of executing the program segment above, each LETTER will contain one of the letters of the alphabet.

R E V I E W . . . .

1. One way of establishing a table of constant values without reading them in through PROCEDURE DIVISION statements is through use of the _____ clause in conjunction with the OCCURS option.

REDEFINES

2. Another approach, by which only the same constant can be entered into all positions of the table, concerns use of the combination of the OCCURS and VALUE clauses. This approach is available only with the [1974 version / 1985 version] of COBOL.

1985 version

3. A table may be filled with zeros or blanks, depending on its PIC description, using the COBOL '85 feature _____ .

INITIALIZE

4. With both versions of COBOL, another way that the VALUE clause can be used, and which permits entry of different constants into different table positions, is to use the VALUE clause at a level [superior / subordinate] to the OCCURS clause.

superior

5. The third approach for entering constants into a table, and by which either the same or different constants can be entered, is by use of the _____ verb.

MOVE

·   ·

THE PERFORM VERB AND TABLE HANDLING

The PERFORM verb has already been discussed in several chapters. We now continue our study of the PERFORM verb by introducing additional formats and emphasizing the use of this verb for table-handling applications.

Beginning with an example, suppose that we have monthly sales data for the 12 months of the year, and we wish to compute the average monthly sales. The data have been stored in SALES-TABLE as follows:

```
01  SALES-TABLE.
    02  MONTHLY-SALES   PIC 9(6)V99 OCCURS 12 TIMES.
```

To compute the average monthly sales, we can write
```
            MOVE ZERO TO TOTAL-SALES
            MOVE ZERO TO N
            PERFORM SUMMATION 12 TIMES
            DIVIDE TOTAL-SALES BY 12 GIVING AVERAGE-SALES.
            ·
            ·
            ·
    SUMMATION.
            ADD 1 TO N
            ADD MONTHLY-SALES (N) TO TOTAL-SALES.
```

Instead of an explicit reference, such as PERFORM ... 12 TIMES, we can use an identifier whose value is subject to change. For instance, the previous example could be modified by using K as the identifier that contains the number of months for which we want to compute a sales average:

```
            MOVE ZERO TO TOTAL-SALES
            MOVE ZERO TO N
            PERFORM SUMMATION K TIMES
            DIVIDE TOTAL-SALES BY K GIVING AVERAGE-SALES.
            ·
            ·
            ·
```

```
SUMMATION.
    ADD 1 TO N
    ADD MONTHLY-SALES (N) TO TOTAL-SALES.
```

However, there is a format of the PERFORM verb that provides a more convenient way of processing data in tables. This format is presented in Figure 12-3.

It will be easier to understand the components of this version of PERFORM if we first consider an example. Let us take the example that we have been describing and rewrite those instructions, applying the PERFORM format:

```
    MOVE ZERO TO TOTAL-SALES
    PERFORM SUMMATION VARYING N FROM 1 BY 1
        UNTIL N > 12
     DIVIDE TOTAL-SALES BY 12 GIVING AVERAGE-SALES.
     .
     .
     .
SUMMATION.
    ADD MONTHLY-SALES (N) TO TOTAL-SALES.
```

The use of PERFORM ... VARYING allows us to execute an object paragraph or paragraphs while systematically varying an identifier. Of course, this identifier (in the above example, N) must have been defined in the DATA DIVISION. Most often, the identifier varied also is used as a subscript, as in this example; however, it could be used simply as a counter to control the number of executions of the object of the PERFORM verb. The flowchart in Figure 12-4 portrays the control logic involved in the execution of PERFORM with the VARYING option.

The WITH TEST BEFORE and WITH TEST AFTER options are available only in the 1985 standard. Omitting use of the WITH TEST ... clause defaults to the 1974 standard, which tests the UNTIL condition prior to each iteration. Use of WITH TEST AFTER tests the condition at the end of each iteration.

FIGURE 12-3
Format of the PERFORM ... VARYING Statement

```
PERFORM [procedure-name-1 [{THROUGH} procedure-name-2]]
                           {THRU   }

[WITH TEST {BEFORE}]
           {AFTER }

VARYING identifier-1 FROM {identifier-2}
                          {literal-1   }

    BY {identifier-3} UNTIL condition-1
       {literal-2   }

[imperative-statement-1 END-PERFORM]
```

Also, if no procedure-name is given, we have a 1985 version in-line PERFORM, as in the following:

```
MOVE ZERO TO TOTAL-SALES
PERFORM VARYING MONTH-NUMBER
            FROM 1  BY 1
            UNTIL MONTH-NUMBER > 12
    ADD MONTHLY-SALES (MONTH-NUMBER) TO TOTAL-SALES
END-PERFORM
DIVIDE TOTAL-SALES BY 12 GIVING AVERAGE-SALES.
```

It is worthwhile to consider some further examples to illustrate the potential of PERFORM ... VARYING. Let us say a home mortgage company issues a set of payment coupons at the beginning of each year. There are 12 coupons, numbered 1 to 12, each containing the name of the month in which the payment is due and the amount. What is required to prepare the coupons, then, is a repetitive execution (12 times) of a task with two variable factors: the coupon number (01 to 12) and the month-name. The amount of payment due will be the same for each of the months, and our present example is not concerned with the determination of this amount.

FIGURE 12-4

Flowchart Illustrating the Control Logic Associated with Using the VARYING Option with the PERFORM Verb

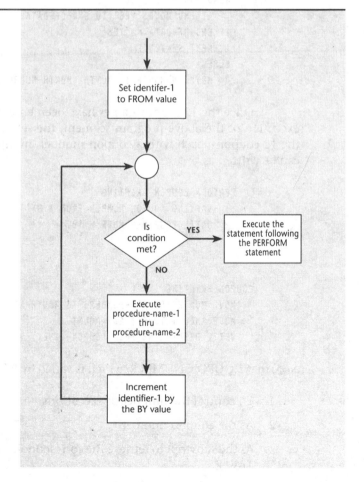

First, let us set up partial DATA DIVISION entries:

```
01  MONTH-NUMBER        PICTURE 99.
01  MONTHS-TABLE.
        02 MONTH            PICTURE X(9) OCCURS 12 TIMES.
01  COUPON-LINE.  (fillers omitted for simplicity)
        02 COUPON-NUMBER    PICTURE 99.
        02 MONTH-NAME       PICTURE X(9).
        02 EDITED-AMOUNT    PICTURE $$,$$9.99.
```

The MONTHS-TABLE will be filled with the names of the 12 months. Assume that the names are to be read from a file, the first record containing the name JANUARY and the twelfth record containing the name DECEMBER, in a field called IN-MONTH. The following PROCEDURE DIVISION program segment can be used to accomplish this task:

```
PERFORM MONTH-READING
    VARYING MONTH-NUMBER FROM 1 BY 1
    UNTIL MONTH-NUMBER > 12.
    .
    .
    .
MONTH-READING.
    READ MONTH-FILE RECORD
        AT END MOVE 'YES' TO END-OF-DATA.
    IF END-OF-DATA = 'YES'
        NEXT SENTENCE
    ELSE
        MOVE IN-MONTH TO MONTH (MONTH-NUMBER).
```

Once the 12 month-names have been entered in the MONTHS-TABLE by execution of the above program segment, the set of statements required to print the 12 coupons, each with a coupon number, month-name, and edited amount, can be written as

```
PERFORM COUPON-PRINTING
    VARYING COUPON-NUMBER FROM 1 BY 1
    UNTIL COUPON-NUMBER > 12.
    .
    .
    .
COUPON-PRINTING.
    MOVE MONTH (COUPON-NUMBER) TO MONTH-NAME.
    MOVE AMOUNT TO EDITED-AMOUNT.
    WRITE PRINT-LINE FROM COUPON-LINE.
```

Note that COUPON-NUMBER, which is varied by PERFORM, is used in three ways:

1. To control the number of executions

2. As the coupon number

3. As the subscript to retrieve the corresponding month-name from MONTHS-TABLE

It now is appropriate to review the overall procedure by which the VARY-ING option is carried out, as already outlined in the flowchart in Figure 12-4. The procedure is as follows:

1. The identifier to be varied is set at its initial value, the value indicated by the following clause:

$$\underline{\text{FROM}} \left\{ \begin{array}{l} \text{identifier -2} \\ \text{literal} \end{array} \right\}$$

2. If the 1974 standard is used, or the 1985 option WITH TEST BEFORE applies, a test is made to determine if the condition specified by UNTIL is met. If it is met, PERFORM is skipped and control passes to the next statement. If the condition is not met, then the paragraph(s) specified is(are) executed once.

3. The value of the varied identifier is incremented by the amount shown in the following clause:

$$\underline{\text{BY}} \left\{ \begin{array}{l} \text{identifier -3} \\ \text{literal} \end{array} \right\}$$

4. If the 1985 option WITH TEST AFTER is used, then a test is made to determine if the condition specified by UNTIL is met. If it is met, PER-FORM is skipped and control passes to the next statement. If the condition is not met, then the paragraph(s) specified is(are) executed once and step 3 is repeated.

5. If the 1974 standard or the 1985 WITH TEST BEFORE is used, then the procedure in steps 2 and 3 is repeated.

The condition need not refer to the value of the identifier-1, which is varied, even though the examples given illustrate only such cases. The condition can refer to other identifiers, but in all cases it must refer to identifiers that have their values altered by the paragraphs under PERFORM control. Otherwise the loop will repeat indefinitely, as in the following example:

```
        MOVE 10 TO AMOUNT
        PERFORM ABC VARYING L FROM 1 BY 1
            UNTIL AMOUNT > 20.
    ABC.
        MOVE AMOUNT TO REPORT-LINE
        WRITE REPORT-LINE.
```

The problem with this segment is that, whereas the value of L is being incremented, the value of AMOUNT is being tested. Since AMOUNT never is altered by the ABC paragraph, there will be no end to the loop!

Now consider one more example that further illustrates use of the VARY-ING option and utilizes the STRING verb described in Chapter 7. Suppose that a header is to be centered with respect to column 40 of a printed page. The size of the header is variable, but it is always 20 or fewer characters long. The header is stored in the field called HEADER, and we wish to move it and print it from the output record called OUTPUT-RECORD.

Consider the following DATA and PROCEDURE DIVISION entries:

```
01  CHECK-FIELD          PIC X.
01  I                    PIC 99.
01  HEADER.
    02 INDIV-CHAR        PIC X OCCURS 20 TIMES.
        .
        .
        .
    MOVE SPACE TO CHECK-FIELD
    PERFORM DETERMINE-SIZE VARYING I FROM 20 BY -1
            UNTIL CHECK-FIELD NOT = SPACE
                  OR I = ZERO.
    ADD 1 TO I
    COMPUTE I = 40 - (I/2)
    MOVE SPACES TO OUTPUT-RECORD
    STRING HEADER DELIMITED BY SIZE
        INTO OUTPUT-RECORD
        WITH POINTER I.
    WRITE OUTPUT-RECORD ...
        .
        .
        .
DETERMINE-SIZE.
    IF INDIV-CHAR (I) NOT = SPACE
        MOVE 'X' TO CHECK-FIELD.
```

The PERFORM DETERMINE-SIZE statement results in searching the HEADER field, character by character, from the right end of the field. The negative increment value in the PERFORM ... VARYING I FROM 20 BY -1 causes I to assume the values 20, 19, 18, etc. Thus we can vary a variable by either adding a value to it or subtracting a value from it. When a nonblank character is encountered or the entire field has been searched, the search is terminated. A value of 1 is then added to I to restore it to the value that identifies the proper length. For example, if the data in HEADER consisted of ACME COMPANY, the Y character would cause an "X" to be moved to CHECK-FIELD. Then, by nature of the PERFORM VARYING, I would be incremented by -1 and would become 11 before the UNTIL test was executed. Thus the ADD 1 to I would restore I to the true length value of 12. Next, the procedure shows that we divide I by 2 and subtract this integer quotient from 40, which is the centering column. In this example the data in HEADER is 12 characters long and I would be I = 40 - (12/2) = 34. Then use of the WITH POINTER I clause in the STRING verb would move the HEADER data into OUTPUT-RECORD, beginning with column 34.

R E V I E W . . . .

1. In general, use of the PERFORM ... VARYING verb allows
    _____ execution of program modules.

    repetitive

2. When using PERFORM ... VARYING, control of PERFORM is associated with
    systematically incrementing the value of a(n) _____ .

    identifier

3. The key programming word that indicates that an identifier is to be systematically incremented in value is the COBOL reserved word _____ .

VARYING

4. The test made to determine if the condition specified for terminating PERFORM control has been met is indicated by the COBOL reserved word _____ .

UNTIL

5. In the 1985 standard two more options are available with the PERFORM ... VARYING that are not part of the 1974 version. One of these options allows omission of a reference to procedure-name, thereby forming a(n) _____ PERFORM structure.

in-line

6. Continuing from #5, above, the other option has to do with the point in time that the UNTIL condition is evaluated during each iteration; it is expressed with one of the two options WITH TEST _____ or WITH TEST _____ .

BEFORE; AFTER

·   ·

SAMPLE PROGRAM I — FORECASTING

The example we present in this section illustrates an application of tables and subscripts. The function of the program is to output a sales forecast for the next several months, as specified, by month. The input values are

- NEXT-MONTH: A numeric value that designates the first month to be included in the forecast

- HOW-MANY-MONTHS: A 2-digit number that designates the number of months to be included in the forecast

- BASE: A dollar value used as the base for the forecast formula

- COEFFICIENT: A numeric coefficient used in the forecast formula

The forecasting formula used is

$$F_i = B + cN$$

The forecast for month i (F_i) is equal to the base (B) plus a coefficient (c) times the number of months (N) from the starting point. If the first month is 2 (February), then the forecast for May will be

$$F_{May} = B + c(3)$$

Thus N = 3 in this case, since May is 3 months after February, which is the starting month.

If the following input were used, the resulting output would be as shown in Figure 12-5.

```
NEXT-MONTH              05
HOW-MANY-MONTHS         09
BASE                    0010000000
COEFFICIENT             0000025.000
```

FIGURE 12-5
Illustrative Computer Output

```
                        PROJECTED SALES

        MAY             100250.00
        JUNE            100500.00
        JULY            100750.00
        AUGUST          101000.00
        SEPTEMBER       101250.00
        OCTOBER         101500.00
        NOVEMBER        101750.00
        DECEMBER        102000.00
        JANUARY         102250.00
```

A sample program listing for the forecasting task is given in Figure 12-6. Notice that the setting up of the MONTH-TABLE in the WORKING-STORAGE SECTION is the same as presented in the earlier section of this chapter.

In the PROCEDURE DIVISION, the paragraph called 010-CALCULATION-ROUTINE is performed HOW-MANY-MONTHS times. In this case the input field, HOW-MANY-MONTHS, contains the number of desired executions of the forecasting computation.

The MONTH-FROM-NOW field corresponds to the N in the forecasting formula $F_i = B + cN$. Finally, the subscript WHICH-ONE is used to reference the name of the month relating to each successive line of output. Since we have only 12 months, we may need to "wraparound" the MONTH-TABLE entries. For instance, if NEXT-MONTH = 5 and HOW-MANY-MONTHS = 9, the last month is not the thirteenth (4 + 9); rather, it is the first month of the next year. Thus, when the month subscript called WHICH-ONE exceeds 12, we subtract 12 from it to "bend" it down around the table.

SAMPLE PROGRAM II — PRINTER GRAPHIC OUTPUT

This section of the chapter presents a sample program that utilizes table-handling concepts to produce graphic printer output in the form of a bar chart. The output format is illustrated in Figure 12-7. For each common stock issue, we print a bar whose length corresponds to the percent yield of the stock.

The yield is computed as the percent ratio of the dividend-per-share to the price-per-share. It is assumed that no yield can exceed 50 percent, but if the computed yield does exceed this percentage, a special message is printed.

The input consists of records containing the stock name, the stock price, and the dividend. Figure 12-8 presents the program listing. The graphic output is prepared in the two paragraphs named 030-FILL-BAR and 040-MOVE-X-TO-BAR.

```
        030-FILL-BAR.
            MOVE SPACES TO BAR-CHART
            PERFORM 040-MOVE-X-TO-BAR VARYING I FROM 1 BY 1
                            UNTIL I > PERCENT-YIELD.
        *
        040-MOVE-X-TO-BAR.
            MOVE 'X' TO BAR-CELL (I).
```

We first clear the group field BAR-CHART by filling it with spaces. Since it is the group-name that includes the entire BAR-CELL table, the 50 entries in the table will be filled with blank spaces. Then the PERFORM ... VARYING varies the

FIGURE 12-6
Sample Forecast Program

```
*
    IDENTIFICATION DIVISION.
    PROGRAM-ID. FORECAST.
*
    ENVIRONMENT DIVISION.
    CONFIGURATION SECTION.
    SOURCE-COMPUTER. ABC-480.
    OBJECT-COMPUTER. ABC-480.
*
    INPUT-OUTPUT SECTION.
    FILE-CONTROL.
        SELECT INPUT-DATA  ASSIGN TO CARD.
        SELECT OUTPUT-FILE ASSIGN TO PRINTER.
*
    DATA DIVISION.
*
    FILE SECTION.
*
    FD  INPUT-DATA    LABEL RECORDS ARE OMITTED
                      DATA RECORD IS INCARD.
    01  INCARD.
        02  NEXT-MONTH        PIC 99.
        02  HOW-MANY-MONTHS   PIC 99.
        02  BASE             PIC S9(8)V99.
        02  COEFFICIENT      PIC S9(8)V99.
        02  FILLER           PIC X(56).
*
    FD  OUTPUT-FILE   LABEL RECORDS OMITTED
                      DATA RECORD IS OUT-LINE.
    01  OUT-LINE             PIC X(132).
*
    WORKING-STORAGE SECTION.
*
    01  WHICH-ONE            PIC 99.
    01  MONTHS-FROM-NOW      PIC 99.
    01  SALES               PIC S9(9)V99.
    01  DATA-END            PIC X(3).
*
    01  HEADER.
        02  FILLER           PIC X(15) VALUE SPACES.
        02  FILLER           PIC X(15) VALUE 'PROJECTED SALES'.
*
    01 PRINT-RECORD.
        02  FILLER           PIC X VALUE SPACES.
        02  MONTH-NAME       PIC X(12).
        02  FILLER           PIC X(5) VALUE SPACES.
        02  EDIT-SALES       PIC ------99.99.
*
```

FIGURE 12-6

Sample Forecast Program
(continued)

```
01 MONTH-TABLE.
   02  JANUARY                PIC X(9) VALUE 'JANUARY  '.
   02  FEBRUARY               PIC X(9) VALUE 'FEBRUARY '.
   02  MARCH                  PIC X(9) VALUE 'MARCH    '.
   02  APRIL                  PIC X(9) VALUE 'APRIL    '.
   02  MAY                    PIC X(9) VALUE 'MAY      '.
   02  JUNE                   PIC X(9) VALUE 'JUNE     '.
   02  JULY                   PIC X(9) VALUE 'JULY     '.
   02  AUGUST                 PIC X(9) VALUE 'AUGUST   '.
   02  SEPTEMBER              PIC X(9) VALUE 'SEPTEMBER'.
   02  OCTOBER                PIC X(9) VALUE 'OCTOBER  '.
   02  NOVEMBER               PIC X(9) VALUE 'NOVEMBER '.
   02  DECEMBER               PIC X(9) VALUE 'DECEMBER '.
*
01 MONTHS REDEFINES MONTH-TABLE.
   02  MONTH                  PIC X(9) OCCURS 12 TIMES.
*
PROCEDURE DIVISION.
*
000-MAIN-ROUTINE.
    OPEN INPUT INPUT-DATA
         OUTPUT OUTPUT-FILE
    MOVE 'NO' TO DATA-END
*
    READ INPUT-DATA RECORD
        AT END MOVE 'YES' TO DATA-END.
*
    IF  DATA-END = 'NO'
        WRITE OUT-LINE FROM HEADER AFTER PAGE
        MOVE SPACES TO OUT-LINE
        WRITE OUT-LINE AFTER 1 LINE
        MOVE ZERO TO MONTHS-FROM-NOW
        MOVE NEXT-MONTH TO WHICH-ONE
*
        PERFORM 010-CALCULATION-ROUTINE
              HOW-MANY-MONTHS TIMES
    ELSE
        MOVE 'NO DATA AVAILABLE' TO OUT-LINE
        WRITE OUT-LINE AFTER 1 LINE
    END-IF
*
    CLOSE INPUT-DATA, OUTPUT-FILE
    STOP RUN.
*
010-CALCULATION-ROUTINE.
    ADD 1 TO MONTHS-FROM-NOW
    IF  WHICH-ONE IS GREATER THAN 12
        SUBTRACT 12 FROM WHICH-ONE
    END-IF
    COMPUTE SALES = MONTHS-FROM-NOW * COEFFICIENT
    ADD BASE TO SALES
    MOVE MONTH (WHICH-ONE) TO MONTH-NAME
    MOVE SALES TO EDIT-SALES
    WRITE OUT-LINE FROM PRINT-RECORD AFTER 1 LINE
    ADD 1 TO WHICH-ONE.
```

FIGURE 12-7

Sample Graphic Output for The Stock-Yield Program

```
                           PERCENT YIELD
                    0   5   10  15  20  25  30  35  40  45  50
     STOCK NAME     I   I   I   I   I   I   I   I   I   I   I
                    I
FORD MOTOR CO.      IXXXXXXXXXX
                    I
GENERAL MOTORS CORP. IXXXXXXXXXXXXXXXXXXX
                    I
CONTROL DATA CORP.  IXXXXXXXX
                    I
IBM CORP.           IXXXXXXXXXXX
                    I
SPERRY RAND CORP.   IXXXXXXXXXXXXXXXXXXXXXXXXXXXXXXXXXXXXXXXX
                    I
HONEYWELL CORP.     IXXXXXXXXXXX
                    I
DIGITAL EQUIPMENT CO IXXXXXXXXXXXX
                    I
EXAMPLE ERROR-1     IINVALID INPUT DATA
                    I
EXAMPLE ERROR-2     IINVALID INPUT DATA
                    I
JACK-POT CORP.      IYIELD HIGHER THAN 50%
```

FIGURE 12-8

Listing of the Program for Graphic Output

```
        IDENTIFICATION DIVISION.
        PROGRAM-ID. GRAPH.
    *
        ENVIRONMENT DIVISION.
    *
        CONFIGURATION SECTION.
        SOURCE-COMPUTER. ABC-480.
        OBJECT-COMPUTER. ABC-480.
    *
        INPUT-OUTPUT SECTION.
        FILE-CONTROL.
    *
            SELECT STOCK-FILE ASSIGN TO CARD.
            SELECT REPORT-FILE ASSIGN TO PRINTER.
    *
        DATA DIVISION.
    *
        FILE SECTION.
    *
```

FIGURE 12-8

*Listing of the Program for Graphic
Output (continued)*

```
FD   STOCK-FILE    LABEL RECORDS OMITTED
                        DATA RECORD IS STOCK-REC.
01   STOCK-REC.
     02   STOCK-NAME            PIC X(20).
     02   STOCK-PRICE           PIC 9(3)V99.
     02   STOCK-DIVIDEND        PIC 9(2)V99.
     02   FILLER                PIC X(51).
*
FD   REPORT-FILE   LABEL RECORDS OMITTED
                        DATA RECORD IS REPORT-REC.
01   REPORT-REC             PIC X(132).
*
WORKING-STORAGE SECTION.
*
01   END-OF-FILE-SWITCH     PIC XXX    VALUE 'NO'.
     88   END-OF-FILE                  VALUE 'YES'.
*
01   PERCENT-YIELD          PIC 99.
*
01   I                      PIC 99.
*
01   GRAPH-LINE.
     02   FILLER            PIC X(5) VALUE SPACES.
     02   STOCK-NAME        PIC X(20).
     02   FILLER            PIC X(2 ) VALUE SPACES.
     02   FILLER            PIC X     VALUE 'I'.
     02   BAR-CHART.
          03   BAR-CELL OCCURS 50 TIMES PIC X.
*
01   HEADING-1.
     02   FILLER            PIC X(40) VALUE SPACES.
     02   FILLER            PIC X(13) VALUE 'PERCENT YIELD'.
*
01   HEADING-2.
     02   FILLER            PIC X(27) VALUE SPACES.
     02   FILLER            PIC X(51) VALUE
          '0    5    10   15   20   25   30   35   40   45   50'.
*
01   HEADING-3.
     02   FILLER            PIC X(10) VALUE SPACES.
     02   FILLER            PIC X(10) VALUE 'STOCK NAME'.
     02   FILLER            PIC X(7)  VALUE SPACES.
     02   FILLER            PIC X     VALUE 'I'.
     02   FILLER            PIC X(50) VALUE ALL '....I'.
*
01   EMPTY-LINE.
     02   FILLER            PIC X(27) VALUE SPACES.
     02   FILLER            PIC X     VALUE 'I'.
*
PROCEDURE DIVISION.
*
```

FIGURE 12-8

Listing of the Program for Graphic
Output (continued)

```
000-MAIN-ROUTINE.
    OPEN INPUT STOCK-FILE
         OUTPUT REPORT-FILE
*
    PERFORM 010-READ-STOCK-REC.
*
    WRITE REPORT-REC FROM HEADING-1 AFTER PAGE
    WRITE REPORT-REC FROM HEADING-2 AFTER 2
    WRITE REPORT-REC FROM HEADING-3 AFTER 2
*
    PERFORM 020-PRINT-GRAPH
        UNTIL END-OF-FILE
*
    CLOSE STOCK-FILE
          REPORT-FILE.
*
    STOP RUN.
*
010-READ-STOCK-REC.
    READ STOCK-FILE RECORD
        AT END MOVE 'YES' TO END-OF-FILE-SWITCH.
*
020-PRINT-GRAPH.
    WRITE REPORT-REC FROM EMPTY-LINE
*
    IF  STOCK-PRICE NOT NUMERIC
        OR STOCK-DIVIDEND NOT NUMERIC
        OR STOCK-PRICE NOT > ZERO
        MOVE 'INVALID INPUT DATA' TO BAR-CHART
    ELSE
        COMPUTE PERCENT-YIELD ROUNDED =
            STOCK-DIVIDEND * 100.0 / STOCK-PRICE
*
        IF  PERCENT-YIELD > 50
            MOVE 'YIELD HIGHER THAN 50%' TO BAR-CHART
        ELSE
            PERFORM 030-FILL-BAR
        END-IF
    END-IF
    MOVE STOCK-NAME OF STOCK-REC
        TO STOCK-NAME OF GRAPH-LINE
*
    WRITE REPORT-REC FROM GRAPH-LINE
    WRITE REPORT-REC FROM EMPTY-LINE
*
    PERFORM 010-READ-STOCK-REC.
*
030-FILL-BAR.
    MOVE SPACES TO BAR-CHART
    PERFORM 040-MOVE-X-TO-BAR VARYING I FROM 1 BY 1
                        UNTIL I > PERCENT-YIELD.
*
040-MOVE-X-TO-BAR.
    MOVE 'X' TO BAR-CELL (I).
```

variable I, which is used as the subscript for BAR-CELL. A stock for which the percent yield is 4%, for example, will thus result in four X characters being moved to the first four locations of the BAR-CELL table.

SUMMARY

This chapter was concerned with the basic concepts and methods used in defining tables and manipulating the associated table data. Only *single-level* table handling was considered. That is, our focus was on *one-dimensional tables*. Chapter 18 presents more advanced methods and language features for table handling, including higher-level tables.

The OCCURS clause in the data description indicates the number of entries in the table for that data item. Consider the following data description:

```
01  REGION-OUTLETS-TABLE.
    02 REGION-OUTLETS OCCURS 6 TIMES.
       03 REGION   PIC X(8).
       03 OUTLETS  PIC 9(3).
```

The table above has six entries. However, each of the entries is subdivided into two elementary fields: one with the REGION name, and the other with the number of OUTLETS in that region. Reference to REGION-OUTLETS-TABLE is a reference to the entire table of data. Reference to REGION-OUTLETS (4) is to the name of the fourth REGION *and* the number of OUTLETS in that region. Reference to REGION (4) is to the name of the fourth REGION, but *not* to the number of outlets. Even though the data item with the OCCURS clause is subdivided into two elementary fields, the table in this example, nevertheless, is a single-level table.

Variable data or constants can be entered into a table by use of the READ command. However, there are three other ways by which constants can be entered into a table. One way of establishing a table of constant values without reading them in through PROCEDURE DIVISION statements is by use of the REDEFINES clause in conjunction with the OCCURS option. Another approach concerns using the OCCURS and VALUE clauses in combination; depending on how these are used, either the same constant will be entered into all positions of the table, or different constants will be entered into different positions. The 1985 verb INITIALIZE can be used to fill a table with zeros or blank spaces. A final approach for entering constants into a table is with the MOVE verb.

Use of the VARYING option with the PERFORM verb makes possible the repetitive execution of program modules. The VARYING option permits us to systematically increment the value of an identifier (subscript) for a data item that is part of a table. The UNTIL option can be used to determine if the condition specified for terminating the PERFORM has been met.

The chapter concluded with two sample programs. The function of the first program was to output a monthly sales forecast for the next several months. The function of the second program was to perform graphic output for table data in the form of a bar chart.

EXERCISES

12.1 Write DATA DIVISION entries to set up a table that is to contain annual dollar sales for 12 years. Use the data-name ANNUAL-SALES at the 01 level and then use a name of your choice for the table. No value will exceed $100,000,000.00.

12.2 Write DATA DIVISION entries to set up a table to contain dollar and unit sales for the years 1980–1992. We want to be able to reference the dollar sales or the unit sales individually for each year, as well as to reference as a group the dollar sales and unit sales pertaining to a given year. The general format of the table is as follows:

YEAR	DOLLAR SALES	UNIT SALES
1980		
1981		
.	.	.
.	.	.
.	.	.
1992		

Do not insert the YEAR values through the DATA DIVISION definition. Instead, write a paragraph called STORE-YEARS that will store the year values in the appropriate place in the table.

12.3 Use DATA DIVISION entries to form a table containing the names of the days of the week so that the names are referenced by a subscript; thus Monday would be referenced by a subscript for which the value is 1, and Sunday would be referenced by a subscript value of 7.

12.4 Assume that TAX-TABLE contains 30 values (V999). Write the PROCE-DURE and DATA DIVISION statements required to print the contents of the table. Write appropriate DATA DIVISION descriptions needed for the tasks below:

a. Print the 30 values in one column of 30 lines.

b. Print the 30 values at the rate of seven per line for as many lines as are needed.

12.5 For the following table write the necessary program instructions to find the smallest value and to place it in SMALLEST. Disregard the possibility of ties.

```
02 TABLE OCCURS 50 TIMES    PICTURE X(12).
```

Write DATA DIVISION descriptions for any additional data-names necessary for the task.

12.6 A sales file contains the following types of data:

COLUMNS	FIELD DESCRIPTION
1	Quarter during which sales occurred; PIC 9, values are in range of 1–4.
2–6	Sales amount; PIC 999V99.

Write a program to read such a sales file and produce the following type of report:

QUARTER	TOTAL SALES	% OF YEAR TOTAL
1	100.00	20%
2	50.00	10%
3	300.00	60%
4	50.00	10%
YEAR TOTAL	$500.00	100%

Use a table to store the quarterly sales; do *not* use four individual data-names. Each value in the TOTAL SALES column may represent the sum of several sales values. In other words, there may be several records that have the same quarter, as, for instance:

QUARTER	SALES
1	20.00
2	35.00
1	10.00
4	100.00

In this example the total sales for the first quarter would be 30.00. As the example demonstrates, the data are not in any order.

12.7 A customer file contains customer names, among other data. We are interested in conducting a frequency analysis of the first letter of customer names. In other words, a table such as the following is to be produced:

BEGINNING LETTER	NUMBER OF NAMES
A	10
B	15
.	.
.	.
.	.
Z	1

Input records have the following format:

COLUMNS	FIELD DESCRIPTION
1–12	Customer name
13–80	Other data

Write a program to do the above task.

13

An Expanded Example of Sequential File Processing

INTRODUCTION

OVERVIEW OF THE TASK

THE PROGRAM TO CREATE THE
   MASTER FILE

DAILY MASTER PROCESSING

MONTHLY PROCESSING

IN THIS CHAPTER *you will study an expanded file-processing example to accomplish two main objectives. First, such an example provides you with the opportunity to review and apply a large number of the statements that you studied in previous chapters. Second, and more important, the example demonstrates what is often missing in a student environment: a system of **interrelated programs**.*

*When initially learning COBOL, it is only natural to be involved in studying and writing individual, fairly short programs. However in the "real world" of programming practice, data processing tasks are complex enough to be developed as **systems** consisting of several programs.*

INTRODUCTION

In this chapter we define and illustrate a system of three interrelated programs. Nevertheless, this is still a limited, if not trivial, example in terms of the size and complexity of real-world computer programming. However, if we attempted to tackle a system of realistic size and complexity, it would require a large and wasted amount of time on your part. For instance, in the sample program we define a limited number of data fields, and we screen input data for a few error conditions. In a realistic program we might have, say, 30 data fields and over 100 error-condition possibilities. Our viewpoint is that if we understand programming logic with respect to three data fields and four error conditions, there is no special benefit to a larger example. Thus, given the limited time available to a student, we try to strike a balance between realism and practical simplicity.

OVERVIEW OF THE TASK

The example deals with a business environment in which we have customers who are involved in such transactions as purchases and payments. We could think of a retail store as the assumed environment. The example is structured as three programs.

The first program illustrates the *creation of a master file* for customer records. We input records from a source file, we screen them for a number of possible errors, and we write the correct records onto a new master file. We then sort the master file in order of the account number in each customer record.

The second program demonstrates a *daily process*. Each day we have sales transactions involving the customers. For purposes of the daily processing, we have an abbreviated version of the customer master file. In this file we store the account number used for identification, the authorized credit limit, and the current balance. The thinking is that because the daily processing is frequent and therefore extensive, we need not do unnecessary processing. Thus the abbreviated daily customer file does *not* contain the customer address. In a realistic setting, the difference in record size would be much greater than simply omitting the address, but the basic point is the same.

As part of the daily processing, we read the daily transactions file and we update the daily master. In the course of the program execution we produce a daily transaction register on paper for managerial review, we generate a report on any error transactions, and, of course, we update the daily master file with the new customer balance. Customers whose current balance exceeds their authorized credit limit are reported for managerial review. Finally, today's daily transactions are merged with the ones from the days before. As is typical in this kind of environment, we have a monthly billing cycle. During each business day of the month we accumulate transactions that are then processed at the end of the month to update the full customer file and to generate monthly billing statements.

The *monthly processing* is the subject of the third programming task in the example. The accumulated monthly transactions are processed against the full (not the abbreviated daily) master file. In the process the full master file is updated, any errors are reported, and monthly billing statements are produced. Actually, this last programming task is illustrated only in part, saving its full detail as an exercise at the end of the chapter.

THE PROGRAM TO CREATE THE MASTER FILE

The first program illustrates creation of the customer master file. Figure 13-1 outlines the main processing steps. The original data are in a source file. Figure 13-2 shows sample input and output, while Figure 13-3 presents the complete program.

The 300-CREATE-MASTER paragraph in the PROCEDURE DIVISION in Figure 13-3 is rather routine. We read the records in the source file and we check

FIGURE 13-1

Overview of File Create Task

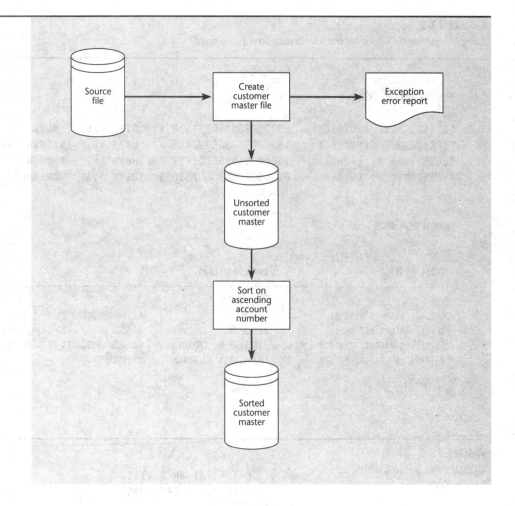

FIGURE 13-2

Sample Input and Output for the File Create Task

INPUT FILE

```
12345JOHN L. ANDERSON     080000000150251020 N. 10TH STREET   MESA     AZ 85280
13345                     0003450000000505 S. ROOSEVELT RD. TEMPE     AZ 85280
33456LINDA M. BREWSTER    100000000500001929 NORTHERN AVE.   TUCSON    AZ 85701
23465LESLIE J. CROWN      050000         400 WASHINGTON BLVD.  MESA     AZ 85202
32222PAT N. THOMPSON      0004000400000010 EAST PLAZA RD.  ANYTOWN    AZ 85281
41231ELMER J. GUSTON      090000000450002350 SOUTHERN AVE.    CHANDLER    AZ 85501
18234JAMES J. JONES       11000000045050
19876JEAN L. PENDLETON    400000002300002888 W. PLAZA RD.   ANYTOWN    AZ 85702
```

UNSORTED MASTER

```
12345JOHN L. ANDERSON     080000000150251020 N. 10TH STREET   MESA     AZ 85280
33456LINDA M. BREWSTER    100000000500001929 NORTHERN AVE    TUCSON    AZ 85701
41231ELMER J. GUSTON      090000000450002350 SOUTHERN AVE.   CHANDLER  AZ 85501
19876JEAN L. PENDLETON    400000002300002888 W. PLAZA RD.  ANYTOWN   AZ 85702
```

FIGURE 13-2

Sample Input and Output for the File Create Task (continued)

```
NEW (SORTED) MASTER

12345JOHN L. ANDERSON    080000000150251020 N. 10TH STREET   MESA     AZ 85280
19876JEAN L. PENDLETON   400000002300002888 W. PLAZA RD.  ANYTOWN  AZ 85702
33456LINDA M. BREWSTER   100000000500001929 NORTHERN AVE.  TUCSON   AZ 85701
·41231ELMER J. GUSTON    090000000450002350 SOUTHERN AVE.   CHANDLER  AZ 85501


ERROR REPORT

               EXCEPTION REPORT
    ERROR MESSAGE                      INVALID RECORD
-----------------------------------------------------------------------------------

    CUSTOMER NAME IS MISSING          13345            0003450000000505 S. ROOSEVELT RD. TEMPE  AZ 85280
    BALANCE AMOUNT NOT VALID          23465LESLIE J. CROWN   050000       400 WASHINGTON BLVD.  MESA    AZ 85202
    CUSTOMER'S BALANCE EXCEEDS LIMIT  32222PAT N. THOMPSON  0004000400000010 EAST PLAZA RD.  ANYTOWN  AZ 85281
    CUSTOMER ADDRESS IS MISSING       18234JAMES J. JONES   11000000045050
```

FIGURE 13-3

COBOL Program to Create the Master File

```
            IDENTIFICATION DIVISION.
            PROGRAM-ID.  CREATMAS.
        *
            ENVIRONMENT DIVISION.
            CONFIGURATION SECTION.
            SOURCE-COMPUTER. ABC-480.
            OBJECT-COMPUTER. ABC-480.
        *
            INPUT-OUTPUT SECTION.
        *
            FILE-CONTROL.
        *
                SELECT CUST-SOURCE-FILE   ASSIGN TO SOURCE-FIL.
                SELECT CUST-MAST-FILE     ASSIGN TO CUST-MAS.
                SELECT ERROR-FILE         ASSIGN TO PRINT-ERR.
                SELECT NEW-MASTER-FILE    ASSIGN TO NEW-MAS.
                SELECT SORT-FILE          ASSIGN TO SORT-WORK.
        *
            DATA DIVISION.
        *
            FILE SECTION.
        *
            FD  CUST-SOURCE-FILE
                    LABEL RECORDS ARE OMITTED
                    DATA RECORD IS CUST-SOURCE-RECORD.
        *
```

FIGURE 13-3
COBOL Program to Create the
Master File (continued)

```
01   CUST-SOURCE-RECORD.
     02  CUST-ACCOUNT-NO        PIC 9(05).
     02  CUST-NAME              PIC X(20).
     02  CUST-CR-LIMIT          PIC 9(04)V99.
     02  CUST-BALANCE           PIC S9(06)V99.
     02  CUST-ADDRESS           PIC X(40).
     02  FILLER                 PIC X(01).
*
FD   CUST-MAST-FILE
         LABEL RECORDS STANDARD
         DATA RECORD IS CUST-MAST-RECORD.
*
01   CUST-MAST-RECORD          PIC X(80).
*
FD   ERROR-FILE
         LABEL RECORDS OMITTED
         DATA RECORD IS ERROR-RECORD.
*
01   ERROR-RECORD.
     02  FILLER                PIC X(132).
*
SD   SORT-FILE
         DATA RECORD IS SORT-RECORD.
*
01   SORT-RECORD.
     02  S-ACCOUNT-NO          PIC 9(05).
     02  FILLER                PIC X(75).
*
FD   NEW-MASTER-FILE
         LABEL RECORDS STANDARD
         DATA RECORD IS NEW-MASTER-RECORD.
*
01   NEW-MASTER-RECORD         PIC X(80).
*
WORKING-STORAGE SECTION.
*
01   END-OF-FILE-INDICATOR     PIC X(03)  VALUE 'NO'.
     88  END-OF-FILE                      VALUE 'YES'.
*
01   ERROR-FLAG                PIC X(03)  VALUE 'NO'.
     88  NO-ERROR-FOUND                   VALUE 'NO'.
     88  ERROR-FOUND                      VALUE 'YES'.
*
01   EXCEPTION-RECORD-FORMAT.
*
     02  ERROR-HEAD1.
         03  FILLER            PIC X(20)  VALUE SPACES.
         03  FILLER            PIC X(16)  VALUE
             'EXCEPTION REPORT'.
*
```

FIGURE 13-3
COBOL Program to Create the
Master File (continued)

```
                              02  ERROR-HEAD2.
                                  03 FILLER              PIC X(05) VALUE SPACES.
                                  03 FILLER              PIC X(13) VALUE
                                     'ERROR MESSAGE'.
                                  03 FILLER              PIC X(22) VALUE SPACES.
                                  03 FILLER              PIC X(14) VALUE
                                     'INVALID RECORD'.
                          *
                              02  ERROR-HEAD3.
                                  03 FILLER              PIC X(04) VALUE SPACES.
                                  03 FILLER              PIC X(115) VALUE ALL '-'.
                          *

                              02  ERROR-BLANK.
                                  03  FILLER             PIC X(132) VALUE SPACES.
                          *
                              02  ERROR-DETAIL-LN.
                                  03  FILLER             PIC X(05) VALUE SPACES.
                                  03  ERROR-MESSAGE      PIC X(35).
                                  03  FILLER             PIC X(01) VALUE SPACES.
                                  03  ERROR-SOURCE-RECORD PIC X(80).
                      *
                       PROCEDURE DIVISION.
                      *
                       100-PROGRAM-SUMMARY.
                           PERFORM 200-START-UP
                           PERFORM 300-CREATE-MASTER
                      *
                           CLOSE CUST-SOURCE-FILE
                                 ERROR-FILE
                                 CUST-MAST-FILE.
                      *
                           SORT SORT-FILE ON ASCENDING KEY S-ACCOUNT-NO
                                USING CUST-MAST-FILE
                                GIVING NEW-MASTER-FILE.
                      *
                           STOP RUN.
                      *
                       200-START-UP.
                           OPEN INPUT  CUST-SOURCE-FILE
                                OUTPUT ERROR-FILE
                                OUTPUT CUST-MAST-FILE.
                      *
                           WRITE ERROR-RECORD FROM ERROR-HEAD1 AFTER PAGE
                           WRITE ERROR-RECORD FROM ERROR-HEAD2 AFTER 2 LINES
                           WRITE ERROR-RECORD FROM ERROR-HEAD3 AFTER 1 LINE
                           WRITE ERROR-RECORD FROM ERROR-BLANK AFTER 1 LINE.
                      *
                       300-CREATE-MASTER.
                           PERFORM 400-READ-SOURCE
                      *
```

FIGURE 13-3
COBOL Program to Create the
Master File (continued)

```
        PERFORM 500-CHECK-WRITE-READ
            UNTIL END-OF-FILE.
*
  400-READ-SOURCE.
     READ CUST-SOURCE-FILE RECORD
          AT END SET END-OF-FILE TO TRUE
     END-READ.
*
  500-CHECK-WRITE-READ.
     PERFORM 600-VALIDATE-FIELDS
*
     IF  NO-ERROR-FOUND
          WRITE CUST-MAST-RECORD FROM CUST-SOURCE-RECORD
     ELSE
          MOVE CUST-SOURCE-RECORD TO ERROR-SOURCE-RECORD
          WRITE ERROR-RECORD FROM ERROR-DETAIL-LN AFTER 2
     END-IF
*
     PERFORM 400-READ-SOURCE.
*
  600-VALIDATE-FIELDS.
     SET NO-ERROR-FOUND TO TRUE
*
     EVALUATE TRUE
          WHEN CUST-ACCOUNT-NO IS NOT NUMERIC
               SET ERROR-FOUND TO TRUE
               MOVE 'ACCOUNT NUMBER NOT NUMERIC' TO ERROR-MESSAGE
*
          WHEN CUST-NAME IS EQUAL TO SPACES
               SET ERROR-FOUND TO TRUE
               MOVE 'CUSTOMER NAME IS MISSING' TO ERROR-MESSAGE
*
          WHEN CUST-CR-LIMIT IS NOT NUMERIC
               SET ERROR-FOUND TO TRUE
               MOVE 'CREDIT LIMIT NOT VALID' TO ERROR-MESSAGE
*
          WHEN CUST-BALANCE IS NOT NUMERIC
               SET ERROR-FOUND TO TRUE
               MOVE 'BALANCE AMOUNT NOT VALID' TO ERROR-MESSAGE
*
          WHEN CUST-ADDRESS IS EQUAL TO SPACES
               SET ERROR-FOUND TO TRUE
               MOVE 'CUSTOMER ADDRESS IS MISSING' TO ERROR-MESSAGE
*
          WHEN NO-ERROR-FOUND
               IF  CUST-CR-LIMIT < CUST-BALANCE
                    SET ERROR-FOUND TO TRUE
                    MOVE 'CUSTOMER'S BALANCE EXCEEDS LIMIT'
                         TO ERROR-MESSAGE
               END-IF
*
     END-EVALUATE.
*
```

for five types of errors in the EVALUATE statement of 600-VALIDATE-FIELDS. The first four types of errors pertain to the individual contents of fields. The fifth type of error compares CUST-CR-LIMIT to CUST-BALANCE to ascertain that when we create a new customer record the credit limit is consistent with the balance owed, if any, by the customer. Notice that if we find an error, we do *not* continue with that record to determine if there are any other errors in the same record. Changing the program to check for *all* five error types in each input record is asked as the first exercise at the end of the chapter.

In 100-PROGRAM-SUMMARY we see that after the CREATE-MASTER process has been completed, we close the three files that were involved (CUST-SOURCE-FILE, ERROR-FILE, and CUST-MAST-FILE) and we proceed with

```
SORT SORT-FILE ON ASCENDING KEY S-ACCOUNT-NO
     USING CUST-MAST-FILE
     GIVING NEW-MASTER-FILE.
```

Thus the customer master file is sorted in ascending order of the account number fields in its records.

DAILY MASTER PROCESSING

Figure 13-4 presents an overview of the daily master update program. The old daily customer master file and the transactions for the day serve as the initial input. There are two printed reports, the Daily Transaction Register and the Transaction Error Report, both of which are illustrated in Figure 13-5. As you can see in the sample transaction register, there are four types of transactions: Purchase, Payment, Return, and Adjustment. The asterisks on the fourth line of the transaction register example signify that the authorized credit limit has been exceeded by that customer.

Sample related input and output data for the daily master processing are shown in Figure 13-6.

Continuing with Figure 13-4, the update process results in a new version of the daily master file. After the update process has been completed, a file merging operation is done conditional on there being an optional transaction file from previous days. On the first day of each month, for instance, the "today's transaction" file would be the only such file, and so a merge operation would not be required.

Figure 13-7 presents the complete program for the daily processing task. The 070-UPDATE-MAST paragraph in the PROCEDURE DIVISION is executed until the transactions and old daily master files have been completely read in. In this paragraph we use the EVALUATE statement to select which of the three conditions is true. If OLD-ACCOUNT-NO = TRANS-ACCOUNT-NO, we enter a loop of PERFORMing 080-APPLY-TRANSACTION UNTIL either we have a transaction for a new customer or it is the end of the transaction file. Thus, on the expectation that we may have several transactions for the same account number, we keep the program logic control for reading and processing possibly *several* transactions at this level, rather than returning to the main PERFORM 070-UPDATE-MAST in the 000-PROGRAM-SUMMARY paragraph. This is a typical way to design the program logic for handling multiple transactions for the same master record.

Because there may be error conditions encountered in processing the transactions, in the 070-UPDATE-MAST procedure we check the following:

```
IF WRITE-REC
   WRITE DAILY-MAS-REC FROM WORK-MAS-REC
```

FIGURE 13-4
Overview of Daily Master Update
Program

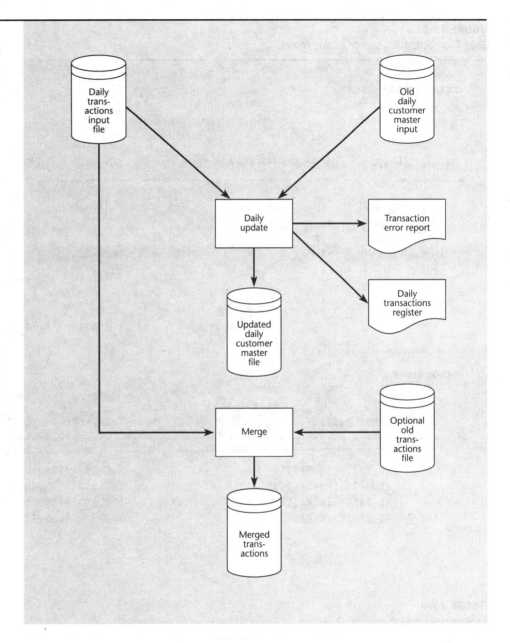

The WRITE-REC condition-name is set to false (SET NOT-WRITE-REC TO TRUE) in the WHEN OTHER alternative of the EVALUATE statement in the 070-UPDATE-MAST procedure. The WORK-MAS-REC is the WORKING STORAGE area in which we prepare the new master record. Alternatively, we could have used the record area in the updated master file (DAILY-MAS-REC in DAILY-MASTER).

The processing logic for the transaction register and the error transaction report have been combined in 100-WRITE-TRANS-REC. Provision for a page heading has been made for the transaction register but not for the error report (being optimists about the number of errors!).

As a last comment on the sample program in Figure 13-7, the paragraph 110-WRITE-TOTALS illustrates limited use of table-processing relating to the last two lines of the transaction register output. In the DATA DIVISION we set up two tables under the headings DAY-TOTAL1 and DAY-TOTAL2. These tables are to contain the total number of transactions and the dollar value for each type of transaction: Purchase, Payment, Return, and Adjustment. The 110-WRITE-TOTALS

FIGURE 13-5

Daily Transaction Register and Error Report

```
TRANSACTIONS REPORT

                              DAILY TRANSACTION REGISTER
                                     06/13/89

     ACCOUNT    DATE    PRODUCT NO    QUANTITY    PRICE    PURCHASE    PAYMENT    RETURN    ADJUSTMENT
     ---------------------------------------------------------------------------------------------------

       19876   05/28/89   0608            1      $100.00   $100.00
       19876   05/28/89                                               $2,400.00
       19876   05/29/89   0011           10      $100.00                         $1,000.00
  **** 33456   06/01/89   8333            1    $8,000.00 $8,000.00
       33456   06/10/89                                                                     $900.00
       41231   06/19/89                                               $400.00

                              TRANSACTIONS PROCESSED       2           2          1           1
                              TOTAL DOLLAR AMOUNTS     $8,100.00   $8,100.00  $1,000.00   $8,000.00



ERROR REPORT

                         ERROR TRANSACTION REPORT
              ERROR MESSAGE                     TRANSACTION RECORD
     ---------------------------------------------------------------------------------------------------

         NO MATCH IN MASTER            12341104218801000001005000
         INVALID TRANSACTION CODE      12345504218800000001000000
         NO MATCH IN MASTER            2000030529895589111155555500240000
         NO MATCH IN MASTER            5000010710899998000101000000040000
```

FIGURE 13-6

Sample Input and Output for Daily Master Processing

OLD TRANSACTION — INPUT FILE	DAILY TRANSACTION — INPUT FILE
19876106108902320010002350	12341104218801000001005000
19876X06108902300100000235	12345504218800000001000000
33456106138967770100003000	19876105288906080001010000
334562061489 00500000	198762052889 00240000
41231106178900450020000300	19876305298900110010010000
412314062089 00011000	2000030529895589111155555
	33456106018983330001800000
	334564061089 00090000
	412312061989 00040000
	50000107108999980001010000

FIGURE 13-6

Sample Input and Output for Daily Master Processing (continued)

OLD MASTER — INPUT FILE

```
12345JOHN L. ANDERSON      080000000150251020 N. 10TH STREET   MESA
AZ 85280
19876JEAN L. PENDLETON     400000002300002888 W. PLAZA RD.
ANYTOWN  AZ 85702
33456LINDA M. BREWSTER     100000000500001929 NORTHERN AVE.
TUCSON  AZ 85701
41231ELMER J. GUSTON       090000000450002350 SOUTHERN AVE.
CHANDLER  AZ 85501
```

DAILY MASTER — OUTPUT FILE

```
12345JOHN L. ANDERSON    08000000015025
19876JEAN L. PENDLETON   40000000100000
33456LINDA M. BREWSTER   10000000760000
41231ELMER J. GUSTON     09000000005000
```

COMBINED TRANSACTION — OUTPUT FILE

```
12341104218801000001005000
12345504218800000001000000
19876106108902320010002350
19876105288906080001010000
198762052889          00240000
19876305298900110010010000
19876X06108902300100000235
20000305298955891111555555
33456106138967770100003000
33456106018983330001800000
334562061489          00500000
334564061089          00090000
41231106178900450020000300
412312061989          00040000
412314062089          00011000
50000107108999980001010000
```

paragraph is used to do the appropriate processing for outputting the results. First, we fill the DAY-NO-TRANSACTIONS and DAY-TRANS-AMOUNTS tables with spaces. Then we use the INITIALIZE statement to move zeros to the numeric fields in the two tables. Actually, since we MOVE data to the subscripted numeric fields DAY-TOTAL-NO and DAY-AMOUNTS in the second and third PERFORM VARYING statements of 110-WRITE-TOTALS, there is no need to INITIALIZE them with zero values. But we do so anyhow to illustrate use of the statement.

FIGURE 13-7

*COBOL Program for the Daily
Processing*

```
        IDENTIFICATION DIVISION.
        PROGRAM-ID. UPDMAS.
    *
        ENVIRONMENT DIVISION.
        CONFIGURATION SECTION.
        SOURCE-COMPUTER. ABC-480.
        OBJECT-COMPUTER. ABC-480.
    *
        INPUT-OUTPUT SECTION.
    *
        FILE-CONTROL.
    *
            SELECT OPTIONAL OLD-TRANS-FILE  ASSIGN TO OLD-TRANS.
            SELECT DAILY-TRANS-FILE         ASSIGN TO DAY-TRANS.
            SELECT MERGE-FILE               ASSIGN TO MERGE-FILE.
            SELECT OLD-MASTER               ASSIGN TO OLD-MAS.
            SELECT DAILY-MASTER             ASSIGN TO DAY-MAS.
            SELECT NEW-TRANS-FILE           ASSIGN TO COMBINED-TRANS.
            SELECT ERROR-FILE               ASSIGN TO PRINT-ERR.
            SELECT REPORT-FILE              ASSIGN TO REPORT-FIL.
    *
        DATA DIVISION.
    *
        FILE SECTION.
    *
        FD  OLD-TRANS-FILE
            BLOCK CONTAINS 50 RECORDS
            LABEL RECORDS ARE OMITTED
            DATA RECORD IS OLD-TRANS-RECORD.
    *
        01  OLD-TRANS-RECORD            PIC X(34).
    *
        FD  DAILY-TRANS-FILE
            BLOCK CONTAINS 50 RECORDS
            LABEL RECORDS ARE OMITTED
            DATA RECORD IS DAY-TRANS-RECORD.
    *
        01  DAY-TRANS-RECORD.
            02  TRANS-ACCOUNT-NO        PIC X(5).
            02  TRANS-CODE              PIC 9.
            02  TRANS-DATE              PIC X(6).
            02  TRANS-PRODUCT-NO        PIC 9(4).
            02  TRANS-QUANTITY          PIC 9(4).
            02  TRANS-PRICE             PIC 9(4)V99.
            02  TRANS-PMT-ADJ-AMT       PIC 9(6)V99.
    *
        FD  OLD-MASTER
            BLOCK CONTAINS 50 RECORDS
            LABEL RECORDS OMITTED
            DATA RECORD IS OLD-MASTER-RECORD.
    *
```

FIGURE 13-7
COBOL Program for the Daily
Processing (continued)

```
01  OLD-MASTER-RECORD.
    02  OLD-ACCOUNT-NO        PIC X(5).
    02  FILLER                PIC X(20).
    02  OLD-CREDIT-LIMIT      PIC 9(4)V99.
    02  OLD-BALANCE           PIC S9(6)V99.
*
FD  DAILY-MASTER
    BLOCK CONTAINS 50 RECORDS
    LABEL RECORDS STANDARD
    DATA RECORD IS DAILY-MAS-REC.
*
01  DAILY-MAS-REC            PIC X(39).
*
FD  NEW-TRANS-FILE
    BLOCK CONTAINS 50 RECORDS
    LABEL RECORDS ARE OMITTED
    DATA RECORD IS COMBINED-TRANS-REC.
*
01  COMBINED-TRANS-REC       PIC X(34).
*
FD  ERROR-FILE
    LABEL RECORDS OMITTED
    DATA RECORD IS ERROR-RECORD.
*
01  ERROR-RECORD            PIC X(132).
*
FD  REPORT-FILE
    LABEL RECORDS OMITTED
    DATA RECORD IS REPORT-RECORD.
*
01  REPORT-RECORD           PIC X(132).
*
SD  MERGE-FILE
    DATA RECORD IS MERGE-TRANS-RECORD.
*
01  MERGE-TRANS-RECORD.
    02  MERGE-ACCOUNT-NO     PIC X(5).
    02  MERGE-TRANS-CODE     PIC X(1).
    02  FILLER               PIC X(28).
*
WORKING-STORAGE SECTION.
*
01  END-OF-TRANS            PIC X(3) VALUE "NO".
    88  TRANS-ENDED         VALUE "YES".
*
01  END-OF-MASTER           PIC X(3) VALUE "NO".
    88  MASTER-ENDED        VALUE "YES".
*
01  WRITE-TRANS-SWITCH      PIC X(3) VALUE "YES".
    88  WRITE-TRANS         VALUE "YES".
    88  NOT-WRITE-TRANS     VALUE "NO".
*
```

```
01    WRITE-FLAG                    PIC X(3) VALUE "YES".
      88  WRITE-REC                 VALUE "YES".
      88  NOT-WRITE-REC             VALUE "NO".
*
01    WORK-MAS-REC.
      02  WORK-ACCOUNT-NO           PIC X(5).
      02  FILLER                    PIC X(20).
      02  WORK-CREDIT-LIMIT         PIC 9(4)V99.
      02  WORK-BALANCE              PIC S9(6)V99.
      02  FILLER                    PIC X(41).
*
01    WS-DATE-ITEMS.
      02  WS-DATE.
          03  WS-YR                 PIC 9(2).
          03  WS-MO                 PIC 9(2).
          03  WS-DA                 PIC 9(2).
*
01    END-OLD-TRANS-FLAG            PIC X(3) VALUE "NO".
      88  END-OF-OLD-TRANS          VALUE "YES".
      88  NOT-END-OF-OLD-TRANS      VALUE "NO".
*
01    WS-SUBSCRIPTS.
      02  SUB                       PIC 9(2) VALUE ZERO.
*
01    SUMMARIZE-TRANS-TABLE.
      02  TRANS-TYPE                OCCURS 4 TIMES.
          03  TRANS-TOTAL-AMOUNT    PIC 9(6)V99.
          03  TRANS-TOTAL-NUMBER    PIC 9(3).
*
01    WS-NUMERIC-ITEMS.
      02  LN-COUNTER                PIC 9(2) VALUE ZERO.
      02  PAGE-SIZE                 PIC 9(2) VALUE 35.
      02  WS-TRANS-AMOUNT           PIC 9(6)V99.
*
OUTPUT REPORT RECORD DESCRIPTION:
*
01    DAILY-REPORT-FORMAT.
*
      02  DAY-HEAD1.
          03  FILLER                PIC X(44) VALUE SPACES.
          03  FILLER                PIC X(27) VALUE
              "DAILY TRANSACTION REGISTER".
*
      02  DAY-HEAD2.
          03  FILLER                PIC X(55) VALUE SPACES.
          03  D-MONTH               PIC 9(2).
          03  FILLER                PIC X(1) VALUE "/".
          03  D-DAY                 PIC 9(2).
          03  FILLER                PIC X(1) VALUE "/".
          03  D-YEAR                PIC 9(2).
*
```

FIGURE 13-7
COBOL Program for the Daily
Processing (continued)

```
        02  DAY-HEAD3.
            03  FILLER              PIC X(5) VALUE SPACES.
            03  FILLER              PIC X(7) VALUE "ACCOUNT".
            03  FILLER              PIC X(5) VALUE SPACES.
            03  FILLER              PIC X(4) VALUE "DATE".
            03  FILLER              PIC X(5) VALUE SPACES.
            03  FILLER              PIC X(10) VALUE "PRODUCT NO".
            03  FILLER              PIC X(8) VALUE SPACES.
            03  FILLER              PIC X(8) VALUE "QUANTITY".
            03  FILLER              PIC X(6) VALUE SPACES.
            03  FILLER              PIC X(5) VALUE "PRICE".
            03  FILLER              PIC X(7) VALUE SPACES.
            03  FILLER              PIC X(8) VALUE "PURCHASE".
            03  FILLER              PIC X(6) VALUE SPACES.
            03  FILLER              PIC X(7) VALUE "PAYMENT".
            03  FILLER              PIC X(7) VALUE SPACES.
            03  FILLER              PIC X(6) VALUE "RETURN".
            03  FILLER              PIC X(7) VALUE SPACES.
            03  FILLER              PIC X(10) VALUE "ADJUSTMENT".
    *
        02  DAY-HEAD4.
            03  FILLER              PIC X(132) VALUE ALL "-".
    *
        02  DAY-BLANK.
            03  FILLER              PIC X(132) VALUE SPACES.
    *
        02  DAY-DETAIL.
            03  FILLER              PIC X(1) VALUE SPACES.
            03  FILLER1             PIC X(4) VALUE SPACES.
            03  FILLER              PIC X(1) VALUE SPACES.
            03  D-ACCOUNT           PIC X(5).
            03  FILLER              PIC X(4) VALUE SPACES.
            03  D-DATE              PIC XX/XX/XX.
            03  FILLER              PIC X(6) VALUE SPACES.
            03  D-PRODUCT-NO        PIC X(4).
            03  FILLER              PIC X(13) VALUE SPACES.
            03  D-QUANTITY          PIC X(4).
            03  FILLER              PIC X(6) VALUE SPACES.
            03  D-PRICE             PIC $$,$$9.99 BLANK WHEN ZERO.
            03  FILLER              PIC X(4) VALUE SPACES.
            03  D-PURCHASE          PIC $$$,$$9.99 BLANK WHEN ZERO.
            03  FILLER              PIC X(4) VALUE SPACES.
            03  D-PAYMENT           PIC $$$,$$9.99 BLANK WHEN ZERO.
            03  FILLER              PIC X(4) VALUE SPACES.
            03  D-RETURN            PIC $$$,$$9.99 BLANK WHEN ZERO.
            03  FILLER              PIC X(4) VALUE SPACES.
            03  D-ADJUSTS           PIC $$$,$$9.99 BLANK WHEN ZERO.
    *
```

FIGURE 13-7
COBOL Program for the Daily
Processing (continued)

```
            02  DAY-TOTAL1.
                03  FILLER              PIC X(36) VALUE SPACES.
                03  FILLER              PIC X(25) VALUE
                    "TRANSACTIONS PROCESSED   ".
                03  DAY-NO-TRANSACTIONS OCCURS 4 TIMES.
                    04  FILLER          PIC X(11).
                    04  DAY-TOTAL-NO    PIC ZZ9.

            02  DAY-TOTAL2.
                03  FILLER              PIC X(38) VALUE SPACES.
                03  FILLER              PIC X(21) VALUE
                    "TOTAL DOLLAR AMOUNTS".
                03  DAY-TRANS-AMOUNTS   OCCURS 4 TIMES.
                    04  FILLER          PIC X(5).
                    04  DAY-AMOUNTS     PIC $,$$$,$$9.99.
         *
         **ERROR FILE RECORD DESCRIPTION:
         *
          01  ERROR-RECORDS.
             02  ERROR-HEAD1.
                03  FILLER              PIC X(26) VALUE SPACES.
                03  FILLER              PIC X(24) VALUE
                    "ERROR TRANSACTION REPORT".
         *
             02  ERROR-HEAD2.
                03  FILLER              PIC X(10) VALUE SPACES.
                03  FILLER              PIC X(13) VALUE
                    "ERROR MESSAGE".
                03  FILLER              PIC X(27) VALUE SPACES.
                03  FILLER              PIC X(18) VALUE
                    "TRANSACTION RECORD".
         *
             02  ERROR-HEAD3.
                03  FILLER              PIC X(80) VALUE ALL "-".
         *
             02  ERROR-BLANK.
                03  FILLER              PIC X(132) VALUE SPACES.
         *
             02  ERROR-DETAIL.
                03  FILLER              PIC X(10) VALUE SPACES.
                03  ERROR-MESSAGE       PIC X(40).
                03  ERROR-TRANS         PIC X(82).
         *
          PROCEDURE DIVISION.
         *
          000-PROGRAM-SUMMARY.
             PERFORM 010-STARTUP
             PERFORM 040-READ-FIRST-PAIR
             PERFORM 070-UPDATE-MAST UNTIL
                TRANS-ENDED AND MASTER-ENDED
             PERFORM 110-WRITE-TOTALS
             CLOSE DAILY-TRANS-FILE,
                   OLD-MASTER,
                   DAILY-MASTER,
                   ERROR-FILE,
                   REPORT-FILE.
```

FIGURE 13-7
`COBOL Program for the Daily
Processing (continued)

```
     *
              OPEN INPUT OLD-TRANS-FILE.
              READ OLD-TRANS-FILE RECORD
                   AT END SET END-OF-OLD-TRANS TO TRUE
              END-READ
     *
              CLOSE OLD-TRANS-FILE.
     *
              IF  NOT-END-OF-OLD-TRANS
                  MERGE MERGE-FILE ON ASCENDING KEY MERGE-ACCOUNT-NO
                                    ON ASCENDING KEY MERGE-TRANS-CODE
                     USING OLD-TRANS-FILE, DAILY-TRANS-FILE
                     GIVING NEW-TRANS-FILE
              END-IF.
     *
              STOP RUN.
     *
          010-STARTUP.
              OPEN INPUT  OLD-MASTER
                          DAILY-TRANS-FILE
                   OUTPUT DAILY-MASTER
                          ERROR-FILE
                          REPORT-FILE.
     *
              MOVE ZEROS TO SUMMARIZE-TRANS-TABLE
              MOVE ZEROS TO D-PURCHASE, D-PAYMENT, D-RETURN, D-ADJUSTS
     *
              ACCEPT WS-DATE FROM DATE
              MOVE WS-YR TO D-YEAR
              MOVE WS-MO TO D-MONTH
              MOVE WS-DA TO D-DAY
     *
              PERFORM 020-WRITE-TRANS-HEADINGS
              PERFORM 030-WRITE-ERROR-HEADINGS.
     *
          020-WRITE-TRANS-HEADINGS.
              WRITE REPORT-RECORD FROM DAY-HEAD1 AFTER PAGE
              WRITE REPORT-RECORD FROM DAY-HEAD2 AFTER 1
              WRITE REPORT-RECORD FROM DAY-HEAD3 AFTER 2
              WRITE REPORT-RECORD FROM DAY-HEAD4 AFTER 1
              WRITE REPORT-RECORD FROM DAY-BLANK AFTER 1
              MOVE 6 TO LN-COUNTER.
     *
          030-WRITE-ERROR-HEADINGS.
              WRITE ERROR-RECORD FROM ERROR-HEAD1 AFTER PAGE
              WRITE ERROR-RECORD FROM ERROR-HEAD2 AFTER 2
              WRITE ERROR-RECORD FROM ERROR-HEAD3 AFTER 1
              WRITE ERROR-RECORD FROM ERROR-BLANK AFTER 1.
     *
          040-READ-FIRST-PAIR.
              PERFORM 050-READ-TRANS
              PERFORM 060-READ-MASTER.
```

FIGURE 13-7
COBOL Program for the Daily
Processing (continued)

```
*
050-READ-TRANS.
    READ DAILY-TRANS-FILE
        AT END MOVE HIGH-VALUES TO TRANS-ACCOUNT-NO
        SET TRANS-ENDED TO TRUE
    END-READ.
*
060-READ-MASTER.
    READ OLD-MASTER
        AT END MOVE HIGH-VALUES TO OLD-ACCOUNT-NO
        SET MASTER-ENDED TO TRUE
    END-READ.
*
070-UPDATE-MAST.
    EVALUATE TRUE
        WHEN OLD-ACCOUNT-NO = TRANS-ACCOUNT-NO
            MOVE OLD-MASTER-RECORD TO WORK-MAS-REC
            PERFORM 080-APPLY-TRANSACTION
                UNTIL (OLD-ACCOUNT-NO NOT EQUAL TRANS-ACCOUNT-NO)
                    OR TRANS-ENDED
            PERFORM 060-READ-MASTER
        WHEN OLD-ACCOUNT-NO < TRANS-ACCOUNT-NO
            MOVE OLD-MASTER-RECORD TO WORK-MAS-REC
            PERFORM 060-READ-MASTER
        WHEN OTHER
            MOVE OLD-MASTER-RECORD TO WORK-MAS-REC
            SET NOT-WRITE-REC TO TRUE
            PERFORM 090-TRANS-ERROR
                UNTIL (OLD-ACCOUNT-NO NOT > TRANS-ACCOUNT-NO)
                    OR TRANS-ENDED
    END-EVALUATE.
*
    IF  WRITE-REC
        WRITE DAILY-MAS-REC FROM WORK-MAS-REC
    ELSE
        SET WRITE-REC TO TRUE
    END-IF.
*
080-APPLY-TRANSACTION.
    IF  TRANS-CODE IS NUMERIC AND
        (TRANS-CODE > 0 AND TRANS-CODE < 5)
        IF  TRANS-CODE = 1 OR TRANS-CODE = 3
            MULTIPLY TRANS-QUANTITY BY TRANS-PRICE
                GIVING WS-TRANS-AMOUNT
        END-IF
        ADD WS-TRANS-AMOUNT TO TRANS-TOTAL-AMOUNT(TRANS-CODE)
        ADD 1 TO TRANS-TOTAL-NUMBER(TRANS-CODE)
        SET WRITE-TRANS TO TRUE
    END-IF
*
```

FIGURE 13-7
COBOL Program for the Daily
Processing (continued)

```
            EVALUATE TRUE
                WHEN TRANS-CODE = 1
                    MOVE WS-TRANS-AMOUNT TO D-PURCHASE
                    ADD WS-TRANS-AMOUNT TO WORK-BALANCE
                    IF  WORK-BALANCE > WORK-CREDIT-LIMIT
                        MOVE "****" TO FILLER1
                    END-IF
                WHEN TRANS-CODE = 2
                    MOVE TRANS-PMT-ADJ-AMT TO D-PAYMENT
                    SUBTRACT TRANS-PMT-ADJ-AMT FROM WORK-BALANCE
                WHEN TRANS-CODE = 3
                    MOVE WS-TRANS-AMOUNT TO D-RETURN
                    SUBTRACT WS-TRANS-AMOUNT FROM WORK-BALANCE
                WHEN TRANS-CODE = 4
                    MOVE TRANS-PMT-ADJ-AMT TO D-ADJUSTS
                    SUBTRACT TRANS-PMT-ADJ-AMT FROM WORK-BALANCE
                WHEN OTHER
                    SET NOT-WRITE-TRANS TO TRUE
            END-EVALUATE
        *
            PERFORM 100-WRITE-TRANS-REC
            PERFORM 050-READ-TRANS.
        *
         090-TRANS-ERROR.
            MOVE "NO MATCH IN MASTER" TO ERROR-MESSAGE
            MOVE DAY-TRANS-RECORD TO ERROR-TRANS
            WRITE ERROR-RECORD FROM ERROR-DETAIL AFTER 1
            PERFORM 050-READ-TRANS.
        *
         100-WRITE-TRANS-REC.
            IF  WRITE-TRANS
                MOVE TRANS-ACCOUNT-NO TO D-ACCOUNT
                MOVE TRANS-DATE TO D-DATE
                IF  TRANS-CODE = 1 OR TRANS-CODE = 3
                    MOVE TRANS-PRODUCT-NO TO D-PRODUCT-NO
                    MOVE TRANS-QUANTITY TO D-QUANTITY
                    MOVE TRANS-PRICE TO D-PRICE
                ELSE
                    MOVE ZEROS TO D-PRODUCT-NO, D-QUANTITY, D-PRICE
                END-IF
                IF  PAGE-SIZE < LN-COUNTER
                    PERFORM 020-WRITE-TRANS-HEADINGS
                END-IF
                WRITE REPORT-RECORD FROM DAY-DETAIL AFTER 1
                ADD 1 TO LN-COUNTER
                MOVE ZERO TO D-PAYMENT,
                             D-PURCHASE,
                             D-ADJUSTS,
                             D-RETURN
                MOVE SPACES TO FILLER1
            ELSE
                MOVE "INVALID TRANSACTION CODE" TO ERROR-MESSAGE
                MOVE DAY-TRANS-RECORD TO ERROR-TRANS
                WRITE ERROR-RECORD FROM ERROR-DETAIL AFTER 1
                SET WRITE-TRANS TO TRUE
            END-IF.
```

FIGURE 13-7

COBOL Program for the Daily
Processing (continued)

```
*
   110-WRITE-TOTALS.
      PERFORM VARYING SUB FROM 1 BY 1
          UNTIL SUB > 4
          MOVE SPACES TO DAY-NO-TRANSACTIONS( SUB ),
                         DAY-TRANS-AMOUNTS( SUB )
          INITIALIZE DAY-NO-TRANSACTIONS( SUB ),
                     DAY-TRANS-AMOUNTS( SUB )
      END-PERFORM
*
      PERFORM VARYING SUB FROM 1 BY 1
          UNTIL SUB > 4
          MOVE TRANS-TOTAL-NUMBER ( SUB ) TO DAY-TOTAL-NO( SUB )
      END-PERFORM
*
      WRITE REPORT-RECORD FROM DAY-TOTAL1 AFTER 2
*
      PERFORM VARYING SUB FROM 1 BY 1
          UNTIL SUB > 4
          MOVE TRANS-TOTAL-AMOUNT( SUB ) TO DAY-AMOUNTS( SUB )
      END-PERFORM
*
      WRITE REPORT-RECORD FROM DAY-TOTAL2 AFTER 1.
*
```

MONTHLY PROCESSING

Figure 13-8 outlines the monthly processing. The daily transactions have been merged as part of the daily processing during the month. The combined transactions file for the month is used as input along with the full-version customer master file. Recall that we distinguished between the abbreviated master used on a daily basis and the full master file used once during the monthly processing. In a more realistic example, we would include transactions to update the full master file with respect to the addition of new customers, name and address changes, and deletion of customer records. However, for the sake of simplicity, we limit the type of transactions to those processed during the daily runs: purchases, payments, returns, and adjustments. As a result of the processing, the customer balance field in the master file is updated, a billing statement is produced, and error transactions are reported.

Figure 13-9 shows sample input and output for the monthly processing. The sample output includes billing statements and an error transaction report. Since the daily processing program checked transactions for error codes, we should not have any at the end of the month. However, it is not unusual to have redundant checking, as illustrated in this case. It may be that the monthly transaction file contains error transactions due to inadvertent merging of error transactions, mislabeling of files, and other hard-to-predict error possibilities. Because processing financial data is a critical operation, it is usually wise to include testing logic to screen out error data if there is any possibility that such data could have slipped through the system.

Figure 13-10 presents the first three divisions of the COBOL program for the monthly processing task. Writing the PROCEDURE DIVISION is left as an exercise.

FIGURE 13-8

Overview of Monthly Processing

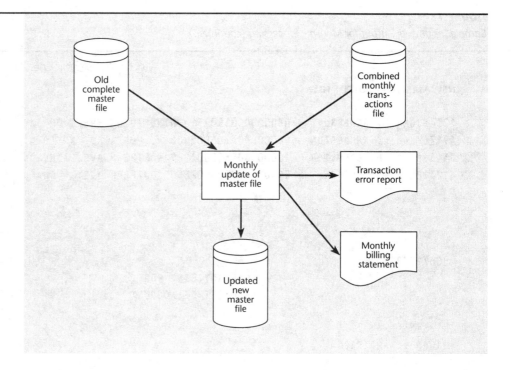

FIGURE 13-9

Sample Input and Output for
Monthly Processing

OLD MASTER — INPUT FILE

```
12345JOHN L. ANDERSON    080000000150251020 N. 10TH STREET  MESA
 AZ 85280
19876JEAN L. PENDLETON   400000002300002888 W. PLAZA RD.   ANYTOWN
AZ 85702
33456LINDA M. BREWSTER   100000000500001929 NORTHERN AVE.   TUCSON
AZ 85701
41231ELMER J. GUSTON     090000000450002350 SOUTHERN AVE.
CHANDLER AZ 85501
```

COMBINED TRANSACTION — INPUT FILE

```
123411042188010000010050000
123455042188000000001000000
198761061089023200100002350
198761052889060800010100000
198762052889          00240000
198763052989001100100100000
19876X06108902300100000235
200003052989558911115555555
334561061389677701000003000
334561060189833300018000000
334562061489          00500000
334564061089          00090000
412311061789004500200000300
412312061989          00040000
412314062089          00011000
500001071089999980001010000
```

FIGURE 13-9
Sample Input and Output for Monthly Processing (continued)

NEW MASTER — OUTPUT FILE

```
12345JOHN L. ANDERSON      080000000150251020 N. 10TH STREET  MESA    AZ 85280
19876JEAN L. PENDLETON     400000000765002888 W. PLAZA RD. ANYTOWN    AZ 85702
33456LINDA M. BREWSTER     100000005600001929 NORTHERN AVE.   TUCSON  AZ 85701
41231ELMER J. GUSTON       090000000000002350 SOUTHERN AVE.   CHANDLER AZ 85501
```

```
 06/13/89                                                           PAGE  1
                                ACME ANYTHING CORP.
                               STATEMENT OF ACCOUNT


 12345
 JOHN L. ANDERSON


 SALE DATE        PRODUCT NO         PURCHASE      PAYMENT     RETURN    ADJUSTMENT
 --------------------------------------------------------------------------------


                       **** NO ACTIVITY IN THIS PERIOD ****


                             NEW BALANCE      $150.25
                       AVAILABLE CREDIT LINE  $649.75




 06/13/89                                                           PAGE  1
                                ACME ANYTHING CORP.
                               STATEMENT OF ACCOUNT


 19876
 JEAN L. PENDLETON


 SALE DATE        PRODUCT NO         PURCHASE      PAYMENT     RETURN    ADJUSTMENT
 --------------------------------------------------------------------------------


   06/10/89         0232             $235.00
   05/28/89         0608             $100.00
   05/28/89                                       $2,400.00
   05/29/89         0011                                      $1,000.00


                             NEW BALANCE      $765.00CR
                       AVAILABLE CREDIT LINE  $4,000.00
```

FIGURE 13-9

Sample Input and Output for Monthly Processing (continued)

```
06/13/89                                                      PAGE  1
                         ACME ANYTHING CORP.
                         STATEMENT OF ACCOUNT

33456
LINDA M. BREWSTER


SALE DATE       PRODUCT NO        PURCHASE      PAYMENT      RETURN      ADJUSTMENT
--------------------------------------------------------------------------------


06/13/89        6777           $3,000.00
06/01/89        8333           $8,000.00
06/14/89                                      $5,000.00
06/10/89                                                                 $900.00


                         NEW BALANCE      $5,600.00
                   AVAILABLE CREDIT LINE       $0.00



06/13/89                                                      PAGE  1
                         ACME ANYTHING CORP.
                         STATEMENT OF ACCOUNT

41231
ELMER J. GUSTON


SALE DATE       PRODUCT NO        PURCHASE      PAYMENT      RETURN      ADJUSTMENT
--------------------------------------------------------------------------------


06/17/89        0045              $60.00
06/19/89                                       $400.00                   $110.00
06/20/89


                         NEW BALANCE          $0.00
                   AVAILABLE CREDIT LINE     $900.00
```

ERROR REPORT

```
                    ERROR TRANSACTION REPORT
         ERROR MESSAGE                       TRANSACTION RECORD
--------------------------------------------------------------------------------


      NO MATCH IN MASTER             12341104218801000001005000
      INVALID TRANSACTION CODE       12345504218800000001000000
      INVALID TRANSACTION CODE       19876X06108902300100000235
      NO MATCH IN MASTER             20000305298955891111555555
      NO MATCH IN MASTER             50000107108999980001010000
```

FIGURE 13-10

First Three Divisions of the COBOL
Program for Monthly Processing

```
          IDENTIFICATION DIVISION.
          PROGRAM-ID. MONTHUPD.
      *
          ENVIRONMENT DIVISION.
          CONFIGURATION SECTION.
          SOURCE-COMPUTER. ABC-480.
          OBJECT-COMPUTER. ABC-480.
      *
          INPUT-OUTPUT SECTION.
      *
          FILE-CONTROL.
      *
              SELECT OLD-MASTER              ASSIGN TO OLD-MAS.
              SELECT COMB-TRANS-FILE         ASSIGN TO COMBINED-TRANS.
              SELECT NEW-MASTER              ASSIGN TO NEW-MAS.
              SELECT ERROR-FILE              ASSIGN TO PRINT-ERR.
              SELECT REPORT-FILE             ASSIGN TO REPORT-FIL.
      *
          DATA DIVISION.
      *
          FILE SECTION.
      *
          FD  COMB-TRANS-FILE
              BLOCK CONTAINS 50 RECORDS
              LABEL RECORDS ARE OMITTED
              DATA RECORD IS COMB-TRANS-RECORD.
      *
          01  COMB-TRANS-RECORD.
              05  TRANS-ACCOUNT-NO          PIC X(5).
              05  TRANS-CODE                PIC 9.
              05  TRANS-DATE                PIC X(6).
              05  TRANS-PRODUCT-NO          PIC 9(4).
              05  TRANS-QUANTITY            PIC 9(4).
              05  TRANS-PRICE               PIC 9(4)V99.
              05  TRANS-PMT-ADJ-AMT         PIC 9(6)V99.
      *
          FD  OLD-MASTER
              LABEL RECORDS OMITTED
              DATA RECORD IS OLD-MASTER-RECORD.
      *
          01  OLD-MASTER-RECORD.
              02  OLD-ACCOUNT-NO            PIC X(5).
              02  OLD-NAME                  PIC X(20).
              02  OLD-CREDIT-LIMIT          PIC 9(4)V99.
              02  OLD-BALANCE               PIC S9(6)V99.
              02  OLD-ADDRESS               PIC X(40).
              02  FILLER                    PIC X(1).
      *
          FD  NEW-MASTER
              LABEL RECORDS STANDARD
              DATA RECORD IS NEW-MAS-REC.
      *
          01  NEW-MAS-REC                   PIC X(80).
```

FIGURE 13-10

First Three Divisions of the COBOL
Program for Monthly Processing
(continued)

```
*
FD  ERROR-FILE
    LABEL RECORDS OMITTED
    DATA RECORD IS ERROR-RECORD.
*
01  ERROR-RECORD                PIC X(132).
*
FD  REPORT-FILE
    LABEL RECORDS OMITTED
    DATA RECORD IS REPORT-RECORD.
*
01  REPORT-RECORD               PIC X(132).
*
WORKING-STORAGE SECTION.
*
01  END-OF-TRANS               PIC X(3) VALUE "NO".
    88  TRANS-ENDED            VALUE "YES".
*
01  END-OF-MASTER              PIC X(3) VALUE "NO".
    88  MASTER-ENDED           VALUE "YES".
*
01  ACTIVITY-FLAG              PIC X(3) VALUE "NO".
    88  ACTIVITY-ON            VALUE "YES".
    88  NO-ACTIVITY            VALUE "NO".
*
01  WRITE-TRANS-SWITCH         PIC X(3) VALUE "YES" .
    88  WRITE-TRANS            VALUE "YES".
    88  NOT-WRITE-TRANS        VALUE "NO".
*
01  WRITE-FLAG                 PIC X(3) VALUE "YES".
    88  WRITE-REC              VALUE "YES".
    88  NOT-WRITE-REC          VALUE "NO".
*
01  WORK-MAS-REC.
    02  WORK-ACCOUNT-NO         PIC X(5).
    02  FILLER                  PIC X(20).
    02  WORK-CREDIT-LIMIT       PIC 9(4)V99.
    02  WORK-BALANCE            PIC S9(6)V99.
    02  FILLER                  PIC X(41).
*
01  WS-DATE-ITEMS.
    02  WS-DATE.
        03  WS-YR               PIC 9(02).
        03  WS-MO               PIC 9(02).
        03  WS-DA               PIC 9(02).
*
01  WS-NUMERIC-ITEMS.
    02  LN-COUNTER              PIC 9(2) VALUE ZERO.
    02  PAGE-SIZE               PIC 9(2) VALUE 35.
    02  WS-TRANS-AMOUNT         PIC 9(6)V99.
    02  PG-COUNTER              PIC 99 VALUE ZERO.
    02  WORK-AVAILABLE-LIMIT    PIC 9(6)V99.
*
```

FIGURE 13-10

First Three Divisions of the COBOL Program for Monthly Processing (continued)

```
OUTPUT REPORT RECORD DESCRIPTION:
*
01  STATEMENT-REPORT-FORMAT.
    02  STATE-HEAD1.
        03  FILLER              PIC X(02) VALUE SPACES.
        03  S-MONTH             PIC 9(02).
        03  FILLER              PIC X(01) VALUE "/".
        03  S-DAY               PIC 9(02).
        03  FILLER              PIC X(01) VALUE "/".
        03  S-YEAR              PIC 9(02).
        03  FILLER              PIC X(62) VALUE SPACES.
        03  FILLER              PIC X(5) VALUE "PAGE ".
        03  S-PAGE              PIC Z9.
*
    02  STATE-HEAD2.
        03  FILLER              PIC X(30) VALUE SPACES.
        03  FILLER              PIC X(19) VALUE
            "ACME ANYTHING CORP.".
*
    02  STATE-HEAD3.
        03  FILLER              PIC X(29) VALUE SPACES.
        03  FILLER              PIC X(20) VALUE
            "STATEMENT OF ACCOUNT".
*
    02  STATE-HEAD4.
        03  FILLER              PIC X(2) VALUE SPACES.
        03  S-ACCOUNT-NO        PIC X(5).
*
    02  STATE-HEAD5.
        03  FILLER              PIC X(2) VALUE SPACES.
        03  S-NAME              PIC X(20).
*
    02  STATE-HEAD6.
        03  FILLER              PIC X(2) VALUE SPACES.
        03  FILLER              PIC X(9) VALUE "SALE DATE".
        03  FILLER              PIC X(6) VALUE SPACES.
        03  FILLER              PIC X(10) VALUE "PRODUCT NO".
        03  FILLER              PIC X(9) VALUE SPACES.
        03  FILLER              PIC X(8) VALUE "PURCHASE".
        03  FILLER              PIC X(7) VALUE SPACES.
        03  FILLER              PIC X(7) VALUE "PAYMENT".
        03  FILLER              PIC X(7) VALUE SPACES.
        03  FILLER              PIC X(6) VALUE "RETURN".
        03  FILLER              PIC X(5) VALUE SPACES.
        03  FILLER              PIC X(10) VALUE "ADJUSTMENT".
*
    02  STATE-HEAD7.
        03  FILLER              PIC X(90) VALUE ALL "-".
*
    02  STATE-BLANK.
        03  FILLER              PIC X(132) VALUE SPACES.
*
```

FIGURE 13-10

First Three Divisions of the COBOL Program for Monthly Processing (continued)

```
        02  STATE-DETAIL.
            03  FILLER              PIC X(4) VALUE SPACES.
            03  S-DATE              PIC XX/XX/XX.
            03  FILLER              PIC X(09) VALUE SPACES.
            03  S-PRODUCT-NO        PIC X(4).
            03  FILLER              PIC X(10) VALUE SPACES.
            03  S-PURCHASE          PIC $$$,$$9.99 BLANK WHEN ZERO.
            03  FILLER              PIC X(4) VALUE SPACES.
            03  S-PAYMENT           PIC $$$,$$9.99 BLANK WHEN ZERO.
            03  FILLER              PIC X(4) VALUE SPACES.
            03  S-RETURN            PIC $$$,$$9.99 BLANK WHEN ZERO.
            03  FILLER              PIC X(04) VALUE SPACES.
            03  S-ADJUSTS           PIC $$$,$$9.99 BLANK WHEN ZERO.
            03  FILLER              PIC X(4) VALUE SPACES.
    *
        02  STATE-DETAIL2.
            03  FILLER              PIC X(28) VALUE SPACES.
            03  FILLER              PIC X(36) VALUE
                "**** NO ACTIVITY IN THIS PERIOD ****".
    *
        02  STATE-TOTAL1.
            03  FILLER              PIC X(31) VALUE SPACES.
            03  FILLER              PIC X(12) VALUE "NEW BALANCE ".
            03  STATE-BALANCE-NOW   PIC $,$$$,$$9.99CR.
    *
        02  STATE-TOTAL2.
            03  FILLER              PIC X(22) VALUE SPACES.
            03  FILLER              PIC X(21) VALUE
                "AVAILABLE CREDIT LINE".
            03  STATE-CR-AMT        PIC $,$$$,$$9.99.
    *
    **ERROR FILE RECORD DESCRIPTION:
    *
     01  ERROR-RECORDS.
        02  ERROR-HEAD1.
            03  FILLER              PIC X(26) VALUE SPACES.
            03  FILLER              PIC X(24) VALUE
                "ERROR TRANSACTION REPORT".
    *
        02  ERROR-HEAD2.
            03  FILLER              PIC X(10) VALUE SPACES.
            03  FILLER              PIC X(13) VALUE "ERROR MESSAGE".
            03  FILLER              PIC X(27) VALUE SPACES.
            03  FILLER              PIC X(18) VALUE
                "TRANSACTION RECORD".
    *
        02  ERROR-HEAD3.
            03  FILLER              PIC X(80) VALUE ALL "-".
    *
        02  ERROR-BLANK.
            03  FILLER              PIC X(132) VALUE SPACES.
    *
        02  ERROR-DETAIL.
            03  FILLER              PIC X(10) VALUE SPACES.
            03  ERROR-MESSAGE       PIC X(40).
            03  ERROR-TRANS         PIC X(82).
```

SUMMARY

In this chapter we presented and discussed a system of three interrelated COBOL programs concerned with sequential file processing.

The first program illustrated the creation of a master file for customer records. The second program demonstrated the processing of daily transactions and updating of the daily master. The third program was concerned with monthly activities, and processed the transactions for the month against the full master file.

The expanded example was intended to provide you with a programming illustration that goes beyond the usual, more-limited text examples. Although the system of programs in this chapter are not at the level of complexity to be "real-world" examples, they serve to illustrate some of the practical issues that guide program development in organizations.

EXERCISES

13.1 Modify the sample program in Figure 13-3 so that each input record is checked for *all* five possible errors. Each error encountered should be included in the error report.

13.2 Write the PROCEDURE DIVISION for the monthly processing program, using the first three divisions in Figure 13-10 as well as the task description in the last section of the chapter.